CRISIS AND TRANSFORMATION IN CHINA'S HONG KONG

HONG KONG BECOMING CHINA

Ming K. Chan and Gerard A. Postiglione
Series General Editors

Ming K. Chan is Research Fellow, and Executive Coordinator of the Hong Kong Documentary Archives, Hoover Institution, Stanford University.

Gerard A. Postiglione is Associate Professor of Education, University of Hong Kong.

In view of Hong Kong's remarkable historical development under British rule, its contemporary global importance as an economic hub and communication center on the Pacific Rim, and because of its new status as a Special Administrative Region (SAR) of the People's Republic of China since July 1, 1997, M. E. Sharpe has launched this multivolume series for an international readership. This series aims at providing both expert analysis and the relevant documentary basis for an informed appreciation of the key issues and major dimensions of Hong Kong's developmental experience. The life and work, hope and fear of the seven million people in the Hong Kong SAR as a free society, capitalist economy and cosmopolitan community under socialist Chinese sovereignty should be of direct relevance to those interested in Chinese affairs. The "one country, two systems" formula that has guaranteed the HKSAR's high degree of autonomy is also the cornerstone policy of the PRC's cherished peaceful reunification with Taiwan. As such, Hong Kong's record of performance as a part of the PRC is of crucial significance to the prospects of Greater China and the Asia-Pacific region in the twenty-first century.

The books in this series:

THE HONG KONG BASIC LAW: BLUEPRINT FOR "STABILITY AND PROSPERITY UNDER CHINESE SOVEREIGNTY?
Ming K. Chan and David Clark, editors

EDUCATION AND SOCIETY IN HONG KONG: TOWARD ONE COUNTRY AND TWO SYSTEMS
Gerard A. Postiglione, editor

THE COMMON LAW SYSTEM IN CHINESE CONTEXT: HONG KONG IN TRANSITION
Berry Hsu

PRECARIOUS BALANCE: HONG KONG BETWEEN CHINA AND BRITAIN, 1842–1992
Ming K. Chan, editor

RELUCTANT EXILES? MIGRATION FROM HONG KONG AND THE NEW OVERSEAS CHINESE
Ronald Skeldon, editor

THE HONG KONG-GUANGDONG LINK: PARTNESHIP IN FLUX
Reginald Yin-Wang Kwok and Alvin Y. So, editors

HONG KONG'S REUNION WITH CHINA: THE GLOBAL DIMENSIONS
Gerard A. Postigline and James T.H. Tang, editors

CRISIS AND TRANSFORMATION IN CHINA'S HONG KONG
Ming K. Chan and Alvin Y. So, editors

CRISIS AND TRANSFORMATION IN CHINA'S HONG KONG

MING K. CHAN AND ALVIN Y. SO

EDITORS

FOREWORD BY LYNN T. WHITE, III

香港大學出版社
HONG KONG UNIVERSITY PRESS

M.E. Sharpe
Armonk, New York
London, England

An East Gate Book

First published in the United States in 2002 by M.E. Sharpe, Inc.

First published in Hong Kong in 2002 by Hong Kong University Press,
14/F Hing Wai Centre, 7 Tin Wan Praya Road, Aberdeen, Hong Kong
(for exclusive distribution in China, Hong Kong, Macau, and Taiwan).

Library of Congress Cataloging-in-Publication Data

Crisis and transformation in China's Hong Kong / edited by Ming K. Chan and Alvin Y. So.
    p. cm.
    Includes bibliographical references and index.
    ISBN 0-7656-1000-0 (alk. paper) : ISBN 0-7656-1001-9 (pbk.: alk. paper)
        1. Hong Kong (China)—Politics and government—1997–   I. Chan, Ming K.
II. So, Alvin Y., 1953–

DS796.H7C75 2002
951.25′05—dc21   2002019092

ISBN 962-209-607-7 (soft cover, Hong Kong University Press, Hong Kong)

Printed in the United States of America

The paper used in this publication meets the minimum requirements of
American National Standard for Information Sciences
Permanence of Paper for Printed Library Materials,
ANSI Z 39.48-1984.

∞

MV (c)   10   9   8   7   6   5   4   3   2   1
MV (p)   10   9   8   7   6   5   4   3   2

Contents

List of Tables and Figures

Tables

Figures

Series General Editors' Foreword

As Hong Kong commemorates the fifth anniversary of its retrocession from British colonial rule to Chinese sovereignty, it is time for a reflective evaluation and detailed examination of this budding Special Administration Region (SAR) of the People's Republic of China (PRC). Indeed, much has changed since July 1, 1997, under the leadership of Chief Executive Tung Chee-hwa, who is about to embark on his second five-year term at the helm.

Rocked by two painful, back-to-back recessions over a span of four years, Hong Kong is beset with the bitter task of economic restructuring. This once potent Asian economic tiger has been humbled by ballooning budget deficits, an unprecedented rise in unemployment, a continuing deflationary spiral, the seriously depressed property market, and near negative growth. The "Hong Kong economic miracle" which characterized the territory's remarkable growth and development for nearly half of a century since the end of World War II now seems a distant memory. Yet, these economic woes constitute only part of the new Hong Kong story. Reality has been altered on various fronts. Environmental deterioration, competition from other regional centers, issues of citizenship and right of abode, frustration over educational reform, civil servants unrest, social dislocation, and popular discontent have contributed to a crisis atmosphere that is engulfing postcolonial Hong Kong. The community's yearning for sure-footed guidance and effective relief measures has yet to be met by the new SAR administration.

Management blunders, administrative scandals, policy reversals and bureaucratic incompetence only deepened widespread pessimism about economic prospects, especially at a time when the local populace feels left behind while post-WTO mainland Chinese metropolises are poised to surpass Hong Kong's snail-paced economic growth. How is it that its once prosperous luster and vibrant self-confidence have faded? Have these crises really shaken Hong Kong to the core? To what extent and in what sense has Hong Kong been transformed? How much should the regime change be blamed for the HKSAR malaise? What will be the long term impact of the current crises on the social, cultural, political, and economic life of the SAR's seven million? Finally, will the SAR be able to hold the course for full reintegration with the Chinese mainland by 2047? Undoubtedly, emerging trends and unfolding events in the SAR will have profound significance both for the PRC's drive toward economic globalization and domestic market reforms, and for Hong Kong's many external economic partners. Thus, careful delineation and informed assessment of Hong Kong's first phase as a SAR of the PRC should be of direct international relevance.

The present volume of over a dozen substantive chapters by Hong Kong-based and overseas scholars provides insightful analysis and expert critique through pertinent case studies and cogent interpretations of the key dimensions of the crises and transformations molding China's Hong Kong since mid-1997. As long as the "one country, two systems" formula still effectively underwrites the SAR polity and socioeconomic life as well as center-region interface, a high degree of local autonomy for a free, capitalist but only semi-democratic Hong Kong would seem to remain a cornerstone commitment of the PRC leadership. However, this formula's original purpose as designed by Deng Xiaoping—the mainland's cherished peaceful reunification with Taiwan—is no more attractive to a majority of the people on that island now than it was before 1997. As such, Hong Kong's record of performance under Chinese sovereignty should be of great interest and even strategic concern to the entire Asia-Pacific region.

We are truly delighted that this collective volume on vital issues defining Hong Kong's early experience as a part of China is the latest as well as the first twenty-first century title in the Hong Kong Becoming China series. Coincidentally, the publication of *Crisis and Transformation in China's Hong Kong* at this juncture in the HKSAR's challenging development also helps to celebrate the first decade of this series, which was launched in autumn 1991 to enhance academic understanding and international appreciation of the mainland China–Hong Kong integrative dynamics and the emergence of Greater China.

Ming K. Chan & Gerard A. Postiglione
Spring 2002

Foreword

Lynn T. White, III

"Hong Kong, China" is the new address. Its important part is the comma.

Separation between the former British Crown Colony and the large Chinese mainland has been essential to Hong Kong's growth ever since this city was founded in the 1840s. Current worries in Hong Kong still concern dangers of imported authoritarianism, mass migration from China that might swamp the city and threaten its high per-capita income, and competition from other coastal cities, especially Shanghai. Hong Kong has attracted people because it has long been liminal, peripheral, wealthier than China while still Chinese, and politically safe for refugees from revolutions.

Connection across the border, however, has been no less essential to this city. Hong Kong's authoritarianism became vice-regal in the structures of two different empires, and since 1997 Beijing has been the only capital. This city's population has long included a few Westerners, Japanese, and Indians — but the vast majority is Chinese. Hong Kong's quickest growth of wealth, during the last quarter of the twentieth century, has depended on moving low-productivity parts of the city's economic processes into China, keeping high-wage jobs in the city. Migration by tycoons, especially from Shanghai, has often been welcomed in Hong Kong. A very large metropolitan suburb, Shenzhen, has grown in the mainland just across the border. Guangdong is now the PRC's richest province because of Hong Kong's capital and global marketing skills. This "Special Administrative Region" administers far more than itself. It manages growth in China's fastest-growing part. For much of the PRC, Hong Kong is now the economic capital, the gem of the South.

Hong Kong's "borders" are also overseas. The entrepreneurs of this city, together with those from Taiwan who come to the mainland through Hong Kong, organize most of the world's trade with China. This pattern has become a basis for tremendous prosperity, and it has also become a cultural conveyor belt, exporting Chinese films and songs along with toys and shoes —and importing foreign styles that range from bluejeans through *sushi* to elections.

Just as the "Hong Kong breeze" (*Gangfeng*) is of great concern to Communist stalwarts in China who want their Party go on forever, the mainland political breeze worries Hong Kong democrats. Subtle pressures have come from Beijing, whose leaders still call their regime a "dictatorship of the proletariat" even though they are now very unconvincing proletarians. In the "one country, two systems" model, the mainland system is run by state capitalists. These leaders have much in common with the tycoon capitalists who have for decades run Hong Kong's dominant networks, paternalistic family corporations that are outside of the government.

Now Hong Kong's middle-income groups have expanded, however, as blue collar jobs have shifted to China. As many parts of the first five chapters of this book show, the increased number of better-educated office workers make demands on a political structure that has until recent years been under the nearly unchallenged control of businesses.

Modern policies for a complex society like Hong Kong are likely to be effective only if the people who give force to them have consented to them and have some sense of ownership over them. A secret of democracy, to the limited extent that form of government is practiced anywhere, is that nothing mobilizes support better than political struggle. A fight (e.g., an election) is an event that can attract attention to public problems. Discord can bring people out of their smaller networks, when issues arise that more extensive public cooperation alone could fix. Legitimate contest, not wisdom by itself, lets governors take public decisions on complex issues, where modern interdependency usually creates short-term losers even if the decisions are for the long-term good.

Authoritarian policy making of the "top-down" sort therefore cannot ensure either that decisions will be made during crises, or that they will be widely supported. If all politics were mere administration, a Chinese corporate CEO might be a fully legitimate Chief Executive for Hong Kong (more legitimate, surely, than the appointed foreign governors of the British days). Administrators with brilliant policies can still, however, lack the support to have these measures implemented; and if so, they get nowhere.

The United Nations Development Program publishes a list of countries according to a "Human Development Index," a broad gauge of modernity that mixes income, education, and health data in statistically equal parts. Of the top thirty on this roster, all but Hong Kong and one other are completely unapologetic liberal democracies.[1] (The other is Singapore, half Hong Kong's size, where free speech for ethnic mobilization could mean external as well as internal disaster.) Hong Kong's small elite of "soft authoritarians" really cannot hope to run their rich and pluralized city effectively as if it were just a banana republic without the bananas.

The substantive problems that they face are modern: The city's demographic structure is aging, and its health care needs will become far more expensive in the next few years. Land is scarce, and the government still manages much of the housing that it built and subsidized long ago (then trying to boost local companies' competitiveness by lowering wage costs for blue collar jobs these companies have now moved to China). The Education Department needs to promote more instruction in standard Chinese (Mandarin), while honoring the newly rich region's "mother tongue" (obscurely called the *muyu*, meaning Cantonese) and also trying to maintain standards in the language of most buyers in the trade networks that Hong Kong oversees (English). A seemly modern degree of independence among academics and journalists is essential, if the city is to remain an open door for China to the outside world.

Random jolts such as the "bird flu" scare or the Asian financial crisis, and especially the consequent deep collapse of real estate values, are public dangers because the parts of a modern society like Hong Kong are linked to each other. When the Thai *bhat* fell and other economies from Indonesia to Korea to Russia to Brazil ran aground, the Hong Kong government scaled back its plan to build more apartments and to subsidize local people buying their rented flats. Eventually, as this official backtracking slowly became evident in public, the poorer half of the city's population was naturally disappointed. The richer half of the population became disaffected at the same time, because the drop of the value of their flats reduced their wealth sharply. In truth, these problems did not start with the Hong Kong government — but the Chief Executive was widely criticized anyway. He lacked the legitimacy that would, regardless of performance, have come from a clearly wide and popular mandate.

Hong Kong's constitution, the Basic Law, hesitantly acknowledges this kind of problem. It establishes one-man rule, in effect. Article 45 nonetheless suggests that in the future, "The ultimate aim is the selection of the Chief Executive by universal suffrage. . . ." Annex I, Part 7, implies that 2007 might be a time for amendment in this direction (although the Beijing-confirmed Chief Executive would have to agree, as would two-thirds of the oddly constructed Legislative Council). The joker in this deck is that nobody yet knows the modal ideas of the Beijing and Hong Kong elites in 2007, 2012, or 2017 when this matter of Chief Executive selection will surely come up perhaps more than once. The chapters of this book relate the many parts of Hong Kong's public life to each other. They show that none of their topics stands separate from the others.

Hong Kong borders both China and the world, and its internal dynamics make a metaphor of life because they are "on the edge" between different external influences. Every chapter of this book brings out this liminal quality of the world's most attractive city-state. The editors have assembled a truly glorious group of scholars to survey the many aspects of Hong Kong's transformation as its borders become even more permeable. Together, these writers have put into your hands the very best treatment of Hong Kong's new story.

Note

1. Hong Kong, number twenty-six on this list including all UN members, is the sole non-sovereign entry. See UNDP, *Human Development Report 2000* (New York: Oxford University Press, 2000), p. 157.

Acknowledgments

This volume of collective scholarly efforts grew from a symposium hosted by the Division of Social Science, Hong Kong University of Science and Technology (HKUST), on its scenic campus, December 15–16, 2000. For extending such enjoyable hospitality and providing careful logistical arrangements to all participants, the HKUST community deserves our note of gratitude. In particular, we extend appreciation to the dean of the School of Humanities and Social Science, Professor Pang-hsin Ting, for funding to underwrite this intellectual congregation. We must also record here the highly efficient and extremely conscientious service rendered by the Social Science Division's Ms. Josephine Wong. Her efforts were indispensable to many areas of this joint undertaking, from preconference liaison and preparation to postconference manuscript revision and reformatting.

We wish to express our profound appreciation for the contributions from academic colleagues and professional experts who served as chairs or discussants at the symposium: Elaine Chan, Thomas Chau, Dora Choi, Greg Felker, James Kung, Jane Lee, Tai-lok Lui, Ngai Pun, Ming Sing, Benjamin Tsou, Yiu-ming To (who became a chapter coauthor in the revision process), Angelina Yee, and David Zweig. We are deeply grateful to Lynn White, our external editorial referee, for his illuminating comments on the chapters and his encouraging overall assessment of the volume. We are also thankful for the inputs from the learned legal minds of Berry Hsu and Ann Cheung, our editorial consultants on Benny Tai's chapter on constitutional issues, which was commissioned after the symposium. Finally, in our editorial task, while Alvin Y. So was ably supported by Josephine Wong in Hong Kong, Ming K. Chan had benefited from the computer skills of Sean Leow, his research assistant at Stanford.

CRISIS AND TRANSFORMATION IN CHINA'S HONG KONG

1

Introduction

The Hong Kong SAR in Flux

Ming K. Chan

This multidisciplinary volume aims to assess the major crises confronting and the crucial transformative processes reshaping China's Hong Kong since July 1, 1997. While drawing definitive characterization of or rendering a summary verdict on the overall performance of the Hong Kong Special Administrative Region (HKSAR) of the People's Republic of China (PRC) would be premature, its five years of local autonomy under Chinese sovereignty did yield some sufficiently clear indicators on the actualization of the "one country, two systems" formula as being practiced in the HKSAR.

Despite many of the pre-1997 doomsayers' dire predictions about Hong Kong's inevitable loss of political autonomy and basic freedoms as part of Communist China, the worst did not happen. So far Beijing has exercised considerable restraint and avoided any overt interference in the HKSAR's internal administration. Yet the highly optimistic forecast of post-1997 Hong Kong's "better tomorrow" with undiminished "stability and prosperity" also has been far off the mark. In fact, the most serious crises that have assaulted the HKSAR came from an almost totally unexpected area—the economy. Since late 1997, the HKSAR has been engulfed by rising unemployment, negative growth, widening budget deficits, rapid equity depreciation, and unprecedented price deflation. Such economic woes stemmed at first from the autumn 1997 pan-Asian financial turmoil and the subsequent bust of the twin economic bubbles—the overheated local property market and runaway stock market speculation. Such serious threats to the livelihood of Hong Kong's populace were also partly due to the painful and long-term fundamental economic restructuring that has been unfolding since the late 1980s. More recently, the already deeply depressed local economy was dealt another devastating blow by the global fallout effects of the September 11, 2001, terrorist attacks in the United States, Hong Kong's foremost international economic partner. Even though both the worst and best post-1997 scenarios failed to materialize, popular expectations, collective self-confidence, and common aspirations of the nearly seven million HKSAR residents did undergo very drastic changes within the last five years. A disturbing mood with the public fearful about the deteriorating employment picture, with little prospect of either immediate relief or near-future improvement, and a widespread sense of helplessness and inability to cope with the deepening economic crisis have hit the entire HKSAR community, from the hard-squeezed middle class to the still more deprived grassroots.

On the surface, the daily life of the great majority of the local populace in the early SAR era seems to remain little changed from the pre–July 1, 1997 colonial days. Other than the replacement of the British Union Jack by the five-star PRC national flag, the sovereignty retrocession has not been particularly noticeable in a physical sense. Even the once-worrisome stationing of People's Liberation Army (PLA) troops has become a nonissue, as the local PLA garrison is almost invisible behind its barracks. Despite this façade of apparent normalcy, Hong Kong, its institutions, and its residents have been negotiating tight and delicate processes of subtle changes and uneasy adjustments, sometimes in response to unexpected external forces, other times due to the need to conform to administrative and constitutional requirements framed by the Basic Law. In fact, the HKSAR's autonomous status under PRC sovereignty has reshaped institutional structure and personnel decisions of the Hong Kong polity, while the need to manage a growing community and complex economy necessitated novel undertakings in infrastructure projects, government programs, and public services. As an organic and dynamic functional hub and economic center of global significance, Hong Kong should change and has changed since the sovereignty retrocession. Depending on the specific criteria and particular perspectives, however the changes have not always been for the better in the early HKSAR era.

If change indeed belies the reality of China's Hong Kong, the past five years saw the SAR regime under Chief Executive Tung Chee-hwa confronted with more than its fair share of devastating crises and major disasters. These challenges placed his administration under considerable strain and stress, often magnifying hidden faultlines and revealing sheer incompetence on the part of both the SAR leadership's governing capacity and the entrenched civil service's emergency response capabilities. These crises included the pan-Asia financial meltdown that resulted in deficit budgets for the SAR government; the 1997–98 bird flu; the 1998 new airport opening fiasco; the unsafe construction of public housing estates scandal; and other glaring cases of serious misdeeds by government personnel, agencies, and public bodies.

They testified to the grave crisis mismanagement of the new regime's civil bureaucracy that was inherited from the British colonialists. In addition, the conservative, paternalistic, and interventionist Tung Chee-hwa regime also suffered from self-inflicted wounds in that he tried, at the very start of his reign, to launch numerous far-reaching reforms in various vital policy fields almost simultaneously; these fields included education, housing, welfare, and the civil service. Tung's too-much, too-soon, all-at-once, multifront chain of reforms provoked stern opposition and determined resistance from almost all affected quarters; many of them, such as teachers and civil servants, even resorted to public protests on the streets. Coming together, all these constituted many of the basic causes underlining a clearly discernable crisis of governability that has troubled the HKSAR regime under Tung's leadership from its early days.

If the 1985–97 transition period had been overshadowed by the Beijing–London–Hong Kong political discords on disputed sovereignty and contested democratization, then it should be natural that the new SAR leadership would deem it desirable to refocus public efforts on, and to reallocate official resources to, various necessary but long-delayed domestic reforms ignored or avoided by the departing British sunset regime. The very rigid and restrictive Basic Law provisions do not yield much room for the Tung administration, even if it were ever so inclined, to attempt many major changes in the political system, at least not until the premandated 2007 constitutional and electoral review. Rather, it is in the socioeconomic realm that the SAR regime supposedly can enjoy much more room to maneuver.

In fact, on the domestic front, the HKSAR has a completely free hand to move forward to seek breakthroughs, to unleash new initiatives, and to chart fresh courses for both novel undertakings and exploration of untapped opportunities, as well as to remedy colonial defects and address past inadequacies in order to make Hong Kong a better place under Chinese rule. However, as the first local-led administration that was inaugurated with very strong Chinese national goodwill and high local expectations, the Tung regime's performance on the domestic front so far has been quite disappointing. It not only failed to inspire public confidence and enhance people's trust in the government amid the worsening economic crisis, but unrelenting public criticisms of his misguided policies and administrative failures became so severed and widespread that Beijing was compelled to step into the fray in order to buttress the tattering Tung regime and salvage the "one country, two systems" experimentation in the HKSAR.

To rescue Tung from plummeting popularity, senior PRC leaders on different occasions repeatedly expressed strong approval of his performance. Aimed specifically at countering the very loud calls from all quarters in Hong

Kong demanding Tung not to seek another term of office, Beijing's top brass, including President Jiang Zemin, even openly issued clear endorsements to support his reelection as HKSAR chief executive for a second five-year term starting July 1, 2002. Such high-profile signals, if not high-handed intervention, from the PRC central government did have a direct deterrent effect in preempting other credible and qualified potential candidates from joining the March 24, 2002, contest to challenge Beijing's preordained Tung Chee-hwa. Nonetheless, even though the prospect that Tung would easily be "reelected" without opposition as the sole candidate for the chief executive's office was very high, there could be no guarantee that Tung would automatically receive an overwhelming share of votes from the eight hundred members of the Election Committee as a show of popular support. A near-nightmarish scenario would have Tung win unopposed but receive little more than four hundred votes out of eight hundred. This would reflect an approval ratio in line with Tung's about 50 percent popularity rating in various public opinion polls during the past two years. Had that been the case, it would reconfirm the legitimacy crisis that has been haunting the Tung regime and has further complicated its governability problems. In early March 2002, as the only nominated candidate (by 7 of 794 electors), Tung was deemed the winner without the need to conduct the actual voting.

While Tung is undoubtedly a very decent, sincere, and honest person, his questionable democratic legitimacy as the first SAR leader (anointed in late 1996 by Beijing's hand-picked HKSAR Selection Committee of four hundred) was compounded by his strong aversion to political parties, electoral campaigns, and parliamentary politics; his noncharismatic leadership style, coupled with an acute lack of public communications skills (along with an equal lack of desire to communicate); and his submissively overt pro-Beijing (as against staunchly pro–Hong Kong) slant on many sensitive political matters. All these factors did little to enhance his political effectiveness and public credibility, or to make his task in implementing sweeping reforms any easier. Nor have his belated crisis alertness, narrow and shallow attempts, and generally meager responses with incoherent policies or ad hoc half-measures to refloat the deeply depressed and still-fast-deteriorating economy proved to be timely and effective.

Reflecting his grand capitalist origins, big business career experience, and clear tycoon sympathies, but handicapping unfamiliarity with the plight of the grassroots, critics were justified in labeling many of Tung Chee-hwa's economic relief policies as aiming more at "saving the market" for the business elites but doing little at "saving the victimized people" from unemployment, wage freeze or salary reduction, and negative equity burdens.

Eventually, the cumulative effects of his sudden policy shifts and secretive about-faces on key issues (such as the fiasco over his housing policy with a targeted eighty-five thousand new units annually), self-contradictory official pronouncements, ill-thought-out proposals, biased decisions, and counterproductive measures alarmed and disturbed even those in the business world, including many of his previous elite supporters, in addition to the already alienated middle class and the hard-pressed grassroots.

On top of its various administrative debacles and policy missteps, the HKSAR regime, in its search for administrative expedience or political correctness, also seriously undermined judicial independence and the rule of law in two mainland China–related cases in the eyes of many legal practitioners and informed observers. The first was the by-now-notorious case of the right of abode for Hong Kong residents' mainland children, against whom the SAR regime resorted to requesting the PRC National People's Congress to reinterpret Articles 22 and 24 of the Basic Law in order to invalidate the HKSAR Court of Final Appeal's January 1999 ruling in their favor. This in fact amounted to opening the front gate to invite Beijing's direct judicial interference in order to save the SAR executive arm from certain defeat on purely legal ground in vital matters of great consequence.

The second case occurred in spring 2001, when Tung Chee-hwa, carefully toeing Beijing's official line, openly condemned the Falun Gong as "definitely a devious cult," without any solid factual proof, and without proper legal justifications regarding the probable unlawfulness in the Falun Gong's activities according to the HKSAR's own laws. Such deliberate actions by the SAR leadership's "looking to Beijing" for an easy exit from the unwelcome practical consequences of due legal process as administered by the SAR's supposedly independent judiciary system or in an anticipatory attempt with political correctness to seek Beijing's approval on controversial matters could only erode the independence of the judiciary and hamper the fair administration of justice for all, which are the key pillars supporting Hong Kong's rule of law to guarantee basic freedoms and economic fair play. Such actions also would run counter to the true sprit and real intent of the one country, two systems design in the legal and administrative spheres. These are but two of the more alarming examples of questionable political judgment, leadership inadequacies, and legal lapses that have tarnished the SAR regime's early record and contributed to a potentially fatal constitutional crisis undermining the SAR's much cherished high degree of autonomy.

Another SAR malaise has been manifested in a serious lack of confidence in near-future prospects among Hong Kong's populace, whose trust in the SAR regime has been sharply declining. In turn, the officialdom itself also suffered from both a growing public credibility gap and pervasive civil service demoralization, while desperately trying to confront the many crises and challenges in the post-1997 era. Unlike the prehandover era's common fear of Chinese communism under the negative China Factor, this new confidence crisis is much more than just the normal and expected teething pains for the new HKSAR community while undergoing the inevitable political and constitutional transformation and long-term economic restructuring. In large measure, this stemmed from the populace's collective sense of desperate victimization and panic helplessness as well as the Tung regime's proven incapacity and even ineptness in relieving the majority's threatened livelihood and alleviate the common economic sufferings, which were first set in motion by the 1997 pan-Asia financial turmoil and further intensified by the post–September 11, 2001, global downturn.

Within the SAR's highly autonomous domain in domestic affairs, the new regime has ushered in several deliberate measures of drastic institutional change such as the December 1999 abolition of the Urban Council (which had the longest history of local elected representation) and Regional Council, and the reintroduction of appointed members to the previously all-elected District Boards (renamed District Councils). From July 1997 through April 1998, the SAR was also burdened with an unelected and extra-constitutional (as it was not provided for in the Basic Law) "provisional legislature" (PLC) which replaced the all-elected Legislative Council (Legco) formed in 1995 under British auspices. This PLC of dubious legitimacy and low public esteem, after repealing a host of prehandover era liberal laws on labor protection and civil rights, enacted a set of regressive electoral rules for the creation of future HKSAR legislature.

When the first ever HKSAR Legco elections were held in May 1998, they were conducted according to new rules under which almost a million voters in some of the thirty functional constituencies were disenfranchised. As for the twenty directly elected geographic constituencies, a new proportional representation system was adopted to marginalize the democratic camp and to effect a divisive partisan alignment to retard the emergence of a single majority party. So serious was this deliberately crafted electoral mandate-legislative representation disconnect under the new SAR rules, that while the democratic activists in May 1998 still captured the same two-thirds of the popular votes as they did in 1995, they were entitled to only one-third of the Legco seats, down from their near majority in 1995. All these electoral twists and turns supposedly would fit in well with Tung's often-repeated emphasis on "depoliticizing" Hong Kong public affairs and on refocusing the populace's energies on socioeconomic undertakings in order to mitigate Hong Kong's rapid politicization during the 1985–97 transition era, which was marked by Sino-British conflicts on local democratization. Thus, a continuing crisis of democracy interacted with the crisis of legitimacy to deepen the new SAR regime's own crisis of governability.

Despite's avowed "depoliticization," the SAR regime is about to formally politicize its own administrative top echelon and overhaul the entire policymaking system with plans for political appointees on contract terms to head key government policy bureaus. Serving a fixed term and occupying a seat on the Executive Council (Exco), these appointees would be directly accountable to the chief executive in a "pseudoministerial system" that should become effective by July 2002, at the start of the chief executive's second term. Perhaps this new system, first suggested by Tung Chee-hwa in his October 2000 fourth policy speech and more clearly outlined in his Legco public speech on April 17, 2002, will enhance the chief executive's overall personal control of the policy formulation, decision-making, and public promotion processes currently undertaken by career bureaucrats who are ill suited for such overt political and even partisan functions.[1] The earlier-than-planned April 2001 departure of Anson Chan (the most senior of the colonial era handover officials) from the post of chief secretary for administration and the appointment of an experienced banker, Anthony Leung, as financial secretary to replace Donald Tsang (who became Chan's successor) in fact had already enabled Tung to enlist personally loyal and politically "patriotic" talents from the private sector to fill two of the top three portfolios in the SAR regime under him.

These personnel decisions could be taken as the vital first steps toward a political appointees–dominated cabinet form of executive-led government, allowing the chief executive much stronger direct command over the entire policy machinery, which for the first four years of his tenure had not been functioning optimally while staffed by colonial-groomed civil servants. Of course, after this new system is inaugurated, Tung Chee-hwa would no longer have as a convenient pretext for policy failures the lack of full cooperation from or smooth coordination among someone else's senior officials whom he had simply inherited. As such, he would have to be fully responsible for all the decisions he made with his own hand-picked appointees. Yet, this new system, which is labeled by Tung as "improving the quality of administration," while definitely constituting a major political reform, will not necessarily yield greater governmental accountability to the Legco and the public at large. Without the advice of and institutional constraints by a civil bureaucracy top layer, these political appointees could well be selected on the basis of their personal loyalty to and ideological compatibility with the chief executive rather than for their public affairs experience, professional expertise, administrative skills, political wisdom, or developmental visions.

These top officials would be recruited and appointed by, accountable solely to, serve only at the pleasure of, and easily removed from office by the chief executive at will, and yet the chief executive himself or herself is not directly elected by the HKSAR community on a universal franchise. Thus any notion of this system as enhancing genuine "executive accountability" to the public or its elected representatives, the Legco councilors, is far off the mark. It will remain very much a scheme to consolidate more power directly into the hands of the chief executive and thus supposedly to facilitate greater administrative efficiency and policy effectiveness in the executive-led SAR government. Neither would this new system be able to solve a major built-in defect in the SAR polity. The Tung regime's lack of a stable and firm base of support among the political parties in the Legco will continue to strain executive-legislative relations in the SAR, at least until electoral reforms, if any, can be introduced to change the realpolitik dynamics by 2008.

Another significant postcolonial transformation has already been unfolding in the realm of political software—the official ideological tilt and partisan color underlining policy orientation and public affairs mechanism. Despite its avowed wish at depoliticization, the HKSAR leadership has been practicing a new kind of political correctness by increasingly looking toward Beijing, often in an anticipatory and solicitous mood, in purely domestic and hence supposedly "autonomous" matters. As an integral part of this "northern orientation" and perhaps also a concerted effort to rectify the past British slights and compensate for the nearly five decades' repression under the old colonial order, leftist partisans received more than their fair share of HKSAR official appointments to public bodies, political honors, regime patronage, and Tung's personal attentiveness while the democratic camp activists were systematically sidelined and underrepresented in the corridors of power.

Of course, reflecting Tung Chee-hwa's shipping family scion background and very strong pro–big business sympathies, the tycoon elites and their high professional surrogates also took a disproportional large bulk of government appointments, from District Councils seats to membership in supervisory committees, advisory panels, and various statutory organs, much more so than the business circle's pubic affairs leadership role and civic representation during the last three decades of British colonial rule. Such very deliberate and obviously partisan twin criteria—patriotic and big business—monopolization of the communal or sectoral representation and interest articulation channels, as well as public affairs participation mechanism under the Tung regime, can only further intensify the already worsening undercurrents of political tensions and the sharpening social classes schism. It is the very worst kind of the politics of exclusion and divisiveness, definitely not in the true spirit of united front inclusiveness that was so effectively practiced by the founding fathers of the PRC against the Japanese and the

Kuomintang on the mainland more than half a century ago. This unhealthy trend of political correctness and societal polarization along partisan ideological and socioeconomic class lines would compromise the indispensable political pluralism and social harmony buttressing the very core values as the moral foundation of the HKSAR's autonomy under the one country, two systems formula.

The HKSAR government's rather disappointing early record could only diminish its positive showcase effects to facilitate the mainland's peaceful reunification with Taiwan. Indeed, in the realpolitik of the HKSAR's future fate calculus, the real danger would very likely not be coming from Beijing's high-handed direct interference, but rather from the gradual undermining of and even brutal assaults on local autonomy by the pro-Beijing partisans, appeasing politicians, incompetent officials, mainland interest-vested tycoons, and newly minted "patriotic" turncoat elites in the SAR. This is the critical area in which enlightened, farsighted, and courageous political leadership is required to guide the HKSAR in its multifold and complex interactions with the PRC central authorities. This calls for a leader with popular mandate and unquestioned legitimacy to stand firm for Hong Kong, both for its own sake and for the real good of the one country, two systems formula, the true success of which the PRC state and the entire Chinese nation across the Taiwan Straits have much at stake. During these past five years at the helm of the HKSAR ship of state. Tung Chee-hwa has yet to demonstrate such needed leadership qualities, and thus to earn genuine affection and popular acclaim as a great Hong Kong leader and a true Chinese patriot.

Desperate concern about the deepening local economic crisis, coupled with the new-regime culture of an ever-ready and unduly submissive pro-Beijing stance, would be galvanized into an official orientation of "looking to the north" that is fast coming into conflict with an increasingly common private apprehension of the HKSAR's overdependency on the mainland in almost all functional areas at the expense of local autonomy. Such a clash of mindsets and orientations could only further polarize the entire Hong Kong community. The widening of the wealth and poverty gaps since 1997 has already resulted in much sharper class divisions and deteriorating social cohesion. Constricted by such a depressing combination of frail and fragmenting social fabrics, threatened livelihood, and economic insecurity, Hong Kong's populace have become highly skeptical and even cynical of the Tung regime's earlier boastful claims and grand utopian visions of transforming the HKSAR into a world city, perhaps as "Asia's New York or London" and serving the high value-added functions of a "Manhattan plus" (at least before the September 11, 2001, attacks on the World Trade Center twin towers in lower Manhattan).

In his first four policy speeches from 1997 to 2000, Tung Chee-hwa has been trumpeting the wholesale, full-speed-ahead development of high-tech industries, information networks, and knowledge-based and high-value-added economy as the true key to uplift Hong Kong from its current economic restructuring pains and elevate the SAR into a global service superhub, with the Disney theme park and Cyberport projects as landmarks for this new age of Hong Kong. Of course, none of these promised rose gardens of the future can meet the very immediate livelihood demands and dire poverty concerns of the deprived grassroots and alienated middle class who are forced to make do with an emptying rice bowl. Such unbridgeable divergence between the public's urgent survival needs and the regime's futuristic grand projections has not been helpful in raising Tung Chee-hwa's rather low and still plummeting public approval ratings. Indeed, Tung's personal popularity has been dragged down and his political reputation has been tarnished by his ineffective responses to the continuing economic recession; his now notorious indecisiveness and policy flip-flops; his taint with the PRC's harsh stance on sensitive matters; and of course, the many highly publicized cases in serious maladministration in his government and in other public institutions under his purview.

Many of the latter mistakes were not of Tung's own doing, but the earlier (1997–98) crisis mismanagement by his young regime had dissipated much of its public credibility as well as the initial trust and good will from the community that he once enjoyed as the first local Chinese leader inaugurating the new SAR era. Then his inability to effectively contain and mitigate the sweepingly destructive impact on livelihood from the inevitable burst of overblown domestic economic bubbles did not endear Tung, with his pro–big business bias, to a depressed community already laced with social fissures along class lines. The resultant strains and stresses of socioeconomic dislocations further accentuated the many inadequacies and defects within the regime. While many of the recent public grievances against the regime are rice-bowl related, it would be erroneous and irresponsible, as some SAR senior officials have suggested, to place all the blame on the lackluster performance of the Tung regime in dealing with negative external economic forces, especially the 1997 pan-Asian financial crisis and the post–September 11, 2001 downturn. Such economic crises, triggered by an unfortunate combination of two successive powerful assaults from the outside world in the first four years of the HKSAR's infancy, were wholly unexpected.

Before the 1997 handover, senior PRC officials repeatedly emphasized the need for Hong Kong to continue its very useful, Beijing-prescribed role as an economic, but not political, city. The seemingly robust local economy was often hailed as Hong Kong's trump card to a much better tomorrow of lasting "stability and prosperity" locally in the SAR and continuous contribution to the mainland's development nationally. In the countdown to 1997, the conservative tycoons and business elites' support for the reunification had much to do with their enormous China market gains, while they personally have also become the favored targets of Beijing's united front efforts. Rather unexpectedly, external destructive forces unleashed by the Asia financial malaise, coupled with unhealthy property and stock market bubbles, rendered the Hong Kong economy, not the political arena, the crisis frontline for the SAR regime and its sovereign in Beijing. Economic crisis and regime mismanagement have posed the most severe tests for the SAR political order, for without economic prosperity, social and political stability could become elusive. With the Tung regime's "looking-to-Beijing" political correctness and deliberate greater emphasis on the "one country" uniformity requirements at the expense of SAR's promised "high degree of autonomy" under the "two systems," then the once optimistic prospect of mainland-HKSAR interactions as a case of mutually beneficial economic integration without undemocratic political integration simply could not be easily actualized in the short term.

The Hong Kong populace's serious lack of confidence in their domestic economy's near future improving prospects has been further complicated by a growing apprehension among some circles of the HKSAR's increasing dependency on the mainland Chinese economy which has been exceptionally robust and growing steadily at 7 to 8 percent annually. The now very necessary and even inevitable reliance on the mainland market for trade, investment, and source of tourism to compensate for the declining U.S. market and other international business opportunities, and the massive official efforts to promote closer infrastructural integration with the Pearl River Delta (which has always been Hong Kong's natural geo-economic hinterland) foster a new dark undercurrent of uneasiness among some HKSAR minds. Their alarm at the prospect that such a China market dependency, which would soon be reinforced by increasingly extensive functional interfaces with the mainland, would result in the HKSAR's being more fully absorbed into the PRC mainland orbit, not just in a nominal political sense, but also into its powerful, much larger, but less liberal social and cultural loci. Then Hong Kong would gradually lose its unique cosmopolitan outlook and treasured global linkages, eventually becoming just another big city of the PRC. Even though Hong Kong is a Chinese city, many Hong Kong people are increasingly fearful of fierce competition with and ultimately displacement effects by a fast-rising Shanghai as the preeminent Chinese economic and functional hub in the global arena. Thus, it was not surprising that the pride of many Hong Kong persons both inside the SAR and overseas seemed to have been deeply wounded when PRC Premier Zhu Rongji, during his spring 1999 visit to the United States and Canada, called Hong Kong metaphorically "China's Toronto" but not "China's New York" (a title that is commonly given to Shanghai).

In an immediate context, the PRC's recent entry into the WTO may provide timely new opportunities and positive psychological uplift to help ameliorate some of the HKSAR's economic pains. An effective economic helping hand from Beijing did provide beneficial buoyant effects and ensure Tung Chee-hwa's uncontested and easy reelection for a second term as SAR chief in March 2002. Yet, in the deepening crisis of self-doubt and lack of confidence in the SAR's uncertain economic and functional transformation, the "China in WTO" image has also triggered in many Hong Kong hearts and minds a new fear that the once efficient, modern, and productive city dominating the Pearl River Delta would soon be superceded by Shanghai at the apex of the much larger and richer Yangtzi Valley hinterland as the preeminent East Asian megametropolis at the cutting edge of the twenty-first century. Furthermore, with the city of Beijing fully dedicated to the task of hosting the 2008 Summer Olympic Games with massive new construction, extensive infrastructural upgrade, and wholesale environmental refurbishment, very soon Hong Kong might not even qualify as the PRC's most modern and hygienic urban center. The mixture of pessimism about Hong Kong's future vibrancy with not fully justified fears of mainland absorption or Shanghai dominance bodes ill for the emergence of the local populace's new and proud identity as the PRC's HKSAR citizens entitled to a brighter future in China's Hong Kong.

While mainland China's remarkable growth and development might be substantially geared up by WTO membership, HKSAR's functional survival and economic significance depend not only on its competitiveness vis-à-vis Shanghai or Singapore in the business realm, infrastructural hardware, or technological advancement. Rather, the continued vibrancy, creativity, and global relevance of China's Hong Kong must be sustained by the strengthening and refinement of its most treasured assets—the sociopolitical values, mentalities, institutions, processes, and procedures buttressing and empowering a free, fair, open, liberal, pluralistic, and cosmopolitan community that is enjoying basic freedoms under the rule of law. This seems to be the crux of both Hong Kong's past success story and its future course, which has yet to be fully accepted by Tung and understood by many of his tycoon allies and pro-Beijing supporters.

While few would doubt, with the PRC top leadership's openly declared support, the certainty of Tung Chee-hwa's serving a second term as HKSAR's chief executive, the road ahead for his regime and the entire community is full of unknown challenges because of Hong Kong's economic vulnerability to extraneous factors, the volatility in the PRC–U.S. relationship (both [the HKSAR is part of the PRC] being Hong Kong's major economic partners), and the unpredictable PRC leadership realignment and possible policy reorientation scheduled to take place during 2002–03. If the flag-raising ceremony on July 1, 2001, HKSAR's fourth anniversary, could be taken as an omen for the future, then very guarded optimism and generous precautionary margins should be in order. The ceremony, which was presided by Tung and attended by the HKSAR political top brass, took place in the rain, while the number 3 typhoon warning signal was hoisted, hardly the ideal weather for smooth sailing.

On the same day, a seven-hundred-strong democratic camp demonstration demanding the direct election of the SAR chief executive by one-person–one-vote universal franchise unfolded in the wind and rain. Among the marchers were Martin Lee (Democratic Party chair), Sezto Wah (teachers' union kingpin), Lau Chin-Shek (veteran leader of the free labor movement), Emily Lau (famed journalist and the most outspoken local legislator), and six other pro-democratic legislative councilors. This collective protest action signified the still undiminished local demands for political participation despite the economic downturn that often made rice-bowl issues the headline stories and a top priority public concern. Such unwavering commitment to democraticization has also been reinforced by the larger-than-expected turnout (over forty-eight thousand) at the twelfth annual mass candlelight vigil in Victoria Park on June 4, 2001, to commemorate the 1989 Tiananmen Incident (the PRC authorities' armed suppression of pro-democratic activists in Beijing). Perhaps these very public undertakings of demonstration march and mass commemoration vividly symbolized the unchanged hearts and minds, hopes and desires, of many HKSAR citizens seeking greater democracy under Chinese sovereignty. In this sense, Tung Chee-hwa has yet to resolve the democracy crisis that has been directly linked to his own legitimacy crisis.

It was, however, the Tung regime that stole the headlines on this otherwise low-keyed HKSAR fourth anniversary by bestowing the Grand Bauhinia Medal (GBM, the highest official honor awarded by the HKSAR government) on Yeung Kwong, a former head of the pro-Beijing Federation of Hong Kong Trade Unions (FTU), who was a well-known leader (as chair of the ultra-left "All-Hong Kong Anti-British Colonial Atrocity Struggle Committee") of the 1967 riots in Hong Kong where over fifty people were killed by leftist urban terrorism. This latest display of Tung's political correctness and high-profile "looking-toward-Beijing" stance for patriotic legitimacy was perhaps not really intended to become an attempted official reversal of the popular local verdict on the 1967 riots as a nightmarish spillover of the PRC's Cultural Revolution, which itself has already been officially condemned and thoroughly discredited on the Chinese mainland since the late 1970s.

Some observers regard Tung's symbolic gesture as a desperate and even risky but necessary campaign device in order to gain the support of the traditional local leftist hardcore and the pro-Beijing laboring grassroots for his reelection. This partisan honor to Yeung Kwong might also be designed as a goodwill gesture to pacify the "patriotic" unionists, in particular to compensate for Tung's pro-tycoon class bias and to mollify the rank and file about the regime's failure to offer effective economic bailout measures. In making this GBM award, Tung Chee-hwa in effect reopened the far from fully healed old wounds and pained memories of the 1967 leftist rampant violence, a prospect of blatant lawless unrest and societal disturbance that he definitely would not wish to be confronted with as the head of a local government responsible for maintaining law and order. Furthermore by resurrecting in public consciousness this very destructive 1967 disturbance staged by the frenzied local leftist militants, perhaps the single darkest page in the pro–Chinese Communist circle's historical experience in colonial Hong Kong, Tung also violated his own dictum that one should only "look forward" instead of lingering on the unhappy past, as he had repeatedly stressed when trying in vain to dissuade the pro-democratic camp from organizing local commemorations of the 1989 Tiananmen Incident. Despite prolonged public outcries and protest demonstrations, Tung personally bestowed the GBM award on Yeung at an official ceremony on October 13, 2001, ironically exactly one month after PRC President Jiang Zemin publicly stated that the Chinese government was fully determined to cooperate with the world community in eradicating all forms of terrorism.

Perhaps the Tung regime had once again seriously misjudged the public mood, or it was simply too ignorant of the fury and unaware of the power in Hong Kong residents' collective memory, especially in the current circumstances of dire socioeconomic hardship combined with strong antiregime sentiments, which was not unlike the situation in spring 1967. The HKSAR leadership definitely had grossly underestimated fierce public criticism from all areas of the community, except for some members in "patriotic" minority camps of the unrepentant diehard leftist core and various pro-Beijing unionists. Of course, the Tung regime could, with twisted logic and perverted justifications, even try to claim that this exercise in political expedience and naked partisanship was a positive example of his actualization of the "one country, two systems" formula. By giving the GBM award to the nominal head of a radical organization tainted with urban terrorism to undermine Hong Kong's "stability and prosperity," he was in effect demonstrating his independence from Beijing, as he did act against both (1) the PRC's official verdict and societal consensus on the horrors and evils of the Cultural Revolution and all its external ramifications (including the Hong Kong 1967 riots) and (2) the PRC's latest commitment to combat world terrorism, which definitely should include urban terrorism with bomb attacks (as in the 1967 Hong Kong leftist vantage). Of course, all the negative fallout from the ill-considered GBM award would further diminish what little was left of Tung's political capital, leadership legitimacy, and moral authority in the eyes of the HKSAR community and the tribunal of historical justice.

After nearly five years in office, Tung is, according to many informed observers, still lacking in political wisdom; flawed in his perception of the looming crisis ahead and of special hidden opportunities; lacking in judgment on the full implications of his own actions, or, more often, his nonactions; far too willing and much too ready to take the partisanship shortcut and resort to politically correct expedience; and ignorant of or inattentive to the public mood. Some of these leadership attributes and operational traits could well remain with Tung Chee-hwa during his second term as HKSAR chief executive. As Hong Kong and its people have changed considerably during the past five years of the SAR era, so has Tung. In comparing and contrasting his first (1997) and second (1998) with his latest, the fifth (2001), policy speech, the changes in overtone and the direction of the main policy thrust are easily discernable. Largely gone are the grand-vision highlights of an almost utopian future with blueprints for massive undertakings and broad stokes of fundamental reforms in all areas as promised in the 1997–98 versions. Instead, the 2001 speech was finally scaled back to adopt a more realistic approach, and one more firmly grounded in the reality of economic hardship, with some nodding gestures toward the urgent needs of livelihood relief and economic uplift measures. While many critics and Legco councilors deemed the SAR regime's total package of HK$15 billion (about 1 percent of the HKSAR's GDP) in immediate economic relief as merely symbolic and definitely much too little even if not too late, most did agree that by now the Tung regime has finally come to grips with the crisis situation and the plights of the middle class and the grassroots. Some, such as the Democratic Party, even lauded his still firm and unchanged commitment to improving the entire field of education, from primary school to university level, but they also keenly questioned how such noble goals as he outlined could be achieved with dwindling funding from a government burdened with four consecutive deficit budgets. Soon Tung and his political appointees as senior officials must develop a clear strategy to decisively salvage the entire crisis front and uplift the HKSAR people from the many economic ills and social injustices as well as political deprivation, most of which were not fully foreseen on the celebratory moment when Hong Kong became a part of China on July 1, 1997.

All these pressing issues and their yet-to-be-found solutions reflect the profoundly uncertain but definitely exciting journey ahead for the HKSAR, through crisis and transformation in economic, societal, and political realms under Tung's guiding hands for another half-decade. As Premier Zhu Rongji pointedly said, when he shared his views with some Hong Kong journalists on September 3, 2001, the HKSAR must move beyond its past practice of "discussing without deciding, and deciding without acting." He further called upon the HKSAR populace to look for solutions to problems "together," as "it is important for Hong Kong people to unite and discuss solutions in the spirit of democracy. Once a decision is made, everyone should make full efforts to move forward." These comments seemed to constitute both a fair and a perceptive characterization of Tung's first-term performance in many areas and also to be pertinent advice on how to overcome the crux of the problems that undermined that performance. Premier Zhu's exhortations should be regarded as a tall order for Tung, exhorting him to exercise true leadership so as to unite the community in seeking and acting upon the right solutions. In this sense, the final verdict on the early phase of the HKSAR experience must await the completion of the chief executive's second term on June 30, 2007.

So far, it is not clear that Tung Chee-hwa has really recognized the full dimensions of his governance crisis, especially his own leadership style. Recently, in his SAR chief executive reelection campaign, Tung only acknowledged "inadequacy" in three main aspects of his first term administration, namely, appreciation of public opinion, political orientation, and policy research.[2] As revealed in his December 13, 2001 formal declaration to seek a second term and in a late January 2002 booklet sent to the eight-hundred members of the HKSAR Election Committee (that should supposedly elect the next chief executive in March 2002), Tung claimed major achievements in seven areas while only admitting to "administrative inadequacies" of a mere technical or procedural nature, such as in predicting community response to his policies, balancing sectoral interests, and setting clear priorities.[3] Even his pledges for second term "commitments" focus principally on administrative reform and elimination of budget deficits. It remains to be seen if the second Tong Regime could undertake breakthrough efforts to mitigate the many problems experienced in his first term.

While no single academic volume could easily encompass the full dimensions, myriad issues, and complex experiences of the HKSAR in its first four and a half years of existence, the collection of thirteen substantive scholarly essays in this book will vividly delineate and carefully assess the key developments and critical changes unfolding in Hong Kong as a part of China since July 1, 1997. Following this brief introductory and impressionistic sketch are five chapters focusing on the SAR's political, electoral, and administrative systems in action. The next two chapters analyze some of the vital facets of the SAR's legal and constitutional functioning. Then come two chapters that review the territory's economic crisis impact and response, and also land-use planning and developmental politics in the still capitalistic HKSAR. Another two chapters address the pertinent issues in the controversial discourse on language policy and higher education autonomy, and the final two chapters examine media politics and cultural trends in postcolonial Hong Kong. At the end a conclusion first summarizes the major findings and key observations of these essays in the broader context of the HKSAR's overall experience with many crises and unique blessings, and then offers a sweeping vista on the unfolding trends and future prospects of China's Hong Kong in its transformative path toward "soft authoritarian developmentalism."

Together, the thirteen learned chapters that are the core of the book offer expert analysis and keen insights by international scholars, both Hong Kong–based and overseas-based. They provide an informed, balanced, solid, extensive, and multidisciplinary baseline from which one can appreciate, articulate, critique, and evaluate the performance of the new HKSAR regime, as well as the issues, challenges, and opportunities confronting China's Hong Kong in the tumultuous initial phase of its long march toward complete political and socioeconomic reintegration with the Chinese mainland by 2047. Perhaps, by then, the full record of the HKSAR's transformative processes, which it is hoped will be a record of turning adversities into opportunities, making more with less, and creating success out of necessity, as well as building consensus out of divergences, will justify and vindicate the "one country, two systems" experiment promoting unity of the Chinese nation in the new millennium.

Notes

1. *Ming pao*, April 18, 2002.
2. *World Journal*, January 26, 2002, p. A-14.
3. *World Journal*, January 21, 2000, A-12; January 29, 2002, p. A-14.

—————— 2 ——————

Hong Kong and the Reconstruction of China's Political Order

Suzanne Pepper

The suggestion that Hong Kong might someday serve as an experimental test case for China's political development, whether democratic or otherwise, would have been greeted with disbelief and perhaps even amusement throughout most of Hong Kong's 150-year history as a British colony. From approximately 1949 on, disbelief would have been heightened by alarm over the much feared "difficulties and dangers" anticipated with any such course. The alarm took on very real dimensions after 1982, when Beijing announced its intention to resume sovereignty over Hong Kong in 1997. Yet, five years later, having been reconstituted as a Special Administrative Region (SAR) within the larger communist-led Chinese body politic, Hong Kong was defying all the odds and negative expectations.

Central to the SAR's achievement was a functioning, if still embryonic, multiparty system that encompassed partisan loyalties all across the political spectrum. Hong Kong voters were not only electing their own representatives, but also choosing candidates who included pro-Beijing Marxists as well as anticommunist democrats. Not since the abortive peace efforts that ended in all-out civil war between Chinese communism and its enemies during the late 1940s, had any such political development occurred under the auspices of any national Chinese government. It therefore marked a small milestone in twentieth-century China's political history and served as a measure of success for Hong Kong's transition back to Chinese sovereignty. The apparent ease with which the milestone was reached nevertheless belied the complex dynamic responsible for recasting Hong Kong in its unlikely role as a test case for China's modern-day political evolution. Hence the achievement also could not conceal its own inherent negatives and the distance yet to be traveled if the promise of Hong Kong's progress to date is ever to be realized.

Chinese Reconstruction: The Historical Context

In fact, the dialectical complexities of Hong Kong's political role are best introduced via past perspectives. The term "national reconstruction" became the translation of choice for *jianguo*, roughly a century ago, and remained in fashion for several decades.[1] Later, the phrase would give way to more literal translations (construction, development, etc.), but the idea signified by that earlier term has never faded because the aim of national reconstruction has yet to be fully realized. The goal remains, in other words, to build a modern political order comparable in unity, coherence, and strength to the memorialized ideal of the traditional pre-1911 regime. Nor was that ideal a mere nostalgic figment of early twentieth-century Chinese imaginations.

Foreign observers were also wont to marvel at the disparity between contemporary chaos and the coherence of the traditional system. To them, it seemed as if some ancient consensus had melded ideas and institutions into an integral whole. The result was a political order so strong that it endured unbroken by any external or internal challenge for a millennium and more, yet so interdependent that the whole could not function minus any one of its fundamental parts. Western military technology then produced just such a challenge, precipitating between 1900 and 1911, the sequential collapse of Confucian learning, bureaucratic power, and imperial authority.

For half a century thereafter, the ensuing vacuum was perpetuated by internal strife, foreign invasions, and civil war, with the latter culminating in a mainland victory for the Chinese Communist Party (CCP) in 1949 and retreat to Taiwan for its Kuomintang (KMT, or Nationalist Party) rival. Now, even after another fifty years have passed, Chinese communist and noncommunist successors are still at work trying to put the pieces back together again. All the foreign intruders have been expelled and civil strife is at a record low, compared to past experience. Yet the critical mass that formed suddenly against the traditional order, a hundred years ago, has still not reconverged around any one new alternative. Meanwhile, successors continue to be driven first and foremost by a search for consensus strong enough to reproduce, in a new political order, the same unity and coherence that had sustained the old regime.

One major reason for so elusive a quest, of course, is the habit that quickly took hold, a hundred years ago, of substituting contemporary Western precedents for those of China's own discredited Confucian past. This search for the secrets of Western success naturally focused on strengths rather than weaknesses, and these were most easily identified in terms of prevailing Western-inspired world trends. Unfortunately, there have been several dominant world trends during the past hundred years and many painful lessons lay in wait as China's intellectual and political leaders were attracted to one grand paradigm after another before any could be effectively adapted to achieve the desired aims of national reconstruction.

Once finally convinced that they must abandon the traditional order, Chinese leaders thus rejected it wholeheartedly, hastening from one source of inspiration to the next: from Western democracy and science, to fascism, communism, and then back again with the most recent reopening to the Western world. After 1976, post-Mao China experimented with varying degrees of political and economic democratization, only to encounter the multiple crises that provoked the mass protests of 1989. No sooner had Chinese leaders crushed that uprising, by reasserting the draconian powers of a communist state, than all its authoritative props collapsed with the overthrow of communism in Europe between 1989 and 1991. By century's end, therefore, the verdict of history was clear. Democracy and capitalism had emerged triumphant internationally and if twentieth-century precedents are any indication, China's twenty-first-century directives will be written in that Western triumph.

Complicating that end, however, is an antithetical habit derived from the new attachment to world trends. Hence the impatient rush from one to the next actually produced a complex self-critical reaction, which Chinese themselves identify as "mechanical copying" (using such phrases as *shengban yingtao* and *quanpan zhaoban*). The sequence of attraction and reaction has nevertheless continued since the early 1920s, when the first major backlash set in after the first full-scale rush to learn from the West. Interacting with a developing Chinese nationalism, and with the undercurrent of Confucian conservatism that never completely disappeared, these lessons have produced a key dynamic of modern Chinese history.

For China, in other words, the dialectical sequence has become an enduring fact of public life. Someone is always advocating some dominant or rising foreign model as the key to national salvation. This custom has been handed down from one political generation to the next, and none—whether right, left, or center—have been able to escape its temptations. Yet the costs of impatiently enrolling the nation in crash course emulations of foreign models have been so destructive that the mechanical-copy rebuke can also be produced on demand. When the long-discredited demand for "complete Westernization" reappeared suddenly in the mid-1980s, for example, political moderate Wang Meng responded with the caution born of China's twentieth-century experience. As a young writer in the late 1950s, Wang had fallen afoul of Maoist radicalism during the antirightist campaign and would soon find himself again at odds with the ruling establishment over events in 1989. But in 1987, Wang Meng was Minister of Culture when he challenged "complete Westernization" by declaring its promoters naive in their quest. They mouthed high-sounding borrowed phrases with big talk and ambitious plans, he wrote, "as if reform could be achieved with a flick of the wrist, and then China could be saved."[2]

The current post-1989–1991 generation of leaders in Beijing, like many predecessors, has therefore tried to incorporate that old lesson into its strategy of defensive development. Post-Soviet Russia now serves as a negative precedent, to illustrate the dangers, should China similarly succumb to pressures for complete Westernization. But everyone also knows that the end has indeed been written. Past precedents accordingly decree that Chinese leaders can at best bargain for time and try to control the terms of their own reformation, as the CCP's old KMT rival was able to do from its refuge in Taiwan. But to design and establish some viable "eastern" variant will require time, internal stability, and a favorable external environment. In any case, the destructive sequence of rushing to adopt diverse foreign models should moderate as China works toward a set of political and economic fundamentals that is (1) compatible with contemporary world trends, and (2) can bridge the communist-anticommunist divide to win acceptance within all China's disparate parts.

Toward that end, the struggle for consensus over economics has essentially been won, leaving only the political system in serious dispute. During the mid-1980s, Beijing thought it had hit upon an acceptable solution for the political realm as well. The idea at that time, when the trends were already clear but pressures were far less intense, was to establish Hong Kong's capitalist prosperity and depoliticized stability as the model for China's twenty-first–century evolution. Taiwan could then follow in Hong Kong's footsteps, and the reunification of China's national political order could proceed on that basis.

In keeping with their strategy, Chinese leaders and editorial writers also frequently invoked the mechanical-copy rationale as they debated and explained the plans for Hong Kong's future. Deng Xiaoping himself used the argument against those lobbying for Western-style democracy. "Hong Kong's system cannot be completely westernized," he told members of its constitutional convention (otherwise known as the Basic Law Drafting Committee) in April 1987. "It cannot just indiscriminately imitate (*zhaoban*) the West." To copy everything and set up an Anglo-American system of representative government—with a bicameral legislature, multiparty elections, and a division of executive, legislative, and judicial powers—would not be suitable, he continued. Nor did he hesitate to suggest the concrete reasons for this: "The people managing Hong Kong affairs should be Hong Kong people who are patriots loving China and Hong Kong. Can such people really be elected by universal suffrage?"[3]

Deng Xiaoping had obviously done his homework, however, and he also in effect acknowledged Western democracy as the dominant world trend. Conditions were not yet ripe for Western-style democracy in China either, he said, during that same 1987 encounter. For the time being, direct elections were being held only in the countryside, at the county level and below. But he speculated that, fifty years hence, this basic-level political reform would have evolved into a national system of universal suffrage. He nevertheless warned that trying to speed up his timetable and hasten the process by turning Hong Kong into a base for subverting the mainland "under cover of democracy" would not be tolerated. It followed, therefore, that the two developing precedents, for urban and rural political reform, in Hong Kong and the Chinese countryside respectively, might finally lay the foundations necessary to end China's twentieth-century predicament by successfully adapting global pressures for Western democracy to the realities of China's national reconstruction.

Through a Taiwanese Mirror

Alas, the world has turned upside down or is at least a very different place since the final draft of the new Hong Kong SAR's Basic Law constitution was completed in 1990. Not only has the international communist movement collapsed but Taiwan's evolution into a full-fledged electoral democracy has seemingly risen on the global tide, leaving Hong Kong's Basic Law government to tread water in the trough below. So complete was Taiwan's transformation that the KMT's seventy-year reign over the Chinese republican establishment was finally broken with opposition candidate Chen Shuibian's victory in the March 2000 presidential election.

As heir to Taiwan's longstanding movement for full independence, moreover, Chen's Democratic Progressive Party (DPP) was more determined than the KMT in rejecting a Hong Kong–style solution. Beijing had actually offered Taiwan all the same guarantees and more as a basis for reunification, but the DPP's rejection even featured directly in the party's March 2000 appeal to voters. Candidate Chen Shuibian's election eve advertisement in Taibei's *Zhongguo shibao* (China Times) epitomized the main issues at stake for Taiwan. The full-page March 17 ad mocked Hong Kong's political system with a photograph of its chief executive, Tung Chee-hwa (Dong Jianhua).

"We are electing our president, not appointing a special administrative region chief executive," read the caption above his photograph, which continued below: "The president is our own and so is the state. We have struggled all these years just to be able to decide who our president should be and this is why democracy is so highly valued." Thereafter, President Chen and other members of his administration let no opportunity pass without promising "not to let Taiwan become another Hong Kong or another Macau."

Senior officials in Beijing (as well as in Washington) were initially perplexed by Taiwan's rebuff, which remained unwavering despite both blandishments and threats. The solution, of course, concerned neither economics nor everyday rights and freedoms, but was instead about something even more fundamental, namely, the system of government itself. Easy to overlook from Beijing's vantage point and Washington's globalized perspective, the small realities of Hong Kong's post-1997 political life suddenly stood out in sharp relief, silhouetted against the backdrop of Taiwan's presidential election campaign. Hong Kong's system could now be seen, as it was, bound root and branch to that of its new Chinese sovereign in Beijing.

Without Beijing's approval, no major political decision could be made in Hong Kong, nor could any government leader be appointed, nor changes made in Hong Kong's governing arrangements. Officials never publicly contradicted their sovereign while the press, under ever-greater pressure to avoid certain forbidden zones, could not serve as a medium for unfettered political debate. Hong Kong's economy and its society were indeed free to function as before, but only within the political boundaries fixed by Beijing through the institutions it had designed, the people it approved to lead them, and the checks it maintained on their behavior. Without guarantees of true political autonomy on all such counts, Taiwan obviously would never agree to exchange its de facto political independence for the arrangements on offer.

Hence, the hopes that some had entertained—about Hong Kong serving as an inspirational pacesetter to hasten Chinese political reform—seemed dashed. Beijing's rules were effectively constraining pre-1997 prospects for democratic development even within Hong Kong itself, thereby inhibiting any wider demonstration effect as well. Having already progressed further along the reform path by going it alone, Taiwan had reinforced the deflation of expectations by unceremoniously rejecting Hong Kong's Basic Law enshrined "one country, two systems" formula as a basis for reunification. In this way, everyone had disappointments to share, including both Hong Kong democrats and Beijing officials. For Beijing, the cost of curbing Hong Kong's democratic aspirations was registered first and foremost in Taiwan's distrust of a Hong Kong–type solution.

Yet the promise remains. Ironically, Hong Kong's prospects as a model for long-term national reconstruction may have actually been enhanced by the reduction of its pacesetting potential. With all such distractions at least temporarily curtailed, the SAR can stand alone as a clear and present instance of gradual political evolution *within* the communist state. The goal for China as a whole remains unchanged: a quest for ideas, institutions, and authority that will allow the nation to establish a modern reproduction of its ancient coherence. The CCP-led national government remains unchanged as well, firmly entrenched, yet professing itself still committed to the process of its own gradual reformation. Within this context, Hong Kong has become a living test of Beijing's resolve to build a new kind of government— compatible with both contemporary world standards and China's reforming communist system.

Hong Kong's Controlled Experiment in Democratic Reform

The Hong Kong experiment is presented here in two parts. These concern form and function, or the institutional framework and how it has begun to work in practice since July 1997. Due no doubt to the intensity of preparations beforehand, everyone's worst pre-1997 fears did not materialize, the worst being Beijing's fear of democratic disruption and Hong Kong's fear of a 1989-type crackdown. These fears have not been completely laid to rest, of course, but are instead being contained within the constitutional parameters of Hong Kong's new Basic Law government—where direct challenges have become routine events.

All the political fears are thus reflected in an elaborate system of checks and balances best characterized as a mix of British colonial, contemporary Hong Kong, and Chinese mainland. If this hybrid framework defies easy categorization, however, so much the worse for the system in practice. Concerning its chronology, Hong Kong's first year under Chinese rule (1997– 98) was spent, in effect, cranking up all the mechanism's cumbersome parts, which then commenced operating in the form its Chinese designers envisaged, roughly by mid-1998. The working system's "multiparty, two-line" adversarial features then emerged during the next year (1998–99), as a natural result of the contradictions activated by Hong Kong's return to Chinese rule. The key stages of this formative sequence, once preparations had been made during the final years of Britain's reign, included: rebuilding the preparatory foundations in 1996 and 1997, to conform more strictly to Beijing's specifications; confirming Beijing's designs in practice with the midterm election in May 1998; selecting Hong Kong's delegations to the National People's Congress and the Chinese People's Political Consultative Conference, in late 1997 and early 1998, to serve as living links between the national and SAR systems; and finally, the clash of components and commitments, once Hong Kong's new government actually began to function.

British Colonial Structure, Hong Kong Decor, Mainland Fixtures

For various reasons extending back to the earliest days of Hong Kong's existence in the 1840s, London had always decided against political reforms whenever such questions were raised. Hence the colony was never allowed to proceed along the path toward representative self-government typically followed by other of Britain's colonies and dependencies. Consequently, in 1982 when China made known its intention to regain sovereignty by 1997, Hong Kong had grown into a thriving metropolis of several million people but was still being ruled in the old-fashioned nineteenth-century way. The reasons for its stunted political growth need not detain us here, except to note the basic rationale used most frequently to excuse Hong Kong's anachronistic governing arrangements. Commenting on why all the reform proposals raised during his 1947–57 tenure as governor had been abandoned, Alexander Grantham later wrote that electoral reforms, which anticipated local self-government, could not be introduced because Hong Kong's inhabitants were virtually all Chinese. Chinese, he continued were "generally speaking, politically apathetic" preferring "to leave the business of government to the professionals and the comparatively small number of private citizens who, out of civic spirit or the honor and glory they get out of it, are willing to serve on government councils and boards."[4]

Coincidentally, however, Grantham also alluded to the "difficulties and dangers" of introducing a democratically elected legislature.[5] His reference was specifically to a possible spillover of China's life-and-death struggle between the CCP and its KMT rival. Insulating Hong Kong from their civil war politics, or more precisely from communist infiltration, became a major post-1949 preoccupation—highlighting the contradiction between rationale and reality. The reality was, in fact, not too little Chinese interest in politics but too much of the wrong kind, and colonial Hong Kong had no solution for the dilemma save banning all political life while manipulating the myth of Chinese political inertia.

The Evolving Colonial Framework, 1982–97

As to how Hong Kong suddenly took its place in the forefront of China's ponderous drift toward political reform, a few familiar details will again suffice. The metamorphosis from political backwater to cutting edge was accomplished between 1982 and 1997, while Hong Kong was preparing for its return to Chinese sovereignty. At the start, in 1982, British officials when pressed could still rationalize their failure to introduce meaningful political change in Hong Kong with the stock response that there had never been any real demand to do so. By 1997, Hong Kong had acquired its new Basic Law constitution, drafted under Beijing's supervision, which promised universal suffrage as the ultimate aim for selecting Hong Kong's future governors or chief executives (Article 45) and all members of its legislature (Article 68). The Basic Law also promised Hong Kong, among many other things, a "high degree of autonomy" in the management of its own affairs (Article 12). A new slogan—"one country, two systems"—was coined and repeated constantly to reinforce this promise of autonomy within the Chinese state.

Meanwhile, between 1982 and 1997, the British-led government had belatedly sprung to life introducing a reform agenda of its own with which the Basic Law had been more or less designed to dovetail. Hong Kong's changing political framework nevertheless remained within the British decolonizing tradition. Such reforms had typically included a gradual devolution of power from the executive, plus various ingenious devices for producing legislators—without actually electing all of them directly through universal suffrage. These devices may have seemed anachronistic, but they reproduced, in effect, colonial variations on the basic theme of Britain's own two-house Commons and Lords parliamentary establishment, with its mix of elected, inherited, and appointed representatives.

Hong Kong therefore proceeded during the fifteen-year transition period as if through a crash course containing all the lessons in colonial devolution that should have been taught long before. In this way, by 1997, the British bequest to Hong Kong included a three-tier system beginning with eighteen advisory District Boards, all members of which were directly elected through universal suffrage. So, too, were the members of the intermediate Urban and Regional Councils that were responsible for various municipal housekeeping tasks (recreation, culture, sanitation, etc.). The Legislative Council (Legco) was also wholly elected, although not wholly by universal suffrage. Only twenty of its sixty seats were filled by direct election on a one-person, one-vote basis, in synchronization with the Basic Law's post-1997 designs. Two such partial Legco elections had already been held, in 1991 and 1995, and by the time of the second, Hong Kong's nascent electorate numbered almost one million in a city of six million people.[6] But the majority of Legco's seats were filled indirectly via the old corporatist principle of representation. This was adapted for Hong Kong use to produce functional constituencies with the latter weighted heavily in deference to business and finance.

Theoretically, legislators still enjoyed minimal power since the system remained executive-led and its British governor could disallow any bill or override any decision. This he continued to do in consultation with his appointed Executive Council, or cabinet of advisors. Legco had nevertheless moved well beyond the genteel consultation-and-consensus mode of colonial practice, to a more aggressive style of parliamentary discourse. Additionally, both the government and sometimes councilors themselves were introducing and passing a wide range of long overdue civil rights and social reform legislation.

Anomalies had, of course, always abounded in colonial Hong Kong. Except for its system of government as well as associated aspects of political life and education, the territory had actually enjoyed an abundance of rights and freedoms. In Grantham's day, these benefits tended to be stated in minimal terms focusing on the public's alleged minimal demands for law and order, low taxes, and justice in the courts. By 1982, anomalies were more striking, since Hong Kong had become a self-conscious alternative to almost everything that the Chinese homeland was not. After serving for three decades as refuge of choice for those fleeing the political and economic excesses of China's communist revolution, Hong Kong promoters were wont to boast about its laissez-faire economy, rule of law, open society, free press, religious tolerance, and indeed about almost everything—except its system of governance. With Hong Kong's post-1982 political reforms, however, came a realization that many of its much-vaunted rights and freedoms were, relative to evolving world standards, almost as anachronistic in practice as the governing arrangements that sustained them. Following the introduction of a modern Bill of Rights ordinance in 1991, therefore, the rush of new civil rights and social reform legislation rounded out Hong Kong's eleventh-hour effort, at the very end of British rule, to make up for the political time lost during all the years before.

Hong Kong Decor: The Emerging Political Culture

Along with its changing constitutional framework, Hong Kong had also acquired a new political culture strong enough to sustain new popular demands for faster movement than the Basic Law allowed, toward fully elected self-government. The Basic Law stipulated a gradual ten-year progression from 1997, toward direct elections for half the sixty-seat legislature, but failed to include a timetable either for phasing out the thirty functional constituency seats thereafter, or for directly electing the chief executive. In making such demands, Hong Kong's new "democracy movement" had surprised many within the allegedly apathetic local community since political activism seemed to grow quite naturally, in a sequence that proceeded roughly as follows. The British belatedly initiated political reforms, beginning with partial District

Board direct elections in the early 1980s, to serve as a source of protection against possible future mainland interference; local activists then raced ahead to set the pace; and Hong Kong's Chinese elite establishment more or less reluctantly fell in behind.

Partisan politicking had actually commenced as soon as electoral reforms were introduced and these became the foundation upon which Hong Kong's nascent political spectrum began to differentiate. During the debate surrounding its introduction in the 1980s, a favorite conservative argument emerged against Western-style political competition. Chinese shunned open public disagreement, it was said, in deference to social harmony and face-saving consensus, preferably achieved under the watchful eye of benevolent governing elites and their intellectual advisors. This line of reasoning found favor especially within business circles and among some professionals. Their arguments then gained real urgency during the Basic Law drafting process, between 1985 and 1990, once the idea of elected self-government began to take hold.[7] The outline of Hong Kong's current partisan divisions followed accordingly, from the diverse efforts to influence its future constitutional design during these years. Conservatives seemed to be updating the old political apathy rationale, together with its contradictory concern about difficulties and dangers. Hong Kong's business community, in other words, feared not too little partisan enthusiasm but too much of the wrong kind, and so did Hong Kong's future Chinese sovereign. The result was a coalition of "conservative" interests similar to that between government and business in prereform colonial days.

So genuine were conservative assumptions about Chinese social norms, however, that they guided arrangements for Hong Kong's first popular Legislative Council election in September 1991. Only eighteen of the council's sixty seats were to be filled by universal suffrage. The territory was therefore divided into nine electoral districts with two seats per district and each elector allowed two votes. The idea was to minimize partisan bickering and spare everyone the "un-Chinese" necessity of choosing between candidates. Instead, participants took to the contest like ducks to water.

Hong Kong's most popular budding politicians were those, such as Martin Lee (Li Zhuming) and Szeto Wah (Situ Hua) who had made names for themselves as pro-democracy activists while the Basic Law was being drafted. They devised a strategy in the 1991 election's double-seat districts of pairing more and less prominent candidates on democratic tickets. This produced a coattail effect, doubling majority preferences by encouraging voters to tap their favorite politicians—not once but twice. Accordingly, these candidates swept the field ultimately winning (after a by-election) seventeen of the eighteen seats contested. A few candidates tried to go against the tide with more neutral or pro-Beijing platforms, but were swept aside by its force (see Table 2.1). Thus Hong

Table 2.1

Hong Kong's Political Fundamentals

The Voting Public and Its Preferences

Direct Legco elections	Voters[a]	Turnout rate[b]	Democratic camp[c]	Pro-China camp[d]	Conservatives[e]
1991[f] (18 seats)	750,467	39.15	72.01	11.76	16.23
1995[g] (20 seats)	920,567	35.79	63.13	30.31	2.37 (inc.)
1998[h] (20 seats)	1,489,705	53.29	65.94	25.07	6.88
2000[i] (24 seats)	1,331,000	43.57	61.87	30.62	6.65

a. Total number of voters.

b. Percentage of registered voters.

c. Association for Democracy and People's Livelihood, Meeting Point, United Democrats, Democratic Party, 123 Democratic Alliance, Frontier, Citizens Party, Neighborhood and Workers Service Center, Independents (Andrew Wong etc.).

d. Federation of Trade Unions, Democratic Alliance for the Betterment of Hong Kong, Hong Kong Progressive Alliance, Independents (Elsie Tu etc.).

e. Liberal Democratic Federation, New Hong Kong Alliance, Liberal Party, New Territories Alliance, New Century Forum, Independents.

f. *Sources:* Candidates and official returns, in, *South China Morning Post*, September 14 and 16, 1991, respectively.

g. *Sources:* Official returns in, *South China Morning Post*, September 19, 1995.

h. *Sources:* Official returns in, *South China Morning Post* and *Ming Pao Daily News*, both May 25 and 26, 1998; also, "Results of the 1998 Legislative Council Election" (http://www.info.gov.hk/gia/general/199805/25/0525201.htm).

i. *Sources:* Official returns in, *South China Morning Post* and *Ming Pao Daily News*, both September 11 and 12, 2000; also, "2000 Legislative Council Election Results," (http://www.elections.gov.hk/elections/update/result/gc_e.htm).

Kong's "democratic camp" came into being as an informal combination of like-minded political interest groups and independents all devoted to the cause of directly elected government both as an end in itself and also as a safeguard for Hong Kong's post-1997 autonomy.[8]

The complex patterns of Hong Kong's nascent partisan system were all reflected in that 1991 exercise, including both past roots and future branches.[9] On the emerging democratic end of the spectrum, victory was accentuated not only by the double-seat voting districts, of course, but by events just past. Hong Kong had been galvanized as never before by the 1989 Chinese student protests. Their violent suppression in Beijing's Tiananmen Square on June 4 confirmed everyone's worst fears about the dangers of Chinese Communist rule. These fears in turn gave a tremendous boost to the democrats' argument for elected self-government, and its logic seemed further vindicated during the next two years as democratically elected governments succeeded collapsing communist regimes throughout Eastern Europe and the Soviet Union. Finally, reinforcing this new international tide was Hong Kong's post-1949 history as a place of refuge from China's own communist revolution.

Hong Kong had actually become an anticommunist town long before 1989, and the exclusion of its pro-Beijing community bore witness to that reality. Hong Kong's CCP branch remained hidden within this community, by necessity as well as by choice. After the Hong Kong government lifted restrictions on political parties in the early 1990s, this CCP branch remained unacknowledged in deference to local sensitivities. The larger community called itself *aiguo* (patriotic) rather than pro-communist, and its members, even today, will admit to a belief in Marxism but nothing more. The larger community centered around PRC-owned or affiliated enterprises and organizations, the largest being the Hong Kong Federation of Trade Unions (FTU) with an associated membership of about two hundred thousand in the 1980s. Before 1982, members of this community were also effectively excluded from all Hong Kong's leading government, social, and intellectual establishments. Hence these "leftists" or "pro-China" partisans, as they were called, had little choice but to keep to themselves, with the multipurpose Hong Kong office of the *Xinhuashe* (New China News Agency, or NCNA) serving as their political headquarters, social center, and cover for the local CCP branch.[10]

By 1991, some pro-Beijing loyalists had begun to venture beyond the security of their own circle, but the few who stood as candidates that year were overwhelmed by the democratic tide running against them. At this end of the spectrum, defeat vindicated the Chinese leadership's assessment of how best to guarantee its own post-1997 rule over Hong Kong. That conclusion had been articulated by Deng Xiaoping himself in the above-cited 1987 comment on why he had no intention of allowing a fully elected government to be established in Hong Kong any time soon. Those running the SAR should be "patriotic," he had noted with reference to this community, and he had estimated correctly that they would not be the first choice of Hong Kong voters.

The restrictive Basic Law formula therefore emerged as an interim solution for indefinite duration. Its design reproduced the existing executive-led government, augmented by a slowly evolving legislature to be dominated for at least ten years through a controllable majority of indirectly elected representatives. Chinese leaders were bound by their promise not to rule directly from Beijing and constrained by the isolation of their natural allies in Hong Kong. A conservative coalition thus continued to develop as the search for partners extended to anyone whose interests or inclinations might similarly conflict with the rising populist tide. The resulting mixed marriage of convenience joined Hong Kong's patriotic community (which began differentiating itself as the "traditional left") with the previously antithetical "old right." This latter included leading members of business and the professions or the reigning establishments of colonial Hong Kong.

In this way, the new "conservative–pro-Beijing" coalition was formed, based on a mutual interest in economic and political stability, and shared perceptions of Hong Kong's new democratic populism as a threat. The conservative partnership was also based on a common assumption that the memory of 1989 would fade and that Hong Kong's conservative Chinese fundamentals would ultimately prevail, thereby reducing the democrats' popular advantage. Meanwhile, Legco may have emerged as the central focus of political debate and reform. But conservatives could remain secure in their domination of that body through the functional constituency device, which disproportionately favored business and professional sectors.

Hong Kong's partisan divisions were thus already in place when Conservative Party leader Christopher Patten was appointed in 1992 to serve as the colony's last British governor. That Beijing and its Hong Kong allies nevertheless blame him for all that happened next is indicative of the political dynamic his tenure provoked. Rather than build bridges of convergence with China's Basic Law plans, as promised, Britain's Conservative Party government turned against its conservative Hong Kong business partners and transferred its loyalties to their rising democratic opposition. So enthusiastically did Patten pursue this new course during his five-year term of office that, by 1997, adversarial "two-line" politics had become part of Hong Kong's new reality.

It would be an exaggeration to say that Patten's mission—to hasten the pace of democratic reform beyond the Basic Law's original intent—polarized Hong Kong. Nor is it even possible to conclude that his efforts accomplished more for the cause of democratic development than might have been achieved gradually under the Basic Law's intended convergence formula. What the controversy he provoked did accomplish, however, was the politicization of Hong Kong to a degree unanticipated by either the Chinese or the British prior to 1992. Hence the details of Patten's reform agenda and the ensuing Sino-British dispute may be well known, but the story of their continuing impact on Hong Kong's political evolution has yet to be concluded, much less told.

To summarize, Patten's reforms were introduced unilaterally and implemented without Beijing's approval, but were advertised at the time as modest variations on Basic Law themes.[11] The variations, more accurately, exploited loopholes and empty spaces within the Basic Law to achieve a top-to-bottom renovation of Hong Kong's evolving constitutional order. Most important were its three levels of government, namely, the eighteen District Boards, two municipal councils, and Legco. The two lower tiers became fully and directly elected during his tenure; the residual practice of appointing some members was dropped. Since the Basic Law did not prescribe arrangements for either of these two levels, the question of violating its intent seemingly did not arise. The same could not be said for Legco, however, where Basic Law drafters, Hong Kong activists, and latterly British negotiators had fought long and hard to achieve the stipulated design. This included the twenty directly elected members in the sixty-seat chamber as of 1997, with an increase to thirty such members over the subsequent decade. Instead of this arrangement, Patten manipulated loopholes to innovate for nineteen of the forty functional constituency-based seats, and then applied his innovations to create the 1995 transitional legislature. According to prior agreements on convergence, its four-year term was not to be interrupted by the 1997 divide. But Patten's variations sought to create the closest equivalent possible to direct elections for nineteen additional seats, thereby significantly disrupting the Basic Law's "safe" functional constituency majority.

Additionally, Patten exploited his skills as Hong Kong's first-ever politician governor to the fullest, setting the pace with an unprecedented schedule of press conferences, monthly question-and-answer sessions in the Legislative Council, and so on. His Executive Council contained the same mix of local notables as before, but they retreated into the shadows of their old "consensus and confidentiality" work mode. By contrast, Legco assumed pride of place as the centerpiece of Hong Kong's new interest in democratic reform, which featured direct popular participation, open debate, competing interests, and accountable government.

Equally significant was the impact of this new political culture on the entire emerging spectrum: left, right, and center. However restricted, the Basic Law did promise eventual universal suffrage and specifically thirty such Legco seats within ten years. Unless they were willing to forfeit all those seats to the democrats without a fight, conservatives themselves would have to join the electoral fray. Beijing therefore allowed its Hong Kong loyalists to establish their own political party. The Democratic Alliance for Betterment of Hong Kong (DAB), set up in 1992, was led by avowed Marxist Tsang Yok-sing (Zeng Yucheng) and drew support from the entire pro-Beijing community including all FTU-affiliated labor unions.[12] Sympathizers within the business community were further encouraged by NCNA staffers to set up political action groups much as democratic activists had done in the 1980s. Additionally, conservative businesspeople, who were less closely associated with the pro-Beijing community and its large labor contingent, organized the Liberal Party, led by Allen Lee Peng-fui (Li Pengfei).

Partisan loyalties were also managed with a skill that belied the inexperience of those responsible. Despite much provocation, for example, pro-Beijing candidates remained models of political civility throughout the sequence of council elections held under Patten's reformed rules in 1994 and 1995. Meanwhile, the dubious benefits of "negative campaigning" were left to Hong Kong's pro-Beijing press, with its exclusive partisan readership and editorial writers skilled in the rhetorical invectives of China's revolutionary past. Here, the democrats' implacable stand against the potential dangers of Chinese rule was repaid many times over in columns that regularly vilified Hong Kong's most popular democratic politicians by name, as traitors, slaves, and running dogs of their British and American colonial masters. In response, however, 1994–95 vote counts for the local and legislative councils revealed a pro-Beijing community that had turned out in force—and with far greater success than its pro-business partners—to confront the democratic challengers on their own popular turf.

Turnout rates overall nevertheless remained unimpressive. The highest ever recorded in colonial Hong Kong after limited direct elections were introduced at the District Board level in the early 1980s, was 36 percent for the twenty directly elected Legco seats in 1995 (see Table 2.1). Some 2.57 million had registered to vote, in a city of six-and-a-half million, giving conservatives enough cause to continue projecting outcomes based on assumptions of political apathy and silent majorities. But in absolute terms, Hong Kong's new political culture could be measured in the number of voters that continued to increase, from 750,000 in the 1991 Legco election to 920,500 in 1995. Pro-democracy candidates still topped the poll. They included like-minded independents and members of the new Democratic Party (DP), led by Martin Lee, Szeto Wah, and others. The democratic candidates, well-known activists all, took more than 60 percent of the votes cast for the twenty directly elected seats, and won fourteen. Two other seats went to another small pro-democracy party, the Association for Democracy and People's Livelihood (ADPL), which insisted on maintaining a less confrontational stance toward Beijing than most other democrats.

Pro-Beijing candidates and their declared allies won 30 percent of the popular vote, which netted them only two directly elected seats under the revised 1995 rules. These were now based on single-seat districts and winner-take-all plurality representation. The two remaining directly elected seats were filled by the pro-business candidate, Allen Lee, and conservative democrat Professor Andrew Wong. Pro-Beijing candidates nevertheless won fourteen of the functional constituency and other indirectly elected seats created through Patten's innovations. By contrast, democrats won only a handful of seats in all the small constituencies combined, most of which had been handcrafted for the benefit of business and professional interests. Overall, twenty-five seats were solidly in the democratic camp (nineteen DP and six others), plus four won by the ADPL. The pro-Beijing coalition won sixteen seats; pro-business candidates won ten; and the balance was held by moderately conservative independents.[13]

In this manner, two historic political barriers were finally crossed during the last years of British rule. Fear of direct elections was as old as Hong Kong itself, reinforced after 1949 by fear of communism and the legacy of China's civil war living on beneath the surface of Hong Kong's émigré society. Neither of its once and future sovereigns distinguished themselves in confronting this challenge. Indeed, only the combined force of late-twentieth century world trends and historical circumstances had finally compelled the breakthrough. Nevertheless, the barriers really had been broken. Hong Kong by 1997 had acquired a one-million-strong electorate and a self-conscious new political life style to go with it. Equally historic, even if unheralded, the electorate and its new political culture encompassed partisan loyalties all across the political spectrum. As a consequence of the 1994–95 election sequence during Patten's tenure, Hong Kong not only showed itself capable of continuing to elect its own representatives. Hong Kong had also elected both avowed pro-Beijing Marxists and anti-communist democrats, who then proceeded to work together without incident in council chambers throughout the territory.

Mainland Fixtures: Enforcing Beijing's Rules

That voters and candidates were easing so smoothly into the routines of democratic reform nevertheless constituted only the first act of this political drama. After the British refused to abandon Patten's reform agenda, Chinese leaders announced in 1993 that all his innovations would be dismantled come July 1997. Patten had attempted to hasten the pace of Hong Kong's democratic evolution; in the process, whether intended or not, he also furthered the cause of partisan political development. Beijing's aims were just the opposite, namely, to depoliticize and discourage the activism he had fostered, and to build Hong Kong's new constitutional order more strictly in accordance with Beijing's interpretation of the Basic Law.

Chinese leaders and their local Hong Kong allies set to work immediately in 1993, thereby ensuring that Patten's reforms were accompanied at each step by plans for their negation. Details were announced piecemeal beginning two years in advance of the main Preparatory Committee, which was formally empowered by the Basic Law with responsibility for "preparing the establishment" of Hong Kong's new SAR government. Ultimately, Beijing decided that provisional bodies would be created to replace Legco as well as the lower-level boards and councils elected in 1994 and 1995, until all could be reconstituted in accordance with Beijing's rules.

Official decisions, formal and informal press releases, and unauthorized politicking by many different participants combined initially to create little more than a discordant theme running parallel to Patten's reform agenda. Set amid the multiple distractions of that time, China's polemics and irregular procedures were symptomatic of the transition itself as an interregnum between one regime's ending and its successor's beginning. Such uncertainties nevertheless disguised the specific constitutional renovations that were under way, as Chinese leaders and their Hong Kong partners moved methodically to expunge every last detail of Patten's designs.

Ironically, partisan behavior came easily in this climate. Pro-Beijing participants now set about their work as if they had suddenly won a majority mandate, even though their professed aim was to turn back the political clock or, in official Chinese parlance, try to recreate Hong Kong's old ethos as an apolitical "economic city." Constitutional revisions were managed throughout by a sequence of committees organized on the authority of the State Council's Hong Kong and Macau Affairs Office (HKMAO) in Beijing, with the help of the Hong Kong NCNA branch. "Bipartisan" cooperation with Hong Kong's democratic camp had essentially ended after the departure of Martin Lee and Szeto Wah from the Basic Law Drafting Committee, as a gesture of protest in 1989. Appointments throughout were by recommendation and/or carefully managed selection procedures. Qualifications included primarily pro-Beijing loyalties or conservative associations. The modus operandi was based on Hong Kong's familiar prereform principles of consultation and consensus, while coordination was reinforced via mainland-style overlapping memberships and concurrent positions. Finally, whereas legislative reform had been the centerpiece of Patten's agenda, with the creation of Legco's interim rival, in 1996, the new provisional council became just another of the appointed formative committees. As such, it served the cause of constitutional renovation by publicly debating and endorsing executive decisions in the old-fashioned way.

The chief interim body was the HKSAR Preparatory Committee (PC), and its deceptively simple mandate was implemented with all-inclusive effect. Formed in December 1995, this 150-member group comprised ninety-four Hong Kong representatives and fifty-six from mainland China. Most prominent among the latter were mainland members of the two organizations directly responsible for Hong Kong work, namely, the HKMAO and NCNA's Hong Kong branch. HKMAO director Lu Ping headed the central PC secretariat, which coordinated all work, while Chinese Vice Premier and Foreign Minister Qian Qichen was named committee chairman. Business people made up the majority of Hong Kong's contingent; the remainder were mostly professionals. More significantly, about thirty members of the Hong

Kong contingent held concurrent membership in one or the other of the PRC's two national representative bodies, that is, the National People's Congress (NPC) and the Chinese People's Political Consultative Conference (CPPCC). These delegates, all from Hong Kong's "traditional left" patriotic community, served thereafter as mainstays in all the transitional formations. In that way, they also became direct links between the two ostensibly separate mainland and Hong Kong systems.

Hong Kong's most popular politicians, by contrast, were nowhere to be seen. Organizers blamed the democrats' absence on their unequivocal support for Patten's reforms, which the incoming sovereign was pledged to negate and the PC required to dismantle. Within Hong Kong's democratic camp, only the small ADPL agreed to these negative requirements and received two seats in return. The pro-business Liberal Party was allocated four seats. Shipping tycoon Tung Chee-hwa, already rumored to be Beijing's choice for Hong Kong's first post-1997 chief executive, was named a PC vice chair.[14]

The PC's work included, most visibly, creation of the HKSAR Selection Committee (SC), which was itself responsible initially for just the one task of naming Hong Kong's first chief executive. This Basic Law stipulation was subsequently amended by Beijing to include selection of the provisional legislature as well. Later, the SC was given one additional building assignment, namely, the creation of Hong Kong's NPC delegation. The four-hundred-member SC was organized in accordance with stipulated proportions of 25 percent each for four broad functional categories: business, industry, finance; professionals; labor, grassroots; and political figures, including specifically all of Hong Kong's incumbent NPC delegates and a selection of its CPPCC representatives. At this point, political criteria were formally added to underline the cost of supporting Patten's reforms, with all SC candidates required to accept the legitimacy of the provisional legislature. A few young hopefuls were disqualified after testing this rule by indicating on their application forms a willingness to select the chief executive only, in accordance with the original SC mandate as stipulated in the Basic Law.

Otherwise, restrictions were minimal and interest great, with some fifty-seven hundred people accepted as candidates, although the PC quickly reduced this number to a short list of only 409. Its secretariat produced the short list, conveniently divided into the four categories, which even ranked candidates by order of preference within each category. This left little for the 150 PC members to do at their November 2, 1996 meeting, except check the first eighty-five names in each category on the final ballot, to produce 340 successful candidates. The additional sixty needed to produce the four-hundred-strong SC were reserved for NPC and CPPCC delegates.[15]

After much informal consultation and a period of formal public debate, the SC in mid-December 1996 endorsed Beijing's choice for chief executive. The Provisional Legislative Council emerged in much the same manner. A semblance of continuity was maintained by promising seats to as many incumbent Legco members as were willing to endorse the dismantling of Patten's reforms. Ultimately, thirty-three incumbents were among those chosen by the SC in late December 1996, but except for ADPL councilors, no others from the democratic camp were among them. Only six provisional legislators had been directly elected, in 1995, reinforcing the distinction between popularly elected democrats and indirectly elected others, since most crossover incumbents were also those who had won their seats in 1995 via the old functional constituencies.

Additionally, the provisional council was noteworthy for its mainland-style overlapping and concurrent memberships. Of the sixty provisional legislators, fifty-four had worked in the various Beijing-appointed transitional bodies, including fifty-one who were SC members and had therefore simply selected themselves. Most significant of the overlapping memberships, however, was the first direct link they created between the SAR's emergent legislative establishment and China's counterpart in the form of nine provisional councilors who were concurrently incumbent members of either the NPC or CPPCC.

In late 1997, after being expanded somewhat and reconstituted as a 424–member Electoral Conference, the SC then created Hong Kong's first formal delegation to the NPC. Previously, Hong Kong's twenty-some delegates had been appointed from within its patriotic community and attached to the delegation of neighboring Guangdong province. In the suddenly relaxed post-July 1997 atmosphere, an olive branch was tentatively extended to the Democratic Party in the form of an invitation to join the NPC delegate selection contest. The party responded, however, with a lengthy platform statement carefully itemizing all its goals for democratic reform not just in the Hong Kong SAR but also in China as a whole.[16] DP nominees were promptly disqualified by failing to secure the requisite number of sponsoring endorsements. The new enlarged thirty-five-member NPC delegation thus reproduced the familiar mix of pro-Beijing and conservative talents, as did Hong Kong's appointed 136-member contingent to the companion CPPCC. A total of nineteen such delegates were concurrently members of the Hong Kong SAR sixty-seat provisional legislative council. Among the ten NPC and nine CPPCC delegates holding dual positions was Rita Fan (Fan Xu Litai), who had been elected by the provisional body to serve as its president.

Besides serving as founder for all the new SAR government's essential organizing bodies, the Preparatory Committee also issued a series of decisions to guide the way forward.[17] These decisions, in effect, helped Hong

Kong interpret the Basic Law by clarifying Beijing's "legislative intent." Indeed, the full extent of the PC's legal authority to serve as Basic Law interpreter only emerged two years later. At that time, in early 1999, one PC "opinion" was cited repeatedly and even issued in a rare English translation by the SAR Justice Department, pursuant to its case in a dispute with Hong Kong's Court of Final Appeal over qualifications for permanent SAR residency status.[18] Yet even in their original presumed form as mere guidelines, the PC's various decisions anticipated all the actions and major pieces of legislation necessary to inaugurate the new order and purge Patten's reforms from its system. The Provisional Legislative Council then moved off to a head start in carrying forward this work during its preparatory sittings between January and June 1997, which were devoted to readying, on PC recommendation, a host of bills for passage as soon as possible after July 1, 1997.

Obviously embarrassed as they then moved into seats vacated only a few days previously by their elected predecessors, provisional councilors were at pains to proclaim their adherence to all the old rules of parliamentary procedure and their determination not to be seen as "rubber stamps." Still, the charge was difficult to escape, especially since it became the favorite chant of countless protest demonstrations organized outside the Legco chamber. Inside, provisional councilors quibbled over their motions and amendments, but rarely voted down bills requested by the Tung Chee-hwa administration and demonstrated little courage in tabling their own. The administration's requests, in turn, mirrored faithfully all the PC's earlier decisions on constitutional renovation, which for their part sometimes even exceeded Basic Law expectations. One such case arose precisely because the Basic Law had not even mentioned Hong Kong's District Boards and municipal councils, alluding to them only as district consultative organizations, "which are not organs of political power" (Article 97). Patten had, however, transformed them into the directly and wholly elected foundations of an integrated three-tier representative structure, a change that was interpreted by Beijing as empowering the local bodies and thereby contravening Article 97.

The PC had consequently devised an ingenious but little publicized solution for negating Patten's new wholly elected foundations. Accordingly, the chief executive would be responsible for transforming all the lower-level boards and councils into provisional bodies, pending future permanent disposition, by formally appointing all members after July 1, 1997. All incumbents, including democrats, would be eligible for such appointment. Additionally, the total membership of each body should be increased by up to 25 percent. The provisional legislature then obliged with the necessary enabling ordinance for this PC recommendation and Tung Chee-hwa proceeded to make the new appointments without hesitation. He did retain all existing members, including democrats, but made new appointments with the aim of diluting their influence. Besides guaranteeing a safe conservative balance within each body, this maneuver also ensured that whatever power and authority basic-level bodies possessed derived not from the people but from their executive.[19]

Epitomizing these formative ventures was, of course, the complex Legislative Council Bill. This prescribed the rules governing fresh elections, to be held in May 1998, which would finally create a Legco in accord with the Basic Law's true intentions. The bill, gazetted on August 15, 1997, and passed in September, seemingly left no hole unplugged in its efforts to reduce democratic margins of victory. Yet little was left to legislative chance since the Beijing-led PC and its political small group had already drawn up precise guidelines, which were followed in every detail.[20]

The full implications of the Basic Law model now emerged clearly, with the functional constituency concept taking center stage since it was responsible for filling forty of Legco's sixty seats. All the Patten era innovations were eliminated, leaving thirty seats to be filled in the old-fashioned way. Another ten were allocated for the functional constituency-based Election Committee where the only "new" component added to the Basic Law's general prescriptions was the bloc of more than a hundred NPC and CPPCC delegates mandated for inclusion within the eight-hundred-member body. Not content with the nearly forty-seat conservative–pro-Beijing majority these arrangements guaranteed, the new election rules then stepped beyond the Basic Law, following PC recommendations, to specify proportional representation for the directly elected seats. This replaced the simple majority voting method used in 1995, and the double-seat, double-vote alternative of 1991, and was designed to increase the pro-Beijing voting minority's chance of winning a proportionate number of seats. Patten had maneuvered one-way, expanding suffrage and thereby exploiting to maximum advantage the democrats' popularity with ordinary voters. The new election ordinance maneuvered in the opposite direction with built-in constraints designed to restrict that advantage. The aim overall was to guarantee a "safe" Legco majority for the conservative pro-Beijing coalition by ensuring that democratic candidates could win no more than about one-third of all the council's sixty seats.[21]

Partisan Politics in Action

For all intents and purposes, then, Hong Kong's new political life began in the early 1980s, as a response to the prospect of reunification with China. By

1984, the British Hong Kong government had begun promoting political reform as a source of protection and local activists transformed that cause into an article of public faith. Beijing naturally resented the rationale and Hong Kong's Chinese business establishment, already exploiting the new opportunities for cross-border economic integration, soon came to accept political reunification as well. Once formed, however, the ensuing division between democrats and conservatives took on a life of its own.

The reality of this new partisan dynamic has still not been fully accepted by all the Hong Kong participants themselves, although Beijing sensed the change, evident by the mid-1990s, when it railed against Hong Kong's new "political city" culture.[22] Yet, even as they deplored that development, Chinese leaders and their Hong Kong allies also seemed unable to escape its logic. Given the Basic Law's promise of universal suffrage and thirty directly elected Legco seats by the year 2007, and considering the democrats' landslide victory in 1991, pro-Beijing partisans had no choice but to join the electoral competition or forfeit that field. The stakes were then raised, once the Chinese decided to match Patten's unilateral reform agenda with one of their own. Now it was the democrats who forfeited the field, albeit temporarily, by refusing to acknowledge the legitimacy of China's provisional arrangements. These were pursued, in turn, with a determination that belied the conservative pro-Beijing coalition's political inexperience and proclaimed distaste for partisan combat. Hence the democrats were not only excluded from all formal Beijing-led transitional work between 1989 and 1997. As a result of that exclusion, they also contributed in no way to drafting the rules that would govern their formal reentry into the SAR's political system via the 1998 Legco election.

With the stakes raised in this way and the deck so clearly stacked against Hong Kong's favorite politicians, in retrospect only a Draconian crackdown of the kind they had worked for over a decade to prevent could have halted the partisan dynamic that was under way. Consequently, the key to Hong Kong's continuing political evolution was the still unexplained decision not to activate sanctions that had been prepared or at least threatened by Chinese officials. Those sanctions were epitomized in Article 23 of the Basic Law, which mandated specific local legislation to prohibit subversion against the central government, the theft of state secrets, and political activities by foreign organizations, as well as ties between them and counterparts in the SAR.

Article 23 thus aimed at the heart of Hong Kong's own democracy movement since the Democratic Party's organizational life was closely entwined with that of the Hong Kong Alliance in Support of the Patriotic Democratic Movement in China. The Alliance was set up in May 1989, to support the cause of Tiananmen protesters and like them was declared subversive by

Beijing authorities, a charge that has yet to be rescinded. As of 1997, moreover, the ever-vigilant pro-Beijing press in Hong Kong reported that twelve of the Alliance's twenty core leaders were concurrently DP members. The two groups were also still being accused of being, in effect, one, with the joint aim of "wanting to overthrow the Central Government and its Communist Party leadership."[23] If Article 23 of the Basic Law was to be implemented as stated, and interpreted as similar legal concepts are elsewhere in China, the implications would therefore be great indeed for Hong Kong's political life. The result would be prison terms, an underground existence, or at least drastically curtailed freedoms of speech and association for Hong Kong's most popular political leaders.

Among the greatest post-1997 surprises, therefore, were the Chinese decisions to allow everything associated with Hong Kong's democratic center of political gravity to continue unhindered, despite numerous pre-1997 indications to the contrary. Specifically, the preconditions for a "normal" political life followed from the decision not to invoke the powers granted by Article 23, plus related decisions to allow the press, public demonstrations, and political groups to carry on essentially as before. Once all these conditions had been met and the new SAR government's willingness to implement them was clear, roughly by late 1997, the next big uncertainty was how Hong Kong would respond. For all intents and purposes, then, Hong Kong's "multiparty, two-line" political system commenced functioning within the Chinese state roughly at that same time.

NPC Delegate Selection

The selection of Hong Kong's delegates to the PRC's Ninth National People's Congress provided a good indicator of the way forward. As noted, the DP was invited to join the competition and then hastily disinvited after its nominees failed to qualify due to their platform. The exercise overall was important as the PRC's first ever relatively transparent selection of a congress delegation. For Hong Kong, moreover, the experience contained several clues to the nature and limits of its emerging adversarial system. First, everyone was on their best behavior as they moved hesitantly into this uncharted territory, meaning that political substance did not change but levels of intensity were scaled back considerably. The old angry rhetoric was absent from the DP's thoughtful twenty-four-page platform, which had nevertheless spelled out all the familiar demands: democratization, an end to CCP monopolistic control of China's government, human rights protection, and so on. The only direct Chinese response was provided by Hong Kong's Beijing-owned newspaper, the *Wen Wei Po* (*Wenhuibao*). Its writers, however, seemed suddenly reborn as models of editorial decorum with their careful description of the continuing ties between "a certain party's" unnamed leaders and the Hong Kong Alliance, which persisted in its unacceptable demands to replace one-party rule in China with Western-style parliamentary democracy.

Next, the actual selection process in November and early December 1997 provided even more striking illustrations of tolerance and diversity. Hong Kong's mainstream press, now regaining its equilibrium, seemed fascinated by the study in contrasts this "election" presented, along with the rare opportunity to witness firsthand "mainland political culture" in action. Suddenly, Hong Kong could compare the difference directly, as NPC and NCNA managers struggled valiantly to adapt Beijing conventions to Hong Kong's new political norms. Hence the democrats remained free to kibitz and criticize despite their disqualification. Additional sources of levity came from among the approved candidates and their 424 selectors, since these participants contained a fair cross section of the pro-Beijing community's new conservative allies. The latter, however, included enough Liberal Party and ADPL members, plus moderate independents, to ensure a steady steam of sardonic commentary and leaks from within the otherwise self-contained selection establishment itself. In this way, the contrast was articulated repeatedly, between Hong Kong's own political culture with its new norms of openness, discipline, and free-wheeling debate, by comparison with mainland-style "small-circle" selection, standardized candidate pledges, preordained voting lists, and guaranteed safe results.[24]

Still, there were points beyond which local critics would not go and lines of argument they failed to exploit. The most significant of the latter concerned the overlapping memberships between Hong Kong's own legislature and the NPC and CPPCC delegations that were rooted in Hong Kong's patriotic CCP-led minority. The SAR had been promised autonomy under the "one country, two systems" principle, and Hong Kong's new democratic ways had been promoted as the best guarantee thereof. By contrast and by Beijing's own admission, Hong Kong's NPC and CPPCC delegations were part of the socialist system that did not operate in Hong Kong. Yet once this direct real-life contradiction established itself within Hong Kong's Legco chamber, the contradiction was accepted without a single word of public debate. Such living links between the two legislative systems were seemingly taken for granted, as a new feature of life within the Chinese state. Only mainland-style political culture was not allowed to enter unchallenged—even though the contradiction became self-perpetuating since once established, the ties guaranteed that mainland-style political culture would be introduced as well!

NPC delegate selection illustrated the careful balance all were trying to maintain, even while also maintaining all their diverse partisan commitments.

The democrats persisted in demanding reform in China, albeit at the cost of continued exclusion from the new governing establishment. Yet, sensitive to the conservative charge that their aggressive confrontation with China had become the chief threat to Hong Kong's stability, democrats also moderated their approach, even allowing some relevant issues to remain unchallenged. Similarly, the SAR establishment was unwilling to remove the subversive label Beijing had attached to the democrats' demands for reform in China overall, even while granting them complete freedom of movement within a Hong Kong system wherein multiple measures had nevertheless been activated to curb their influence. The next major tests, then, would be the 1998 midterm election necessitated by China's refusal to allow the 1995 Legislative Council to complete its four-year term of office, and then the SAR's first "regular" cycle of district and Legco elections in 1999 and 2000.

The May 1998 Legco Election: Partisan Affirmation

After the one-year interregnum dominated by the Tung Chee-hwa administration and its supportive provisional legislature, conservative conventional wisdom remained little changed, albeit now based partly on continuing assumptions about the silent majority's political apathy and partly on a one-dimensional assessment of their opponents' strength. Democrats had built their movement in Hong Kong on the potential dangers of Beijing's rule. Since none had materialized, the democratic rationale stood discredited and its adherents were being denied all access to the rewards of public office. By conservative reckoning, therefore, the democrats' popularity was bound to wane and their resolve to weaken. Actually, even the democrats could not be confident that such logic would not prevail. The uncertainty persisted until polling day itself since, whether by accident or by design, all prior indicators seemed inspired by the same conservative assumptions.

Campaigning was low keyed since all the participants remained on their best rhetorically subdued behavior. Uniformity also settled over the exercise, which minimized political differences and focused on common livelihood concerns induced by the local impact of Asia's worsening economic downturn. Campaign rallies had to be scaled back due to flagging interest, and record-low turnout rates were predicted, along with torrential downpours, which turned out to be the one threat that actually did materialize. Hong Kongers defied all the odds with a 53 percent turnout rate for the twenty directly elected Legco seats, even while demonstrating the same 60+ percent preference for democratic candidates as in 1991 and 1995 (see Table 2.1). In absolute numbers, some 1.5 million of Hong Kong's 2.8 million registered voters (in a city of 6.5 million) went to the polls on May 24, with the democrats' share totaling about 982,000 votes.

Having failed to predict the outcome, pollsters were equally unsuccessful in pinpointing reasons. Because of the endemic Hong Kong fear of social conflict, political public opinion surveys do not usually question or at least publicize the socioeconomic backgrounds of respondents. Until recently, this habit pervaded all poll results on questions related to the new partisan divisions and perhaps for this reason, the most reliable postelection survey in 1998 indicated blandly that a great majority of its respondents (59.7 percent) turned out on election day to "fulfill civic responsibility." The second most common response (14.8 percent) was "to support certain political parties."[25] Whatever their reasons, in any case, Hong Kong voters provided a clear verdict and its implications seemed intensely partisan.

Heading into the election, political configurations remained unchanged, albeit somewhat more sharply defined than in 1995, and thus might have served to caution conservatives hoping for a return to harmony. The liberal-conservative dividing line had, of course, been accentuated by the transitional arrangements, and some minor political party developments had contributed further to that effect. Consequently, the habit of thinking in terms of "camps" was now firmly established, effectively ordering the multiplicity of groups and parties into three categories: democratic, business, and pro-Beijing. The latter two were further recognized as coalition partners who usually, but not always, stood together in opposition to the democrats. Reflecting Hong Kong's post-1997 conceptions, the term "pro-China" has been slow to change but is giving way gradually in everyday usage to the more politically correct "pro-Beijing" designation.

The political parties themselves remained small and fragmented, signifying their common origins in the interest and action groups of the 1980s. Largest within the democratic camp was the DP, with only about six hundred participating members and a platform that remained unchanged in its basic demands for various economic and political rights, including a faster transition to full universal suffrage than mandated by the Basic Law. "Radical" independent democrat, Emily Lau (Liu Huiqing) had formed her own group, called the Frontier in English but more appropriately *qianxian* (front line) in Chinese, befitting her aggressive stand, especially on political causes. Democratic reform in mainland China was not among them, however, which set her apart from the DP and its Hong Kong Alliance colleagues. Independent democrat Christine Loh (Lu Gonghui) had also formed a new group, the Citizens Party, which sought to avoid direct political and economic confrontation by focusing on environmental issues. Allen Lee continued to head the pro-business Liberal Party, and the DAB still led the pro-Beijing forces of the old patriotic left in alliance with the FTU. Meanwhile, several pro-Beijing business people and groups had joined together, with active encouragement from the NCNA, to form a "new left" party, the Hong Kong Progressive Alliance. The small ADPL remained with a foot in both (democratic and pro-Beijing) camps.

Whether Hong Kong's complex political arena had taken shape in response to the Legislative Council's equally complex design or vice versa seemed irrelevant. The two were evolving together and each now reinforced the other, as demonstrated by the 1998 election results. These provided a near-perfect mirror image of Hong Kong's mixed record of political evolution to date. Not only did the 60+ percent democratic voting majority hold, but public commitment to electoral politics actually seemed to strengthen, even as fear of China receded. Proportional representation nevertheless fulfilled its promise, keeping the democrats' share of directly elected seats to fourteen. All pro-Beijing candidates contesting in this category united under the DAB banner, as they had not before, and netted a somewhat lower proportion of the direct vote (25 percent) than in 1995. Nevertheless, DAB candidates won five directly elected seats, or one in each of the five electoral districts into which the territory was divided. The Election Committee also fulfilled its purpose, with the help of NCNA managers and the Hong Kong Progressive Alliance, by returning a majority of pro-Beijing councilors. Finally, pro-business candidates and conservative independents regained their pride of place by sweeping the functional constituency sector. Yet they failed to win a single directly elected seat despite fielding candidates in most districts. The Liberal Party was alone among business groups who did so, and the defeat of its chairman, Allen Lee, marked the end of his political career. An even worse fate befell the ADPL, which failed to win a single seat in any category.[26]

Basic Law drafters and Preparatory Committee enforcers could therefore rest content that all the designs and guidelines had achieved their intended aims. Overall, the 1995 "Patten" legislature had divided more or less evenly between the democratic camp and the conservative/pro-Beijing coalition. The 1998 Basic Law rules, by contrast, clearly shifted the balance, producing roughly a 23 : 37 seat division in favor of the conservative and pro-Beijing majority. Underlying hopes and assumptions were something else again, however, since just as all indicators prior to May 1998 suggested that conservative hopes for an apolitical outcome might prove correct, so all signs afterward pointed to something quite different. They suggested a new public interest in electoral participation as an end in itself, rather than merely a safety net for Hong Kong's uncertain political future. The signs also suggested more determined partisan loyalties than had previously been apparent.

Since pollsters dutifully avoided divisive questions, we lack corroborating evidence, but voters evidently treated the 1998 election as a referendum on the provisional legislature. The public, in effect, rewarded every candidate who had spoken out unequivocally for stronger democratic institutions, and especially rewarded those candidates who had boycotted the interim appointed legislature. As a rough rule of thumb, the more forceful a candidate's commitment, the more votes received. Accordingly, Emily Lau's margin of victory was great enough to elect her virtually unknown running mate as well, under the transferable vote method of proportional representation that had been introduced to protect the minority's support for pro-Beijing candidates. By contrast, Christine Loh, who did more than any other democratic candidate to curb her pervious confrontational stance on political issues, just barely regained the seat she had won easily in 1995. Voters were even less kind to Allen Lee and ADPL members who had joined all the formative transitional bodies including the provisional legislature, which Christine Loh did not. In this manner, then, a clear partisan polarization had taken hold. With pro-Beijing forces able to mobilize all their grassroots trade union supporters to stand against a democratic majority determined to reward its favorite politicians, Hong Kong's old apolitical epicenter no longer had enough space for those who tried to keep a foot in both camps.

Lines in the Sand

Buoyed by the unexpected turnout and their majority share thereof, democrats hastened to exploit their "mandate" from the May 1998 election with calls for a constitutional convention, or a referendum, or whatever else it might take to circumvent the Basic Law's constraints on democratic development. Within a month, however, the Tung Chee-hwa administration had done everything it could to kill all such talk, by refusing even to consider hastening the pace of progress scheduled to reach thirty directly elected seats by Legco's 2004–07 term. The political facts of SAR life were thus quickly realized. Much like the election itself, the system could be seen to have fulfilled the intentions of its conservative creators by effectively checking and balancing Hong Kong's competitive political instincts.

Also like the election, however, Hong Kong's new system was probably as inefficient and unwieldy as any ever devised—and it seemed calculated to produce at least one result precisely the opposite of that originally intended. Such an end was achieved by setting conservatives against democrats in a way that, short of barring their competitive urges altogether, could only heighten the tensions between them. By the end of its second year under Chinese sovereignty, in any case, Hong Kong showed no signs of returning to its pre-1982 idealized past. The new "political city" culture was, if anything, more firmly entrenched than in Patten's time, and was being reinforced by an almost daily sequence of adversarial challenges for which conservatives and pro-Beijing partisans were as responsible as the democrats. Multiple examples might be used to illustrate this strengthening polarization, but two will suffice. One concerns the democrats' tenuous relationship with Tung Chee-hwa himself; a second is the related ongoing campaign for a faster pace of democratic development.

Under Hong Kong's Basic Law system, the chief executive is all powerful. Legco, by contrast, is barred from introducing virtually all substantive legislation and is limited in its work to passing government-initiated bills, approving the government's budget, raising questions, debating issues, and entertaining complaints from the public. By Basic Law mandate, Legco lives in the chief executive's shadow and Tung Chee-hwa is inclined to keep it that way. As a conservative businessman, Tung himself had always been successful in keeping a foot in all camps, that is, mainland China, colonial Hong Kong, and Taiwan, and was tapped by Beijing precisely for that reason. Hence by temperament and political inclination, he was Patten's antithesis in all respects. Initially, Tung ignored not only the democrats but all politicians and the Legislative Council as well. He even shunned public commentary, whether extemporaneous or otherwise, which he dismissed as "putting on a show." Or perhaps he was genuinely surprised to discover just how far removed he was from Hong Kong's new political culture.

During his second year in office, however, Tung came to accept the necessity of public relations, even if not political communication. Above all, he too learned that Hong Kong was no longer a place for people who preferred the middle ground. He therefore proceeded to acquire the subtle partisan skills of symbolic gesture and behind-the-scenes lobbying. For example, he keeps his periodic meetings with democratic politicians to a formalistic minimum, while socializing openly with their pro-Beijing opponents. More significant, even while complaining that it cannot rely on a single vote in Legco, Tung's administration quickly became adept at whipping its fractious two-thirds conservative and pro-Beijing majority into line. Consequently, even if they pass the strict vetting procedures and are allowed by Legco President Rita Fan, democratic motions and amendments routinely go down to defeat.

One noteworthy example in this respect was the motion of no confidence in Secretary for Justice Elsie Leung (Liang Aishi). Tung had maintained the colonial custom of appointing a lawyer from private practice to head the Justice Department, but this was not a disinterested choice. Leung was a prominent member of the pro-Beijing community and an NPC delegate as well, prior to her appointment. Afterward, a series of seemingly partisan decisions marked her tenure and the motion of no confidence actually seemed set to pass—until concerted last-minute lobbying by the Tung administration among the functional constituents succeeded in turning Liberal Party legislators to her defense.[27]

Less dramatic but more determined has been the protracted debate over Hong Kong's democratic evolution. Assigned to represent the government in this debate is the head of the Constitutional Affairs Bureau, Michael Suen Ming-yeung (Sun Mingyang). It was Suen who had immediately ended all postelection euphoria in 1998 by declaring that a faster pace toward universal suffrage would mean amending the Basic Law, procedures for which had yet to be studied, much less determined. Undeterred, democrats sponsored a motion debate on direct elections soon after the first regular Legco term began in July 1998. Not only did procedures need careful study, continued Suen, but amending the Basic Law was too drastic a step to take so soon.[28]

Determined to keep the question alive, democrats have continued to raise motions and sponsor debates, albeit to no avail. Perhaps most significant of these failures were the attempts to bloc or dilute the Tung administration's arbitrary decisions to abolish Hong Kong's second-tier Urban Council and Regional Council and restore appointed members as permanent features of the third-tier District Boards. Although not specifically mandated by the Basic Law or by the Preparatory Committee in its formal resolutions, these decisions followed from the above-mentioned interim provisional arrangements. All reflected Beijing's opposition to wholly and directly elected bodies at any level in Hong Kong on grounds that they set precedents for local political organizations rooted in popular sovereignty. Illustrating democratic efforts was the attempt to amend a mild motion on the relationship between executive authorities and Legco, sponsored by nonaffiliated legislator Ambrose Cheung (Zhang Yongsen). Cheung was the Urban Council's representative in Legco, and his motion reflected the controversy generated by Tung's "final solution" for the two municipal councils, which was debated in the fall of 1998 along with District Board reorganization.

Cheung's September 1998 motion nevertheless called only for more trust and cooperation between the executive and legislative branches. Frontier legislator Lee Cheuk-yan (Li Zhuoren) offered an amendment arguing that friendly persuasion was not enough since the Basic Law design itself was to blame for denying those who had won a popular mandate the right to make policy. Lee's amendment therefore demanded a directly elected chief executive and legislature. He also called for an end to the restrictions on private members' bills, plus an end to Legco's dual voting mechanism whereby private bills, motions, and amendments must all be approved by a majority of each of two groups (with the functional constituency councilors voting as one group, and directly elected legislators diluted by Election Committee members forming the second).[13] As anticipated, Lee's amendment failed to pass, but the debate served its purpose by elevating Hong Kong's constitutional development from a transitional question to a permanent political issue. Michael Suen, Legco conservatives, and the government all shifted their moderate pleas for "consultation and consensus" to an adversarial mode, and the political parties responded further in kind, with this issue marking the basic line of division on either side of which everyone took up a position.

The polarization trend also came close to provoking a split in the DP, between "Young Turks" demanding aggressive stands in the Frontier mold and the more moderate old-timers, among whom Martin Lee and Szeto Wah suddenly found themselves. Although the split had not yet erupted into open rebellion, its diverse styles were already evident in the September 1998 Legco debate. Lee Cheuk-yan's rhetoric was reminiscent of the mid-1990s, with its blunt charges of legislative castration, DAB duplicity, executive hegemony, and loyalty to Beijing rather than to the people of Hong Kong. Martin Lee, by contrast, had offered a professorial discourse on Basic Law checks and balances, reflecting the DP's less confrontational post-1997 style. Ultimately, an interim compromise was reached to pacify radicals impatient over the futility of debating society politics. The young Turks had argued that withdrawing from Legco altogether would be preferable. Henceforth, the DP would try to play a dual role by accommodating the new Basic Law system in Legco, while speaking out more forcefully there and simultaneously keeping the popular movement alive "from the streets," where the causes to champion and energies to tap now seemed limitless. Democrats thus ended their first legislative year under SAR rule (1998–99), defeated but not subdued. The final sitting had ended in across-the-board failure for all democratic initiatives on legislation governing the next Legco election, to be held in 2000.

Conservatives were less torn by conflicting commitments, although both the DAB and the Liberal Party were faulted for "turning in the wind" by saying one thing to please their constituents and another when Tung Chee-hwa needed Legco votes. Business people generally demonstrated no such qualms, however. Emboldened by the shifting power balance in their favor, a chief executive who was one of their own, and the economic downturn, business leaders quickly dusted off their favorite laments about democratic politics, articulating them with a confidence not heard in public since 1989. Reinforcing this line of argument, pro-Beijing stalwarts for their part marked Legco's first anniversary under SAR rule with the accusation that democratic forces had tried to dominate the government by reason of their popular mandate. The government owed no such deference to directly elected legislators and should strengthen its executive leadership against them by more energetically mobilizing senior civil servants, public relations, and Legco's conservative majority.[30]

Taking their cues accordingly, some civil servants nevertheless responded in the manner to which they had long been accustomed. Just as the business community was recycling its old laments, so Michael Suen revived the conservative colonial logic that could be traced back to Alexander Grantham and beyond. Details were adapted for contemporary use but the familiar old themes of apathy, danger, and difficulty ran throughout. In his June 1999 speech at a Harvard conference on Asian and international relations, Suen declared that some in Hong Kong were arguing "loudly and eloquently" for a faster pace of democratization. In truth, he said, there was a "low level of interest in this matter in the community at large," understandably since economic issues were of greatest concern. Referring to the Legco debates, he noted disingenuously that they "did not manage to achieve any consensus." Finally, he referred to the difficulties and alluded to dangers. Hong Kong's political parties were nowhere near ready to assume power, direly deficient as they were in terms of organization, funding, and experience. Their "initial metamorphosis" would require at least another decade and even then it was difficult to anticipate how a fully elected legislature could fit into Hong Kong's executive-led system. "The longer the time scale," he concluded, "the better their prospects."[31]

A Pro-Beijing Offensive

By 1999, partisan divisions were also being reinforced through increasingly pointed overtures not only from local pro-Beijing opinion leaders, but specifically from members of Hong Kong's NPC and CPPCC delegations, and also from Hong Kong-based Beijing officials within the old NCNA organization. In particular, this upsurge seemed to quicken after the NCNA branch underwent a rectification of names in January 2000. Emerging after five decades of "undercover" existence, the NCNA's political leadership functions were separated from its news media work and placed under the umbrella of the new Hong Kong SAR Central Government Liaison Office. Although this change went largely unchallenged, it seemed to contravene the Basic Law, which stipulates that only the Chinese People's Liberation Army and the central government's Foreign Ministry shall maintain direct representation in Hong Kong. The local CCP branch nevertheless remains unacknowledged and presumably continues to function under cover of the NCNA's successor.

Leading members of the new *Zhonglianban* (Central Liaison Office), including both locals and those assigned from mainland China, were also more inclined to venture forth in a manner that seemed further to compromise one country, two systems autonomy. They began by speaking out routinely at community functions in support of the beleaguered Tung Chee-hwa and more forcefully on certain specific issues. In April 2000, a deputy director, Wang Fengchao, issued a tough public warning to the news media against reporting on Taiwan independence. His statement was provoked by a Hong Kong cable television interview with Taiwan's just-elected vice president, Annette Lu (Lu Xiulian), who had ventured some forthright comments on Taiwan's differences with the mainland. Despite a countercurrent of local protest in this instance against so clear an interference with press freedom by a Beijing official, the warning served its purpose. Lu's comments continued to be published as reported elsewhere. But no local news organization dared risk a direct follow-up interview with the outspoken Lu, who was being excoriated in equal measure by the Beijing press and by its Beijing-backed Hong Kong counterparts. Hong Kong's economic freedoms were defended more authoritatively after a similar stern warning by a lower-ranking Liaison Office official, He Zhiming, against business people who did not choose their Taiwan partners carefully.

Other subjects took more direct hits, however, including three well-known individuals who had long been targets of partisan editorial wrath. All three—Cheung Man-yee (Zhang Minyi) of Radio Television Hong Kong (RTHK), Robert Chung (Zhong Tingyao) of Hong Kong University, and *South China Morning Post* (SCMP) journalist Willy Lam (Lin Heli)—met turbulent fates in 1999 and 2000, after years of political pressure from Beijing-friendly sources. Of the three, only Robert Chung emerged victorious if not unscathed after a brief but searing public confrontation over an apparent attempt by a Tung Chee-hwa aide to stifle Chung's routinely publicized opinion poll chronicle of Tung's declining popularity. Chung was fortunate to have inadvertently mobilized widespread press, academic, legal, and community support.[32]

The circumstances of Cheung Man-yee's struggle were less auspicious. Her nemesis was CPPCC member and magazine publisher Xu Simin, who articulated the pro-Beijing community's grievances against RTHK as the territory's only government-owned broadcaster. Xu maintained that it had been a propaganda tool for the colonial authorities before 1997, and should have made a more concerted effort to tone down its critical anti-Beijing line thereafter. Director Cheung Man-yee, a holdover from the pre-1997 past, was targeted as the cause of RTHK's recalcitrance and "promoted" to other work in December 1999. Xu's crusade against her finally prevailed after RTHK granted airtime to a Taiwan representative for the purpose of explaining the "two Chinas theory" of then Taiwan president Lee Teng-hui (Li Denghui). Although RTHK is now a mere shadow of its former critical self, demands that it better reflect SAR government policies nevertheless are ongoing.[33]

Willy Lam was the least fortunate of all, doubtless because his detractors included national as well as local leaders. After 1989, Lam covered China in the old-fashioned "China-watching" way, that is, from Hong Kong, and his writing reflected its mainstream critical concerns throughout the 1990s. For example, Lam wrote the story as he saw it when Beijing called a group of thirty Hong Kong tycoons to a special meeting with President Jiang Zemin in June 2000. Jiang reportedly enjoined them to support their much-criticized leader Tung Chee-hwa. Coincidentally, many of these tycoons were core members of the Election Committee establishment, which would be called upon again, in 2002, to endorse Tung's second term. One of those present was SCMP controlling shareholder Robert Kuok Hock Nien (Guo Henian), who was angry enough to send a blistering letter to the editor, accusing Lam of gross distortions. Soon thereafter, Lam's position fell victim to reorganization, a mainland China-trained editor was assigned to supersede him, American editor-in-chief Robert Keatley decided to vet Lam's copy, and he resigned in November.[34] Keatley, too, soon moved on, but not before he had redesigned the paper to suit its publisher's specifications with a new "lite" infotainment format. The result, given other changes among Hong Kong's news providers, has been to leave the territory without a reliable source of information on government and politics, whether local, national, or international, in any language.

These three cases, including the politicking that precipitated them and the accompanying publicity in the pro-Beijing press, paralleled a similar Beijing-directed upsurge of editorial orthodoxy that was under way in China as a whole. Each of these cases also reaffirmed the same contradictory pattern that had been first glimpsed during Hong Kong's NPC delegate selection in late 1997. The SAR had been promised autonomy under the one-country, two-systems principle and its parameters had been spelled out in the Basic Law. Yet, once unanticipated compromises were introduced, in the form of Hong Kong's NPC and CPPCC delegations and the Central Liaison Office, these were accepted without dissent or even debate. Such direct links between the two systems were seemingly taken for granted as new facts of political life despite their dubious constitutional pedigree; only the mainland-style political culture that inevitably followed from those facts was not allowed to enter unchallenged.

The 1999–2000 Election Cycle: Democratic Stagnation

The first regular SAR election cycle took place on November 28, 1999, and September 10, 2000, for the reconstituted District Councils and Legco, respectively. If the 1998 midterm poll measured the adversarial system's capacity to survive 1997, the next cycle tested the democrats' ability to stand indefinitely against the forces now ranged against them. Perhaps the best analogy to illustrate the essential contours of this cycle is the November 2000 U.S. presidential contest between Democrat Albert Gore and Republican George W. Bush. In fact, American Democrats enjoyed majority support for their ideas and policies, inclusive of Ralph Nader on their extreme left. They were nevertheless placed on the defensive due partly to their own mistakes and misfortunes, and partly to their Republican opposition's irreducible strengths. Similarly, Hong Kong democrats continue to enjoy majority support, but by 1999–2000 that support was beginning to show signs of wear and tear. Activists were being forced onto the defensive due to the combined effect of their own lapses and the strength of the new SAR establishment now united determinedly in opposition to them.

The defensive democratic posture was most evident at the district level, where its candidates, in effect, ceded the field. Clues to their abnegation actually lay in the energetic and well-funded campaign run by pro-Beijing forces in the previous 1994 District Board elections. Democrats won 32 percent of the 346 seats contested that year, and declared pro-Beijing candidates won only 14 percent. Yet most of the independents (who captured 48 percent, or 167 seats) also leaned one way or the other. In fact, between 110 and 120 new District Board members were inclined toward the pro-Beijing camp, reflecting residential patterns and longstanding leftist sympathies in many working-class neighborhoods.[35]

With the foundations thus laid, pro-Beijing forces enjoyed a considerable incumbency advantage in 1999. They could also count on recently appointed members to reinforce the ethos of conservative strength. Despite their protests and motions, democrats in Legco had been unable to block or even modify the government decision to abolish the two municipal councils and reconstitute the local boards as District Councils with only three-quarters of the seats directly elected (390 of 519 total seats). For democrats, these calculations were compounded by the government's failure to increase the District Councils' limited advisory powers as initially pledged when the municipal councils' abolition was being debated. Christine Loh, for example, acknowledged that virtually no one in her small new party was inclined to contest the election. Ever forthright, Emily Lau dismissed the exercise as a waste of time, and her Frontier group fielded only nine of the total 798 candidates vying for the 390 directly elected seats.

Ultimately, democrats overall were able to field 219 candidates to the pro-Beijing camp's 201. But the democratic share of seats actually won fell slightly by comparison with 1994, to 30 percent, or about 117 seats. Democrats also suffered some unexpected high-profile defeats, while pro-Beijing parties won 29.5 percent of the seats (about 115) in a dramatic increase over 1994.[36] Momentum had clearly shifted from one camp to the other and was reinforced by the conservative inclinations of virtually all the independents and others. The result was then compounded by Tung Chee-hwa's failure to include any democrats on the list of 102 appointed district councilors he submitted to Beijing for approval in December, and by the twenty-seven additional conservative "rural" ex-officio representatives of Hong Kong's original precolonial residents. The SAR's new District Councils were now safe and secure under government control, which had been accomplished through a series of intricate maneuvers that owed as much to Hong Kong's tradition of colonial management as to Beijing's fear of democratic disruption. When leaders of the eighteen councils were selected in January, all were either pro-Beijing or conservative, with the exception of one each for the DP and ADPL.[37]

That Hong Kong's democrats have been placed on the defensive is not surprising given the strength of the national and local forces aligned against them. Before 1997, they had actually braced for much worse. By the September 2000 Legco election, however, they were being criticized by friend and foe alike for failing to adapt more quickly to their changed surroundings. Democratic strength was consequently being both eroded and squandered by their opponents' success and by errors for which democrats had no one to blame but themselves. Indeed, what seemed most lacking was neither smart strategies nor clever tactics but something their opponents had in abundance, namely, conceptual clarity—of goals and of purpose.

Both before and after 1997, pro-Beijing patriots and conservatives rallied easily around the watchwords "stability" and "prosperity," as defined by officials in Beijing and Hong Kong. Before 1997, the democratic cause was equally clear and understood by all: elected self-government was not just a source of protection against Beijing's interference but also a means of linking China and Hong Kong and every individual with mainstream twentieth-century world history. The cause was at once long term and immediate, and everyday lives were inspired by its promise. After 1997, as fear of China diminished, the multiple struggles for democratic reform remained ongoing sources of political energy. Yet, instead of being exploited as such, that energy began to fragment into a multitude of details and distractions, while the larger cause like the forest was often lost for the trees. Christine Loh's surprise retreat from electoral politics provides a clear case in point.

The unexplained withdrawal of so articulate a voice from the campaign hustings might have been seen as a blow to the democratic cause and a victory for Tung Chee-hwa's depoliticization efforts had Loh not damned his administration as she went, for obstructing Legco's work at every turn. But democrats then failed to take their cue and turn the 2000 election into a referendum on political reform—since plans will have to be laid and popular interest mobilized during Legco's 2000–04 term if the promised 2007 review is to materialize with substantive results. Hence the public headed to the polls on September 10 with a passive impression of legislative futility rather than active proposals for what to do about it, leading one local sympathizer to complain that Hong Kong democrats seemed to have given up the struggle and decided to wait for Beijing to hand them universal suffrage on a silver platter! Little wonder that turnout fell back from the 53 percent high of 1998 to a more standard "colonial" norm of only 43.57 percent (see Table 2.1). Little wonder, too, that the democratic camp (ADPL) managed to win only one of the four new directly elected seats and the DP saw its share of the total vote slashed from 43 percent in 1998, to 35 percent, amounting to a "loss" of about 172,000 votes.

The 2000 election differed from that of 1998 only in that four additional seats were added to the directly elected category, to make a total of twenty-four returned from the same five electoral districts. Election Committee seats were accordingly reduced from ten to six; thirty seats remained to be filled by individual functional constituencies. The 800-member KHSAR Election Committee was itself elected, as before, with a guaranteed pro-Beijing bloc of at least 100 by reason of the NPC-CPPCC link. Overall, the results were also similar to those in 1998, with a 23 : 37 or 21 : 39 split (depending on how a few independents are calibrated) between seats won by the democratic camp and by its pro-Beijing conservative rivals, respectively. The democratic camp's 60+ percent majority of the total vote count also held. But these similarities obscured the shifting dynamic, worth roughly a 5 percentage-point gain for pro-Beijing forces. The similarities also obscured the continuing polarization pressures at work.

Translated into real votes, and bearing in mind the higher turnout rate in 1998, democratic candidates, all inclusive, had won some 982,289 votes, or 66 percent of the total cast that year, in comparison with 373,428 votes for all pro-Beijing candidates. In 2000, the figures were 823,551 and 407,576, respectively. Between 1998 and 2000, pro-Beijing candidates thus picked up 34,000 additional votes, while the DP's loss of 170,000 evidently accounted for most of the 10 percentage-point decline in voter turnout over the period.

This shifting dynamic is all the more significant, however, because it suggests not so much voter apathy as unfulfilled partisan aspirations. Certainly, such sympathies contributed to the rise in pro-Beijing turnout, with loyalists rallying strongly around DAB vice chair Gary Cheng (Cheng Jienan). Their determination "not to lose a single vote" paid off and then some, after the pro-democracy *Apple Daily* (*Pingguo ribao*, August 23, 24, 25, and 26, 2000) scooped his influence peddling and personal indiscretions in an exposé shortly before election day. Handsome and well spoken, Gary Cheng cultivated an upright image and helped the DAB gain acceptance beyond its core constituency, where his longstanding indiscretions were a well-kept secret among close colleagues. When the incriminating evidence was produced in documentary form, allegedly by a vengeful ex-girlfriend, the candidate's chances of retaining his Legco seat appeared to be doomed. Instead, supporters were galvanized by the emergency and by another surge of inflammatory rhetoric about spies and conspiracies and a future too terrible to contemplate should "radical" democrats succeed in their "plot" to take over Hong Kong.

The Gary Cheng exposé, in fact, seemed to vindicate such Chinese-style negative campaigning, and conspiracy became a leitmotif of the pro-Beijing camp's election drive throughout the summer. The Robert Chung inquiry and Willy Lam's critical articles, plus an ongoing series of small but noisy street protests by students and others over various issues, were all rationalized as deriving from a democratic plot. This argument, traced to unnamed "sources" and widely repeated by word of mouth, accused democrats of trying to revive their own fortunes in advance of the September Legco poll by exploiting Tung Chee-hwa's ever-declining popularity with the aim of driving him from office, destabilizing Hong Kong society, and seizing power for themselves. Gary Cheng's running mate, Choy So-yuk (Cai Suyu), used this logic to shrill effect during the closing days of the election campaign, and the final drive was, in any case, more than enough to save all leading DAB candidates including Cheng himself.

Patriotic nightmares did almost come true, however, with the near success of Trotskyite Leung Kwok-hung (Liang Guoxiong), alias Long Hair. A fervent nationalist and critic of both capitalism and Beijing-style communism, Leung's nickname followed from a vow made in 1989 not to cut his hair until Beijing reversed its verdict against the Tiananmen protest. After serving a brief sentence for disturbing the peace, Leung emerged from prison shorn of his waist-length locks but no longer content to shout slogans from Legco's public gallery. He resolved instead to continue his struggle from the floor of the council chamber itself and chose to contest the election in Emily Lau's five-seat constituency, thereby making her a victim of her own success. Leung proved surprisingly popular with university students in the district and took 18,000 of Lau's votes, not quite sufficient to win a seat himself but enough to slash her usual surplus and deprive her running mate of his expected coattail victory. Leung's hastily organized campaign was also the only one in town daring enough to challenge the conspiracy theorists head on by calling openly for Tung Chee-hwa's departure. In 1998, Hong Kong did not reward candidates who had tried to find a safe middle ground somewhere along the pro-Beijing/pro-democracy divide. Two years later, both the DP and Emily Lau paid a similar price after they, too, began temporizing between confrontation and accommodation.

Finally, in one last bitter footnote, Gary Cheng resigned his seat and democrats united behind the candidacy of independent lawyer Audrey Eu (Yu Ruowei) who insisted on campaigning as a moderate for the December 2000 by-election. In what was essentially a two-horse race with DAB candidate Christopher Chung (Zhong Shugen), she was unable to achieve the usual 60 percent democratic majority share even in the predominantly pro-democratic Hong Kong Island constituency. Instead, the contest produced a 52.1 percent–37.6 percent division of votes cast for Eu and Chung respectively. The by-election returns for all candidates were: democratic camp, 54.5 percent, and pro-Beijing plus conservatives, 45.2 percent.

Whither Hong Kong's New Democracy?

Questions about why earlier talk of mainland China's inevitable "Hong Kong-ization" is no longer heard, and why Taiwan has rejected the Hong Kong model of reunification, can now be addressed more clearly. The pre-1997 anticipation of Hong Kong's likely impact on China had, of course, been encouraged by the success of economic integration, plus the pervasive assumption that thriving market economies are bound to be associated sooner or later with pluralistic societies and Western style democracies. Hong Kong had, in any case, enjoyed so long a period of growth that people could begin to assume the economy was invincible and would guarantee everyone's political future as well. Hence Hong Kong's confidence was badly shaken upon discovering its vulnerability to the Asian economic downturn and China's relative insulation therefrom. Simultaneously with that realization, moreover, Hong Kong on its own had to begin applying in the political realm all the lessons it had learned so hastily between 1982 and 1997, and had to master a few other fundamentals as well.

The British were gone, along with all sense of urgency, the international spotlight was turned off; and in the absence of any major disruption to its way of life, Hong Kong had become just another relatively minor concern on the periphery of the world's relationship with China. Meanwhile, in Hong Kong itself, the economy's managers were not the guarantors of Western-style democratic development but its adversaries. If the democrats and their cause were to survive at all, they would have to stand alone and adjust to a massive shift in the power balance against them. Thus, before they can begin to think again about serving as any kind of political precedent or inspiration for China, they must guarantee their own survival in Hong Kong itself.

By extension, the same uncertain prospects for democratic survival that pertained in Hong Kong also lay at the heart of Taiwan's rejection. China had originally offered the one country, two systems formula as a guarantee of autonomy. In reality, by the year 2000, Hong Kong seemed to be undergoing the same sort of political integration that the economy had experienced a decade earlier, when China and Hong Kong were becoming one another's largest investors and trading partners. The SAR itself now seemed more like "one territory with two political cultures" locked in an unequal contest, the rules of which were being turned inexorably against Hong Kong's new democratic norms.

Yet, ironically, with democratic confidence at low ebb, the second and third years of political life under SAR rule may have actually established conditions for the survival of those same norms. The conditions, in other words, might have dissipated at any one of several points. As a worst-case scenario, Beijing might have insisted on a strict implementation of Article 23, leaving the SAR government no choice but to comply. Second, a best-case scenario might have been just as debilitating by granting democrats such attractive terms that they would have been unwittingly coopted by the new SAR establishment. Third, the public might simply have lost interest and failed to vote, or abandoned their loyalty to democratic candidates. Instead, none of the above occurred. The new authorities obliged by maintaining all the old rights and freedoms. But they also obliged in every other way possible, by reducing democratic margins of victory in Legco, by abolishing spheres of competitive influence at the municipal level, and by diluting elected district representation.

The net result was to make life considerably more difficult for the democrats, while at the same time strengthening partisan tensions between them and their adversaries, which should be sufficient (assuming constraints do not intensify) to perpetuate the political dynamic indefinitely. This is because tensions are routinely reinforced, among other things, by Legco's adversarial voting procedures, which guarantee defeat for democrats on every partisan issue. The system also separates directly elected democrats from indirectly elected conservative and pro-Beijing loyalists on every motion and amendment raised by councilors themselves. In this manner, the rationale for elected local self-government as protection against the dangers of Chinese rule has easily transited the 1997 divide and evolved into a general democratic demand, regardless of party affiliation, for universal suffrage and directly elected government.

Finally, that democrats in particular must continue balancing along so fine a line between confrontation and resignation suggests another condition necessary for the long-term survival of this adversarial system. Thus it seems to be not only self-generating in terms of sufficient partisan energies to sustain momentum, but self-regulating as well—given all participants acceptance of their new places within the mainland Chinese state. Accordingly, the "one country, two systems" formula has become a convenient rhetorical device that is no longer taken literally. This is because the points of contact and interaction are too numerous, and acquiescence is too great, on all sides to permit literal systemic division. Integration, in fact, began with the Beijing-appointed Preparatory Committee's detailed partisan prescriptions for establishing the SAR government. Thereafter, the ties have been strengthened by the government's heavy reliance on Hong Kong's conservative business community with its extensive cross-border economic interests, and also by Hong Kong's increasingly outspoken pro-Beijing loyalists, ensuring multiple direct links that have been absorbed essentially without dissent. All have been accepted as part of the new foundation upon which Hong Kong's adversarial system must operate.

Taiwan is understandably wary of such a result, because it stands in direct contradiction to the island's genuinely autonomous and fully elected alternative. Beijing will therefore have to improve dramatically on the terms of its "one country, two systems" proposal or persist with an offer that Taiwan cannot but refuse. In terms of China's own long-term political evolution, however, the aim is not so much about keeping the Hong Kong and mainland systems separate as about finding viable means of maintaining and improving Hong Kong's governing arrangements *within* the greater Chinese body politic.

Toward that end, the disagreements among democrats over strategy and tactics should be seen as a source of flexibility and strength rather than an impulse to self-destruct. DP leaders were initially uncertain about how long the post-1997 "honeymoon" should last, and whether some coalition arrangement might allow them to be represented in Tung Chee-hwa's Executive Council. The party therefore maintained its low-keyed transitional style until activists forced a logical confrontation. Everyone had only to contemplate the high-profile popularity of Emily Lau and her trade unionist Frontier colleagues, underscored by Leung Kwok-hung's meteoric success, to grasp the continuing link between unequivocal democratic stands and electoral support.

Meanwhile, no one needed to be reminded either about the growing strength of the pro-Beijing competition, now able to mobilize 400,000 loyalist votes of its own whenever necessary. Exploiting the opportunities provided by Hong Kong's new activist political culture, members of the pro-Beijing community were speaking out and making their influence felt as never before. Even Beijing leaders, including President Jiang himself, were unable to resist political temptation. Nor were they inhibited by the "one country, two systems" scruples as they lobbied Hong Kong tycoons and civil servants directly on Tung Chee-hwa's behalf.

If all these conditions are to fulfill their promise for Hong Kong's ongoing political evolution, however, democratic leaders as a whole—rather than just a few individuals among them—must find a more dynamic balance within the new Basic Law order. They need to revive the political commitments and skills that connected activist leaders with their popular base through 1998, but have now begun to stagnate. Currently at risk, in other words, are certain intangible resources that if not tapped more fully will continue to atrophy and once lost will be all the more difficult to rebuild for lack of public confidence. Such resources include not only the street-level activism that energized Hong Kong's new democratic political life during the 1980s and has become, after democratic losses in 1999 and 2000, the focus of conventional wisdom on reviving democratic fortunes. Equally important is the larger historic aim of establishing a participatory system of governance, the aim that inspired imaginations between 1989 and 1997 but has been honored since more as a ritualized item on Legco's calendar than an activist article of faith.

Yet, just as Hong Kong surprised itself on Election Day, 1998, so the new SAR system is defying all the odds. It may have one of the most cumbersome forms of government ever devised, and Hong Kong may be suffering a period of indecisive leadership as a result; but the awkward new regime is also a reflection of the obstacles that have been surmounted in creating it. Consequently, it has registered achievements no one would have thought possible even a decade ago, most notably the establishment of a multiparty system that encompasses partisan loyalties all across the political spectrum. This system is still in its infancy and the conditions necessary for long-term survival are not yet secure. Nevertheless, Hong Kong under Chinese rule is electing its own representatives who include both pro-Beijing Marxists and anticommunist democrats. The fears that have kept those two orientations divided for most of this century are being contained within the constitutional framework of a new government that is as unprecedented, if not as spectacular, as Taiwan's election of a non-KMT president. All the ensuing challenges have not been laid to rest in Hong Kong, but they have been reduced to more or less routine facts of daily political life—which must surely be one major prerequisite for the reconstruction of China's twenty-first-century political order.

Notes

1. For example, Sun Wen, *Jianguo fanglue* (Plans for national reconstruction), (Shanghai: Shangwu, 1930).

2. Wang Meng, "Mantan gaige ticai wenxue" (Discussing reform themes in literature), *Renmin ribao, guonei* (People's daily, domestic edition), Beijing, September 8, 1987. The insights on twentieth-century China's dialectical attraction to paradigmatic world trends are derived from an earlier study of Chinese revolutionary history. See Suzanne Pepper, *Radicalism and Education Reform in 20th Century China* (New York: Cambridge University Press, 1996, 2000).

3. Deng Xiaoping, "Huijian Xianggang tebie xingzhengqu jibenfa qicao weiyuanhui weiyuan shi de jianghua" (Talk to members of the Hong Kong SAR Basic Law drafting committee), April 16, 1987, in *Lun Xianggang wenti* (On Hong Kong questions) (Hong Kong: Sanlian, 1993), pp. 38–39.

4. Alexander Grantham, *Via Ports: From Hong Kong to Hong Kong* (Hong Kong: Hong Kong University Press, 1965), pp. 111–12.

5. Ibid., pp. 112, 136–96.

6. Changes in Hong Kong's governing arrangements can be followed through the consecutive editions of Norman Miners, *The Government and Politics of Hong Kong* (Hong Kong: Oxford University Press, 1975, 1981, 1986, 1991, 1995).

7. For a useful review of the 1985–90 period, see Mark Roberti, *The Fall of Hong Kong: China's Triumph and Britain's Betrayal*, rev. ed., part 2 (New York: John Wiley, 1996). Legislative Council debates provide the best extant record of conservative fears articulated during the 1980s, albeit in less colorful language than that used in less formal settings. See, for example, *Hong Kong Hansard: Reports of the Sittings of the Legislative Council of Hong Kong* (hereafter, *Hong Kong Hansard*), August 2, 1984, pp. 1352–412.

8. Rowena Y.F. Kwok, Joan Y.H. Leung, and Ian Scott, ed., *Votes without Power: The Hong Kong Legislative Council Elections, 1991*, (Hong Kong: Hong Kong University Press, 1992); see also Lau Siu-kai and Louie Kin-sheun, ed., *Hong Kong Tried Democracy: The 1991 Elections in Hong Kong* (Hong Kong Institute of Asia-Pacific Studies, Research Monograph no. 15, Chinese University of Hong Kong, 1993).

9. See Lo Shiu-hing, *The Politics of Democratization in Hong Kong* (New York: St. Martin's Press, 1997).

10. The only direct acknowledgment of Hong Kong's CCP branch, to date, was that made by Xu Jiatun, NCNA Hong Kong director in the 1980s, after his defection to the United States in the aftermath of the 1989 Tiananmen upheaval. According to his memoirs, there were over six thousand CCP members in Hong Kong as of 1983, and "more than two-thirds were local party members." See *Xu Jiatun Xianggang huiyilu* (Xu Jiatun's Hong Kong memoirs), (Taibei: Lianhebao, 1993), vol. 1, pp. 66–79. Although no history has yet been written of Hong Kong's patriotic community, leading members have recently begun publishing personal Chinese-language memoirs and commentaries. For a firsthand bilingual sketch, see "Zuopai renshi" (The leftist community), in Zeng Yucheng (Tsang Yok-sing), *Zhi yen ji: lun Xianggang wenti* (Straight talk: A collection of essays on Hong Kong affairs), (Hong Kong: Tiandi tushu, 1995), pp. 156–61.

11. The only available document outlining Patten's program in full is his introductory policy speech: "Our Next Five Years: The Agenda for Hong Kong," *Hong Kong Hansard*, October 7, 1992, pp. 14–49; on implementation, see Jonathan Dimbleby, *The Last Governor* (London: Little, Brown, 1997).

12. Since Hong Kong's Communist Party branch remains "underground," having never been publicly acknowledged by anyone except Xu Jiatun (see note 10), the identity of CCP members remains a matter of much local speculation. DAB leader

Tsang Yok-sing and his journalist brother Tsang Tak-sing (Zeng Decheng) are among the few who acknowledge their continuing adherence to Marxism. See also "Brothers in Arms," *Sunday Morning Post Magazine*, May 2, 1993, pp. 10–14; Tsang Yok-sing, "Coming of Age in '67," in *Hong Kong Remembers*, Sally Blyth and Ian Wotherspoon, ed. (Hong Kong: Oxford University Press, 1996), pp. 92–101.

13. Based on official election returns in, *South China Morning Post* (SCMP), *Hong Kong Standard*, and *Wen Wei Po* (*Wenhuibao*), all Hong Kong, all September 19, 1995.

14. *Wenhuibao*, SCMP, and *Hong Kong Standard*, all December 29, 1995. Also, "Quanguo renmin daibiao dahui Xianggang tebie xingzhengqu choubei weiyuanhui zucheng renyuan mingdan" (Hong Kong Special Administrative Region Preparatory Committee of the National People's Congress, membership list) and "Xianggang tebie xingzhengqu chouwei gongzuo guize" (Work regulations of the Hong Kong SAR Preparatory Committee), both in *Xianggang guodu shiqi zhongyao wenjian huibian* (A compilation of important documents on Hong Kong's transition period) (hereafter, *Important Transition Documents*), Yuan Qiushi, ed. (Hong Kong: Sanlian, 1997), pp. 379–80 and 261–65, respectively.

15. *Wenhuibao*, SCMP, and *Hong Kong Standard*, all November 3 and 4, 1996. A few Chinese-language newspapers printed the secretariat's ranked short lists, e.g., *Xianggang jingji ribao* (Hong Kong economic daily) and *Xingdao ribao* (Sing Tao Daily), both November 2, 1996.

16. *Luoshi minzhu xianzheng, tuidong Zhongguo fazhi: women dui guojia fazhan de ruogan yijian* (Some of our opinions on implementing democratic constitutional government and promoting the rule of law in China), (Hong Kong: Democratic Party, November 1997), 24 pp.

17. Official minutes or full records of its proceedings and small-group deliberations during the PC's eighteen-month life span, from January 1, 1996 to July 1, 1997, have not been placed in the public domain. The only available PC documents are the decisions, resolutions, opinions, etc., that were formally adopted at its ten plenary meetings and were published originally in various issues of *Zhonghua renmin gongheguo guoyuwyuan gongbao* (State Council gazette), in Beijing. These materials are reprinted in *Important Transition Documents*, pp. 266–310.

18. "Chouweihui guanyu shishi 'Zhonghua renmin gongheguo Xianggang tebie xingzhengqu jibenfa' diershisi tiao dier kaun de yijian" (Preparatory Committee opinion on implementing Article 24, Section 2, of the Basic Law of the Hong Kong SAR of the People's Republic of China), passed by the fourth plenary meeting of the Hong Kong SAR Preparatory Committee of the NPC, August 10, 1996, in, *Important Transition Documents*, pp. 279–81.

19. "Chouweihui guanyu sheli Xianggang tebie xingzhengqu linshixing quyu zuzhi de jueding," (Preparatory Committee decision on establishing the SAR's provisional district organizations), passed by the PC's eighth plenary meeting, February 1, 1997, in *Important Transition Documents*, pp. 301–02; and "1997 nian quyihui (xiuding) tiaolie" (District Boards [amendment] ordinance 1997), in, *SAR Gazette Extraordinary*, July 1, 1997, pp. 105–29.

20. "Chouweihui guanyu sheli Xianggang tebie xingzhengqu shoujie lifahui chansheng banfa xiaozu de jueding" (Preparatory Committee decision on establishing the small group for creating the Hong Kong SAR's first Legislative Council), passed by the PC's sixth plenary meeting, November 2, 1996, in *Important Transition Documents*, pp. 294–95; and "Chouweihui guanyu Zhonghua renmin gongheguo

Xianggang tebie xingzhengqu diyijie lifahui de juti chansheng banfa" (Preparatory Committee's concrete methods for producing the first Legislative Council of the Hong Kong SAR, of the People's Republic of China), passed by the PC's ninth plenary meeting, May 23, 1997, in *Important Transition Documents*, pp. 304–7.

21. Legislative Council ordinance in, *Government of the Hong Kong Special Administrative Region Gazette*, Legal Supplement, no. 1, October 3, 1997, pp. 435–621; see also Linshi lifahui (Provisional Legislative Council), *Huiyi guocheng zhengshi jilu* (Official record of proceedings), September 27, 1997 (draft).

22. Beijing's political city fears were first publicly articulated by Lu Ping during his 1994 visit to Hong Kong. For the text of Lu's speech, see SCMP, May 7, 1994.

23. "Liangfen zhenggang, yige mudi" (Two political platforms, one objective), *Wenhuibao*, November 12, 1997.

24. See Suzanne Pepper, "Hong Kong Joins the National People's Congress: A First Test for One Country with Two Political Systems," *Journal of Contemporary China* 8, no. 21 (July 1999): 319–43.

25. *Minyi kuaixun: haowai* (*PP Express*: extra), Public Opinion Program, Social Sciences Research Center, University of Hong Kong, June 11, 1998, p. 6.

26. Details and analysis of the 1998 election are available from a variety of perspectives, for example: *Report on 1998 Legislative Council Elections*, Human Rights Monitor, Hong Kong, December 1998, 50 pp.; *Power Transfer and Electoral Politics: The First SAR Legislative Election in Hong Kong*, Kuan Hsin-chi, Lau Siu-kai, Louie Kin-sheun, Wong Ka-ying, ed. (Hong Kong: Chinese University Press, 1999); Shiu-hing Lo and Wing-yat Yu, *Election and Democracy, in Hong Kong: The 1998 Legislative Council Election* (College Park: University of Maryland, Occasional Papers in Contemporary Asian Studies, no. 4, 1999); Richard Baum, "Democracy Deformed: Hong Kong's 1998 Legislative Elections," *China Quarterly*, June 2000.

27. For example, SCMP, March 10, 11, 13, 17, 20, and 23, 1999.

28. See "Direct Elections" (Debate), in *Legislative Council: Official Record of Proceedings*, Hong Kong, July 15, 1998, pp. 505–98.

29. See, "Relationship Between the Executive Authorities and the Legislature" (debate), *Legislative Council: Official Record of Proceedings*, September 23, 1998, pp. 1762–836.

30. For example, Gu Xinghui, "Tequ zhengfu ying jiaqiang xingzheng zhudao" (The SAR government should strengthen executive leadership), *Jingbao yuekan* (Mirror monthly), no. 7 (1999), pp. 6–7.

31. Michael Suen, "Asia at the Crossroads: Rising to the Challenges of Reform," speech at the Harvard Project for Asian and International Relations 1999 Conference, June 8, 1999 (http://www.info.gov.hk/gia/general/199906/08).

32. Robert Chung is director of the public opinion program at the University of Hong Kong's journalism and media studies center. His surveys are among the most respected of those conducted by local pollsters, but democratic sympathies were evident in his frequent press commentaries and he had long been a target for criticism by Beijing loyalists. Dr. Chung's first public allegation of pressure to stop his Tung Chee-hwa popularity polls was made in a SCMP commentary (July 7, 2000). He was ultimately vindicated by a formal university inquiry in August, with university head and CPPCC member Patrick Cheng Yiu-chung (Zheng Yaozong) emerging as conduit for the pressure from Tung Chee-hwa's office. Cheng resigned his university position amid charges of "cultural revolutionary harassment" by loyalists, while Robert Chung continued as director of polling but has ceased his press commentaries thereon. See

"Report to the Council of the University of Hong Kong by the Independent Investigation Panel," August 26, 2000, 40 pp. A selection of anti–Robert Chung views is in *Jingbao yuekan* (Mirror monthly), no. 8 (August 2000, pp. 8–13). *Jingbao* is published by Xu Simin, an octogenarian CPPCC member and self-proclaimed critic at large on behalf of the patriotic left.

33. Xu Simin began escalating his campaign against RTHK by raising the issue at the first 1997 convocations of the NPC and CPPCC in Beijing during March 1998. Responding to his efforts, national leaders publicly reminded Hong Kong delegates that in deference to the one-country, two-systems principle, they were not supposed to meddle in Hong Kong affairs (*Mingbao*, March 5, 6, 7, 8, 9, and 10, 1998). Undeterred, Xu and others have persisted in their campaign against RTHK, which remains too independent for their liking. See also *Hong Kong Standard*, January 24, 2000, and March 3, 2000; Zhong Yan, "Xianggang diantai bixu gai xie" (RTHK must change its evil ways), *Jingbao yuekan* (Mirror monthly), no. 9 (September 2000), pp. 10–11.

34. For the relevant accounts of the Willy Lam story, see: SCMP, June 28, 2000 (Lam's article, "Marshalling the SAR's Tycoons"); SCMP, June 29, 2000 (Robert Kuok's letter); SCMP, July 1, 2000 (joint letter by seven other businessmen present at the Beijing meeting, also criticizing Lam); *Asian Wall Street Journal*, Hong Kong, November 10–12, 2000 (Lam's account of his resignation from the *SCMP*); and AWSJ, November 17, 2000 (Keatley's defense).

35. Based on official election returns in, SCMP and *Hong Kong Standard*, both September 20, 1994; also, *Mingbao* (Ming Pao daily news), Hong Kong, September 21, 1994.

36. Based on official election returns in, SCMP, *Hong Kong Standard*, and *Ming Pao Daily News*, all November 30, 1999.

37. SCMP, December 31, 1999, *Hong Kong Standard*, December 28 and 31, 1999, January 15, 2000. For a full account, see Wing-yat Yu, Kwok-fai Wan, and Shiu-hing Lo, "The 1999 District Councils Elections," chapter 5 of this volume.

3

Realpolitik Realignment of the Democratic Camp in the Hong Kong SAR

Ming K. Chan

Five years, indeed, can be a very long time in politics, especially for the democratic camp in Hong Kong. The past fifty-some months since Hong Kong's retrocession to People's Republic of China (PRC) sovereignty in July 1997 have witnessed four seasonal changes for the democratic camp in both electoral maneuvers and realpolitik struggles.[1] The first phase, July 1997–April 1998, saw almost all the major prodemocratic figures absent from PRC-appointed Special Administrative Region (SAR) provisional legislature (PLC). The second phase, May 1998–April 1999, was a rebound for the democratic camp returning to the arena on their first SAR Legislative Council (Legco) elections victories. The third phase, from spring 1999 to summer 2000, was marked by the democratic camp's marginal performance in the District Council (DC) elections, the abolition of the Urban Council and Regional Council, and bitter internal strife on economic policy and electioneering. The most recent fourth phase, still unfolding since the September 2000 second SAR Legco elections, has been a period of retrenchment for the democratic camp against the ascendancy of the pro-Beijing bloc and public disenchantment with political parties.

A common trend linking these four phases of the democratic camp's experience is the rising level of frustration and internal discontent among its rank and files due to the restricted political space and diminishing parliamentary effectiveness in the SAR. By design, the Legco is the institutional forum for the SAR's political parties to establish themselves as nonruling parties to enact law and to debate policies only. They have little direct input into the selection of the SAR rulers. The deformed SAR polity of the Basic

Law–dictated, executive-led system created serious problems for the democratic camp to function effectively as a parliamentary opposition. The limited autonomy the SAR has so far enjoyed in charting the future course of constitutional reform and further democratization reflects Beijing's determination to marginalize the Hong Kong democratic camp. Indeed, the democratic camp, despite its popular electoral support during the past decade, is now facing uncertain prospects after the September 2000 elections, amid the combined challenges from the pro-Beijing political forces, the Tung Chee-hwa regime's deliberate slights, and the unpredictable effects of a slow but discernable economic upturn.

This chapter aims to delineate and examine the key dimensions of the democratic camp's realignment during the past five SAR years, and to highlight the institutional obstacles and realpolitik pressures impacting on the Hong Kong's prodemocratic activists as a viable political force on Chinese soil. These analytical efforts shall provide an informed and timely basis to articulate the second SAR Legco election results and the trends of party politics realignment. In this regard, comparisons with the May 1998 first SAR Legco election and the November 1999 first SAR DC election results can be useful measurements of the democratic camp's performance in an altered political landscape. The first part of this essay will review the SAR's political and economic realities. The second part will look at the democratic camp's platform reorientation and dual strategies while in retreat. The third part will examine the May 1998 Legco election results confirming a democratic camp rebound. The fourth part will chart the internal divisions of the democratic camp under the SAR's deformed polity and distorted electoral rules. The fifth part will review the democratic camp's marginal gains in the 1999 DC elections. The sixth, final part will highlight the September 2000 Legco election results and longer-term implications. The flagship of the democratic camp, the Democratic Party (DP), will provide the major case examples in this essay.

Altered SAR Political Landscape and Economics Realities

The sovereignty retrocession on July 1, 1997, not only ushered in the SAR regime but also introduced a new set of political institutions and rules of game which mitigated many of the key factors underlining the rapid growth and impressive expansion of the democratic camp during the 1985–97 transition era. Briefly, the pre-1997 factors propelling the dramatic rise of the democratic camp and contributing to their popular appeals include:

1. The British decolonization process encompassing localization and partial democratization which opened up the electoral arena for grassroots political participation and gave birth to party politics.[2]

2. The "fear of China" factor, especially after the June 4, 1989, Tiananmen Incident, galvanized popular support for local democracy as a defense against Chinese communism. The PRC's lopsided united front effort aimed at attracting the illiberal, antidemocratic elites and big business interests, thus provoking the grassroots to seek electoral mandate and legislative representation for socioeconomic counterbalance and political safeguard.[3]

3. The PRC's stern stance in the Sino-British discords over transition affairs reinforced the negative impact of the China factor. This was especially true for the electoral reforms of last British colonial governor, Chris Patten, which directly benefited the democratic camp in 1992–97 but derailed the "through-train" institutional and personnel continuity transcending the 1997 handover.

The seemingly smooth final moments of the sovereignty transfer and superficial tranquility in the new SAR's early operations should not mask the fundamental and significant changes unfolding on the political scene since July 1, 1997. This altered political landscape introduced new elements and unpredictable variables into the realpolitik power equation that redefined the effect and impact of these transition era factors. At the risk of oversimplification, the new SAR political realities harbor the following noteworthy features:

First, the demise of the colonial regime rendered the Sino-British discords almost irrelevant to realpolitik, even though suspicion of residual colonial influence and distrust of British-groomed institutions and personnel still persisted among the PRC officials and their diehard local supporters. Thus, the prehandover political axis of the pro-democracy forces versus the conservative, illiberal forces was often manifested in a simplified polarity of a British colonial–Western agenda versus a "patriotic"–pro-Beijing stance.[4] The promotion of SAR democratization would no longer carry the stigma of being part of the alleged British colonial conspiracy and Western imperialist plot to undermine China's actualization of sovereignty over Hong Kong.

Second, the PRC's nonintervention in HKSAR affairs for the first twenty-three months since the handover has greatly diminished the negative China factor impact. Such remarkable self-restraint not only earned high marks locally and internationally for the PRC's "one country, two systems" formula but also significantly blunted the democratic camp's major appeal in building democracy as a defense against Beijing's encroachment. However, on June 26, 1999, at the request of the SAR government, the National People's Congress (NPC) Standing Committee in Beijing reinterpreted the Basic Law provisions on the right of abode in the SAR of Hong Kong permanent residents' mainland children. This action effectively overturned the HKSAR Court of Final Appeal's January 29, 1999, ruling on these children's unrestricted abode rights. In a single stroke, this drastically changed the central government-SAR relationship and also called into question the Beijing noninterference assumption.[5]

Third, the PRC's decision to dismantle Patten's electoral reforms, especially the replacement of the last colonial Legco elected in September 1995 with a SAR PLC signaled more than an end to British-sponsored democratization but an actual antidemocratic rollback and disenfranchisement. The proceedings of the PRC's SAR Preparatory Committee and the PLC left no doubt that the new SAR institutional structure and rules of game were deliberately designed to ensure a pro-Beijing, conservative majority and also to reduce the representation and influence of the democratic camp in all tiers of electoral organs. The reintroduction of appointed seats to both the eighteen District Boards (renamed District Councils in 1999) and the Urban Council and Regional Council, and the installation of an unelected PLC in July 1997, pulled the electoral carpet out from under the democratic camp. To survive the SAR's regressive, antidemocratic new order, the democratic activists had to search for new strategies and seek fresh resources to continue their crusade for democracy in Hong Kong under Chinese rule.

On the other side of the coin, it was the unexpected economic downturn stemming from the Asian financial crisis soon after the handover that created new class tensions and rapidly widened existing social fissures along class lines in the HKSAR. This economic crisis necessitated a more interventionist touch by the SAR regime under Tung Chee-hwa, which harbored a very conservative and paternalistic approach on livelihood issues and political reforms. The inept crisis management performance of the SAR regimes on such nuts-and-bolts everyday matters as the bird flu epidemic in the winter and spring of 1997–98, and the chaos in the new airport operation in summer 1998 drew sharp public criticism of post-handover maladministration. Thus, economic deterioration and the rice-bowl bottom line gradually emerged as the paramount concerns of the SAR political elites and the populace.[6] This socioeconomic front constitutes a fruitful new dimension with great mass appeal, and with electoral mobilization potential that could help the democratic camp to maneuver in the restrictive SAR political arena with its deliberately biased rules.

It is a main argument of this chapter that, while these socioeconomic concerns have been of great significance to the HKSAR's public discourse and policy debates, they do not really displace or fully eclipse the China factor in the popular support for political reform and democratization. Rather, livelihood concerns and rice-bowl issues amid an economic crisis have reinforced some of the justifications for democratization and added new vocabulary and urgent relevance to the democratic camp's articulation of public interests in the SAR. In other words, attached to and perhaps imposed on top of the pro-democracy versus conservative/illiberal axis is another tycoon–big business versus grassroots–middle class axis. Analytically, the combined operation of these two sets of overlapping axis can be a useful perspective from which to appreciate the twisting course of the democratic camp's realignment from retreat to rebound to retrenchment in the SAR toward the twenty-first century.

The Democratic Camp in Retreat, 1997–98

With the sole exception of the grassroots-based Association for Democracy and People's Livelihood (ADPL), the full array of democratic camp Legco members firmly opposed the PLC as an illegitimate, extraconstitutional organ not provided for in the Basic Law. They boycotted the proceedings of the PRC-appointed SAR Selection Committee that selected Tung Chee-hwa as the SAR Chief Executive and the sixty members of the PLC in December 1996. Rather than compromising their long-held stance on full-scale democratization with popular direct election of the chief executive and the entire legislature, the democratic camp Legco members elected in 1995 won considerable local and international sympathy for their principled opposition to the nonelected PLC. In retrospect, their chosen path of temporary retreat from the SAR's undemocratic order can be regarded as a necessary and dignified tactical move. Of significance was their relatively short ten-month retrenchment, which did not become a period of passive inaction and acceptance of the fate of displaced former political activists. Rather, a majority of these ex-Legco members took advantage of their "outside-the-establishment" status to sharpen their public image as the principled and even martyred opposition against antidemocratic regression. They became vocal critics of the SAR regime and the PLC while continuing their high-profile advocacy of full democracy.

The PLC nonparticipation of the ex-Legco members did much to enhance their credentials as the "collective conscience of Hong Kong democracy" while at the same time depriving the PLC of any claim to a fig leaf of electoral legitimacy. In fact, the PLC, from start to finish, suffered an acute lack of popular approval. Neither its extraconstitutional origins and nonelected membership nor its "rubber-stamp" performance in support of the SAR executive branch's invalidation of pre-handover legislation on civil liberty and labor welfare did anything to remedy its dubious legality or lack of public credibility. The Legco electoral results in May 1998 would vindicate the democratic camp's tactical retreat at ten months earlier, as ADPL leader

Frederick Fung, the only democratic camp politician to serve in the PLC, was defeated in the contest for a directly elected seat in West Kowloon, his political citadel for over two decades.[7]

Of more profound longer-term implications was the democratic camp's strategic repositioning of itself and the subsequent campaign platform reorientation during the period of retreat. This strategic reformation was as much a matter of survival necessity in the hostile SAR political realities as it was making use of the new opportunities afforded by the economic crisis. The experience of the DP, the democratic camp flagship with the largest party membership and number of seats in the Legco and, until late 1999, in the Urban Council and Regional Council and District Boards can be illuminating. In a nutshell, the DP has adopted a new "walking-on-two-legs" strategy with a double-track approach—democracy and socioeconomic justice.

Strategic Repositioning: Democracy and the China Factor

Not forfeiting its proven public appeal of fighting for full democracy in Hong Kong, the DP leadership subtly modified its previous hostile stance toward the PRC officialdom from harshly critical and (following the June 4 Tiananmen Incident) condemning to a more moderate but still critical tone. No longer burdened with an alleged British colonial dark tint as in the once-bitter Sino-British discord, the DP leadership, especially the veteran teachers' union kingpin Szeto Wah and DP chair prominent barrister Martin Lee, emphasized the fact that they were among the first wave of local public figures in the early 1980s to support Hong Kong's 1997 sovereignty retrocession to China, hence their undoubted "patriotism." What drove them and the PRC officialdom apart was the democratic activists' unyielding insistence on retrocession with democracy both before and after 1997 against Beijing's preference for sovereignty retrocession without genuine democracy.[8] By reclaiming their patriotic legacy in the post-colonial SAR, the DP leaders attempted to refurbish their public image vis-à-vis both the PRC officialdom and the local pro-Beijing bloc which, in addition to the traditional leftist hard core, also harbored many recent converts of opportunists, colonial turncoats, coopted conservative elites, and China market-minded tycoons. This was an important DP tactical move aiming at narrowing the deep gulf over the sensitive area of "patriotism" between them and the pro-Beijing bloc, which has become the favored political mainstream in the SAR new order. In other words, the democratic camp refused to be type-casted by their opponents as "anti-China" simply because of its vigorous campaign for full democracy in Hong Kong, and hence passively yielded the patriotic high moral ground to the pro-Beijing bloc. Rather than being trapped in the false polarity of a mutually exclusive choice between either patriotism (i.e., supporting Hong Kong's reintegration with China) or Western-style democracy as the pro-Beijing bloc and conservative elites have constructed, the democrats must reaffirm their unwavering commitment to full democracy but without any unwelcome stigma of being labeled "unpatriotic."

To the DP leaders, full democracy would help make Hong Kong a much better community under Chinese sovereignty and thus would directly contribute to the success of the "one country, two systems" model as a positive example facilitating the PRC's cherished peaceful reunification with Taiwan. In this light, to promote the well-being of the HKSAR with its nearly seven million people through democratization would be the duty of any patriotic HKSAR citizens among whom the democrats have been at the forefront.[9] Reflecting this modified and updated approach, the post-handover DP leadership shifted from a confrontational stance targeting the PRC officialdom as the prime evil repressing local democratization to a more moderate advocacy of building local democracy as a patriotic duty of the SAR citizenry. The new focus of DP's moral wrath and political assault was on the illegitimate PLC and the SAR regime under Tung Chee-hwa which had joined forces to enact the antidemocratic rollback. Inept crisis mismanagement, from the bird flu to the new airport chaos to the economic downturn, provided ample ammunition for the DP and other democratic activists' fierce criticism of the Tung regime during the first year of the SAR. Since there was little hard evidence on Beijing's direct interference in the SAR's internal affairs during this period, Beijing was often spared the fire from the democratic camp.

In fact, as local confidence in the "one country, two systems" formula gradually increased and the "fear-of-China" factor receded in importance, the democratic camp's battle cry of democracy as a defense against interference from Beijing's Communist dictatorship also declined in popular appeal.[10] Against such a major shift in public sentiments and also utilizing the postcolonial space to remount the high moral pedestal of patriotic legacy, the DP leadership rearticulated the relationship between their quest for democracy and the China factor, which has assumed new meanings and relevance since the handover. Their new DP line on democracy in Hong Kong without overt hostility or deliberate provocation toward Beijing changed the DP's stance from a confrontational mood to a moderately critical tone on the still sensitive China factor.

At the same time, the DP's gear shifting also meant internalizing and localizing the politics of contested democratization from an international issue in the pre-1997 Sino-British discord to the domestic realm of central-regional interactions as well as local power plays among the SAR political forces. Without the entanglement in Sino-British politics, the democratic camp's new patriotic twist to its democracy crusade could help to desensitize the China factor and yield fresh opportunities for potential contacts with Beijing, even though the PRC officialdom has yet to relax its stern attitude toward most of the democratic activists. As a defense mechanism, this new approach to Beijing has helped the DP to defuse some of the pressure from the pro-Beijing bloc and to keep the DP more in tune with the shifting public mood in the SAR in the absence of overt interference from Beijing.

Platform Reorientation: Socioeconomic Justice

A more profound reorientation of the DP strategy is the projection of its high-profile role as champions for socioeconomic justice, especially for the grassroots and the "sandwiched" middle-class interests. This new focus on socioeconomic issues constitutes the second track or the "other leg" upon which the DP engineered its very remarkable rebound. Both domestic built-in factors and external forces enabled the DP to enlarge its party platform to emphasize everyday livelihood concerns of the common folks in order to compensate for the diminishing appeal of its "democracy to protect Hong Kong from Chinese communism" stance. The domestic built-in factors refer mainly to the nature, composition, and vested interests of the new SAR elites, the PLC, and the policy orientation of the Tung regime. These factors, when they interacted with the external forces of the devastating Asia economic crisis, provided the objective conditions and favorable circumstances for the DP to retain its pro-democratic political base and capture more popular support with its additional call for socioeconomic justice.

As a nonelected chief executive enthroned by the tycoons and pro-Beijing elites who dominated the SAR Selection Committee, Tung Chee-hwa could gain public support only through actual performance to attain functional approval to compensate for his lack of electoral mandate and popular legitimacy.[11] However, constrained by the rigid Basic Law framework and keen to depoliticize postcolonial Hong Kong, Tung has little room to maneuver on the political front. He could only seek to earn public approval in domestic social and economic undertakings such as housing, education, and welfare in order to play his own brand of compensatory politics.

Housing, education, and welfare have been the three big budget items and critical policy choices directly affecting a very broad segment of the populace. They are also among the major public policy areas that the colonial regime failed to resolve satisfactorily and Tung's attempt to address them could have given him a promising launch to achieve functional legitimacy. Yet, many of Tung's decisions have been ill considered and counterproductive. For instance, his appointment of Executive Council (Exco) member

C.Y. Leung, a pro-Beijing land surveyor and property agent, to run the housing policy review provoked public conflict of interests outcries. This case is symptomatic of the unrepresentiveness and lack of accountability of the SAR establishment elites.[12]

The SAR Exco and PLC composition reflect the pro-Beijing and pro-business bias of the SAR polity. Their nature as nonelected bodies only deepened their acute lack of public credibility and popular mandate. That Tung Chee-hwa, like many Beijing-anointed elites, came from a big business background with a conservative and antidemocratic agenda further aggravated public distrust of his plutocratic order. Tung has been regarded in popular perception as lacking sympathy for and even understanding of the grassroots' needs but rather was pursuing policies to reward his tycoon supporters at the expense of fair play and socioeconomic justice.[13]

The deepening economic recession and sharply rising unemployment created urgent demands for official relief efforts while decreasing revenues and budget deficits depleted the regime's deployable resources and seriously challenged Tung's vision on social engineering and economic development. For example, half a year after launching his grand plan in October 1997 to provide a promised total of 85,000 new units per year to alleviate housing shortage, the collapse of the property market forced Tung to suspended public land auctions and shelved his targeted supply of new units. Critics from the democratic camp rightly characterized Tung's ineffective economic rescue efforts for "only saving the property and stock market (to bail out the tycoon developers) but not helping the people (who suffer high unemployment and deep wage cuts).[14] Eventually, the unannounced cancellation of such housing target would become another policy debacle and public image disaster for Tung in summer 2000.

Capitalizing on the economic downturn generated mass discontents, the DP enlarged its popular appeal as the real champion for the grassroots' threatened livelihood and the middle class' diminished well-being. The DP emphasized its role as the indispensable safeguard and effective counterweight to check and balance the big business–SAR regime axis.[15] As political activists outside the SAR power structure without direct responsibility in governance, the DP leaders did not offer specific proposals for relief measures or detailed policy suggestions for refloating the depressed economy. Rather, the democrats kept their high public profile as vigilant critics to make the Tung regime more responsive to the needs of the depressed masses.

The DP's vital new mission to promote much-needed economic justice for the "silent majority" of the common folks of both the grassroots and the middle class, who had already been disenfranchised in the SAR polity, gained political momentum and popular support as the economic crisis worsened.

The inept management of public services and the lack of effective relief efforts by a Tung regime commonly viewed as the willing captive of the big business lobby only served to make imperative the democrats' added functions as defenders of the people against the double exploitation of democratic regression and socioeconomic deprivation by the same pro-Beijing plutocratic SAR establishment. In vowing to return to an elected SAR Legco, the DP leaders skillfully played up the class interests issue as a new dimension of their party platform reorientation, using the urgent and direct relevance of socioeconomic justice amid high unemployment, business failure, and wage reduction to galvanize new public support to compensate for the diminishing democracy versus China factor appeal. This also enabled them to mitigate the negative impact of the Tung regime's deliberate attempt at depoliticization, such as the proposed abolition of the Urban/Regional Councils. The DP's unwavering commitment to democracy could thus be combined and enhanced with an organic linkage and even with integration into its new populist socioeconomic crusade. The vast experience and public credibility of some DP leaders, such as veteran labor unionists Szeto Wah and Lau Chin-shek, as effective grassroots champions and mass mobilizers contributed much to the creation and implementation of the DP's dual-track–bifocal new platform "to fight for democracy to obtain socioeconomic justice" and "to ensure socio-economic justice through the safeguard of democratic representation."[16] The May 1998 elections would soon vindicate the DP's walking on two legs new strategy to return to Legco.

The 1998 Elections and Democratic Rebound

The May 24, 1998 elections for the first SAR Legco were indeed very remarkable in several respects.[17] Historically it was the first open and free election conducted on Chinese soil under the PRC regime, even though the electoral rules enacted by the PLC and Tung regime were biased to marginalize the electoral gains and legislative presence of the democratic camp. The voter turnout rate for the twenty directly elected seats (one-third of Legco total) in the five geographic constituencies reached a record-breaking 53.3 percent (about 1.5 million) of registered voters, a totally unexpected high yield when compared with the 39 percent for the 1991 and 36 percent for the 1995 elections.

The entire democratic camp managed to receive about 65 percent of the total votes in the direct elected seat contests, a level of popular support similar to their 1991 and 1995 electoral gains.[18] However, due to the new and complex proportional representation (PR) system (with various party lists of ranked candidates) deliberately designed to put the democratic camp at very considerable disadvantage, the directly elected seats won by prodemocratic candidates actually decreased from sixteen to fourteen. In addition, the democratic camp managed to get only five seats (down from eight seats in 1995) in the thirty-seat functional constituencies. This was due to the new 1988 electoral rules of "corporate voting" to replace the 1995 individual members voting in most functional constituencies, thus reducing eligible voters by almost 80 percent (from over 1.1 million in 1995 to less than a hundred and forty thousand in 1998), and also the replacement of several professions and occupational groups with others in this category. Furthermore, the democratic camp did not win any of the ten seats in the Election Committee category, losing the two seats it had won in 1995. Again, this was due to the change from the 1995 Election Committee electorate of four hundred elected District Board, Urban Council, and Regional Council members to the 1998 Election Committee of eight hundred members selected from business, professional and "patriotic" elites like NPC deputies. Another major setback was the total rout of the ADPL, which failed to retain any of the four seats it won in 1995 (two directly elected, one functional, and one Election Committee). This was partly due to the new electoral rules but also because its leader Frederick Fung compromised his democratic stance by serving in the PLC.

In contrast to the democratic camp's reduced Legco seats, the pro-Beijing, middle-class grassroots–based Democratic Alliance for Betterment of Hong Kong (DAB) took a total of ten seats. These include five directly elected seats (up from two in 1995) and, as in 1995, three functional and two Elections Committee–produced seats. The DAB has benefited from the new system, as its popular vote share in the directly elected seats increased to 25.2 percent, from 15.6 percent in 1995. Beijing's noninterference in SAR internal matters considerably reduced the negative China factor pressure on the DAB. Its pro-Beijing stance was further compensated by its prograssroots livelihood platform.

The big business–supported Liberal Party (LP) kept its total number of Legco seats at ten. But its party chair, veteran politician Allen Lee, failed to retain his directly elected seat, the LP's sole Legco representation by popular vote. It held onto the previous nine functional seats and added a single seat in the Election Committee category. The pro-Beijing and pro-business Hong Kong Progressive Alliance (HKPA) gained a total of five seats, up from the three Election Committee seats in 1995 with two newly won functional seats. The new system definitely helped this political group despite its lack of mass base, as it was the only party that did not contest any directly elected seats.

Even though the total number of Legco seats won by the democratic camp was down from the 1995 near-majority of twenty-nine to nineteen in 1998, the democratic camp has mounted an impressive campaign.[19] What characterized this as a democratic camp rebound was the undiminished extent of its popular support, with the similar 65 percent share of popular votes that it has enjoyed since 1991. This has shown the still very strong public preference for the democratic camp, notwithstanding the sovereignty transfer and significantly altered electoral system. A closer examination of democratic camp electoral yields offers further indications underlining their rebound.

The DP's popular vote share actually increased slightly, from 42.3 percent in 1995 to 42.9 percent in 1998. The ADPL's significant drop from 9.6 percent in 1995 to 4 percent in 1998 corresponded to its rout, which signaled the diminished yet still significant China-factor effects among the grassroots voters who had been its solid supporters. The four-seat gain and 12.6 percent share of the new Frontier group (established in 1996) with two of its winners, Lau Chin-shek and Lee Cheuk-yan, from unionist background and another winner, former journalist Emily Lau, with a proven middle-class draw confirmed a fruitful biclass (grassroots and middle class) and bifocal (democracy and socioeconomic justice) combination of broadened popular appeal leading to victory. If the directly elected seat won by grassroots activist Leung Yiu Chung (with 38,627 votes) is included, the Frontier's results were even more impressive. Leung had to run on his own ticket as the new PR system would greatly diminish his winning chance had he remained on the Frontier's list as its second candidate after first-ranked Lee Cheuk-yan, who won easily with 46,496 votes.

It is clear that the PR system could work against the larger parties if they field more than one or two candidates in the same directly elected multiseat geographical constituency. This would create problems, as it did, for the DP as the largest party in the democratic camp, both internally over the ranking of candidates on the party list and also in its relations with other prodemocratic parties. The above example of the Frontier's Leung and Lee, despite its happy ending, is a good case in point. Another democratic camp success story is DP chair Martin Lee's carefully coordinated campaign efforts with the new Citizens Party (established in 1997) to ensure the victory of its founder Christine Loh in her May 1998 contest for a directly elected seat in Hong Kong Island where Lee and DP vice chair Yeung Sum easily won their own seats on wide margins. This is an exemplary instance of democratic camp interparty collaboration to deny the pro-Beijing bloc an additional Legco seat.[20]

The democratic camp's 1998 electoral victory vindicated their new emphasis on socioeconomic issues to preserve their popular support previously derived mainly from the democracy versus China factor effects. However, it would be wrong to assume that the democratic camp had belatedly "discovered" the livelihood issues only after the handover when the negative China factor receded in importance or when the Asian economic crisis hit the SAR. Rather, many prominent prodemocratic figures were well-known social activists with a strong track record in fighting for labor rights, community concerns, and grassroots grievances as well as bread-and-butter issues long before they became advocates for democracy in the late 1980s. Many of the democratic camp elements were intensively politicized by the 1997 retrocession. Baptized by the 1987–88 campaign for direct elections, the Basic Law drafting process, the Sino-British discord, and especially the Tiananmen Incident local mobilization, they were transformed into front-line prodemocratic partisans. The convergence of grassroots social activism with democratic advocacy among many democratic camp elements took shape in the realpolitiks maneuvers of the late 1980s and early 1990s.

As the democrats' action agenda throughout 1990–97 was dominated by the paramount transition-era China factor and democratization concerns in a society experiencing economic prosperity and enjoying new opportunities for electoral participation, livelihood issues often became less urgent and of lower priority. Yet socioeconomic issues and class interest articulation were not entirely absent in the public debates on electoral reforms during 1987–88 and 1992–94 or in the 1991 and 1995 Legco elections. This was especially true for the ADPL, whose leader Frederick Fung rode on his popularity with the "public-housing" lobby to victory in the 1991 and 1995 Legco contests. Yet Fung's 1998 defeat can be attributed in part to noneconomic but political concerns, mainly questionable commitment to democracy due to his much criticized PLC service.

At the other end of the ideological spectrum, the DAB has a substantial grassroots base, mainly through interlocking membership and leadership with the pro-Beijing Hong Kong Federation of Trade Unions (FTU, with 113 affiliated unions and a combined membership of 245,700 in 1997, the largest labor organ in HK). In fact, one of the DAB top three leaders is a unionist party, vice chair Tam Yiu-chung, who also sits on the SAR Exco, was a FTU vice president, while the other two, party chair Tsang Yok-sing and secretary-general Gary Cheng, are educators. They have been outspoken on socioeconomic issues from middle-class and grassroots perspectives. Their collective defeat in the 1995 Legco directly elected seats contests could be attributed to their pro-Beijing stance. In the 1998 Legco elections, all three won their directly elected seats, no doubt benefiting from the PR electoral system and the receded China factor. Ironically, the DP-generated popular backlash against the SAR plutocracy and the nonelected PLC also indirectly contributed to the DAB's electoral success.[21]

As the contrasting fates of the ADPL and DAB in the 1995 and 1998 elections suggested, any successful maneuver in compensatory politics to balance the China factor–democracy card with socioeconomic appeals would require considerable skill, experience, and public credibility. The democratic camp's remarkable rebound in the 1998 polls did not stem from a superficial, instant reinvention of platforms or an about face in strategic orientation. The SAR plutocratic order and the economic recession yielded the unique space and opportune time for the DP and its allies to fine-tune and reemphasize their existing socioeconomic agenda and populist repertoire not as a substitute for, but rather in an organic symbiotic link up with their undiminished democratic push.

Deformed Polity and Internal Divisions, 1998–99

The return of the democratic camp to Legco in July 1998 ushered in a new power realignment, partisan polarization, and elite fragmentation in the SAR.[22] Despite a popular vote share similar to that in the 1991 and 1995 elections, the democratic camp occupies only nineteen seats in the first SAR Legco instead of the twenty-nine-seat near-majority in 1995–97. It is clear that the PR system adopted for the 1998 Legco election's twenty directly elected seats had worked well to punish the democratic camp and reward the pro-Beijing bloc. Furthermore, it opened the floodgate to bitter rivalries and prolonged conflicts among candidates in the democratic camp and even inside the same party. Under the PR system, a political party participating in the direct election is required to put up a candidate list; if there is more than one candidate, then the party candidates must be listed in ranking order for a specific geographical constituency. The candidates ranked at the top on the party list naturally stand a much better chance of getting elected than those with lower ranking. The need for the party leadership and membership to work out an official party list of ranked candidates to contest direct elections brought into open the factional discords, personality clashes, and policy disagreements within the DP which was engulfed in internecine strife in early 1998.[23]

In December 1997, the DP's lists of candidates for the 1998 Legco direct elections were first voted on at a party general meeting. Then, exercising its right of veto and approval, the DP Central Committee in January 1998 endorsed and overturned some of the general meeting's voting results on the listings. For example, the DP Central Committee placed unionist Lau Chin-shek at the top of the list of the Kowloon West constituency, instead of in his original third place, with the justification that Lau's public prominence and grassroots popularity would help to gain more votes for the DP ticket there. Also, the DP Central Committee reversed the ranking of two New Territories West candidates Albert Chan (from third down to fourth) and Wong Wai-yin (from fourth up to third). While Lau Chin-shek's new ranking was accepted by DP members, the decision to lower Chan's ranking provoked strong reaction. Chan accused DP vice chair Anthony Cheung for forming a faction with ex–Meeting Pointing elements within the DP against him. Finally, a DP extraordinary meeting in February 1998 settled this case by restoring Chan to his original third place and Wong back to the fourth place on the party list.[24] Both Chan and Wong lost in the May 1998 contest, but their case clearly illustrated the very bitter internal discord and intraparty struggles within the democratic camp due to electoral pressures created by the new SAR polity.

The reentry into the SAR power structure supposedly opened new opportunities and added fresh momentum for the democratic camp to participate more directly in the governance process. Yet, the severely restricted access to the executive-led SAR regime's decision-making center, and their seriously disproportionate legislative presence (fewer than one-third of the sixty seats) to their electoral mandate (almost two-thirds of the popular votes) soon frustrated many democratic activists. Feeling politically disempowered or even legislatively crippled, they tried to seek a breakaway alternative to the parliamentary forum in the SAR's deformed democracy. In their December 1998 party congress some DP Young Turks proposed a long-term walkout from both the Legco and the eighteen District Boards, and also proposed to take their fight against the Tung regime directly into the street with public protests and mass demonstrations. As most of them had staged such direct collective actions over political and socioeconomic issues in the colonial era, this call to arms for street politics and popular mobilization was no empty talk but threatened to split the DP.[25]

This intraparty strife was further complicated by the new election and almost immediate resignation of veteran unionist and "street fighter" Lau Chin-shek as DP vice chair.[26] Lau's stepping down was partly aimed at preventing further discord within the DP ranks, but it also stemmed from his dual links with both the DP and the Frontier in violation of DP rules. Despite Lau's inclination to exit the DP, his late 1998 election to DP vice chair on Young Turks' support did depose vice chair Anthony Cheung whose softer approach to the PRC officialdom had long been resented by the Young Turks. Lau's subsequent resignation from the vice chair post did not return Cheung to the DP leadership. Rather Cheung also resigned form his DP central committee post. Albert Ho, a lawyer and Legco member with strong prodemocratic credentials, was elected DP vice chair to fill Lau's slot as a compromise choice acceptable to both the Young Turks and the DP mainstream.

The crisis within the DP was temporarily resolved in January 1999 when party chair Martin Lee and his moderate mainstream reconciled with the militant Young Turks to agree on a joint approach. The DP decided that it would continue its Legco and District Board functions to fulfill its electoral mandate as a responsible opposition with a critical voice to promote democracy and socioeconomic justice vis-à-vis the SAR regime. The DP's grassroots linkages and mass mobilization resources should be reenergized both to prepare for the 1999 DC and the 2000 Legco elections and to actualize the DP's socioeconomic commitments.[27] The new emphasis on livelihood issues and empathy with the grassroots' economic concerns, while crucial to the DP's electoral rebound also provoked a divisive intraparty struggle for its heart and soul—its desired social base, class identity, and operational mode.

Pulling from the brink of an open split, the DP for the moment seemed to have turned these internal debates over strategy and tactics into sources of flexibility and strength which could have provided it with new wisdom and determination to forge ahead in SAR politics. As Suzanne Pepper has observed, "the controversy appeared to help ease the democrats' transition from their old 'freedom fighter' mode toward the more careful balance needed to survive under Basic Law rule. These allow like-minded partisans to play complementary roles by accommodating the new order, while simultaneously keeping their popular movement alive 'from the streets' where the causes to champion and energies to tap are now seemingly limitless."[28]

However, the partisan frustrations, limited democratization prospects, and legislative ineffectiveness created by the SAR's executive-led system resulted in continuous discords within the DP and among democratic camp elements throughout 1999. In fact, the problems of Lau Chin-shek continued to plague the DP's internal unity. Lau repeatedly toyed with the idea of withdrawal from the DP in order to form a new labor party. As Lau had already been placed on a one-year "inactive member" status in May 1999 and resigned from all leadership posts within the DP, his eventual exit from the DP would be a matter of time, only the manner of his exit and his future relationship with DP elements remained to be decided. But his CTU partner Lee Chuek-yan remains unenthusiastic about the formation of a labor party and prefers to keep their nonparty, loose coalition Frontier links which do not conflict with their unionist duties.[29] Lau's problems also added fuel to the DP's simmering discords over strategies, class identity, and labor policy to intensify intraparty tensions.

The deep divide between the two wings of the DP did not improve but rather was further complicated by the discord between the DP central leadership and its many local branch offices where the frontline links with the masses assumed increasing importance in the preparation for the November 1999 DC elections. Once again, candidate selections and campaign resources allocation imposed very heavy strain and stress on the already-frayed DP solidarity. Realpolitik pressures on the DC electoral competition also distorted the DP's relations with other prodemocratic organs and activists, thus further fragmenting the democratic camp's cohesion vis-à-vis the pro-Beijing bloc. As the eighteen DCs are district-level advisory and consultative organs on local affairs such as public facilities and essential services, hence neighborhood concerns and livelihood matters naturally assume greater and more direct relevance to the district constituencies (which are much smaller than Legco's geographic constituencies) than political maneuvers and territorywide policy debates in the Legco contests. This was particularly true in the early posthandover era when the sharp economic downturn combined with an obvious silence from the previous Sino-British political crossfire and the lack of direct intervention from Beijing propelled the rice-bowl issues to the forefront of public concerns as campaign topics. This new socioeconomic emphasis, while fitting well with the democratic camp's dual strategies, also became another major fissure for inter- and intraparty strife.

The Young Turks versus mainstream conflicts over the DP's future course of action (street protests or parliamentary maneuvers) in late 1998 and early 1999 actually extended far into another critical dimension. That is the fundamental question about the primary social base of the DP. The party's effective 1998 dual strategies did not provoke much internal debate on its commitment to SAR democratization. However, the DP platform on socioeconomic justice and its avowed functions to counterbalance the SAR plutocracy naturally raised the class issue and intensified the party's soul searching for its class identity, the major social base of its popular appeal and electoral support, and by extension its basic stance and overriding guidelines on socioeconomic issues.

The mixed membership backgrounds of the DP which was formed by the amalgamation of several groups in 1994 were a root cause of its internal polarization on socioeconomic policies and targeted social bases.[30] DP chair Martin Lee has been a champion for the party fulfilling middle-class aspirations for democracy through electoral campaigns and parliamentary participation. The more populist DP elements, some with rich mass movement repertoire, preferred more militant direct collective actions in the economic crisis when rising unemployment endangered grassroots livelihood. The PLC's rollback of colonial sunset era labor legislation and the underrepresentation of democratic elements in the SAR Legco despite their electoral majority accelerated the radicalization of the Young Turks who wished to gear the DP to be a more populist political body for the masses.[31]

Such polarization among DP members erupted over the debate on the proposed minimum wage legislation during mid-1999. In April 1999, CTU secretary-general Lee Chuek Yan (not a DP member) tabled a Legco motion calling for the enactment of minimum wage and right to collective bargaining legislation. Immediately, Lee's proposal lit the fuse that blew open the

DP's sharp internal disagreements on minimum wage and larger socioeconomic policies. Stage managed by DP Legco labor affairs spokesman Cheng Kar-foo, there were extensive consultations within the DP ranks, involving Legco, Urban Council, Regional Council, and DB office holders, and central committee as well as local branch members. The DP labor policy panel also held meetings with party members and conducted seminars with scholars and experts, both supporting and opposing the minimum wage law. [32]

Basically, the Young Turks had been firm in their support for a legal minimum wage, especially amidst the tidal wave of wage freeze and salary reduction in the economic crisis which necessitated official protection of the basic rights and legitimate interests of the low-income grassroots. However, the party's central leadership, mindful of its middle-class appeal, harbored strong reservations.[33] While Cheng himself supported the minimum wage law proposal, he acknowledged the great difficulty in pushing the entire DP toward supporting the measure. In fact, his was a minority view among DP Legco members. The DP secretary-general Law Chi-kwong (a social work professor and Legco member for the social welfare functional constituency) questioned the practical and net effects of any minimum wage law which could undermine small business and even worsen unemployment in the short term.

After heated and prolonged debates among the DP ranks, the mainstream leadership under party chair Martin Lee held an extraordinary general meeting on September 18, 1999, to settle this sharp internal policy discord. It drew 140 DP members, who voted to decide the party's official stance. At the end, 114 votes supported DP Legco economic policy spokesman Sin Chung-kai (information technology functional constituency) who opposed Cheng Kar-foo's motion for DP endorsement of a minimum wage law, which received only 94 votes. Among these 208 votes, 81 were proxy votes and another 6 were abstain votes. Thus, 214 DP members, a very substantial portion of its membership, took part to decide the issue through democratic procedures. Although Martin Lee hailed this as a genuinely healthy exercise in practicing democracy and a breakthrough for any local political party to settle internal divisions and reach consensus through democratic means, the DP did not fully heal its factional wounds.[34] The democratic camp's dual strategies have become a sharp double-edged sword, cutting its own practitioners.

In an open letter to his fellow DP members at the meeting, Legco member Lee Wing-tat (New Territory West directly elected seat) laid bare the factional strife that had almost paralyzed the party for the past nine months. Lee's letter was particularly critical of a Young Turk radical, Andrew To (a former student union leader and a DB member), who attacked the DP mainstream leaders in newspaper articles as "no different from the June 4 Tiananmen butchers" for their highhandedness in party affairs. Lee deplored the Young Turks' anonymous press attacks on Martin Lee and Yeung Sum's personnel arrangements and their attempts to seize control of local branches. The deep distrust and open animosity within DP ranks, according to Lee, had resulted in the public perception of the DP as a party of conflicts and contradictions with no real consensus.[35]

The one-year "inactive party member" status placed on Lau Chin-shek saved him from being embroiled in this DP strife over the minimum wage issue. Not only was this crisis ignited by Lau's CTU colleague Lee Chuek-yan's motion, but many of the DP Young Turks in their penchant for grassroots collective action were keenly looking forward to the formation of a "labor party."[36] Defeated in his attempt to enlist DP support for the minimum wage measure, Cheng Kar-foo (New Territory East geographical constituency) also felt frustrated by his lack of sway over his DP colleagues in Legco proceedings. Instead of concentrating on DP central affairs, Cheng devoted his main efforts to galvanize support at the local level ahead of the November 1999 DC election.[37]

On the other track of its dual strategies, a regalvanzied DP adroitly practiced its hand in compensatory politics with the China-factor–patriotism card as illustrated by two public events in spring 1999. Reacting to the news of the May 8, 1999, North Atlantic Treaty Organization (NATO) bombing of the PRC embassy in Belgrade, which killed three and wounded more than twenty Chinese, the DP staged a mass protest march on May 11. It drew almost a hundred party members and supporters to the U.S. consulate-general in Hong Kong where DP chair Martin Lee read an open letter condemning the incident and calling for an immediate end to the air raids.[38] In this undertaking, the DP hoped to reemphasize its patriotic, nationalistic (i.e., pro-Chinese but not pro-CCP) credentials and to cast off its "pro-Western" label as affixed by the pro-Beijing bloc, especially on Martin Lee personally due to the international support for his democratic crusade. In this instance, the DP's open letter carefully paralleled Tung Chee-hwa's May 8 statement of condolence to the bombing victims and support for the PRC official stance.

The DAB and the FTU staged two protest demonstrations on May 9 and 11, drawing larger crowds filled with pro-Beijing students than the DP's protest. On May 12, the SAR Legco unanimously passed a resolution condemning the bombing and demanding a full investigation after forty-one members had spoken against the NATO military operation. Not wasting any opportunity for partisan assault, DAB chair Tsang Yok-sing criticized Martin Lee for acknowledging U.S. President Bill Clinton's apology and for linking this incident with the NATO operation against Serbian genocide in Kosovo, a stance paralleling the U.S. government position on this matter.[39] It seemed that the DAB, already in neck-to-neck combat with the DP for popular support, refused to yield its self-proclaimed monopoly on grassroots patriotism to the DP's attempt to gain a foothold in this cherished turf.

Three and a half weeks later, on June 4, 1999, the DP leaders, including Martin Lee, Lau Chiu-shek, Albert Ho (who replaced Lau as vice chair), and other democratic camp figures such as Lee Cheuk-yan, gathered on the podium at the Tiananmen Incident tenth-anniversary commemoration in Victoria Park. This mass assembly, drawing over seventy-five thousand participants (larger than the fifty thousand in the last prehandover event on June 4, 1997) was organized by the Hong Kong Alliance in Support of the Patriotic Democratic Movement in China and presided over by its chair, Szeto Wah, who is the DP chief whip.[40] Although Martin Lee resigned from the Alliance's executive committee in the early 1990s to distance his new party (then called "United Democrats of Hong Kong") institutionally from the "subversive" Alliance, the presence of the entire DP leadership at this commemorative gathering definitely signaled their undiminished commitment to democracy in Hong Kong and in China as a whole. This was a significant symbolic gesture to reassure the pro-democratic "silent majority" that the DP (which unlike the ADPL) has not been compromised by the SAR political-legal restrictions under PRC sovereignty.

The June 4 legacies, and by extension, the whole China factor political and ideological package, still set the DP apart from the DAB, and help to sharpen and perpetuate the DP's identity and public image as the bona fide populist pro-democracy flagship in HK politics, both before and after 1997. However, these still impressive democratic credential assets could not make up for the democratic camp's very alarmingly marginal performance in the late November 1999 DC elections and their inability to derail the Tung regime's attempt to abolish the Urban Council and Regional Council, thus removing the middle layer of Hong Kong's three-tiered electoral representation.

The District Councils Electoral Setbacks

The first DC elections in the SAR were held on November 28, 1999, for 390 of the bodies' 519 seats. The record 35.82 percent voter turnout rate was a slight increase over 33.1 percent in 1994 and 32.5 percent in 1991.[41] A relatively subdued affair when compared with the Legco contests, this round of DC elections is still of political significance, as it confirmed the relative strength of the democratic camp and the pro-Beijing bloc among the grassroots, both trying to gain popular support over rice-bowl matters.[42]

Many of the DC candidates regarded these polls as a warm-up for the

September 2000 Legco elections for themselves and their political parties. This was a timely test of voters' interest and public response to the Tung regime's controversial decisions on two counts: first, the abolition of the middle-tier Urban Council and Regional Council at the end of 1999 to reduce the SAR's three-tiered elected governance bodies into two, supposedly to streamline public health, municipal services, and cultural-recreational administration; second, to revive the discontinued (since September 1994) colonial practice of filling a share (about 20 percent, 102 out of 519) of DC seats by government appointment. (There were another 29 ex-officio seats.) With the demise of the municipal councils, the DCs would provide the only local-level electoral experience and public service training ground for future political activists and also would become useful anchorages for the political parties' grassroots support networks.

A record 799 qualified DC candidates (including thirteen Legco members) registered by October 20, 1999. Of the 390 DC seats to be filled by direct elections, 76 were returned without contest, as the incumbents faced no opposition. The other 314 seats were hotly fought. A brief review of the DC election results will illuminate the very substantial shifts in the SAR's neighborhood politics at the expense of the democratic camp.[43]

1. The pro-Beijing DAB fielded the largest number of candidates—176, of whom 17 were returned unopposed and another 66 were elected. It enjoyed an improved winning rate of 47.2 percent as compared to 44.5 percent with 37 winners out of 83 candidates in the 1994 District Board polls.

2. The DP put up a total of 172 candidates, of whom 6 were unopposed and another 80 were victorious. Its winning rate of 49 percent was down from the 56.3 percent with 75 winners among 133 candidates in 1994.

3. The ADPL entered 32 candidates, of whom 4 were unopposed and another 15 were elected. Its winning rate of 59.3 percent was much less than the 72.5 percent with 29 winners among 40 candidates in 1994.

4. The pro-Beijing conservative HKPA fielded 35 candidates, of whom 7 were unopposed and another 14 were elected. Its winning rate of 70 percent was an advance from 20 percent with a single winner among 5 candidates in 1994.

5. The pro-business LP sponsored 34 candidates, of whom 2 were unopposed and another 13 were elected. Its winning rate of 45 percent more than doubled the 20.9 percent with 18 winners out of 86 candidates in 1994.

From the above delineation of the five major parties' DC poll results, it is clear that the pro-Beijing bloc emerged as the clear winner, while the pro-business LP, which is acceptable to Beijing, also had done well. A tabulation of the total gain of DC seats and success rates of the various groups yields the following: pro-Beijing bloc, 99 seats, or 49.3 percent; LP, 16 seats, or 45.7 percent; democratic camp, 117 seats, or 53.4 percent; independent and others, 158 seats, or 46.1 percent.[44]

While numerically the democratic camp still commands the largest number of elected DC seats, its previous relative strength vis-à-vis the pro-Beijing and pro-business axis was gone. For the DP in particular, a once mythical overwhelming electoral success record was finally broken. In comparison with 1994, the DP's 1999 success rate, at 49 percent, represented a significant drop of 7.3 percent. It also fell behind the democratic camp's 1999 combined rate, at 53.4 percent. Perhaps the DP could draw some comfort that it still has the largest number (86) of elected DC members, 3 seats ahead of its arch-rival DAB, but the previous gap of the DP's 75 seats versus the DAB's 37 seats in 1994–99 no longer existed. In terms of popular votes, the DP's 1999 share of 24.7 percent (22.8 percent in 1994) was only slightly ahead of the DAB's 23.1 percent (11.8 percent in 1994), with the LP declining to 3.2 percent (from the 7.3 percent in 1994).[45] The only positive indication of the DP's residual strength was in the 95 single-seat DC contests in which DP candidates directly confronted DAB challengers, the DP won 55 seats at a success rate of 58 percent.[46] Furthermore, the ADPL managed to return its chair, Frederick Fung, to a DB seat, an important step in his Legco rebound.[47]

At the micro level of individual candidates, two well-known and long-tenured Legco politicians, the DP's Fred Li (Legco Kowloon East geographical constituency) and the LP's Selina Chow (Legco Wholesale and Retail functional constituency), lost their DC bids. To some observers, this spelled the end of any "superstar effects" of political heavyweights in popular electoral contests.[48] As the DP has maintained the most powerful galaxy of political superstars, such as Martin Lee, Szeto Wah, and Lau Chin-shek, this was indeed an alarming sign. Other democratic camp superstars, such as Emily Lau and Lee Cheuk-yan, might have to rearticulate their coattail effects on fellow Frontier contestants even if their own Legco election prospects were not seriously threatened by such new trends. Yet, another kind of "star effect" worked to enhance the DC victories of a DP newcomer who is a singer, a TV actor–turned DAB candidate, and a TV historical drama commentator who defeated Selina Chow.[49] The 1999 DC exercise was not good to the DP Young Turks, as five of them lost their incumbencies (and four became unemployed, because they were full-time politicians).[50]

In postelection statements, the DP leadership admitted to a rather disappointing performance, while the DAB and the local leftist press boasted of the tremendous gains by the "patriotic forces."[51] A closer analysis can identify several major factors underlining this remapping of the SAR's political landscape, which make the 2000 Legco elections and the further realignment of the democratic camp even harder to forecast.

The DAB's victories are built upon a combination of external circumstances and internal resource mobilization, coordination strategies as well as superior grassroots linkages. Externally, the absence of Beijing's overt interference into HKSAR affairs greatly reduced the China-factor negative impacts of DAB's patriotic stance. As DAB chair Tsang Yuk-sing said, "Voters in the past needed the DP as a bulwark against China. But as the fear of intervention subsides, they are turning to vote for us."[52] Another favorable factor was the economic downturn that caused livelihood issues, unemployment, and wage reduction to become voters' priority concerns.

The DAB's solid image as a patriotic grassroots organ, working closely with the pro-Beijing FTU (with 136 unions and a combined membership of 286,904 in 2000), enabled it to make the most of its working-class appeal, especially in the industrial areas. In fact, two of the four best known DAB Legco members started their careers as FTU unionists: DAB vice chair Tam Yiu-chung, who is the only SAR Exco member with a Legco seat, and female labor leader Chan Yuen-han. The joint DAB-FTU efforts in overlapping or interlocking leadership also extended into their shared local networks, penetrating into the eighteen DC zones. DAB district offices often worked hand in hand with FTU local branches or affiliated unions in the localities for electoral campaigns and other patriotic mobilizations. The pro-Beijing grassroots also enjoyed strong financial support with a well-funded war chest for elections and local network building. Contributions from PRC-linked business and elites provided much for the DAB's material resources while pro-Beijing schools, enterprises, and unions yielded valuable manpower to weave an extensive territorywide local network to mount electoral campaign and turn out sympathetic voters.[53]

After the 1998 Legco elections, the DAB set up intensive training programs on a HK$4 million budget for party members and office-seeking candidates, the only such systematic efforts among HKSAR political parties. The candidate and cadre training programs and the penetrative power of the DAB-FTU networks indeed paid handsome dividends at the DC polls.[54] The economic downturn that made livelihood, unemployment, and wage reduction worries into priority concerns for the voters definitely yielded room for the pro-Beijing camp to cultivate grassroots support through local networks for community service and "social unionism" leading to electoral victories.

In sharp contrast to the DAB's human and financial resources, the DP operated with an extremely meager party coffer and with inadequate numbers of effective campaign workers and few well-trained DB candidates of whom many were recent recruits into the party.[55] More damaging than anticipated by its partisans, the well-publicized internal strife between the Young Turks and mainstream leadership had projected a public image of the DP as a highly divided and confused political group, unsure of its own class identity and main socioeconomic constituencies, and unable to provide any clear platform on rice-bowl issues. The intraparty conflicts also derailed systematic attempts to reach down into the neighborhoods and build up a solid grassroots network for party loyalty and electoral support. With the exception of Szeto Wah and Lau Chin-shek, both of whom were veteran unionists and street activists, few of the DP's superstar mainstream leaders devoted sufficient effort to local affairs and district organizations.

Furthermore, the fiasco over the minimum wage motion and Lau Chinshek's uncertain status also undermined the DP's effectiveness in drawing working-class support, even in an economic downturn. Thus, the combination of an overall lack of resources, inadequate local linkages and mobilization, internal strife with blurred class identity, and contradictory socioeconomic platforms seriously diminished the DP's domestic appeals. By late 1999, the once-effective dual strategies responsible for the DP's May 1998 rebound had nearly crippled one of its two legs.[56] While the post-1997 China factor had receded in direct relevance, the DP's assets from the legacy of its democratic commitment perhaps saved it from even more disastrous DC electoral results.

Not only falling short of its internal preelection projection of obtaining at least ninety elected DC seats, the DP in fact was soon replaced by the DAB as the single largest party in the DC system.[57] In late 1999, the SAR government appointed another 102 DB members, among them 11 DAB members, 12 HKPA members, and 9 LP members; the rest were mainly businessmen and professionals.[58] While Tung defended this reintroduction of appointed members as an effective way to absorb talents and recruit specialists to serve the local communities, the DP took a principled moral stance by refusing to accept any DC appointments for its members.[59] By not compromising its democratic credentials with the SAR regime's antidemocratic counterreformation (to invalidate the British eleventh-hour democratic reform under Governor Chris Patten), the DP allowed the DAB, with ninety-four seats (eighty-three elected and eleven appointed) to emerge as the top party in the DC. This would yield advantages to the DAB and other pro-Beijing organs such as the HKPA in the election of DC chair by members of each of the eighteen councils, and hence would give the pro-Beijing bloc extra resources in local consolidation ahead of the 2000 Legco contests.

The year 1999 closed with another institutional setback for the democratic camp in its uphill struggle against the Tung regime's antidemocratic counterreformation. Seizing as pretext the mismanagement of the bird flu crisis in 1998 and, by extension, the administrative inefficiency of the Urban Council and Regional Council in public hygiene and municipal services, the SAR government decided to abolish these councils at the end of 1999.[60] Despite vocal and stern opposition from the councilors and the democratic camp parties and politicians, on December 3, a municipal services ordinance was passed by the Legco mandating the abolition of the two councils on December 31, 1999. It was passed by a narrow margin of thirty-one votes for and twenty-seven votes against, following two days of heated debates in the Legco. All the DP and other democratic camp Legco members voted against this ordinance. So did two top DAB leaders, Tsang Yuk-sing and Gary Cheng. Yet, two other DAB leaders with strong FTU ties, Tam Yiu-chung (who as an Exco member had to either abstain or support the bill introduced by the government) and Chan Yuen-han, voted for this ordinance on the abolition of the councils.[61] This opportunistic 2 : 2 equal-split vote by the DAB leadership did not endear the party to antiabolitionists. The fact that other than these two DAB "loyalists," almost all the directly elected Legco members voted against the abolition did not matter at the end.

Once again, the SAR's deformed policy of electoral majority but legislative minority enabled the Tung regime to proceed with its counterreformation, disenfranchising voters from participation in the middle-tier elected organs (which in the Urban Council's case, had the longest record of local elections since 1887). It seemed that the democratic camp ended the old millennium with deep scars and heavy hearts. Perhaps some of the wounds were self-inflicted, but they were mostly triggered off by the distorted rules and restricted space prescribed by the Basic Law and enforced by the conservative plutocracy, with the help of the patriotic bloc of pro-Beijing loyalists.

The 2000 Legco Elections

At the new millennium's dawn the local press was filled with DP stories colored by a pessimistic tone. These stories ranged from the Young Turks' fierce attacks on DP vice chair Yeung Sum, to DP intrigues and power plays on the splitting of the candidate lists for Legco elections.[62] The press headlines soon focused on the DP's difficulties in preparating for the Legco contests—including funding shortages as well as jockeying for selection, and nomination list ranking of prospective candidates.[63] In April and May, the press on DP electioneering turned decidedly gloomy, with accounts of factional maneuvers and disappointed members' exits from the DP after they failed to achieve electoral listing.[64] A depressed atmosphere enveloped the democratic camp after Citizens Party founder Christine Loh decided to stand down in July 2000 when her Legco term ended, citing legislative impotence as her reason.[65] In June, after a year's freeze, Lau Chin-shek exited the DP for refusal to end his concurrent Frontier ties.[66] Thus, three years into the SAR era, the democratic camp was not faring well. The slow economic upturn might further lessen its socioeconomic appeal. In this summer of shadows and doubts, the democratic activists unfolded their Legco election campaign.

The second SAR Legco elections on September 10, 2000, did not drastically alter the partisan legislative alignment but did yield significant indicators for compensatory politics. The overall voter turnout rate of 43.57 percent for the twenty-four seats in the five direct-election geographical constituencies was almost 10 percent lower than that of 1998 but was still higher than the pre-handover figures (39 percent in 1991 and 36 percent in 1995). Though the DP was still the largest party, retaining twelve of its thirteen seats in Legco, its share of popular votes declined from 42.9 percent in 1998 to only 34.7 percent. Yet, despite the conflict of interests scandal of vice chair Gary Cheng, the DAB became a clear winner, capturing an impressive 29.7 percent of the popular vote, up from 25 percent in 1998. The DAB took a total of eleven seats—seven in direct elections, three functional, and one election committee seat.[67] (Cheng soon resigned his Legco seat under pressure. After losing the December 10, 2000, by-election, the DAB commanded only ten Legco seats).

The public's strong concerns for livelihood greatly facilitated the victory of prograssroots and labor-linked candidates. For instance, three of the FTU winners were DAB-FTU joint candidates: Tam Yiu-chung and Chan Yuen-han (both of whom retained their 1988 directly elected seats), and Chan Kwok-keung (who took the new, third labor union functional seat). In the democratic camp, four of the direct-election winners had strong unionist credentials: Szeto Wah (DP), Lee Cheuk-yan, and Lau Chin-shek (both CTU; despite his DP exit, Lau still ran on the DP ticket with James Tu, his 1998 DP electoral partner in Kowloon-West, and both won easily in 2000), and independent Leung Yiu-chung. (Leung, Lau and Lee are Frontier members.) The DP's Cheung Man-kwong, head of the Professional Teachers' Union, again defeated a pro-Beijing candidate to retain his education functional seat. The prodemocratic camp also regained an old member, Frederick Fung, who was defeated in 1998 due to his PLC tint.[68]

The popular vote distribution clearly reflects the latest partisan realignment in the SAR: 61.87 percent democratic camp, 30.62 percent pro-Beijing, and 6.65 percent conservative.[69] While the leftist front kept to the 1998 level, the DAB has rationalized its organization and brought most of the pro-Beijing elements under its banner, such as the FTU and HKPA for the direct election contests. However, the democratic camp's small but alarming decline in public support may point to a longer-term trend of retrenchment. Its failure to make any gain in the additional four new direct election seats is not a good omen. Perhaps the SAR's deformed polity and biased electoral design have become repressive institutional restraints that rendered the democratic camp's fierce competition with the pro-Beijing bloc in SAR politics an uneven contest.

A case of note was the popular support received by the DAB-FTU's Chan Yuen-han, whose 108,587 votes (47.4 percent) made her the new top vote getter, edging out the DP's Szeto Wah, who won easily with 103,863 votes (45.3 percent) in the same Kowloon-East constituency.[70] This surprisingly strong support for the DAB-FTU despite the Cheng scandal revealed the mobilization capacity of the leftist grassroots network based on social service. In a sense, Cheng's electoral win was partly due to the DAB-HKPA joint effort in placing Cho So-yuk, a HKPA 1998 elected Legco member, as the second ranked candidate (after Cheng) on the DAB's 2000 Legco election list for Hong Kong Island. In this crisis situation Cho was able to mobilize her considerable Fujian natives loyalist network of grassroots supporters to compensate for the damaging Cheng drag at the polls.[71] Without the Cheng scandal, the DAB-FTU bloc could probably have edged out the DP in both seats gained and vote share on its way to become Hong Kong's largest political party and, if the longer-term scenario envisaged by DAB chair Tsang Yoksing could be actualized, even to become the SAR's ruling party one day.[72]

On the other side, the deep schism within the DP and the disunited democratic camp's bickering over personnel and socioeconomic policies seriously undermined their popular appeal and grassroots support. The new DP strategy of splitting its candidates into two or three separate party lists in the two larger New Territories constituencies did not work so well as originally envisioned. The narrow defeat of DP Legco veteran Lee Wing-tat was partially compensated for by the surprise victory of DP 1998 loser Albert Chan, both ran but on separate DP lists in the same New Territories West constituency of six seats. Lee attributed his defeat to overconcentration on high-level Legco duties at the expense of local service and grassroots efforts among his constituents.[73]

The DP's setback, though expected by most observers, was perhaps not as severe as originally feared. The media blitz on the Gary Cheng scandal, which broke out only two weeks before polling, probably depressed enough nonhardcore voters of either camp to salvage some support for democratic camp candidates, including the DP. A closer review of the DP's one-seat loss reveals a slightly different picture, in which the exit of Lau Chin-shek due to party regulation did account for the one seat gone out of the DP, but Lau is still staying in the democratic camp. DP veteran Ho Man-kar's retirement from his Legco health care functional seat was a voluntary decision for family reasons. Thus, these were the two seats which the DP did not retain but not due to electoral defeats. The democratic camp's overall Legco presence still stood at nineteen seats after the September 10 elections. The retirement of Christine Loh and Ho Man-kar, and the defeat of Lee Wing-tat were finely balanced by the return of Albert Chan and Frederick Fung to the Legco, plus the gain of a directly elected seat by DP newcomer Wong Sing-chi in New Territories East. In a desperate struggle for survival, the democratic camp experienced several stressful cases of interparty competition. For instance, the DP's very keen campaign tactic of voting list manipulation made Wong the party's second winner (after first DP winner Cheng Kar-foo, who ran on a separate DP list in the same New Territories East constituency) but denied victory to Choi Yiu-chong, a running mate of Emily Lau on the Frontier's list.[74]

The democratic camp's Legco presence now stands at twenty seats after the December 10, 2001, Hong Kong Island by-election. In that poll, barrister Audrey Eu, supported by the democrats, won a majority of 108,401 votes (52 percent) over her DAB opponent's 78,282 votes (37.6 percent) and four independent contestants' votes from 1,231 to 13,717.[75] Eu's victory was the fruit of collaboration among the democratic parties, which did not field their own candidates in order to put their collective efforts behind Eu. Likewise, the pro-Beijing bloc was united in supporting the DAB candidate, who is a business executive supposedly with middle-class appeal. To mobilize the "patriotic" labor votes, the FTU stationed their top leaders around polling stations at major working-class public housing estates on election day.[76] Perhaps the Hong Kong Island voters (with a 33.27 percent turnout) were more middle class than grassroots, thus the DAB-FTU's extensive deployment of campaign manpower, material resources, and propaganda efforts could not prevent this democratic camp landslide. Eu's professional image with no party affiliation might be an invaluable electoral asset, even though the intensive campaign inputs from the DP, CTU, and Frontier leaders were high profiled and probably crucial in galvanizing the middle-class and working-class voters against the pro-Tung regime "loyalist" DAB. Still, the leftist bloc's December performance indicated substantial improvement over its September record of 72,617 votes at a 27.8 percent share in Hong Kong Island.[77]

This by-election triumph was a rare case of successful joint undertaking within the fractured democratic camp since 1998. Yet, any lingering shadow of bitter internal discords would not enhance the democratic camp's minority status within the 2000–04 Legco vis-à-vis the pro-Beijing loyalist bloc of twenty-four seats, and the conservative plus middle-of-the-road strand of sixteen seats.[78] The SAR democrats indeed face a hazardous journey ahead.

The Democratic Camp in Retrenchment

The DP leadership election at the December 17, 2000, party congress reflected a truce between the factions and a commitment to major reforms. Without any contest, Martin Lee remains DP chair while Yeung Sum and Albert Ho yielded the vice chairs to Law Chi-kwong and Lee Wing-tat. The tranquillity at the DP congress was due to the Young Turks' decision to stay away from the proceedings and the leadership contest, hence avoiding any open strife with the mainstream. Yet, such surface calm could hardly mask the deep down factional faultlines. Martin Lee's reelection as party chair was marked by unprecedented low level of support, with 230 votes for him, 55 votes abstaining, and 7 votes against him, such nonsupport amounted to 10 percent of the membership.[79]

In fact, the Young Turks' absence from the party congress might be a sign pointing to their eventual breakaway from a DP still dominated by the mainstream, with whom they harbored little real hope for reconciliation. After the December 2000 Legco by-elections, a new public affairs organ, "Social Democratic Forum" was established among some democratic camp activists, with many DP Young Turks at its core. While the Forum was not yet a full-fledged political party, it conducted public opinion surveys with policy suggestions on specific issues (such as health care), and fiercely criticized various SAR government decisions, sometimes with high-profile demonstrations like those during the Fortune Magazine global conference in May 2001. Forum members also staged rallies calling for the direct election of the SAR chief executive to protest Tung Chee-hwa's certain reelection (by an election committee of 800) on March 24, 2002. These actions aim at raising the collective identity and public recognition of the Forum and its key members, many of them are likely to run in the 2003 District Councils elections and the 2004 Legco elections as candidates under a non-DP banner. As such, it has been suggested that those Young Turks active in the Forum would ultimately exit the DP before the DC polls. Had they stayed with the DP, their chance of a high ranking on the DP's official list of candidates for the 2004 Legco poll's geographical constituency direct elections would be slim. Under the SAR Legco's proportional representation system, the Young Turks' DP departure thus became a matter of ideological choice and electoral necessity. This final step, taken on April 18, 2002, could resolve the DP's factionalism and might even contribute to the overall strength of the democratic camp as a cluster of several political parties.[80]

As for the DP mainstream leadership, the September 2000 electoral setbacks with a net loss of some 170,000 votes had sounded the alarm for soul searching and extensive reform. The DP launched an exercise called "Listening to the People" during September–December 2000 to collect rank-and-file members' inputs and channel local party offices' views to the central leadership. A detailed report on this exercise was presented to the party congress. Perhaps due to the Young Turks' absence, there was little debate within the DP on its findings. But the clear need to devote greater human efforts to the party ranks and more institutional resource to address communal concerns at the local level had been accepted. Still many of the fundamental problems in the DP's necessary overhaul, such as its strategic repositioning (vis-à-vis Beijing, the SAR regime under Tung, etc.), its own targeted electoral base–social constituency (mainly middle class or middle class cum grassroots) and the corresponding socioeconomic platform, the building of broad-based coalitions and effective popular mobilization for democratization, the structural and tactical approach to electoral campaign together with the internal candidates selection process and the recruitment and nurturing of new blood as well as leadership succession, have yet to be systematically articulated, resolved, and put into effect. These are issues and operational areas crucial to the viability and survival of the DP and the entire democratic camp as an effective opposition force in the SAR political arena.

So far, the DP's postelection record of undertakings offers only tentative gestures and preliminary signals of change and reform. Even though the Young Turks had withdrawn from the leadership contest and much of the policy discussions, some new DP initiatives still provoked criticisms from among its own ranks. Among these DP measures, the most obvious and sensitive reorientation has been its attitude toward the Beijing regime. In order to shake off the increasingly heavy baggage of its "always anti-PRC on all issues" stereotyped label and to project a refurbished public image of itself as a political party of moderation and reason willing to discuss policy differences with those who might disagree, the DP shifted gear on its approach to the PRC authorities.[81] At the March 10–11, 2001, party camp on review and future directions, the DP clarified its positioning as a HKSAR political party with a stance toward the PRC and the SAR government that was "affirmative of their good deeds but critical of their misdeeds" but definitely not wholesale "anti-Beijing" or "anti-Tung."[82] The DP encouraged its members to learn more about the PRC and to visit the mainland to actualize its new emphasis on a "China perspective." In fact, several DP members managed to make private visits to Shanghai in spring 2001, including Legco councilors

Fred Li in January and Wong Sing-chi in April (together with two DP central committee members).[83]

The DP also sent a letter to PRC president Jiang Zemin in late April 2001, ahead of Jiang's third visit to the HKSAR in May to keynote the *Fortune* magazine conference. The letter, which was transmitted to Beijing via Tung Chee-hwa's office, politely welcomed Jiang to Hong Kong so that he could further understand SAR conditions by seeing them firsthand and also asked for better communication between the PRC central government and the DP. To showcase the party's "patriotic" credentials, the letter reiterated the DP's full support for the PRC's peaceful reunification with Taiwan, its entry into the World Trade Organization (WTO), and Beijing's bid to host the 2008 Olympic games. The DP leaders' May 2000 visit to the United States to lobby the American Congress on behalf of the PRC's permanent normal trade relations status was specifically mentioned. Only at the end did the letter touch on such sensitive political matters as the speeding up of Beijing's own political reform, a reversal of the official verdict condemning the Tiananmen Incident, and fair treatment of HKSAR residents arrested on the mainland. Avoiding any mention of the ultrasensitive Falun Gong, the letter closed with a request to end the "black list" banning mainland entry for some HKSAR residents, including DP members and other dissidents. While some criticized the letter as unduly weak and submissive, Martin Lee defended the DP as "firm in our stance but polite in our words," while vice chair Lee Wing-tat explained the nonreference to Falun Gong as meaning that its local handling by the Hong Kong authorities would be a matter clearly within the domain of SAR autonomy. Martin Lee also publicly insisted that DP members should not undertake any action that might "embarrass President Jiang" during his visit.[84]

Perhaps echoing the DP's new moderate approach to Beijing, eighteen local prodemocratic bodies ran joint newspaper advertisements to welcome Jiang's visit with the slogan "sovereignty rests with the people, fortune is to be shared."[85] In sharp contract to the DP's deliberate cordiality, some Social Democratic Forum members chained themselves to a flagpost outside Jiang's conference venue as a defiant protest gesture. They were forcibly removed by HKSAR police, which also arrested a host of other protesters (including several from the Patriotic Alliance) in a very high-handed suppression.[86] Not only were most Young Turks absent from the DP's March camp when the new line toward Beijing was formalized, they also took strong exception to the DP mainstream's restraint over the PRC official's confiscation of three DP central committee members' mainland entry permits. Instead of accepting the DP decision to resolve the matter through private channels, eight Young Turks under the Social Democratic Forum banner staged a public protest outside the PRC Central Government Liaison Office on March 30, 2001.[87] Hence, in addition to the differences on socioeconomic policies, and electoral and parliamentary tactics, the DP stance toward Beijing has become another major cleavage dividing the Young Turks and the mainstream.

Mindful of its need for external moral support, the DP leadership has also shown restraint in its response to the U.S. surveillance plane incident in early April 2001. Instead of demanding an outright U.S. official apology (for the loss of the Chinese airforce plane and the US aircraft's unauthorized landing in Hainan) as the DAB did, at the insistence of party chair Martin Lee (who felt the facts of this incident remained unclear) the DP initially only expressed its "deep regrets" for the Sino-U.S. plane accident. Not unlike the case of Hong Kong's reactions to the 1999 U.S. bombing of the Belgrade PRC embassy, the DP's "unpatriotic" response to the airplane incident was vocally condemned by the pro-Beijing bloc while the FTU and other leftist bodies mounted protests outside the local U.S. consulate to underscore their unquestioned nationalism. It is of interest to note that during the 2001 Sino-US discord, criticisms of the DP's rather "neutral" stance also came from the party's own ranks.[88] Perhaps this reflected some of the early effects of the DP's new "China perspective" and also the gaps within the DP ranks.

On the domestic front, the DP has kept up its vigorous scrutiny of the SAR regime, and from time to time it took the lead in mounting public criticisms or proposing alternative measures to many government decisions and public policies. Many DP figures and their democratic camp Legco colleagues, with an eye on the grassroots' rice-bowl bottom line, worked together to defeat most of the government fees increases in the March 2001 budget. With the still severe economics downturn and high unemployment as justification, the democratic activists were extremely vocal in their stern opposition to the two railways' proposed fare hikes despite huge profits. In this case, they received reinforcement from an expected source, Tung Chee-hwa himself. Perhaps conscious of his negative pro-business image and low public approval ratings which were liabilities in his March 2002 reelection bid, Tung took the unusual step of publicly cautioning the management of the two railways (the government is the sole owner of the Canton-Kowloon southern line and the majority shareholder in the underground mass transit system) to make the "wise decisions" for the well-being of the HKSAR community. Under combined pressure from almost the full political spectrum, the railways' fare hikes were postponed until April 2002, safely after the SAR chief executive election. In February 2002, both railways again deferred their proposed fare increase due to public pressure in a worsening economic recession with rising unemployment and falling price deflation.[89] Thus it seemed that almost everyone in the SAR realpolitik arena took part in the game of compensatory politics over livelihood issues affecting the grassroots and even the impoverished middle class.

In opposing increases in most fees, rates, and fares by government, public utilities, and transport systems, the democratic camp and the pro-Beijing DAB adopted basically identical stances. Their main difference has been more a matter of the timing, style, and intensity of their public postures and media effects than of critical analysis of the issues at hand. For instance, CTU/Frontier leader Lau Chin-shek effectively reinforced his image of standing guard to protect communal interests and promote socioeconomic justice with a fifty-hour hunger strike in late June 2001 at Kowloon Tong station (which is the two railways' only interchange) to protest the fare hike. Besides generating public support and media coverage, Lau also gained political capital from the subsequent fare increase deferment, thus consolidating his champion for the common folks status.[90] Besides lending moral support by visiting Lau during his hunger strike, the DP also took direct actions to galvanize popular support against the fare hike, such as a public signature campaign, protests at forty underground stations, the distribution of flyers inside train carriages, and the threat of a 100- to 200-strong sit-down demonstration on the railway tracks. In contrast, the DAB, while also opposing the fare increase, refrained from public protests. Hence the democratic camp could take far more credit than the DAB for the public pressure leading to the favorable outcome in this fare hike episode.[91]

On another controversial issue, which touches on social behavior and public morality, the government proposal to legalize betting on football games, the DP and its democratic camp allies have joined forces with the DAB to create a common opposition. Both sides mobilized their teachers' organizations to mount a territorywide antifootball gambling joint campaign among school principals, teachers, students, and their parents and families. Legco and DC members of both camps used meetings in council chambers to denounce the SAR officialdom for its biased and deliberately misleading "public consultation" exercise, which is tilted in favor of legalizing football betting. Again under public pressure, Tung Chee-hwa backtracked from this controversial proposal in January–February 2002 during his reelection public relations efforts.[92] Beyond these two areas of livelihood and community concerns, the DP and DAB often locked horns on sensitive political and legal issues, such as amending regressive clauses in the Public Security Ordinance, the SAR regime's hostile stance on the Falun Gong, and the drafting of a law on the SAR chief executive election.[93]

Almost without exception, the DAB would faithfully carry out its expected loyalist functions as the flagship of the patriotic bloc in support of the Tung' regime, especially when he was toeing Beijing's official line,

introducing illiberal measures for tighter social control, or pushing unpopular policies to enhance the "one country" dimension of the SAR polity. On
these matters, the DP and other democratic camp politicians would play the
vigilant role of a principled opposition with social conscience to safeguard
the rule of law, civil liberties, public accountability, democratic entitlements,
and SAR autonomy with the "two systems" emphasis. Besides economic
subjects, these are the key middle-class concerns, which, since the 2000 Legco
elections, have assumed increasing significance in the DP versus DAB rivalry and competition for middle-class support. A major part of the DAB's
post-2000 elections reform is its much-publicized outreach to capture middle-
class votes with a new image refurbishment (such as a more "global perspective" and moderation on the 2007 review on direct elections).[94] The DP's
response to this new challenge from the left is still unfolding.

With the Young Turks' recent departure from the party's hierarchy and functions, DP should move ahead to refine and strengthen its socioeconomic policy
platform and its organizational and operational agenda toward a better-defined
and more clearly focused middle-class orientation. In concentrating more of
its limited human efforts and institutional resources on construction of a solid
and committed middle-class constituency for political mobilization and electoral support, the DP would, by default or design, leave the grassroots and
laboring-class field more open to the Young Turks as new Frontier members
and the CTU's Lau Chin-shek, to pursue more militant collective actions and
street struggles. If resolutions from the March 2001 DP camp could still be a
meaningful guide to the party's future developmental objectives, much is required for the many demanding tasks ahead.

In a nutshell, the DP aimed at a substantial recruitment of 150 new members both to enlarge total party membership (of some six hundred) and to
inject new blood to replace the 50 departed Young Turks. Also, the DP hoped
to construct a local neighborhood liaison network to link up a mass support
base of 25,000 core voters concentrated in various strategic locations. All
the DP branch offices and district councilors' offices would work together to
help set up a total of eighty party volunteer organizations with thirty members each. It hoped to provide 300 places in training and advancement programs for DP district councilors and party members, with at least twenty
annual slots for international training. In addition, the DP targeted an increase of 20 percent (about eighteen seats) in its District Council presence
after the 2003 DC elections. It also promised to issue DP policy white papers
on all the major public policy areas from time to time. In order to support all
these new undertakings, the DP must substantially strengthen its coffers by a
twofold increase in donations to reach an annual sum of HK$1.6 to 1.8 mil-
lion. To meet this target, a stable pool of 3,000 regular donors has to be

maintained. In view of the economic downturn on individual family budgets, the DP lowered the required payroll due from its DC members by 20 percent. The meager but still solvent DP treasury has about HK$3 million in reserve in March 2001 against a projected annual expenditure of HK$7 million (including HK$5 million in regular income from membership fees and public officeholders' payroll dues), with the shortfalls to be provided by outside donations.[95]

In contrast to the healthy financial base of the big business–supported LP and the abundant resource enjoyed by the DAB from mainland-related corporate contributions, the DP has a much smaller war chest to carry out its reforms and to prepare for the 2003–04 elections.[96] It is imperative that the revitalization and rejuvenation of the DP and the entire democratic camp be based on strategic visions, issue analysis and platform designs, personnel deployment, and campaign and mobilization tactics that are manpower intensive but do not necessarily involve big budgets. With such a basis, the democratic camp's retrenchment at the start of the new millennium could still become an interlude for genuine reforms and breakthroughs despite the HKSAR regime's conservative authoritarianism and deliberate marginalization of democratic forces as well as Tung Chee-hwa's personal aversion to political parties and parliamentary proceedings.

Uncertain Prospects for HKSAR Democracy in the Twenty-First Century

If the 2000 Legco election results offer any redeeming lesson to the democratic camp, they reaffirm the importance of systematic local penetration with a clear socioeconomic focus to galvanize voters' support. With the negative 1997 China factor fast fading and the economic downturn still depressing the community, the democratic camp must thoroughly rearticulate its previously effective combination of liberal democratic political appeals with socioeconomic electoral mobilization. The ascendancy of socioeconomic issues has been a significant development in the rising tide of public affairs activism in Hong Kong since 1997. Grassroots unrest and labor militancy over livelihood concerns in an economic recession and restructuring crisis have characterized the social scene in the new SAR, the polity of which is likely to evolve toward an authoritarian corporatist state-society mix. Popularly elected politicians must firmly embrace socioeconomic concerns as the bedrock of political support and electoral platform.

The current recession has necessitated an increasingly interventionist approach by the Tung regime with its strong conservative paternalist instincts. The official commitment to carry out much-needed reforms in education, public housing, welfare, and the civil service, together with massive infrastructure projects, would force the SAR administration to work with the Legco on a wide range of undertakings, particularly over budget allocations. In this regard, a future democratic camp–dominated populist "biclass coalition" will be of importance with the potential for a majority or near majority in the Legco, where more seats will be returned by direct elections. The profound impact of such prodemocratic middle-class–grassroots alliance could reshape HKSAR politics.

As in the recent rail fares case, the existence of a livelihood issue Legco coalition across partisan and ideological lines has exerted sufficient pressure to force Tung Chee-hwa to yield a deferment. If the democratic camp can reform itself to regain harmony and cohesion with broad consensus on the divisive class identity and socioeconomic issues, then the possibility that a united democratic camp will form an issues-based ad hoc alliance with the DAB-FTU on rice-bowl concerns and economic policies is not entirely unrealistic. Such socioeconomic "class unity" in legislative politics will further fragment the already unstable pro-Beijing bloc of leftist mass organs and conservative tycoons which together formed a "loyalist lobby" buttressing the unpopular Tung regime. Thus, Tung Chee-hwa's fourth SAR policy speech on October 11, 2000, with its shifted focus on education, poverty, and bureaucratic accountability can be regarded as a belated attempt to arrest Tung's plummeting public approval in order to prepare for his second term as SAR chief executive.[97] In the same light, Tung's June 2001 "break-the-ice" dinner with DP Legco members could be seen as an attempt at a more accommodating political outreach. Perhaps the DP's "softening" stance on Beijing also had some spin-off effects on Tung's friendlier gesture. The DP leaders at this "very cordial" dinner reciprocated with careful avoidance of sensitive conversation topics such as the treatment of Falun Gong.[98] Tung's award of the Bronze Bauhinia Star to DP moderate figure Anthony Cheung on July 1, 2001, may be a symbolic sign of the SAR regime's thaw toward the more moderate democratic camp elements (or it may be a necessary balancing act to counter the lopsided SAR annual honor list favoring the pro-Beijing elites).[99]

Despite their new "China perspective" reorientation toward Beijing, the DP activists remain firm in their commitment to democratization in the HKSAR and by implication, on the Chinese mainland. If the annual June 4 Tiananmen Incident commemorative activities in post-1997 Hong Kong can be taken as useful indicators of local support for the democratic camp vis-à-vis the China factor, then their latest display of such sentiments right before the HKSAR fourth anniversary is noteworthy. Following the lower-than-expected turnout (of only fifteen hundred participants, five hundred fewer than in 2000) at the May 27, 2001, daytime march to commemorate the

Tiananmen Incident, and alarmed by press reports on recent survey poll findings of sharply declining public support (at 45.8 percent, some 7 percent less than in 2000) for such Patriotic Alliance–sponsored events, those who were still faithful to the democratic cause swiftly responded. A congregation of over forty-eight thousand took part in the twelfth annual Tiananmen Incident commemorative candlelight assembly at Victoria Park on the evening of June 4, 2001. The total attendance was some three thousand more than the year 2000 figure, a significant reversal of the trend that would force local pundits to rethink and regret their premature verdicts on the supposedly rapid dying out of local enthusiasm for the cause of Chinese democracy.[100]

Notwithstanding the sovereignty retrocession and the economic hardship, popular support for local democratization, even with an altered, more positive perception of Beijing, remains an important force in HKSAR politics that must not be underestimated. For the democratic activists, if socioeconomic debates have divided them, then democratization is still the sacred common cause and ultimate battle cry that can galvanize them into joint actions and collective mobilization. Thus, comradeship in political and constitutional struggles may provide an indispensable bond that will help to revive democratic camp solidarity against HKSAR conservative authoritarianism. A July 2001 press account pointed to the attempts to regroup the prodemocratic leaders in the 1987–88 coalition for direct elections as the core of a new grand alliance to mount massive campaigns leading to the 2007 electoral review. If this project could actually materialize, then a revival of democratic camp's political activism might be forthcoming.[101]

However, dramatic events in spring 2002 suggested a rather alarming prospect for a deeply divided and shrinking democratic camp. After the DP held a relatively uneventful annual general meeting in mid-December 2001, another crack soon developed as former vice chair Anthony Cheung set up a "Synergy Net" group with some DP members who were former Meeting Point elements. This provoked strong criticism from mainstream elder Szeto Wah. As Martin Lee will have to step down as DP party chair in December 2002, all these internal discords could be the early signs for intraparty struggles over leadership succession and for control of party policy orientation.[102] In January 2002, the Frontier's Emily Lau admitted to a sharp decline (from more than 100 in 1999 to 59 in 2001) in its membership, which was enlarged by 50 Young Turks in April.[103]

The changing Beijing-HKSAR interactive dynamics combined with socioeconomic realities in the SAR will eventually facilitate the realignment of legislative politics, especially for the democratic camp and the DP, but also for DAB and even the Tung regime. The third SAR Legco elections in 2004 will see a contest for an equal number (thirty) of directly elected and functional seats. The resultant 2004–08 HKSAR Legco will play a direct role in the Basic Law–mandated 2007 constitution review which could ultimately usher in a fully directly elected Legco and even possibly the direct election for the SAR chief executive. By then, the first decade of the HKSAR, a very different electoral game would be a foot, offering new possibilities for a reformed and even reunited democratic camp to transcend the existing system of a caged democracy.

Furthermore, after Tung Chee-hwa was reelected without contest in March 2002, for a second five-year term as HKSAR chief executive, he will introduce a new system of placing political appointees as top officials in charge of the major policy bureaus, to enhance "executive accountability"—which means accountability to the chief executive personally but not to the Legco and the public at large. Nonetheless, this may turn a new page, relieving strained executive-legislature interactions by presenting new opportunities for the SAR's political parties to mount some modified if not entirely different parliamentary game plans in the Legco chamber toward government policies and the new policy makers.

The recent devastating blow to the already depressed local economy by the global fallout effects of the September 11, 2001, terrorist attacks in the United States also compelled the political parties to work much more closely together to forge a remarkable consensus, if not exactly full unity, out of emergency situation crisis response spirit. For instance, after several days of intensive discussion, most of the Legco members joined forces to propose an "all-parties, seven-points" economic rescue package of practical and immediate measures a couple of days before Tung Chee-hwa delivered his fifth policy speech on October 10, 2001,[104] almost exactly a month after the tragedies in New York. While the SAR regime did not adopt many of these seven points in its March 2002 budget, the ability of such intercamp cooperation on urgent solutions to meet the burning livelihood needs of the community would force the SAR executive arm to be more careful about heeding the advice of the Legco as an effective public representative collective interest group. Perhaps in this hour of dire economic circumstance, the unprecedented collective efforts by the political parties could also help to arrest the ongoing trend toward serious public disenchantment with political parties, as evident in the 2000 Legco elections low voter turnout. It seems that the democratic camp, other political blocs, and even the SAR regime would all have opportunities in the current economic crisis to regain public trust and strengthen their political mandate.

The SAR's Basic Law–framed polity is burdened by rigid constitutional restrictions and serious institutional flaws with too many checks and inadequate balance in its "hardware" structure.[105] These structural defects and constraints have rendered the SAR system a very difficult governance mechanism to operate, particularly in the context of a strained executive-legislative relationship. However, in the "software" realm of realpolitik maneuvers on socioeconomic undertakings and bureaucratic reform toward an executive cabinet with political appointees as senior officials and Exco members, there would be opportunities, such as the 2007 electoral review, for the SAR's party politics to unshackle themselves from the present narrow political confines. Perhaps all these might yield a more level arena with fair and open rules for the democratic camp to reform and reenergize itself as the effective mainstream force for socioeconomic justice and democratic progress in HKSAR realpolitik of the twenty-first century.

Notes

1. The term "democratic camp" as used here refers to and is mainly represented by the Democratic Party, the Frontier, the Citizens Party, and the Association for Democracy and People's Livelihood, plus a few pro-democracy Legco independents.

2. On the China factor and the British decolonization and democratization processes, see Ming K. Chan, "The Politics of Hong Kong's Imperfect Transition: Dimensions of the China Factor," in *The Challenge of Hong Kong's Reintegration with China*, Ming K. Chan, ed. (Hong Kong: Hong Kong University Press, 1997), pp. 1–30.

3. On the PRC co-opting of local elites, see Shiu-hing Lo, "Political Opposition, Co-optation and Democratization: The Case of Hong Kong," in *Political Order and Power Transition in Hong Kong*, Pang-kwong Li, ed. (Hong Kong: Chinese University Press, 1997), pp. 127–57.

4. Some scholars use the "politics-of-identity" concept on the battle lines drawn by the "pro-China" (i.e., pro-Beijing) and the "pro-democracy" camps, as Wang Gungwu and John Wong have labeled it in their *Hong Kong: After the Smooth Handover, Now the Hard Part*, [EAI Background Brief No. 18] (Singapore: East Asian Institute, National University of Singapore, 1999). Also see their edited volume, *Hong Kong in China: The Challenges of Transition* (Singapore: Times Academic Press, 1999).

5. *San Francisco Chronicle*, June 28, 1999, p. A-10.

6. A concise review of the economic downturn up to the eve of the May 1998 Legco elections is given by Yi-zheng Lian in "An Economic Roundup of Post-Handover Hong Kong," in Asia Society, *Hong Kong: The Challenges of Change* (New York: Asia Society, 1998).

7. PLC's performance is assessed in James T.H. Tang, "Politics in Hong Kong: Democracy in Retreat," in Asia Society, *Hong Kong: The Challenge of Change*. Also note the near–40 percent negative versus only 11 percent positive public approval rate on the PLC in opinion survey polls conducted near the end of its tenure in April 1998, as reported in *Pop Express*, no. 20, April 1998, pp. 5–6 (Hong Kong: Social Science Research Center, University of Hong Kong).

8. Ming K. Chan, "Democracy Derailed: Realpolitik in the Making of the Hong Kong Basic Law," in *The Hong Kong Basic Law: Blueprint for 'Stability and Prosperity' Under China Sovereignty?* Ming Chan and David Clark, ed. (Armonk: M.E. Sharpe, 1991), pp. 3–35. Also see Martin Lee and Szeto Wah's interview in *Hong*

Kong Economic Journal (hereafter *HKEJ*), July 3, 1999, on their patriotic views but their disagreement with Beijing on democracy.

9. Private discussions with DP chair Martin Lee and vice chair Yeung Sum, both on December 4, 1997, in Hong Kong.

10. According to survey data collected by the Hong Kong Transition Project, 64 percent of respondents in one poll considered the 1997 retrocession with the new SAR system under PRC sovereignty as the best arrangement for Hong Kong. This is reported in the project director's paper: Michael DeGoyler, "Public Opinion and Participation in the 1998 Legco Elections: Pre/Post Colonial Comparisons" (presented at a Chinese University of Hong Kong conference, September 1998). In contrast, in September 1995, 62 percent of respondents in another poll expressed dissatisfaction with the PRC about Hong Kong transition matters.

11. In his search for "functional legitimacy," Tung can be compared with pre-1997 British colonial governors, in particular Murray MacLehose in the post-1967 leftist riots era. For an elaboration of functional legitimacy in Hong Kong's historical context, see Ming K. Chan, "Labor vs. Crown: Aspects of Society-State Interactions in the Hong Kong Labor Movement Before World War II," in *Between East and West: Aspects of Social and Political Development in Hong Kong,* Elizabeth Sinn, ed. (Hong Kong: Center of Asian Studies, University of Hong Kong, 1990), pp. 38–46.

12. Leung first gained political prominence in 1985 when appointed by Beijing as secretary-general of the Hong Kong Basic Law Consultative Committee. Patronized by tycoon developers and the conservative elites as their key political spokesman on various PRC-appointed transition organs, Leung was appointed by Tung to be the SAR Exco convener effective July 1999.

13. This common public perception was skillfully played up by the democratic camp to become a major campaign issue in spring 1998. See Timothy K.Y. Wong "Issue Voting" in *Power Transfer and Electoral Politics: The First Legislative Election in the Hong Kong Special Administrative Region,* Kuan Hsin-chi et al., eds. (Hong Kong: Chinese University Press, 1999), pp. 105–30.

14. These were the exact words of labor leaders Lau Chin-shek and Lee Cheuk-yan in private conservation with the author, December 4, 1998.

15. This author was among the first to suggest this "safeguard and counterweight" concept to the democratic camp at an international labor conference organized by DP and Frontier leaders and hosted by the Hong Kong Confederation of Trade Unions in Shatin, Hong Kong, February 20, 1997. The full text of the author's speech is published as "The Labor Movement and the China Factor in Colonial Hong Kong" in *Asian Food Workers* 27, no. 2 (April–May 1997): 11–12.

16. Private discussions with Martin Lee, Yeung Sum, Lau Chin-shek, and Lee Cheuk-yan, all on December 4, 1998.

17. Unless specified otherwise, all the May 24, 1998, election figures are based on those reported in Elaine Chan and Rowena Kwok, "Democratization in Turmoil? Elections in Hong Kong," *Journal of Contemporary China* 8, no. 20 (1999): 47–65, and in *Hong Kong Economic Daily*, May 25, 1998, p. A-19.

18. On the 1991 election results and analysis, see Ming K. Chan, "The 1991 Elections in Hong Kong: Democratization in the Shadow of Tiananmen," in *China in Transition: Economic, Political and Social Developments,* George T. Yu, ed. (Lanham: University Press of America, 1993), pp. 229–50. On the 1995 election results and analysis, see *The 1995 Legislative Council Election in Hong Kong,* Kuan Hsih-chi et al., eds. (Hong Kong: Hong Kong Institute of Asia Pacific Studies, CUHK, 1996).

19. Private conversations with Martin Lee, May 5, 1999, in Hong Kong. Lee considered the May 1998 election results for his DP and the democratic camp as a whole to be very successful and better than commonly expected, perhaps with the exception of ADPL–Frederick Fung's defeat.

20. Richard Baum, "Democracy Deformed: Hong Kong's 1998 Legislative Elections—and Beyond," *China Quarterly*, no. 162 (June 2000): 439–64.

21. Ibid.

22. In private conversations on May 5, 1999, Lee pointed out that he would not mind seeing the proliferation of a few more pro-democracy parties to contest in the future elections if the PR system remind unchanged. To Lee, it would be much better for the entire democratic camp to gain more Legco seats, even if it meant the DP might suffer a slight drop in its own Legco seats. This point was emphasized in the context of our discussion on the DP internal discord over the dual (DP and Frontier) affiliation of Lau Chin-shek, who had contemplated the idea of resignation from the DP (and the Frontier) to form a new "labor party."

23. On the DP's factional discord and internal strife, see Shiu-hing Lo, "The Democratic Party in the Hong Kong Special Administration Region," *Round Table*, no. 352 (1999): 635–58.

24. Ibid., pp. 640–42.

25. The DP's internal disagreement was widely reported by the press. See *South China Morning Post*, December 30, 1998; *Hong Kong Standard*, December 18, 1998; and *Yazhou Zhoukan* (*Asiaweek*, Chinese edition) December 28, 1998–January 3, 1999, pp. 20–21.

26. Private conversations with Lau Chin-shek, Hong Kong, May 1–2, 1999, and Martin Lee, Hong Kong, May 5, 1999. On May 19, 1999, the DP leadership announced the "freeze" of Lau's active membership, but did not expel him or force him to resign from the party.

27. On the DP's reconciliation of internal functions and the new approach ahead, see *South China Morning Post*, January 12, 1999; and Yazhou Zhoukan, January 18–24, 1999, pp. 14–16. Also private conversations with Martin Lee, May 5, 1999.

28. Suzanne Pepper, "Elections, Political Change, and Basic Law Government" (paper presented at the Conference on Elections in Taiwan, Hong Kong, and Mainland China, Hoover Institution, Stanford, CA, March 5–6, 1999), pp. 28–30.

29. Private meetings with Lau and Lee, May 1–2, 1999, and November 3, 1999.

30. Shiu-hing Lo, *The Politics of Democratization in Hong Kong* (New York: St. Martin's Press, 1997), pp. 143–44, 155–62; Lo, "The Democratic Party," pp. 638–39.

31. Lo, "The Democratic Party," pp. 642.

32. *HKEJ*, April 17, 1999, p. 5.

33. Ibid.

34. *Sing Tao Daily* (U.S. West edition), September 20, 1999; *Yazhou Zhoukan*, September 27–October 2, 1999, pp. 29–30.

35. *Sing Tao Daily*, September 20, 1999; *World Journal*, September 18, 1999, p. A-15; *Next Magazine*, September 24, 1999, pp. 76–81.

36. *Sing Tao Daily*, January 5, 2000, p. A-16.

37. *HKEJ*, January 18, 2000, p. 14.

38. *Sing Tao Daily*, and *World Journal*, both May 11, 1999.

39. *World Journal*, May 12, 1999.

40. *World Journal*, June 4, 1999.

41. The 1999 figure is from *Ta Kung Pao*, November 29, 1999, front page. The

1991 and 1994 figures are from *Hong Kong 1995: A Review of 1994*, ed. Government Information Services (Hong Kong: Government Printer 1995), p. 34.

42. Frank Ching "A Small but Significant Hong Kong Poll," *Far Eastern Economic Review*, December 9, 1999, p. 15.

43. The figures for this and the following sections on the DB polls are based on *Yazhou Zhoukan*, December 6–12, 1999, p. 25; *Ta Kung Pao*, November 29–30, 1999, front page; *HKEJ*, October 21, 1999, p. 5.

44. These figures come from the surveys and tabulations by the team of Robert Chung's Public Opinion Program at the Social Science Research Center, University of Hong Kong. See his article in *HKEJ*, December 8, 1999, which verifies the actual seats won and his projections in this DB poll.

45. *World Journal*, November 30, 1999, p. A-16.

46. *World Journal*, November 29, 1999, p. A-12, November 30, 1999, p. A-16; *Yazhou Zhoukan*, December 6–12, 1999, p. 25.

47. *World Journal*, November 30, 1999, p. A-16.

48. *Sing Tao Daily*, November 29, 1999, A 15; *World Journal*, November 30, 1999, p. A-12; *Yazhou Zhoukan*, December 6–12, 1999. pp. 25–26.

49. *Sing Tao Daily*, November 29, 1999, pp. A-15–A-16; *World Journal*, November 30, 1999, p. A-16.

50. *World Journal*, November 30, 1999, p. A-16.

51. For example, see the front-page headlines and editorial in *Ta Kung Pao*, November 29 and 30, 1999.

52. Quoted in *Asiaweek*, December 10, 1999.

53. Private meeting with Tam Yiu-chung, November 3, 1999. Also see *HKEJ*, December 3, 8, and 11, 1999, for analysis of the DAB victory in the DC polls.

54. Private meeting with Tam Yiu-chung, November 3, 1999. Also see the following analysis for the DAB's victory in the DB election: *HKEJ*, December 3, 8, and 11, 1999; *Tao Kung Pao*, November 30, 1999; *Asiaweek*, December 10, 1999, p. 40; *World Journal*, November 29, 1999, p. 12; *Yazhou Zhoukan*, December 6–12, 1999, p. 26.

55. *Yazhou Zhoukan*, December 6–12, 1999, p. 26.

56. *HKEJ*, December 2 and 8, 1999. Political scientists Shiu-hing Lo, in conducting his research project on the HKSAR grassroots politics in autumn 1999, warned of the DP's coming disaster in the DB polls as early as a month before the polls, in a private memo to the chapter author.

57. Private conversations with Martin Lee and Yeung Sum, November 3 and 4, 1999; both suggested 90 seats as the "passing and acceptable level" in DC seat gains.

58. *HKEJ*, December 31, 1999, p. 4.

59. *Ta Kung Pao*, November 29, 1999, front page.

60. Private meetings with John C.Y. Leung, Principal Assistant Secretary for Constitutional Affairs in charge of the councils' abolition, May 3 and November 10, 1999.

61. *Ta Kung Pao*, December 4, 1999, front page; *HKEJ*, December 3, 1999, p. 15, and October 14, 1999, p. 7.

62. Details on the DP's decision to split into two or three party lists for some geographical constituencies such as New Territories East and West but would keep a single list for the three urban constituencies are given in *HKEJ*, January 10, 2000, p. 7; January 20, 2000, p. 6; January 22, 2000, p. 5; February 3, 2000, p. 8; February 8, 2000, p. 5; February 14, 2000, p. 5; February 15, 2000, p. 11; February 18, 2000, p. 12; and February 21, 2000, p. 8.

63. For example, on the same day, both *HKEJ* and *World Journal* carry stories on

the DP's Legco electoral preparation problems in the directly elected seats' party list split and in the social work functional constituency, *HKEJ*, March 31, 2000, p. 12; World Journal, March 31, 2000, p. A-14.

64. See *HKEJ*, April 10, 2000, p. 6; April 14, 2000, p. 16; April 27, 2000, p. 7; April 28, 2000, p. 11; May 2, 2000, p. 6. See also *Sing Tao Daily*, April 2, 2000, p. A-14; May 8, 2000, pp. A-13–A-15; and *World Journal*, April 10, 2000, p. A-10; April 13, 2000, p. A-12; May 9, 2000, p. A-15. All report the intraparty conflicts over Legco election party lists.

65. *HKEJ*, April 12, 2000, p. 6; *World Journal*, April 12, 2000, p. A-14; *Sing Tao Daily*, April 12, 2000, p. 16.

66. Private conversation with CTU chief executive Elizabeth Tang, June 29, 2000.

67. The 2000 electoral figures are based on reportage in *Ming Pao*, *Sing Tao Daily*, and *HKEJ*, September 11, 12 and 13, 2000.

68. *Ming Pao*, September 11, 2000.

69. Figures provided by Dr. Suzanne Pepper, October 26, 2000.

70. *Ming Pao*, September 11, 2000.

71. *HKEJ*, April 12, 2000, also see *HKEJ*'s April 1 and 5, 2000, reports on this DAB-HKPA dual affiliation for Cho So-yuk, a 1998–2000 Legco member from the HKPA in an election committee–returned seat.

72. Private conversation with Ching Cheong, Hong Kong correspondent for the *Singapore Straits Times*, October 6, 2000.

73. *Ming Pao* and *HKEJ*, both September 12, 2000.

74. *HKEJ*, September 12, 2000, p. 7.

75. *Yazhou zhoukan*, December 18–24, 2000.

76. The author's on-site observation, with Dr Sonny Lo and his University of Hong Kong research team on polling day.

77. *Bauhinia Magazine*, January 2001, p. 13.

78. *HKEJ*, September 12, 2000.

79. On the DP congress, see *HKEJ*, *Sing Tao*, and *Ming Pao*, all December 14–18, 2000.

80. *HKEJ*, June 2, 2001; *Ming Pao*, January 9, 2001; *Sing Tao*, April 19, 2002.

81. *Sing Tao*, December 27, 2000, reports the reorganization of DP's public relations office to improve the party's contact with Beijing.

82. *Sing Tao*, March 12, 2001.

83. *World Journal* and *Sing Tao*, both April 22, 2001.

84. *HKEJ*, *World Journal*, and *Sing Tao*, all May 5, 2001.

85. *Sing Tao*, May 7, 2001.

86. *Yazhou Zhoukan*, May 14–20, 2001, p. 50; *Sing Tao*, May 8, 2001.

87. *World Journal*, March 31, 2001.

88. *HKEJ*, April 7, 2001; *World Journal*, April 5 and May 5, 2001.

89. *World Journal*, June 23 and July 4, 2001; *Ming Pao*, February 7, 2002.

90. *World Journal*, June 22, 2001.

91. *Sing Tao*, June 22, 2001.

92. *World Journal* and *Ming Pao*, both June 23, 2001; and *World Journal*, January 21, 2002, p. A-12.

93. *HKEJ*, December 21, 2000; *Sing Tao*, June 29, 2001; *Apple Daily*, December 19, 2000.

94. *Ming Pao*, June 6, 2001; *HKEJ*, May 1, 2001.

95. *HKEJ*, March 12, 2001; *Yazhou zhoukan*, April 1–17, 2002, pp. 26–27.

96. *Apple Daily*, December 19, 2000. DAB reports its 1999–2000 income amounted to HK$32 million; after expenditures, it enjoyed a surplus reserve of HK$6.7 million in late 2000.

97. *HKEJ*, October 12, 2000.

98. *Sing Tao* and *World Journal*, both June 13, 2001.

99. On the controversial award to a leftist unionist, see *Sing Tao*, July 1, 2001; *Ming Pao*, July 1–6, 2001.

100. *HKEJ*, *Sing Tao*, and *World Journal*, all May 28 and June 2, 4, and 5, 2001.

101. *World Journal*, July 2, 2001

102. *Sing Tao*, January 20, 2002, p. A-13 and *World Journal*, February 24, 2002, A-10.

103. *Sing Tao*, January 28, 2002, p. A-17; *World Journal*, January 28, 2002, p. A-12, January 29, 2002, p. A-14, and April 22, 2002, p. A-10.

104. *Ming Pao* and *Sing Tao Daily*, both October 7–11, 2001.

105. Suzanne Pepper, "Elections, Political Change, and Basic Law Government: The Hong Kong System in Search of a Political Form," in *China Quarterly*, no. 162 (June 2000): 410–38.

4

Changing Political Cleavages in Post-1997 Hong Kong

A Study of the Changes Through the Electoral Arena

Ngok Ma

After Hong Kong became a Special Administrative Region (SAR) of the People's Republic of China (PRC), the political landscape underwent major changes. Before 1997, the China factor as a structural, historical, and socialization factor[1] had been defining the political landscape of Hong Kong. Ironically, after Hong Kong reverted to Chinese sovereignty, the China factor somehow ceased to be the defining cleavage of the Hong Kong political scene. Attitudes toward the SAR government and distributional issues began to assert their significance as major sources of political cleavages in Hong Kong, bringing a more pluralized cleavage structure.

This chapter seeks to examine how the political cleavages in Hong Kong changed throughout the years, especially after 1997, with special focus on the cleavage pattern as reflected from the electoral arena. It argues that the change of sovereignty has reduced the significance of the China factor in determining the political cleavages of Hong Kong. As the uncertainty over Chinese intervention waned, the post-1997 SAR saw a diminishing significance of political issues. Due to the change of the electoral system, we witnessed a more pluralized cleavage structure in Hong Kong after 1997. The change in cleavage pattern would pose a major challenge to democrats in Hong Kong. Facing multiple new fault lines and the new proportional representation system, the democrats would find it extremely difficult to find a new ideological position or issue package that would capture a wide range of supporters across the multiple-issue cleavages, as they were accustomed to before 1997. The new pluralized cleavages would add to the fragmentation of the democracy movement in Hong Kong, facilitating executive control by the SAR government.

The Concept of Cleavages: A Brief Review

There are many definitions for "political cleavage." Simply put, cleavages are "the criteria which divide the members of a community into groups."[2] Here, I follow Moreno's definition of *political cleavages* as "divisions in society of individuals' orientations, attitudes, and behavior toward policy, political groups, and government, and that are expressed through party support."[3] The above definition draws our attention to several properties of political cleavages. First, they are rooted in deeper divisions in society, such as divisions in class, religion, or economic or cultural interests. Second, cleavages are always institutionalized by groups or organizations. Political parties play a special role in transforming social divisions into *political* cleavages by giving coherence and organized political expression to what are otherwise inchoate and fragmentary beliefs, values, and experiences.[4] Party competition usually centers on the dimensions of conflict that reflect the most salient cleavages in society, and parties act as agents that politicize the social cleavages for their own advantage.

As political parties are vital to the formation of political cleavages, competitive elections prove the best arena through which we can observe clearly the alignment of these political cleavages. In an attempt to compete for public support and power, political parties will highlight their political differences with regard to others during elections, in order to mobilize support from the respective social divisions. While the parliamentary arena may provide more room for maneuver and compromise between parties, in the electoral arena parties have no choice but to emphasize the differences between themselves.

It should be noted that not all cleavages may find electoral expression.[5] Parties or candidates generally go through a process of "priming" during elections: they will choose certain issue positions to frame the voters' evaluation toward themselves, so as to put themselves in the best situation to win the election.[6] Nevertheless, to be successful in elections, political parties have to seize the differences or cleavages that could most effectively mobilize support from social groupings, which means electoral struggles would still invariably reflect the dominant interest and value conflicts in society.

There can be various sources of political cleavages: ascriptive (race or caste), attitudinal (values and ideology), or behavioral (through organizational membership).[7] Lipset and Rokkan stated four major forms of cleavages in Western Europe: urban-rural, secular-religious, left-right, and subject-dominant cultures.[8] Inglehart pointed out that the new generation in Western democracies is more concerned with quality of life and self-expression than with economic issues. The difference between this attitude and the traditional focus on bread-and-butter issues is termed the materialist-postmaterialist divide.[9]

While the above seminal studies mostly refer to the experience of mature democracies, in new democracies, the democratic-authoritarian cleavage is usually the dominant cleavage.[10] For transitional democracies such as the Eastern European countries, democracy cannot be taken for granted; thus the major cleavage is between the proreform and antireform groups. Cleavages about policy issues are usually more dominant in developed countries, while structural cleavages are more salient in less developed countries. Democratic consolidation, on the other hand, will make the democratic-authoritarian cleavage less salient as the democratic system becomes more mature.[11]

Hong Kong is an interesting case for the study of political cleavages in this respect. Hong Kong has begun a long democratization process since the mid-1980s, which means that the democratic-authoritarian cleavage should be dominant in Hong Kong (which was the case before 1997). However, after fifteen years of democratization, we were not even close to saying that democracy had come to Hong Kong, let alone become "consolidated." It becomes an interesting research question whether this democratic-authoritarian divide will continue to be the major cleavage between political parties in the post-1997 Hong Kong Special Administrative Region (HKSAR).

This chapter will recapitulate the major changes in the alignments of political cleavages in Hong Kong in the last few decades, with special emphasis on the political cleavages demonstrated during popular elections. The analyses of the cleavages in the past elections were based on past election studies and on extensive surveys of campaign literature and the contents of broadcast forums in the four legislative elections in 1991, 1995, 1998, and 2000.[12] The dominant political cleavages will be identified by analysis of the campaign materials and election forums. Major differences in positions between political parties and political forces on various campaign issues will be ascertained to identify the major cleavage lines that separate the various political forces. Last, the paper will discuss how the alignment of political cleavages in Hong Kong has changed as a result of the change of sovereignty and the long process of democratization.

Political Cleavages Before the 1990s

Before the 1980s, the dominant ideological cleavage in Hong Kong was between the "left" (pro–Chinese Communist Party [CCP] groups) and the "right" (pro-Kuomintang [KMT] groups), a leftover of the mainland civil war. The most serious social conflicts in postwar Hong Kong (e.g., the 1956 and 1967 riots) were instigated by pro-KMT and pro-CCP masses. However, since both groups did not actively seek to influence public policy of Hong Kong, this dominant social cleavage was not effectively brought into the Hong Kong political system. Large businesses, especially British merchants, essentially "captured" the Hong Kong state before the 1970s.[13]

Entering the 1970s and 1980s, this dominant left-right political cleavage began to fade. For a while, the "leftists" became immensely unpopular in mainstream society because of their violent action in the 1967 riots.[14] The influence of pro-KMT groups also began to diminish, as they were unable to actively participate in the social and political movements in the 1970s and 1980s. The reform movements in 1970s and 1980s were spearheaded by the local middle class and professionals, who later formed the backbone of the prodemocracy groups. This new generation, a local-born, better-educated elite, also had a stronger Hong Kong identity, and was more sympathetic to Western values such as democracy, social equality, freedom, and human rights. When the public became more concerned with reforming Hong Kong society, the traditional "leftists" and "rightists" began to lose their appeals as they still set their sights on developments in mainland China and Taiwan. Although the pro-KMT groups were fading in influence, the anticommunist sentiments lingered on.

The Sino-British negotiations over the sovereignty of Hong Kong in 1982–84 triggered a decade-long politicization and mobilization process. The long transition period means that structurally there was a dual authority structure, and the danger of possible mainland Chinese intervention before or after 1997 always loomed large.[15] In face of imminent retrocession of Hong Kong into the hands of communist China, the local population began to worry if the lifestyle of the Hong Kong could be kept after 1997. A democratic system, whatever that means in the minds of the Hong Kong public,[16] had a certain appeal in fending off intervention from mainland China and preserving the freedom and lifestyle of Hong Kong.

The democracy movement in the 1980s was thus a convenient confluence of these anticommunist, Hong-Kong centered, and rising proreform and prodemocracy sentiments in Hong Kong. The "democrats" in the 1980s were in fact a loose pro-social-democratic coalition pushing for social-democratic and political reforms. In pushing for reforms, they met resistance on several fronts. On the political front, they had to bargain with the PRC and Hong Kong governments, the local business conservatives, and the local pro-Beijing groups to fight for a more democratic future political system. On the electoral front, the democrats found themselves confronted with a myriad of conservative local leaders. The 1980s marked the first organized attempts of the democrats to increase their influence through participating in District Board (DB) and Municipal Council elections. Years of administrative absorption[17] means that the colonial government was generally on good terms with the local "gentry" class, the *kaifong* (neighborhood) leaders, and rural leaders. These traditional local elites were sympathetic with the colonial government before the 1990s, politically conservative, and more skeptical to social reform and social movements.

One point is noteworthy. Although the Chinese government opposed a fast pace of democratization in Hong Kong, the democrats largely did not adopt a confrontational attitude against the PRC government before 1989. The local leftists were also not the main enemies of the democrats in local elections. First of all, the local leftists did not participate very actively in local elections in the 1980s. The 1985 DB election marked the first time that leftist organizations mobilized their members to run as candidates and register as voters.[18] Some democrats in fact had good relations with local leftists before 1989, and sometimes had their support in elections. The major opponents of the democrats in local elections in the 1980s were the traditional local leaders, the *kaifong* and rural conservatives. Before 1989, the democrats chose to direct most of their criticisms against the colonial government, as they saw the democracy movement as part of a reform movement to correct the ills and injustices of the colonial system.[19] The democracy movement thus played a role in the plot of "Hong Kong people ruling Hong Kong" after 1997, which was promised by the Chinese government in the Joint Declaration in 1984.

This is not to say the China factor was not important. Anticommunist sentiments and potential oppression and intervention from mainland China were important reasons behind the support for the democracy movement. But if anything, the dominant cleavage in Hong Kong before the 1990s was not one between democrats and pro-PRC groups, but one between proreform and antireform elements in Hong Kong.

From Tiananmen to the 1991 Election: Politicization of the Cleavage

While the democracy movement of the 1980s was not anti-Beijing, the Tiananmen crackdown in 1989 totally changed the picture. The active role played by the Hong Kong democrats in supporting the mainland movement, and the setting up of the Alliance in Support of the Patriotic Democratic Movement in China (ASPDMC), tied the democrats firmly onto the anticommunist stakes. More than one million Hong Kong citizens took to the streets in spring 1989 to support the democracy movement in mainland China. Supporting democracy, defending Hong Kong's freedom and lifestyle, and anticommunism suddenly became synonymous.

The Tiananmen crackdown also brought two parallel developments that reshaped the political cleavages in Hong Kong. It made leading democrats such as Szeto Wah, Martin Lee, and Lau Chin-shek highly visible charismatic leaders and sped up party formation in Hong Kong. The formation of the United Democrats of Hong Kong (UDHK), a part-merger of three prominent prodemocracy groups,[20] united most proreform, prodemocracy forces under the "democrats" banner. On the other hand, the Chinese leaders feared that the democracy movement in Hong Kong might threaten their control on the mainland regime, and denounced Martin Lee and Szeto Wah as "subversives."[21] This condemnation, coupled with the fact that many UDHK leaders were also ASPDMC leaders, confirmed the "anti-China" (or more correctly "anti-Beijing") status of UDHK.

The 1991 election was one about differentiating between "genuine democrats" and "nongenuine democrats." Democrats tried their best to show their credentials in the local democracy movement and in supporting the mainland democracy movement. Independents such as Chan Yuk-cheung and Lee Yu-tai also tried to boast their track records in supporting democracy whenever possible. Pro-Beijing candidates and conservatives, with some of them "disguised" as independents, were invariably asked of their attitude toward the Tiananmen crackdown. Various studies of the 1991 election showed that the attitude toward the PRC leadership was the most determining factor for voters' choice.[22] The supporters of UDHK and Meeting Point (MP) generally expected candidates to dissent with the PRC government, opposed mainland China's intervention into Hong Kong affairs, and supported reforms along the lines of more democracy and better protection of human rights.[23] A study of the platforms of the 1991 candidates showed that most candidates raised social-democratic demands, and there was no significant difference between their positions on distributional issues. The most important differences in the platforms were in issues concerning liberty and democracy, and attitudes toward mainland China.[24]

Although the attitude toward the PRC was a crucial dividing line between candidates in the 1991 election, the pro-Beijing camp was not the largest group of challengers to the democrats. Only three candidates (Chan Yuen-han, Gary Cheng, and Hau Sui-pui) were seen as genuine pro-Beijing candidates. The major challengers to the democrats in the 1991 election were the nonleftist conservatives, which included the pro-business conservatives (Liberal Democratic Foundation, or LDF), rural conservatives (Tang Siu-tong and Tai Chin-wah), traditional *kaifong* leaders (Cecilia Yeung and Poon Chi-fai), and some young professional conservatives (Yeung Fuk-kwong and Kan Chung-nin). The above four categories of conservatives had a total of fourteen candidates, and were the strongest challengers to the democrats in the

Figure 4.1 **Cleavage Pattern in the 1991 Election**

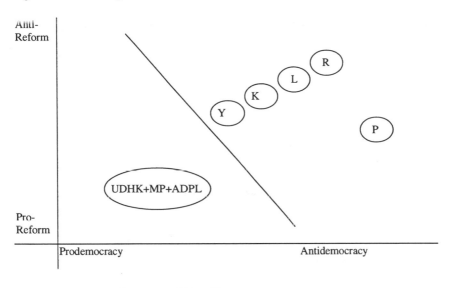

Key: UDHK: United Democrats of Hong Kong
       MP: Meeting Point
       ADPL: Association for Democracy and People's Livelihood
       Y: Young professional conservatives
       K: *Kaifong* leaders
       L: Liberal Democratic Foundation (LDF)
       R: Rural conservatives
       P: Pro-China candidates

1991 election. However, these conservatives did not form a well-coordinated
"united front" against the democrats in 1991. While UDHK and MP ran on
joint tickets and coordinated their candidates in most constituencies, very
few conservatives ran on joint tickets, and the few that did either failed mis-
erably or split seriously in later stages of the campaign.[25]

Figure 4.1 shows the cleavage pattern as reflected from the 1991 campaign. The three major prodemocracy groups, UDHK, MP, and ADPL,
adopted very similar positions on most issues. There was no serious debate
on issues of social policies and economic policies. While the democrats raised
mostly social-democratic demands, it was difficult to distinguish their positions from some other conservatives. The major dividing line was between
who was proreform and prodemocracy, and who was not. A simple democrat-
conservative divide thus can be constructed.

From the Patten Reform to the 1995 Election

The above cleavage pattern was largely continued in the parliamentary arena before governor Chris Patten arrived. The dominant conflict in the Legco before mid-1992 was between the democrats led by UDHK and pro-business conservatives of the Cooperative Resource Center (CRC). The democrats tried to challenge various traditions of consensual politics, push for more social-democratic reforms, and above all else speed up the pace of democratization. The CRC, on the other hand, was mostly supportive of the government in refuting the democrats' demands, earning themselves the nickname "the firemen team."[26]

Several developments in 1992–95 polarized the Hong Kong political scene and changed the dominant cleavage. The most important event of course was the political reform proposed by Chris Patten and the subsequent Sino-British dispute. The debate on Patten's proposal had a strong polarization effect. Beijing's harsh criticisms against Patten were delivered in such nationalist terms that politicians who supported Patten's proposals were deemed pro-British or unpatriotic. Politicians who wanted to be on good terms with Beijing had no choice but to oppose the Patten reform. The debate turned the rural conservatives, the business sector, and *kaifong* leaders, who all used to have good relationships with the colonial government, against the proposal and the British government. The attitude toward Beijing and democracy became the most crucial political issue in the territory.

The debate also led to a reintegration of the prodemocracy camp. It led to an internal split within the MP, with founding members such as Ivan Lau and Tsang Shu-ki quitting MP in protest of its decision to support the Patten proposal. MP used to have a better relationship with Beijing, with chairman Anthony Cheung appointed as one of the Hong Kong Affairs Advisers (see below). The subsequent merger of MP with UDHK to form the Democratic Party (DP) means that a clear line was drawn between DP and the PRC government; it was then relatively difficult to take the position of "moderate democrats" and maintain good relationship with Beijing.[27]

On the other hand, the PRC government began to coopt its supporters with a series of appointments. In 1993, the Preparatory Working Committee for the SAR was formed, accompanied by the appointment of several batches of Hong Kong Affairs Advisers from 1992 to 1994. These appointments served to co-opt the most prominent businessmen and pro-Beijing politicians in the territory. In 1994–95, the PRC government further appointed three batches of Hong Kong District Affairs advisers, which included a collection of about seven hundred district-level leaders. The democrats were largely kept out of these appointed bodies. An "unholy alliance against the democrats,"[28] composed of business representatives, conservative politicians, and local leaders, was thus formed. The polarization brought about by the Patten debate seemed to leave Hong Kong politicians with only two choices: prodemocracy and anti-Beijing, or pro-Beijing and antidemocracy.

The formation of the Democratic Alliance for Betterment of Hong Kong (DAB) in July 1992 consolidated the pro-China forces. Composed mostly of pro-PRC activists, local grassroot leaders, and the pro-PRC Hong Kong Federation of Trade Unions (FTU) leaders, DAB quickly replaced the pro-business conservatives as the greatest rival of the democrats. As an electoral machine, DAB coordinated all pro-Beijing, conservative, and *kaifong* forces during elections, to compete with the democrats. It also had great manpower and monetary support from various pro-Beijing groups and institutions in Hong Kong, which gave it a great edge in resources.

As for the formation of political cleavages of Hong Kong, DAB played a major role in providing a major ideological counterpost to the democrats. In the 1991 election, the prodemocracy sentiment was so overwhelming that the conservatives did not want to admit they were conservatives, and pro-Beijing candidates hesitated in revealing their pro-Beijing affiliations. Seen as spokespersons for the Chinese government, DAB members did a good job of putting forward their pro-Beijing and conservative ideology in political debate in 1992–95. First, DAB claimed that it is natural for the ethnic Chinese in Hong Kong to be "patriotic," or "pro-PRC." Apart from appealing to nationalist sentiments, they purported a pragmatic rationale for being pro-Beijing: China is the future sovereign, and we should be less confrontational against it and keep a good relationship or dialogue with it. The Tiananmen crackdown is history. It is no use to harp on the old themes of Tiananmen. China should look to the future, and, as Chinese, the Hong Kong people should help China to develop rather than continually confronting the PRC government (as the democrats do). Democracy is a good thing, they said, but its development should be gradual lest it should jeopardize the stability and prosperity of Hong Kong. This provided a very important ideological basis for being "pro-Beijing" or at least being more conciliatory toward the PRC government, which managed to rally conservative-minded groups and voters behind it.

The electoral system also helped to reshape the political cleavage. Patten's reform changed the election method of all three tiers of councils—DB, Urban Council (UC) and Regional Council (RC) and Legco—to the single-member constituency, first-past-the-post method. As a rule, this method promotes two-party competition and a more polarized pattern of competition.[29] Parties or groups with similar ideological positions will try to coordinate under the single-member system, for fear of splitting the vote between themselves and creating a lose-lose situation. In the three tiers of elections in 1994–95, both the pro-Beijing camp and the prodemocracy camp tried their best to coordinate their candidates, to the extent that a majority of the seats were contested by two candidates only.[30] For the sake of winning elections, politicians had to choose to coordinate with either the pro-Beijing or the prodemocracy camp, which added to the polarization of the political field in Hong Kong.

The 1995 Campaign: A Polarized Election

The 1995 Legco election was a face-off between pro-Beijing forces and prodemocracy forces. The prodemocracy camp largely succeeded in fielding only one candidate in most of the constituencies, and various groups of conservatives were coordinated into a united front against the democrats.[31] Consequently, eleven of the twenty directly contested seats were one-on-one contests between democrats and pro-Beijing candidates, as close to a two-party competition as it ever was in Hong Kong.[32] Politicians, social groups, and even voters were forced to choose between two rival camps and two rival ideologies.

Li saw the two major cleavages in the 1995 election as the center-periphery cleavage and the collective-individual consumption cleavage, with the former much more dominant. By center-periphery cleavage, Li means the difference between the pro-Beijing stand and the pro-Hong Kong stand.[33] Others showed that by 1995 there was strong party identification on the part of the voters, and the party label in fact had better explanatory power on voters' choice than both the China factor and social and economic policy issues.[34] This showed that, by 1995, DP and DAB, as the flagships of the prodemocracy and pro-Beijing forces, respectively, had consolidated the major cleavage in Hong Kong through electoral and party competition. The 1995 contest became a struggle between two rival ideologies, represented respectively by DP and DAB.

While the "pro-Beijing" label was dismissed as a "kiss of death" in 1991, in 1995 DAB succeeded in purporting the cause of being "pro-Beijing." The handover was near, and with the militancy that the PRC government demonstrated in the late transition era, it seemed unwise to adopt an overly confrontational attitude against Beijing. DAB hence put forward its nationalist and practical logic of being "pro-Beijing." It also emphasized its role as the bridge between Hong Kong and the PRC government. They criticized the democrats for being "anti-China and destabilizing Hong Kong" (*fanzhong luangang*). They claimed that adopting a confrontational attitude against the mainland Chinese authorities, as the democrats did, would enrage Beijing and hurt the stability and prosperity of Hong Kong. They also accused the democrats of having no channel of communication with the PRC government. Electing more candidates who were deemed "acceptable" to Beijing, they claimed, would pacify the mainland and bring about a more stable transition.

At the other end of the spectrum, DP candidates tried to position themselves as politicians who would stand firm for the interests of Hong Kong in face of pressure from Beijing, people who dared to say "no" to the PRC government. They admitted that communication with Beijing was important, but emphasized that it should not be achieved at the expense of the interests of the Hong Kong people. DP's position was best summarized by its historic half-page advertisement on September 13, 1995, four days before polling day:

> During elections, almost every candidate says s-he is supportive of democracy, human rights, rule of law, freedom and grassroot interests. How should voters choose? Voters should judge who can stand firm, unaffected by the people in power, and bravely speak for the people of Hong Kong. On issues like "direct election in 1988," the Bill of Rights, the Tiananmen crackdown, the Court of Final Appeal, and Provisional Legislature, we witnessed many pro-China figures offering beautiful lip-services, but would choose to follow the line of Beijing at the most crucial moment of voting. They may have a kind heart, but they cannot escape the iron grip from above.

The class cleavage was not too salient in the 1995 election. The major class-related issue at the time was the importation of labor from mainland China, which had been government policy since 1990. With the exception of the Liberal Party candidate Allen Lee, almost all candidates were opposed to the scheme, thus this did not pose a major cleavage in the election. Chan Yuen-han of DAB had tried to use the issue of unemployment benefits to attack DP candidate Mak Hoi-wah, but the issue also did not become a salient campaign issue.[35]

Another reason for the low salience of class cleavage was that the democrats chose to "politicize" the class cleavage. The prodemocracy labor unions, represented by the Hong Kong Confederation of Trade Unions (HKCTU), forged an election alliance with DP in the "new nine functional constituencies," which were elected by the 2.7 million working population. The concerted strategy of DP and CTU was to attribute the rising unemployment and the labor importation policy to the slow pace of democratization in Hong Kong. They argued that labor interests were not well protected in Hong Kong because the Legco was not fully elected and was dominated by business interests represented by the functional constituencies. The pro-business conservatives and pro-Beijing politicians were precisely the culprits since they had been opposing a faster pace of democratization since the mid-1980s. "No democracy, no labor rights" was the joint campaign slogan of DP and CTU. The democrats transformed the class cleavage back into the dominant cleavage: the pro-democracy and pro-Beijing cleavage.

Figure 4.2 shows the cleavage pattern reflected from the 1995 campaign. Elsewhere I have used a one-dimensional issue-line to capture the relative positions of the different parties in 1995.[36] With the low salience of class issues, Figure 4.2 is in fact not far from a one-dimensional issue line. The dominant conflict from 1995 to the handover, as was the nature of the Patten debate, was about whether Hong Kong should choose more democracy and autonomy at the price of confronting Beijing, or better relations with Beijing at the expense of more say from the Hong Kong people.

A brief analysis of the voting records of different parties in the 1995–97 Legco would testify the nature of cleavage in this period. An analysis of the most important voting decisions in the 1995–97 Legco shows that, on issues of constitutional development, human rights, and security, DP always adopted positions different from those of the Liberal Party (LP) and DAB. On social policy issues, however, there was a less clear-cut distinction between the parties. DP had quite a few common positions with DAB on issues like social welfare, housing, and health care.[37] Both DP and DAB, together with the Frontier (TF)[38] and ADPL, were more inclined to grassroot interests. These four groups invariably adopted a position on social issues that was different from the positions of pro-business parties such as LP and the Hong Kong Progressive Alliance (HKPA). The dominant political cleavage in 1995–97 was around issues like human rights, democracy, and attitude toward Beijing. The secondary cleavage, which was "hidden" or transformed during the 1995 campaign, was between the pro-grassroots groups (DP, DAB, TF, and ADPL) and the pro-business groups (LP and HKPA).

The Transfer of Sovereignty and the Fading of the China Factor

Although the China factor had been defining the major political cleavages in Hong Kong before 1997, the factor began to fade after Hong Kong reverted to Chinese sovereignty in 1997. Since the central government largely refrained from intervening in SAR affairs after 1997, the uncertainty and fear over the "China factor" before 1997 began to wane afterward. In 1995, DP could persuade voters that they needed someone who could "stand firm" against possible pressure from Beijing, but as Beijing seldom intervened, by 1998 "standing firm" became all too irrelevant for the Hong Kong people.

Figure 4.2 **Cleavage Pattern in the 1995 Election**

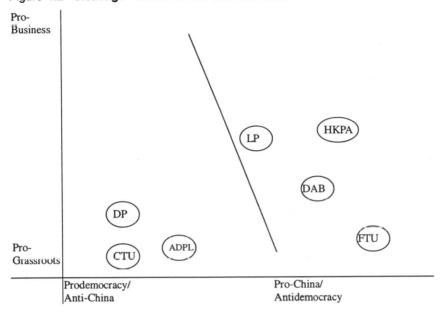

Key: DP: Democratic Party
      CTU: Confederation of Trade Unions
      ADPL: Association for Democracy and People's Livelihood
      LP: Liberal Party
      D'AB: Democratic Alliance for the Betterment of Hong Kong
      HKPA: Hong Kong Progressive Alliance
      FTU: Federation of Trade Unions

The fading of the China factor also stripped DAB of its most powerful card. The relatively peaceful political climate means that it was difficult to convince voters that they had to vote for pro-Beijing politicians to pacify the PRC authorities. Moreover, with the SAR government having direct access to the PRC central government, DAB also lost its role as a bridge between Hong Kong and Beijing.

The fading of the China factor, together with the less than satisfactory performance of the SAR government, transformed the dominant cleavage from pro-Beijing–prodemocracy to one of pro-government–anti-government. On the one hand, dissatisfaction against the PRC government among prodemocracy voters was partly diverted against the SAR government. The chief executive (CE) was not elected by universal suffrage, and Tung Chee-hwa was politically conservative and did not adopt a friendly attitude toward the democrats. This made prodemocracy supporters dislike the CE and the SAR government. As the CE was more or less handpicked by Beijing, some of the anti-Beijing sentiments could be translated into anti-government sentiments. Pro-Beijing parties and politicians, out of political loyalty, had no choice but to defend the performance of the SAR government. They supported some unpopular policies by the SAR government (e.g., abolition of labor-rights legislation) after 1997 and had to bear part of the blame.

The transformation of this cleavage was fully reflected in the 1998 Legco election. DP's general campaign strategy was to discredit the SAR government and the Provisional Legco (PLC).[39] The attitude to China was seldom mentioned in election forums or campaign literature. Cashing in on the low popularity of the PLC and the SAR government, DP claimed that the ills of the first year of SAR governance were due to the inability of the nonelected PLC in supervising the SAR government. It dismissed the PLC as a rubber-stamp of the SAR government and accused it of being biased in favor of business interests. DP claimed that it was necessary to elect democrats back into the Legco to supervise the government. TF mostly adopted a similar strategy to that of DP.

On the other side of the spectrum, DAB was almost the only party on the progovernment side in the 1998 election. The Hong Kong Progressive Alliance, the most progovernment party, did not participate in the direct elections. DAB had once considered positioning itself as a partner of the SAR government, but dropped the plan in view of the low popularity of the government. In defense of its progovernment position, DAB argued that the PLC had its achievements and should not be seen as a rubber stamp. DAB purported a conservative ideology, trying to project an image of being "peaceful and rational." DAB leaders claimed that DAB was a rational party that could maintain a good dialogue with the SAR government, and criticized those who "earned popularity by criticizing the government."

This progovernment-antigovernment cleavage in 1998 was not as salient as the pro-Beijing–prodemocracy cleavage before 1997. First, not all the parties adopted a strong critical attitude against the government or the PLC. Moderate prodemocracy parties such as ADPL and Citizens' Party did not make serious efforts to attack or defend the government or the PLC. On the conservative side, even LP adopted a more critical attitude against the government in 1998. Unlike in 1995, when every party could find its position on the pro-Beijing–prodemocracy axis, in 1998 the difference was more obscure, with DAB as the only progovernment party.

There were other constraints to this transformation from a pro-Beijing–

anti-Beijing cleavage to an antigovernment-progovernment divide. First of all, antigovernment sentiments, in the Hong Kong context, were never as strong as anticommunist sentiments. A survey in 1994 found that among the three governments of Britain, mainland China, and Hong Kong, 52.3 percent of respondents said they had the most confidence in the Hong Kong government in defending their interests. Only 5.5 percent had the most confidence in the PRC government.[40] Thus the deep-rooted anticommunist sentiments in Hong Kong society would not easily make a complete switch into antigovernment sentiments. The anti-Beijing syndrome also had a "Hong Kong–centered" overtone. Unless the SAR government was seen as one that would take orders only from Beijing, this Hong Kong–centered sentiment would not turn into antigovernment sentiments. Moreover, antigovernment sentiment after 1997 was partly due to the less than satisfactory performance of the HKSAR government. If the government improved its performance and popularity, the progovernment-antigovernment cleavage would be less pronounced.

Accompanying the transformation of the PRC-democracy cleavage was the rise in importance of economic issues. The economic downturn brought by the Asian financial crisis had led to more concern on economic and livelihood issues. While many Hong Kong people would cite issues like freedom, political stability and post-1997 corruption as the most concerned issue, by 1998 around 40–56 percent of citizens worried most about economic prospects.[41] Half of the voters in the 1998 election saw the economy as the most important issue.[42]

The rise of importance of economic issues, coupled with the change in electoral system, led to more pluralized competition within the prodemocracy camp. In 1995, the prodemocracy CTU ran on joint tickets with DP, and refrained from competing against DP. Due to the change of the electoral system, in 1998 DP had to compete against prodemocracy labor activists such as Lee Cheuk-yan and Leung Yiu-chung, and other prograssroot democrats such as ADPL. The nine functional constituencies added in 1995, which were elected by 2.7 million of the working population in 1995, were redefined and changed to corporate voting in 1998. The change enabled business groups and organizations in the sectors to regain control of the functional seats, driving prodemocracy candidates such as Lee and Leung to seek other venues of election. The change to a proportional representation system also tempted more prodemocracy groups to compete in the direct election, as a small share of the vote would earn them representation. As a result, with the exception of the Kowloon East constituency, all the constituencies saw competition between different prodemocracy lists in 1998.

This created an intracamp competition within the prodemocracy camp. [43]

Figure 4.3 **Cleavage Pattern in the 1998 Election**

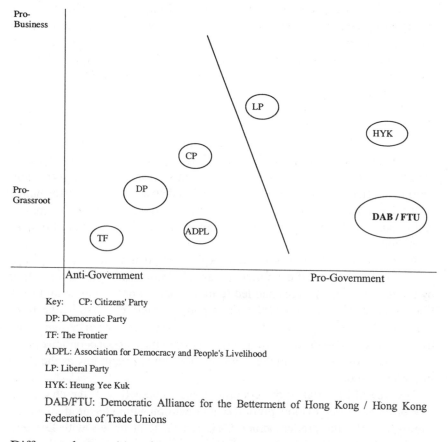

Key: CP: Citizens' Party

DP: Democratic Party

TF: The Frontier

ADPL: Association for Democracy and People's Livelihood

LP: Liberal Party

HYK: Heung Yee Kuk

DAB/FTU: Democratic Alliance for the Betterment of Hong Kong / Hong Kong Federation of Trade Unions

Different class positions began to create a new divide among the democrats. In New Territories West, voters faced seven pro-democracy lists. Most prodemocracy candidates had a strong pro-grassroots image: labor activists Lee Cheuk-yan and Leung Yiu-chung, the pro-grassroots ADPL, and former ADPL member Ting Hin-wah. Comparatively, the DP was less pro-grassroots. In New Territories East, DP also competed against Emily Lau of TF, and the DP campaign team chose to emphasize DP as a party "which cares both about democracy and people's livelihood," implying that they were closer to the grassroots than Emily Lau, who ran on a mostly political agenda.[44]

Figure 4.3 demonstrates this more pluralized cleavage pattern. The class cleavage was still less pronounced than the progovernment-antigovernment cleavage in the 1998 campaign. Although candidates spent a lot of time discussing social and economic issues, there was very little difference between their economic platforms. The major campaign issues remained the

Table 4.1

Number of Members and Unions of Three Major Labor Confederations

Name of confederation	Number of members		Growth rate, %	Number of unions		Growth rate, %
	1997	1999		1997	1999	
HKFTU	257,000	300,000	16.7	130	152	16.9
HKCTU	120,000	145,000	20.8	38	50	31.6
HKTUC	30,000	40,000	33.3	40	52	30.0

Source: Sing Tao Daily News, May 1, 2000.
Key:
HKFTU: Hong Kong Federation of Trade Unions
HKCTU: Hong Kong Confederation of Trade Unions
HKTUC: The pro-Taiwan Hong Kong Trade Union Council

government's performance, Provisional Legco, "Returning to Legco," and so on. The class issue and cleavage, however, would become more salient in the 2000 election.

The Rise of the Social Democratic Field

The 2000 campaign witnessed a rise in salience of the class cleavage. The change was largely due to changing social and economic situation, changing government policies, and party position shifts. The years 1998–2000 saw a further impoverization of the lower class. Real wages were falling, and unemployment hovered around 6 percent throughout the period. Many employees suffered from pay cuts and extended working hours, with as many as 600,000 employees working more than 60 hours a week.[45] The economic situation led to increased concern toward unemployment and the welfare of the lower class. Policy issues such as the minimum wage began to receive widespread discussions within the community. The economic plight also led to more street action and increased unionization. The three major labor union confederations all recorded significant increases in membership in the years 1997–99 (see Table 4.1).

Class or welfare issues were mostly overshadowed by political issues before 1997, but were brought to the forefront afterward partly because of changing government policies. After 1997, faced with a budget deficit, the SAR government tried to improve public-sector efficiency by downsizing the civil service. The government started a new wave of public-sector reforms, including measures such as the contracting out of services, the corporatization of government departments, and the cutting of redundancies in the civil service. The reform was met with strong opposition by civil service unions.

The reforms and the changing economic situation forced various political parties to take position on these class-related issues. Politicians who were affiliated with labor unions (the FTU and CTU leaders) unequivocally stood behind the civil servants and labor interests, but the reforms began to create difficulties for catch-all parties such as DP and DAB. DP was generally supportive of the civil service reform, but its support of the contracting out of public housing management led to vehement criticisms from the ten-thousand-member labor union of the Housing Department and other civil service unions.

Factional struggle and ideological debate within DP also drove it to adopt a more middle-class-oriented position.[46] After late 1998, the "Young Turks" faction within DP, mostly made up of young district-level activists, began to fight the central leadership for a more pro-grassroots platform. In the September 1999 DP general meeting, the Young Turks moved a motion to put "minimum wage legislation" into the 2000 election platform. The party leaders, or the "mainstreamers" as they were called, saw this as a major challenge to their grip on party leadership. They joined hands with former Meeting Point members, who were more middle-class oriented, to defeat the motion. In a motion debate on minimum wage on May 17, 2000, DP voted against Lee Cheuk-yan's motion to push the government to set up minimum wage in Hong Kong, which led to Lee's criticisms of DP's mainstreamers.

The above changes led to a rise in significance of the class cleavage by 2000. As DP moved gradually toward a more middle-class position, it faced competition from other pro-grassroot groups (including CTU and ADPL) within the prodemocracy camp. [47] In the 2000 campaign, ADPL attacked DP on the issue of minimum wage, claiming that "a vote for DP is a vote against minimum wage." DP also had less sympathy and support from the labor unions in 2000. In 1995, DP obtained full support of CTU member unions on the direct election battlefront. In 2000, they got almost no help from the labor unions. Some civil service unions actually campaigned against DP, calling on its members not to vote for DP.

Table 4.2 compares the result of some prolabor candidates in the 2000 election to their results in 1998. It shows that these prolabor candidates, regardless of political affiliation, all got a marked jump in the total number of votes or the vote share (or both). DP got 170,000 fewer votes in the 2000 election compared with 1998, but the three prodemocracy grassroots politicians (Lee, Leung, and Fung) had picked up about 50,000 votes. A new social-democratic political field has emerged, and the loss of the social-democratic vote was a major reason for the unsatisfactory result for DP in 2000.

On the political front, the progovernment-antigovernment cleavage became more pronounced in 2000. The popularity of Chief Executive Tung

Table 4.2

Results of Selected Pro-Labor Candidates, 1998 and 2000

Candidate	Affiliation/Camp	Total votes, 1998	Vote share 1998, %	Total votes, 2000	Vote share 2000, %
Frederick Fung	ADPL/democrat	39,534	19.3	62,717	35.2
Lee Cheuk-yan	HKCTU/democrat	46,696	12.5	52,202	15.2
Leung Yiu-chung	NWSC/democrat	38,627	10.3	59,348	17.3
Chen Yuen-han	FTU/DAB	109,296	41.8	108,587	47.4
Tam Yiu-chung	FTU/DAB	72,587	19.4	101,629	29.6

Chee-hwa grew ever lower in the years 1998–2000, making it very attractive to adopt an antigovernment stand. DP and other democrats (including TF, Lee Cheuk-yan, and Leung Yiu-chung) criticized DAB and other pro-government politicians as "royalists" who would defend SAR government at whatever costs. DP campaigned with the slogan "A vote for DAB is a vote for Tung Chee-hwa," and played an old trick in trying to attribute the economic impasse to political factors. DP candidates claimed that the lower class was in such hardship because the SAR government was not popularly elected and was biased in favor of major business conglomerates. Some candidates used "Oppose corrupt politics" and "Oppose government-business collusion" as campaign slogans.

Because the second SAR chief executive would be elected in 2002, whether Tung should run for a second term became an issue often discussed in election forums. The democrats' common position was that the SAR chief executive should be directly elected as soon as possible, as the often-criticized performance of Tung showed the deficiency of the current system. At the other end of the spectrum, both DAB and HKPA tried to defend the performance of Tung, and said that Tung should be given the chance to run for another term. The Liberal Party adopted a somewhat ambivalent attitude toward the reelection of Tung.[48]

Whereas in 1998 the DAB mostly adopted a defensive attitude about the performance of the SAR government, in 2000 it managed to stage an ideological counteroffensive. Its candidates claimed that the democrats were too radical and confrontational, which would not bode well for Hong Kong's stability and development. DAB positioned itself as a moderate, constructive party, one that made rational suggestions for the government to improve governance, instead of criticizing in public. DAB claimed that it was a "stabilizing force," and condemned the democrats as "radicals" or "extremists" who would destabilize Hong Kong by protesting too much. At the operational level, DAB often cited two incidents to attack the democrats. One was the government's intervention in the stock market in August 1998 to fight off international hedging funds. The other was the government's appeal for the National People's Congress to reinterpret the Basic Law to overrule the verdict of the Court of Final Appeal in January 1999, so as to stop massive numbers of immigrants from the mainland. Both acts had the support of public opinion but were strongly opposed by the democrats. DAB used these two events to show that the democrats were "irrationally" opposing the SAR government at the expense of the interests of the Hong Kong people.

Figure 4.4 shows the new pluralized cleavage pattern as reflected from the 2000 campaign. Two major cleavage lines can be drawn. Within the prodemocracy camp, a new cleavage grew between the more pro-grassroot democrats and DP and TF.[49] On the progovernment side, both HKPA and LP were more inclined toward business interests, an important reason being that both had the functional constituencies as their major battlefield. With wide support from grassroots organizations and the HKFTU, DAB succeeded in absorbing most of the conservative votes in 2000.

Discussion and Conclusions

The above review shows that the China factor has ceased to define the dominant political cleavages in Hong Kong after 1997. Before 1997, attitudes toward Beijing and democratization shaped the major cleavage separating local political forces. Moreno claimed that the proreform-antireform cleavage dominates in the early transition period, but the cleavage will fade after democratic consolidation.[50] We saw that the proreform-antireform or prodemocracy-antidemocracy cleavage did dominate before 1997, but the cleavage declined in significance after 1997. As time goes by, it seems that political issues will decline in significance, while the class cleavage will rise in salience in the post-1997 HKSAR. How can we account for this change?

One important reason of course was that Beijing largely did not intervene into SAR affairs. Another important reason, I argue, was that the uncertainty about the China factor was gone after 1997. The pre-1997 debates about "pro-China"–"anti-China," or prodemocracy-antidemocracy were not debates about values such as democracy or nationalism *per se*, but debates on how to best safeguard Hong Kong's interests and lifestyle *as apart from mainland China*.[51] What was special about the China factor was not what the PRC authorities actually did; it was what Beijing *might* do after 1997. The threat of potential intervention and/or oppression from mainland China (or whatever it might do) was hanging like the sword of Damocles over the heads of most Hong Kong people before 1997. The Tiananmen crackdown and the dispute over the Patten return package pushed these uncertainties to an ex-

Figure 4.4 **Cleavage Pattern in the 2000 Election**

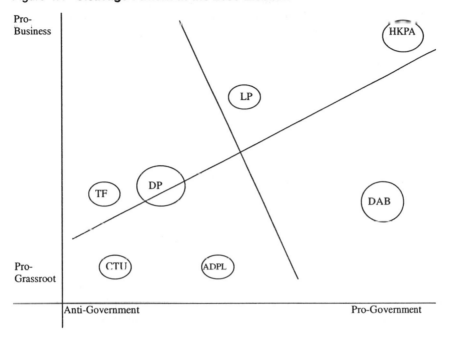

Key: DP: Democratic Party
TF: The Frontier
CTU: Confederation of Trade Unions
ADPL: Association for Democracy and People's Livelihood
LP: Liberal Party
DAB: Democratic Alliance for the Betterment of Hong Kong

treme. Three years into the SAR, this uncertainty over what Beijing might do is largely gone.

The uncertainty over the development of democracy was also less pronounced after 1997. The democratic-authoritarian cleavage dominates in the early democratic transition period largely because of a grave uncertainty about whether the infant democratic regime will be toppled and replaced by an authoritarian regime. This uncertainty fades as democracy becomes "consolidated." After 1997, the prodemocracy-antidemocracy cleavage began to fade in Hong Kong, not because we have a consolidated democratic system. Far from it. But with the pace of democratization defined by the Basic Law, most Hong Kong people are sure that the political system is not going to backtrack or progress dramatically. It is unlikely that Beijing will undo the partially democratic system that is in place in the HKSAR, but it is even more unlikely that we will move rapidly to a fully democratic system, no matter how much Hong Kong people want it. The fear is largely gone, but so is the hope for changing the system.

In this light, the protracted democratization in Hong Kong has a demobilization effect. It will be difficult to mobilize people to fight for more democracy, as they think the system has been fixed for them in the short run. The constitutional review in 2007 may be the next ordeal that will bring some uncertainty, motivating people to participate. On the other hand, economic and employment issues rise in importance due to economic difficulties. In due course other social cleavages may surface as more important cleavages.

This change gives rise to many possibilities of a restructuring of political cleavages in Hong Kong. Figure 4.5 shows a reconstruction of political fields after 1997. A dominant cleavage remains the conservative-progressive cleavage, which will largely overlap with the antigovernment–pro-government cleavage for the time being. The SAR government is likely to adopt a conservative attitude toward political and social-democratic reforms. The pro-Beijing parties and the business conservatives would serve as its major allies. On the other hand, the democrats will continue to push for more progressive-democratic reforms, which is bound to challenge the dominant position of the business sector in the current political system, as it invariably entails a change to the functional constituency system.

With the rising significance of economic issues, an enlarging social-democratic political field evolves. Pluralistic competition within the pro-democracy camp will drive groups to distance themselves from one another in terms of class positions. Figure 4.5 also shows that the pro-business, conservative political field is at present relatively narrow. Both HKPA and LP were insignificant players in the direct election part of the 2000 election. They could get their voices heard in the Legco arena through functional representation, but, lacking electoral machines of any sort, for the time being they would be unable to compete with DAB for the conservative votes.

Notably absent is a party that can fill the liberal-democratic field. There is no party that is both pro-democracy and pro-business–middle class at the same time. Yet the development of this political field is vital to the democratic development of Hong Kong. If pro-business interests can get significant representation through popular elections, the business sector's fear of rapid democratization can be alleviated. There can be two possibilities. Both DP and LP could move to take up that space. Both seem unlikely. LP would have to come out of the protective shell of functional constituencies and embrace a faster pace of democratization.[52] DP would have to move further

Figure 4.5 **Cleavage Pattern in Hong Kong, 2000 and Beyond**

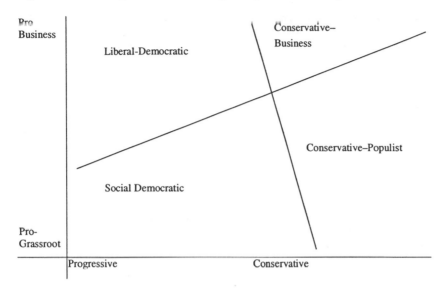

away from the pro-grassroot positions. In view of the relative failure of DP in the 2000 election, it would be a difficult choice for DP to give up the vast and enlarging social-democratic political field. With the rising salience of the social-democratic field, an alliance between the democrats and the business groups is also unlikely.

This brings the democracy movement to an impasse. As other social cleavages may surface, the political cleavage pattern in Hong Kong will continue to pluralize. Besides the vague goal of "ultimate" democratization, the various prodemocracy groups will find less and less common grounds. Under the proportional representation system, it will be difficult for the various prodemocracy groups to reintegrate into a concerted movement to push for more progressive reforms. It would be equally difficult for any political party, in view of the more pluralized cleavage structure, to come up with an issue package that can capture a majority of votes across the various cross-cutting fault lines. The executive branch is in a strong position to control SAR politics, facing a fragmented legislature and a divided opposition movement. This may be precisely what the Basic Law drafters had desired when they designed the Basic Law, an ideal scenario for the perpetuation of an "executive-dominant" system. However, it means that public grievances on various social and economic issues cannot be effectively channeled or aggregated in the political system, which can also be a source of governance crisis for the future SAR government.

Notes

1. Leung, "The 'China Factor' in the 1991 Legislative Council Election," p. 189.
2. Rae and Taylor, *The Analysis of Political Cleavages*, p. 1.
3. Moreno, *Political Cleavages: Issues, Parties and the Consolidation of Democracy*, p. 16.
4. Moreno, *Political Cleavages*, p. 16.
5. Li, *Hong Kong from Britain to China*, p. 12.
6. Jacobs and Shapiro, "Issues, Candidates Image and Priming."
7. Rae and Taylor, *The Analysis of Political Cleavages*, p. 1.
8. Lipset and Rokkan, "Cleavage Structures, Party Systems, and Voter Alignments."
9. Inglehart, *The Silent Revolution*; and Inglehart, *Culture Shift in Advanced Industrial Society*.
10. Moreno, *Political Cleavages*, pp. 2–3.
11. Ibid.
12. In the 1995, 1998, and 2000 campaigns, the author sent out research assistants to collect campaign materials from candidates of major parties and make transcripts of all broadcast election forums. The research team also interviewed candidates and leaders of major parties in the three elections, to understand their campaign operations, the choice of campaign issues, and campaign strategies.
13. Chiu, *The Politics of Laissez-Faire*.
14. Cheung, *Xianggang Liuqi Baodong Neiqing*, pp. 122–24.
15. Leung, "The 'China Factor' in the 1991 Legislative Council Election," p. 189.
16. For a discussion of how Hong Kong people viewed (sometimes erroneously) the concept of democracy, see Kuan and Lau, "The Partial Vision of Democracy in Hong Kong."
17. King, "Administrative Absorption of Politics in Hong Kong."
18. Li, *Hong Kong from Britain to China*, pp. 152–53.
19. A campaign poster of Lee Chik-yuet, a prominent prodemocracy leader at the time, in the 1986 Urban Council election, aptly conveyed this sentiment. The caption on the poster was titled, "It's time for reform!" (*Gaige di shihou daole!*)
20. The three groups were the Meeting Point, the Hong Kong Affairs Society and Association for Democracy, and People's Livelihood.
21. *People's Daily*, July 21, 1989; see also So, "The Tiananmen Incident, Patten's Electoral Reforms, and the Roots of Contested Democracy in Hong Kong," p. 55.
22. Leung, "The 'China Factor' in the 1991 Legislative Council Election"; Tsang, "Who Voted for the Democrats?"; and Kwok, Leung, and Scott, *Votes Without Power.*
23. Tsang, "Who Voted for the Democrats?" pp. 148–49.
24. This somehow showed that in the eyes of many candidates, the 1991 election was the result or natural continuation of a decade of social-democratic reforms. See Lee, "Issue Positions in the 1991 Legislative Council Election."
25. For example, rural conservatives Tai Chin-wah and Tso Shiu-wai ran on a joint ticket, but in later stages of the campaign both Tai and Tso asked their respective supporters to vote for one person only. The only other joint ticket is Wong Man-chiu and Cheung Wai-sun in Hong Kong Island West, who finished with least votes in the six-person contest.
26. Choy and Lau, "The Executive-Legislative Relations in Hong Kong before 1997," p. 243.

27. The Association for Democracy and People's Livelihood (ADPL) led by Frederick Fung, however, continued to pursue this "moderate democrat" position without much success.

28. So, "The Tiananmen, Patten's Electoral Reform, and the Roots of Contested Democracy in Hong Kong," pp. 69–70.

29. Duverger, *Political Parties*; and Katz, *A Theory of Parties and Electoral Systems*.

30. In the 1994 DB election, 296 seats were contested, and 201 of them had only two candidates. The fifty-two contested UC and RC seats in the March 1995 election had thirty-four among them having only two candidates. The 1995 Legco election had twenty directly elected seats, twelve of which were contested between two candidates.

31. For the various groups of conservatives that had run in 1991, some still ran as representatives of pro-business parties (e.g., the Liberal Party, the LDF, or the Hong Kong Progressive Alliance). Some rural conservatives were absorbed by the DAB (e.g., Cheung Hon-chung), and some enjoyed full support of pro-Beijing forces (e.g., Tang Shiu-tong). The traditional *kaifong* leaders and professional conservatives were no longer major contestants in the 1995 election and beyond.

32. For more discussion of the party competition patterns in 1995 and 1998, see Ma and Choy, "Party Competition Patterns."

33. Li, *Hong Kong from Britain to China*, p. 220.

34. Louie, "Party Identification in Hong Kong Elections," pp. 137–64; Wong, "Issue Voting," pp. 106–29.

35. HKFTU and some other candidates (e.g., ADPL) supported unemployment benefits, but the DP opposed it. DAB, however, also did not agree to pushing unemployment benefits, which was the reason why FTU candidates did not use it as a campaign issue to attack DP.

36. Ma and Choy, "Party Competition Patterns," p. 77.

37. Choy and Tsoi, *Selected Vote-Counts of the Legislative Council of Hong Kong*, pp. 485–96.

38. In 1996, some political heavyweights of the prodemocracy camp, including Emily Lau, Lau Chin-shek, and Lee Cheuk-yan, formed the Frontier (TF) as a loose political organization. TF adopted an even more confrontational attitude toward the PRC government than DP, and under the influence of labor unionists like Lee Cheuk-yan, the group adopted a pro-grassroots position.

39. Since the PRC government saw the political reform package proposed by then British colonial governor Chris Patten as in violation of the Basic Law, it refused to recognize the Legco elected in 1995 under Patten's formula. In 1997, it disbanded the Legco elected in 1995 and set up the Provisional Legislative Council, which served as Hong Kong's legislature from July 1997 to May 1998.

40. Wong, *Public Opinion and Politics in Hong Kong in the Transition Era*, p. 5.

41. Hong Kong Transition Project, *Poll-arization*, p. 48.

42. Wong, "Issue Voting," p. 120.

43. Ma and Choy, "Party Competition Patterns."

44. Note that different TF candidates have very different stands on labor issues. Members such as Lee Cheuk-yan, Leung Yiu-chung, and Lau Chin-shek had a strong prolabor stand, but Emily Lau and Cyd Ho had more middle-class–oriented stands and images. When TF was first formed, the members always split when they voted on labor or class issues. In recent years it seems that Emily Lau and Cyd Ho have usually

chosen to vote with Leung and Lee on labor issues. The difference in the personal images is still there, though.

45. *Sing Tao Daily News*, May 1, 2000.

46. For more discussion of the factional struggle in DP, see Ma, "Factionalism and the Democratic Party in the 2000 Election."

47. Some DP candidates admitted that they were moving toward the middle class in postelection interviews, and some (e.g., Lee Wing-tat) saw this as the factor for the loss of some of the prolabor votes.

48. The two LP candidates running in direct election adopted quite different stands. Lau Hing-kee of New Territories East was more ambivalent and largely refrained from criticizing Tung. Yeung Fuk-kwong of New Territories West tried to adopt a more liberal position and said the CE should be directly elected.

49. In 2000, the labor activists in TF, including Lau Chin-shek, Lee Cheuk-yan, and Leung Yiu-chung, all ran as representatives of their respective labor groups and not of TF.

50. Moreno, *Political Cleavages*, p. 3.

51. Mathew, "*Heunggongyahn*," p. 3.

52. The LP lost two seats in the 2000 election, and now has only eight seats in the Legco, all of them functional constituency seats.

Bibliography

Cheung Ka-wai. *Xianggang Liuqi Baodong Neiqing*. (Inside story of the 1967 riot in Hong Kong). Hong Kong: Pacific Century Press, 2000.

Chiu, Stephen W.K. *The Politics of Laissez-Faire: Hong Kong's Strategy of Industrialization in Historical Perspective*. Hong Kong: Hong Kong Institute of Asia-Pacific Studies, 1994.

Choy Chi-keung, and Lau Sai-leung. 1996. "The Executive-Legislative Relations in Hong Kong Before 1997." *Hong Kong Journal of Social Science* 8 (August 1996): 237–66.

Choy Chi-keung, and Richard Y.C. Tsoi, ed. *Selected Vote-Counts of the Legislative Council of Hong Kong (1995–1997)* (in Chinese). Hong Kong: Hong Kong Humanities Press, 1998.

Duverger, Maurice. *Political Parties: Their Organization and Activity in the Modern State*. New York: Wiley, 1963.

Hong Kong Transition Project. *Poll-arization: Election Politics and the Politicizing of Hong Kong*. Hong Kong: Hong Kong Transition Project, 2000.

Inglehart, Ronald. *The Silent Revolution: Changing Values and Political Styles Among Western Publics*. Princeton, NJ: Princeton University Press, 1977.

———. *Culture Shift in Advanced Industrial Society*. Princeton, NJ: Princeton University Press, 1990.

Jacobs, Lawrence, and Robert Shapiro. "Issues, Candidates Image and Priming: The Use of Private Polls in Kennedy's Presidential Campaign." *American Political Science Review* 88 (1994): 527–40.

Katz, Richard. *A Theory of Parties and Electoral Systems*. Baltimore: Johns Hopkins Press, 1980.

King, Ambrose. "Administrative Absorption of Politics in Hong Kong: Emphasis on the Grass Roots Level." *Asian Survey* 15 (1975): 422–39.

Kuan Hsin-chi, and Lau Siu-kai. "The Partial Vision of Democracy in Hong Kong: A Survey of Popular Opinion." *China Journal* 34 (July 1995): 239–64.

Kwok, Rowena, Joan Leung, and Ian Scott. *Votes Without Power. The Hong Kong Legislative Council Elections 1991*. Hong Kong: Hong Kong University Press, 1992.

Lee, Jane C.Y. "Campaigning Themes of the Candidates in the 1991 Legislative Council Election." In *Hong Kong Tried Democracy: The 1991 Elections in Hong Kong*, Lau Siu-kai and Louie King-shuen, ed. Hong Kong: Hong Kong Institute of Asia-Pacific Studies, 1993, 297–315.

Lee Ming-kwan. "Issue Positions in the 1991 Legislative Council Election." In *Hong Kong Tried Democracy: The 1991 Elections in Hong Kong*, Lau Siu-kai and Louie King-shuen, ed. Hong Kong: Hong Kong Institute of Asia-Pacific Studies, 1993, 237–48.

Leung Sai-wing. "The 'China Factor' in the 1991 Legislative Council Election: The June 4th Incident and the Anti-Communist China Syndrome." In *Hong Kong Tried Democracy: The 1991 Elections in Hong Kong*, Lau Siu-kai and Louie King-shuen, ed. Hong Kong: Hong Kong Institute of Asia-Pacific Studies, 1993, pp. 187–235.

Li Pang-kwong. "1995 Legislative Council Direct Election: A Political Cleavage Approach." In *The 1995 Legislative Council Elections in Hong Kong*, Kuan Hsin-chi et al., ed. Hong Kong: Hong Kong Institute of Asia-Pacific Studies, 1996, pp. 245–74.

———. *Hong Kong from Britain to China: Political Cleavages, Electoral Dynamics and Institutional Changes*. Aldershot, UK: Ashgate, 2000.

Lipset, Seymour Martin, and Stein Rokkan. "Cleavage Structures, Party Systems, and Voter Alignments: An Introduction." In *Party Systems and Voter Alignments: Cross-National Perspectives*, Seymour Martin Lipset and Stein Rokkan, ed. New York: Free Press, 1967, pp. 1–64.

Louie, K.S. "Party Identification in Hong Kong Elections: A Further Enquiry." In *The 1995 Legislative Council Elections in Hong Kong*, Kuan Hsin-chi et al., ed. Hong Kong: Hong Kong Institute of Asia-Pacific Studies, ed. 1996, pp. 137–64.

Ma Ngok. "Factionalism and the Democratic Party in the 2000 Election." Paper presented at the Conference on the 2000 Legislative Council Election, Chinese University of Hong Kong, December 11, 2000.

Ma Ngok, and Choy, Chi-keung. "Party Competition Patterns: The 1995 and 1998 Campaigns Compared." In *Power Transfer and Electoral Politics: The First Legislative Election in the Hong Kong Special Administrative Region*, Kuan Hsin-chi et al., ed. Hong Kong: Chinese University Press, 1999, pp. 71–104.

Mathew, Gordon. "*Heunggongyahn*: On the Past, Present, and Future of Hong Kong Identity." *Bulletin of Concerned Asian Scholars* 29, no. 3 (1997): 3–13.

Moreno, Alejandro. *Political Cleavages: Issues, Parties and the Consolidation of Democracy*. Boulder, CO: Westview Press, 1999.

Rae, Douglas, and Michael Taylor. *The Analysis of Political Cleavages*. New Haven: Yale University Press, 1970.

Scott, Ian. *Political Change and the Crisis of Legitimacy in Hong Kong*. Hong Kong: Oxford University Press, 1989.

Sing Tao Daily News. "Longer and Longer Working Hours for Hong Kong People." May 1, 2000.

So, Alvin. "The Tiananmen Incident, Patten's Electoral Reforms, and the Roots of

Contested Democracy in Hong Kong." In *The Challenges of Hong Kong's Reintegration with China*, Ming K. Chan, ed. Hong Kong: Hong Kong University Press, 1997, pp. 49–83.

Sun, Milan T.W., and Timothy K.Y. Wong. "Priming and Election: An Analysis of the 1995 Legislative Council Election." In *The 1995 Legislative Council Elections in Hong Kong*, Kuan Hsin-chi et al., ed. Hong Kong: Hong Kong Institute of Asia-Pacific Studies, 1996, pp. 165–99.

Tsang Wing-kwong. "Who Voted for the Democrats? An Analysis of the Electoral Choice of the 1991 Legislative Council Election." In *Hong Kong Tried Democracy: The 1991 Elections in Hong Kong*, Lau Siu-kai and Louie King-shuen, ed. Hong Kong: Hong Kong Institute of Asia-Pacific Studies, 1993, pp. 115–55.

Wong, Timothy K.Y. *Public Opinion and Politics in Hong Kong in the Transition Era.* Hong Kong: Tin Yuen, 1997.

———. "Issue Voting." In *Power Transfer and Electoral Politics: The First Legislative Election in the Hong Kong Special Administrative Region*, Kuan Hsin-chi et al., ed. Hong Kong: Chinese University Press, 1999, pp. 106–29.

5

The 1999 District Councils Elections

Shiu-hing Lo, Wing-yat Yu, and Kwok-fai Wan

The 1999 District Councils (DC) elections were characterized by a fierce tug of war between the pro-democracy camp and the patriotic forces. The pro-democracy camp is composed of the Democratic Party (DP), the Frontier (TF), the One Two Three Alliance (OTTA), the Citizens Party (CP), and the Association for Democracy and People's Livelihood (ADPL). The pro-Beijing patriotic camp comprises not only the Democratic Alliance for Betterment of Hong Kong (DAB), the Hong Kong Progressive Alliance (HKPA) and the Civil Force (CF) but also the relatively conservative or progovernment parties, such as the Liberal Party (LP) and the New Century Forum (NCF).[1] The goal of this chapter is to analyze the performance and campaign strategies of the pro-democracy camp and the patriotic forces in the District Councils elections held on November 28, 1999. It will also explore the factors shaping the voters' decisions to support the pro-democracy camp or the patriotic forces.

Overview of the Election Results

In comparison with the results of the 1994 District Board elections, the patriotic forces improved their performance and succeeded in catching up with the pro-democracy camp.[2] In Table 5.1, the patriotic forces obtained only 25.1 percent of the total number of votes in 1994, but they narrowed the lead by the pro-democracy camp and succeeded in acquiring 32 percent of the total vote in 1999. On the contrary, the pro-democracy camp got 31.5 percent of the total number of votes in 1994, but its gain was maintained at 32.3 percent in 1999. The DAB's drastic improvement in the performance of its candidates greatly helped the patriotic forces narrow the gap with the pro-democracy forces. The DP sustained its political momentum by securing

Table 5.1

Election Results of District Councils (Boards), 1994 and 1995

	1994					1999				
	Number of votes	Share of vote, %	Number of candidates	Number of seats	Success rate, %	Number of votes	Share of vote, %	Number of candidates	Number of seats	Success rate
DP	157,918	22.8	133	75	56.4	200,185	24.7	172	86	50.0
ADPL	48,364	7.0	40	29	72.5	38,119	4.7	32	19	59.4
The Frontier						9,388	1.2	9	4	44.4
Citizens Party						2,072	0.3	1	1	100.0
OTTA	11,517	1.7	17	4	23.5	11,396	1.4	10	6	60.0
DAB	81,891	11.8	83	37	44.6	190,792	23.5	176	83	47.2
LP	51,186	7.4	89	18	20.2	27,718	3.4	34	15	44.1
HKPA and LDF[a]	28,164	4.1	35	12	34.3	21,488[b]	2.7	30	16	53.3
Civil Force	12,141	1.8	10	10	100.0	19,633[c]	2.4	14	11	78.6

Sources: The 1994 figures are calculated by using the data from Louie Kin-shuen and Shum Kwok-cheung, *Xiang gang xuan ju zi liao hui bian, 1982 nian–1994 nian* (The election data of Hong Kong, 1982–1994), (Hong Kong: Chinese University Press, 1995). The 1999 figures are calculated by using the data from the HKSAR government's official homepage for the 1999 District Councils elections (http://www.info.gov.hk/dcelect99/) on November 30, 1999.

Notes:

[a] The Liberal Democratic Federation (LDF) did not merge with the Hong Kong Progressive Alliance (HKPA) in 1994 District Boards elections. However, the two merged before the 1999 District Councils elections. Therefore, the votes obtained by the two organizations in the 1994 elections are grouped together for comparison.

[b] Choy So-yuk is counted as a member of the HKPA as she did not join the DAB at that time.

[c] Lau Kong-wah of the DAB is not counted as a member of the Civil Force.

24.7 percent of the vote in 1999 as compared to 22.8 percent in 1994. However, the ADPL appeared to lose some popular support from 7 percent of the total vote in 1994 to 4.7 percent in 1999. Overall, the pro-democracy forces failed to enhance their influence and outperform the patriotic forces.

The performance of political parties varied in the 1999 DC elections. Although the DP maintained its share of votes, its success rate declined slightly due to the fact that the party nominated far more candidates than it had in the 1994 elections. The decline of the DP's success rate was attributable to a number of factors, including (1) the shift of some DP incumbents to competition in other geographical constituencies, (2) the mutual distrust between some DP candidates and the local residents, and (3) the strong performance of the opponents of the DP candidates, especially the DAB candidates.[3] Examples showing the failure of DP incumbents changing their constituencies included Ng Wing-fai in Yau Tsim Mong district and Ho Suk-ping in the Shatin district.[4] Ng was defeated by a patriotic candidate and Ho was unseated by a DAB candidate.[5] The mutual distrust between the DP candidates and some residents could be seen in Mei Foo Sun Chuen, where residents complained about the way in which DP incumbents handled the management of their housing estates.[6] The DP competed directly with the DAB in ninety-six constituencies, of which fifty-four were won by the DP candidates, thirty-six by the DAB contenders, and the other 6 by other candidates. Clearly, the DAB constituted a serious threat to the DP.

The other pro-democracy parties such as the OTTA and ADPL failed to achieve any breakthrough in elections. The OTTA increased both its success rate and the number of candidates, but it has only six candidates elected in 1999 as compared to four candidates elected in 1994. It remained a relatively small political party that was eventually abolished in early December 2000 due to the lack of financial support from the Taiwan government.[7] The ADPL was characterized by a decrease in the number of its candidates and in its success rate. This result was attributable partly to the defection of some ADPL members to the DP in 1997 after their internal dispute over the question of whether they should participate in the Provisional Legislative Council (a body established by the People's Republic of China to replace the last legislature of the British rule), and partly to the ADPL's unsuccessful attempt to penetrate into other districts apart from its political base at Shumshuipo.[8] The Frontier and the CP were relatively uninterested in the 1999 District Councils elections. Though the Frontier nominated nine candidates to compete in Shatin and the Eastern districts, only four of them were elected. The CP, on the other hand, remained a political discussion group with only Chan Tim-shing elected in the Eastern district. In brief, the pro-democracy forces appeared to be a loose pile of sand without a political will to grasp more elected seats in the District Councils than before.

The patriotic forces relied on the DAB to check and balance against the pro-democracy camp. The DAB drastically increased its number of candidates from 83 in 1994 to 176 in 1999. Their success rate also rose from 44.6 percent in 1994 to 47.2 percent in 1999—a phenomenon ascribable to the strong grassroots work of the DAB candidates. The LP, on the other hand, improved its performance by decreasing the number of candidates from 89 in 1994 to 34 in 1999, and by enhancing its success rate from 20.2 percent in 1994 to 44.1 percent in 1999. In the past, the LP candidates lacked experience in district elections. But prior to the November 1999 District Councils elections, the LP recruited some candidates who had strong grassroots network in, for example, the Kowloon City and Tsuen Wan districts. In addition, the LP nominated its leaders such as party chair James Tien, legislators Howard Young and Selina Chow to compete in the 1999 District Councils elections. Although Chow was defeated, Tien and Young managed to be elected—a psychological boost to the business-oriented and politically conservative party, which did not have rich experience in electoral participation. The HKPA strategically merged with the now-defunct Liberal Democratic Federation (LDF), nominating fewer candidates than the 1994 District Councils elections and simultaneously improving its previous success rate. The HKPA also captured more directly elected seats than before: sixteen in 1999 as compared to twelve in 1994. The stronghold of the HKPA remained the Kowloon City. The party also expanded its influence to Sai Kung and Shatin districts. The Shatin-based Civil Force slightly increased its number of seats, but its success rate declined from 1994 to 1999. Overall, the pro-Beijing or patriotic forces improved the performance of their candidates and constitute the arch rival of the pro-democracy camp.

It can be said that the DAB, HKPA, and LP constitute a loosely organized patriotic front because they nominated candidates competing against each other in the same constituencies.[9] For example, the DAB candidates competed with the HKPA in four constituencies. The DAB also clashed with the LP in fourteen constituencies. It appeared that compromise between the DAB, HKPA, and LP could not be reached because of political parochialism and personal considerations of the candidates.

Both the pro-democracy and the patriotic forces tried their best to avoid internal competition amongst their like-minded candidates in elections. The DP competed with the OTTA, the TF, the ADPL, and the Neighborhood and Workers' Association in eleven geographical constituencies.[10] While the pro-democracy forces failed to avoid direct confrontation among some candidates, the patriotic forces encountered a parallel difficulty in reaching a compromise between the DAB and the LP. As the LP was keen to nominate candidates to compete in the DC elections and enthusiastic to grasp some directly elected seats, it was natural the LP did not attempt to avoid direct competition with the DAB, which was aggressive in establishing a power base for its future candidates during the Legislative Council elections in September 2000.

The Balance of Power in the Eighteen District Councils:
The Role of Independents and Appointees

The pro-democracy forces and the patriotic camp could capture a majority of the seats in some of the eighteen District Councils. For example, the pro-democracy forces grasped fourteen of the twenty-one directly elected seats in the Shumshuipo DC and fifteen of the twenty-seven directly elected seats in the Tuen Mun DC (see Table 5.2). The patriotic forces, on the other hand, gained twelve of the twenty-two directly elected seats in the Kowloon City DC and twenty-four of the thirty-six directly elected seats in the Shatin DC.

By lobbying for the support of independent candidates who were directly elected, both the pro-democracy and the patriotic camps enhanced their political domination of various District Councils. Independent candidates in the 1999 DC elections could be categorized into three major types: the pro-democracy independents, patriotic independents, and other elected independents. All of them did not want to participate in any political party mainly because they regarded party discipline as too restrictive, and partly due to their perception that an independent image could attract the support of voters who disliked candidates with party background.[11] The pro-democracy independents tend to be the friends and supporters of the democracy movement.[12] The patriotic independents have the proclivity of acquiring support from any force within the patriotic camp, especially the DAB and the pro-Beijing Hong Kong Federation of Trade Unions (FTU).[13] The other independents did not have the explicit support or endorsement of party candidates and politicians.[14] As shown in Table 5.3, there were twenty-nine pro-democracy independents, thirty-six patriotic independents, and eighty-four elected independents. Indeed, it remains to be seen whether the eighty-four elected independents are going to ally with some political groups and parties.

The emergence of the pro-democracy independents and the patriotic independents has complicated the political landscape, directly or indirectly influencing the way in which District Councils are dominated by political forces. For instance, the pro-democracy forces ally with the pro-democracy independents to capture a majority of directly elected seats in the Kwai Tsing DC (nineteen of the twenty-eight elected seats), Tsuen Wan DC (ten of

144

Table 5.2

Numbers of Seats Obtained by Pro-Democracy Camp, Patriotic Forces, and Independents in the Eighteen District Councils

	Pro-democracy camp	Independents (pro-democracy)	Patriotic forces	Independents (patriotic)	Appointed members Patriotic	Appointed members Independents	Other elected Independents	Ex-officio members	Total
Eastern	8	2	16	3	3	6	8	—	46
Wan Chai	2	0	4	2	2	1	3	—	14
Central and Western	6	2	4	0	2	2	3	—	19
Southern	2	0	4	2	1	3	9	—	21
Kwun Tong	9	6	6	9	4	4	4	—	42
Wong Tai Sin	9	2	5	5	3	3	4	—	31
Kowloon City	5	0	12	4	3	2	1	—	27
Yau Tsim Mong	6	0	2	4	2	2	4	—	20
Shamshuipo	14	0	3	0	1	4	4	—	26
Sai Kung	3	1	8	1	1	4	4	2	24
Shatin	6	2	24	0	1	8	4	1	46
Tai Po	5	0	6	2	2	3	6	2	26
Northern	7	1	6	0	1	4	2	4	25
Kwai Tsing	11	8	3	1	2	5	5	1	36
Tsuen Wan	6	4	5	0	1	4	2	2	24
Tuen Mun	15	0	8	0	1	6	6	1	37
Yuen Long	2	1	7	1	2	5	12	6	36
Islands	0	0	2	2	1	3	3	8	19
Total	116	29	125	36	33	69	84	27	519

Table 5.3

Shares of Votes of Pro-Democracy Camp, Patriotic Forces, and Independents in DC Elections, 1999 (in percent)

	DP	ADPL	CP	Frontier	OTTA	Independents (Pro-democracy)	DAB	LP	HKPA	Civil Force	New Century Forum	Independents (Patriotic)	Other Independents	Total
Eastern	26.2					8.7	35.4	2.2	1.7			6.5	15.2	100
Wan Chai	28.2		2.7	1.5			27.3	18.7					25.8	100
Central and Western	40.9				4.2	8.8	33.4	2.9	3.2			23.3	6.5	100
Southern	29.7						10.4	2.1				23.9	34.6	100
Kwun Tong	31.1					13.8	24.0					22.5	7.2	100
Wong Tai Sin	26.4	8.6				8.6	22.5					11.3	11.4	100
Kowloon City	20.2	4.2			1.2	1.2	18.8	21.8	13.4			30.7	7.8	100
Yau Tsim Mong	31.4	2.9			6.1		15.7	1.3				2.3	11.9	100
Shamshuipo	23.9	38.6			2.2		21.3					6.8	11.6	100
Sai Kung	13.7	5.7				5.6	17.0		13.4	24.2		1.1	34.8	100
Shatin	15.0			10.1		4.4	20.7	2.3	7.0			13.7	15.3	100
Tai Po	28.5						19.6	17.9	4.7			1.9	15.6	100
Northern	27.9					4.4	39.6	1.1				4.6	25.2	100
Kwai Tsing	25.1	1.5				19.6	19.5		2.1			5.4	27.7	100
Tsuen Wan	25.8	15.3				15.0	12.7	12.2	1.1		3.2	4.8	24.7	100
Tuen Mun	29.2				7.9	2.6	31.0					2.1	9.1	100
Yuen Long	10.3				6.0	2.1	18.1	1.5				16.9	59.7	100
Islands	13.8						15.4	1.5					52.4	100
Total	24.7	4.7	0.3	1.2	1.4	6.8	23.5	3.4	2.7	2.4	0.1	9.4	19.3	100

the seventeen elected seats), and Central and Western DC (eight of the fifteen elected seats). Hence, the coalition of pro-democracy forces and their like-minded independents has tipped the balance of political power in favor of themselves in some District Councils. However, the patriotic forces also form a loose alliance with the patriotic independents to control most of the seats in the Eastern DC (nineteen out of thirty-seven) and Sai Kung DC (nine out of seventeen).[15] Clearly, political alliance with independents has become a marriage of convenience in the eyes of the pro-democracy forces and patriotic camp, both trying to dominate DC.

Furthermore, the system of appointment made by the government of the Hong Kong Special Administrative Region (HKSAR) and that of ex officios in the District Councils located in the New Territories prevented the pro-democracy camp from dominating DCs. After the injection of 102 appointed and 27 ex-officio seats (ex-officios are the chairs of the Rural Committees of the Heung Yee Kuk in the New Territories, and they are not necessarily pro-Beijing),[16] the pro-democracy forces have lost their domination of some District Councils even though they successfully captured a majority of directly elected seats (see Table 5.4). The balance of power between the pro-democracy and the patriotic forces has been tipped in favor of the latter after the HKSAR government appointed DC members in Kwun Tong, Wong Tai Sin, and Yau Tsim Mong DCs. The pro-democracy forces and their like-minded independents have fifteen, eleven, and six directly elected seats in these District Councils, respectively. Simultaneously, the patriotic forces and patriotic independents gained fifteen, ten, and six seats, respectively, in the three DCs. Above all, in the wake of the HKSAR government's appointments to the Kwun Tong, Wong Tai Sin, and Yau Tsim Mong District Councils, the patriotic front (including the patriotic forces and patriotic independents) has eighteen, thirteen, and eight seats, respectively, thus outnumbering the pro-democracy forces, which cannot gain any extra seats under the appointment system. Meanwhile, although the domination of the patriotic forces appears to have been diluted in the Eastern and Sai Kung DCs after political appointees and ex-officio members were introduced, respectively, they can consolidate their domination of the Wan Chai District Council. On the whole, the injection of political appointees and ex-officio members can curb the influence of the pro-democracy forces and elevate the power of their political foe, the patriotic front.

It must be noted that, while the patriotic forces cannot obtain a majority of the seats in some District Councils, they can still dominate the councils by cooperating with the independents, who are by no means the allies of the pro-democracy camp. The selection of the chair and deputy chairs is a case in point. Each of the eighteen District Councils has a chair and a deputy chair,

Table 5.4

Numbers of Directly Elected Seats Obtained by Pro-Democracy Camp, Patriotic Forces, and Independents in District Councils Elections, 1999

	DP	ADPL	Frontier	CP	OTTA	Independents (Pro-democracy)	DAB	LP	HKPA	Civil Force	New Century Forum	Independents (Patriotic)	Other Independents	Total
Eastern	6			1		2	13	2	1			3	8	37
Wan Chai	2						3	1				2	3	11
Central and Western	5		1		1	2	3	1					3	15
Southern	2						2	2				2	9	17
Kwun Tong	9					6	6					9	4	34
Wong Tai Sin	7	2				2	5					5	4	25
Kowloon City	4	1					3	4	5			4	1	22
Yau Tsim Mong	4	1			1		2					4	4	16
Shamshuipo	3	10			1		3						4	21
Sai Kung	3					1	5	1	3			1	4	17
Shatin	3					2	9	1	3	11		2	4	36
Tai Po	5		3				4		1				6	19
Northern	7					1	6						2	16
Kwai Tsing	10	1				8	2		1			1	5	28
Tsuen Wan	6					4	1	3	1				2	17
Tuen Mun	9	4			2	1	7		1			1	6	29
Yuen Long	1				1		7						12	23
Islands							2					2	3	7
Total	86	19	4	1	6	29	83	15	16	11	0	36	84	390

Table 5.5

Numbers of Chairpersons and Vice-Chairs Affiliated with Political Forces in the Eighteen District Councils, January 2000–December 2003

	Pro-democracy camp	Patriotic forces	Independents	Total
Number of chairpersons	2	10	6	18
Number of vice-chairs	1	13	4	18

Source: Compiled by the authors.

both of whom have seats in the District Management Committee presided over by the District Officer and attended by officials from other government departments.[17] As shown in Table 5.5, the patriotic camp succeeds in grasping ten of the eighteen chair positions and thirteen deputy chairs. The pro-democracy forces merely capture two chairs and one deputy chair. The ability of the pro-democracy and patriotic forces to capture chairs and deputy chairs has symbolic meaning: It demonstrates their success in either occupying most of the seats or obtaining the support of independents. For example, in the Central and Western District Council, the DP members nominated an independent appointed member, Wu Chor-nam, to compete with Chan Chit-kwai, who had been DB chair from 1997 to 1999.[18] Eventually, Wu was elected with eleven votes, whereas Chan got eight votes.[19] The selection of Wu as the Central and Western District Council chair was politically significant to the DP, which was able to capture the council with the cooperation of pro-democracy independents such as Wu.

Campaign Strategies of the Pro-Democracy Forces and Patriotic Camp in the Eighteen Districts

The pro-democracy forces did not have a standardized campaign strategy in all the eighteen districts. The DP tended to decentralize the campaign strategies to the "big brothers" or experienced district councilors. For example, Fung King-man of the DP supported four DP candidates to compete in Kowloon City, and three of them were elected.[20] The Kowloon City district has traditionally been dominated by the patriotic forces. Fung's strategy was to avoid attacking the performance of the DP's opponents, while at the same time emphasizing the DP's past performance and district work.[21] Fung and her party members focused on the economic platform of improving the people's livelihood. She mobilized supporters of the Kowloon City South Women Society, of which she was a vice chair. Fung also made use of political stars like DP party chair Martin Lee to appeal to voters' support. Another example of the DP's reliance on political mentors was the Eastern district, where Tsang Kin-shing, nicknamed the "Bull," supported Leung On-kay and Tang Chui-chung to compete in the elections. Unfortunately, Tsang himself was defeated by a political unknown from the DAB due to his lack of district work.[22] Although Leung was elected, she later withdrew from the DP because of her dissatisfaction with the party's internal dispute. Tang was a young candidate who failed to challenge the DAB incumbent, Chris Chung Shu-kun. The former lost by 1,107 votes and he later helped Tsang campaign in the September 2000 Legislative Council elections.[23] The third example illustrating the use of political mentors in the DP's campaign strategy was the Shumshuipo district, where Wong Tak-chuen and Chan Chung-kong of the DP supported three party candidates. However, all of them including Wong and Chan were defeated, thus leading to the total annihilation of the DP in Mei Foo Sun Chuen.[24] Finally, in the Northern district, Wong Sing-chi of the DP supported seven candidates and six of them were elected—a resounding success for the DP in a district where the DAB had already penetrated 80 percent of the Mutual Aid Committees (MACs).[25]

In fact, the DP was comparatively weaker than the DAB in terms of political support from MACs and other district-based groups. In our preelection survey of DC candidates, 33.3 percent of the forty-eight DP respondents said they got the support of MACs and other district groups, but 81.5 percent of the 27 DAB respondents replied they received such political support (see Table 5.6).[26]

The other pro-democracy forces adopted a more district-based campaign strategy. For instance, the ADPL nominated fourteen candidates and ten of them were elected. Most of the ADPL candidates relied on the appeal of its leader Frederick Fung Kin-kee, who was automatically elected because the DP appeared to lack the confidence to nominate a candidate strong enough to defeat him. An outstanding feature of the ADPL candidates was their diligent district work. In a sense, the ADPL's strategy was similar to the DP in that the former also made use of Fung as the "big brother" or political mentor.

Unlike the ADPL, two pro-democracy parties—the OTTA and TF—adopted a loosely organized campaign strategy. The OTTA nominated ten candidates to compete in the Yuen Long, Kowloon City, Shumshuipo, Tuen Mun, and Central and Western districts. The OTTA candidates ran a relatively individualized campaign strategy, designing their own campaign pamphlets. Seven of the ten candidates competed with the DAB, and five of them were elected. One candidate, Chun Fei-pang, was anxious about the election result; he tried to fully mobilize his supporters as well as residents to vote for him. Consequently, Chun got 724 votes and the DAB contender, Wong Sui-man, obtained 638 votes.[27] Another OTTA candidate, Mak Ip-sing, defeated

Table 5.6

Party Candidates Receiving the Support of Mutual Aid Committees and District-Based Organizations, 1999

	Received support		Did not receive support	
	Number	Percent	Number	Percent
DP	16	33.3	32	44.4
DAB	22	81.5	5	18.5
Independents	34	63.0	20	37.0

Lee Yat-po of the DAB by 844 votes. Mak organized lots of activities for the residents by using the Yuen Long Youth Community Center and the Hoi Wah Service Fund.[28] The OTTA remained a small political party whose electoral performance depended on the efforts by individual candidates.

Similarly to the OTTA, TF nominated eight candidates to participate in the contest in the Shatin district, but only three of them were elected. The Frontier candidates did not have a track record of district work, but they tended to rely on political star Emily Lau. Although Emily Lau went to help some TF candidates, their performance was handicapped by three factors. First, TF committed a strategic error by nominating some middle-class candidates to run in lower-class districts, such as King Cheng King-hung, who failed to challenge the DAB incumbent Wong Mo-tai. Cheng managed to obtain 1,041 votes after eight months of continuous district work, whereas Wong succeeded in mobilizing members of the Shatin Women Society, the Federation of Trade Unions, and the New Territories Association of Societies (NTAS).[29] Cheng's failure also demonstrated TF's strategic error of competing with strong DAB opponents. Wong, for example, has been working at the district since 1972. It was almost impossible for a new candidate like Cheng to unseat her. However, from the viewpoint of Emily Lau, it was perhaps worthwhile to nominate Cheng to challenge Wong, who was viewed as the most senior DAB candidate in the Shatin district. While Lau's plan was understandable, Cheng would stand a better chance to win the election if he were sent to a more middle-class constituency.[30] Second, TF was relatively late in nominating candidates to compete in the elections, thus making them in lack of preparation and district work. On the contrary, TF's contenders had already conducted intensive district work. The party was also divided between some younger radicals who assisted Emily Lau and some relatively mature candidates who thought that TF should be better organized rather than harping on ideological themes.[31] Third, TF could not reach a compromise with the DP, thus leading to the defeat of both of their candidates and to the success of an "independent" in the Sunshine City constituency.[32] Here, TF candidate Lee Poon-shing competed with DP candidate Chan King-ming and independent Lee Chi-wing. Lee Poon-shing got 562 votes; Chan, 702 votes; and Lee Chi-wing, 888 votes. This was a good example of the rivalry among the pro-democracy candidates, resulting in the electoral victory of other candidates.

The patriotic camp also displayed a diversified campaign strategy, ranging from a loosely organized tactic of the LP to a very systematic mobilization by the DAB. The LP was characterized by a decentralized and individualized campaign strategy. Candidates of the LP designed their own pamphlets, platforms, and election engineering. Their campaign style tended to be diversified; some were very hard working in the district, but some appeared to be insufficient. Selina Chow, for example, was no match for her contender, Ronald Fung Kwok-fai, who campaigned on the streets for several months continuously and who waved to drivers and pedestrians early in the morning as well as late in the evening. Fung managed to get 766 votes, while Chow acquired 683 votes, in the Stubbs Road constituency. Another LP candidate who worked hard in the district was Chiang Sai-cheong, who defeated a DAB candidate and an independent in the Oi Chun constituency. Overall, the LP aimed at helping its leader James Tien to be elected. Tien was elected with 774 votes, defeating incumbent Leung Wing-on, who got 412 votes.

The HKPA ran a more district-based campaign than the LP. The former focused on the Sai Kung, Shatin, and Kowloon City districts. The HKPA made use of personal connections in various districts, relying on the support of some rural leaders. Hiew Moo-siew, for example, obtained the support of Sai Kung's rural leaders and was elected.[33] In Kowloon City, the HKPA nominated eight candidates, and five of them were elected. (Of the five, two were automatically elected.) Most of the HKPA candidates relied on the support of the MACs and Owners Corporations (OCs). Because urban development remains relatively slow in Kowloon City, the HKPA's dependence on the MACs and OCs could help its candidates to be elected. A good example was Wong Siu-yee, who could rely on the MAC leaders and members to mobilize residents to vote for him. His contender was a young DP member Tsoi Lai-ling, who was defeated by 495 votes.

The DAB was the best organized political party in the 1999 District Councils elections. The DAB employed full-time district coordinators and deputy district coordinators, organizing various activities for the residents and thus paving the way for candidates to win the elections.[34] These coordinators also help residents to form MACs and OCs, trying to expand the DAB's tentacles into various districts.[35] The DAB's organizational strength could not be excelled by the pro-democracy forces, which lacked sufficient human and financial resources in each of the eighteen districts.

The DAB also constituted the only political party that enjoyed the assistance of various types of supportive organizations. First and foremost, the pro-Beijing FTU provided logistical support for DAB candidates, mobilizing members to campaign for them. When the FTU staff paid regular visits to its members, the former recommended patriotic candidates to the latter in their constituencies.[36] Approaching the election day, the FTU sent a formal letter to each of its members, appealing to them to support a particular patriotic candidate. The letter said:

> The first District Councils elections in the HKSAR will be held on November 28, 1999. This is the first DC elections after the establishment of the HKSAR government. It is highly significant for us to realize the "one country, two systems" and "Hong Kong people ruling Hong Kong," and to maintain Hong Kong's long-term prosperity and stability. Therefore the Federation of Trade Unions appeals to every member to cast his or her vote actively. Now we sincerely recommend Mr. Peter Cheung to you. . . . We firmly believe that Peter Cheung is the best candidate for the first HKSAR District Councilor. So we specially recommend him to you. Please vote for Peter Cheung together with your family members and relatives.[37]

The FTU volunteers also helped some patriotic candidates to contact individual voters, paying home visits and distributing leaflets on the election day. The DAB candidate, Kwok Bit-chun, defeated Li Wah-ming of the DP by 196 votes in Shun Tin West constituency. Li was an urban councilor and a legislative councilor, but Kwok was a very strong candidate working hard at the constituency. The FTU fully mobilized workers to help Kwok, who deliberately avoided the mass media in order to hide his weakness in public relations.[38]

The FTU also mobilized political support for patriotic independents. Law Lai-kuen, a patriotic independent in the Lok Wah South constituency, received the help of at least thirty to forty FTU helpers every week near the election day.[39] In July 1999, she conducted a survey of voters in her constituency and found that her opponent, Hung Chung-fun of the DP, got 70 percent of the support.[40] Law caught up quickly from July to November, defeating Hung narrowly by thirty-five-votes. Hung later admitted that he had underestimated the potential and strength of Law.[41] In any case, the FTU constituted a mobilizational machinery of the DAB and patriotic candidates.[42]

The most impressive hallmark of the patriotic front was a vast array of supportive organizations that became the coordinative nucleus. There were two major pro-Beijing supportive organizations, namely the New Territories Association of Societies (NTAS) and Kowloon Federation of Associations

(KFA), which have 107 and 38 affiliated groups in the New Territories and in Kowloon respectively.[43] The NTAS was formed in 1985 and KFA was founded in June 1997, both with the objectives of organizing district groups in a more coherent way and serving as umbrella organizations for them.[44] Since July 1997, there has been a "restructuring" of united front organizations in the HKSAR.[45] The executive committees of the NTAS and KFA held formal meetings that endorsed the candidates of the patriotic front. The meetings of the executive committees of the NTAS and KFA not only endorsed patriotic candidates to use the names of the two organizations in their campaign pamphlets, but also arranged patriotic independents to compete with the pro-democracy candidates.[46] For instance, Kong Wai-yeung competed with Ip Shu-on of the DP. Kong had a prominent patriotic background; he was a secretary-general of the Federation of Yau Tsim Mong Associations, which was and is affiliated with the KFA.[47] Another good example was Lee Tat-yan, who was rumored to receive the support of the former New China News Agency (NCNA, which has been renamed Liaison Office since 2000) and who defeated Lau San-ching of the DP in the San Po Kong constituency.[48] Apart from coordination and mobilization work, the NTAS and KFA appealed to the members of their affiliated organizations to vote for patriotic candidates.[49] The affiliated organizations mobilized their staff members to campaign for patriotic candidates. A typical example was Chan Chung-kit, who received human and other resources from Tai Kok Tsui District Concern Group during his term as chair, and who defeated Leung Shet-fong of the DP in the Cherry constituency.[50]

Occasionally, the NTAS and the KFA failed to achieve compromise among patriotic candidates who competed with each other. For example, the KFA did not support two patriotic candidates who competed with each other in the same constituency in Kwun Tong.[51] Similarly, in Tuen Mun, the NTAS did not want to interfere with two patriotic candidates confronting each other in the Lung Mun constituency.[52] These two patriotic candidates were Lung Shui-hing of the DAB, a member of the New Territories West Residents' Association affiliated with the NTAS, and Yau Siu-leung, an honorary president of the same residents' association.[53] These were exceptional cases, however.

Furthermore, overlapping memberships are a prominent feature of the leadership stratum in the DAB, FTU, NTAS, and KFS. DAB leaders such as Tam Yiu-chung, Chan Yuen-han, and Wong Kwok-hing are simultaneously the core leading members of the FTU. The executive committee of the KFS in 1999 had at least nine members of the DAB, including Chan Kam-lam, Ip Kwok-chung, Wen Choy-bon, Lam Man-fai, Kan Chi-ho, Kwok Bit-chun, and Poon Kwok-wah.[54] DAB members such as Chau Chuen-heung and

Cheung Hok-ming are also leaders of the NTAS.[55] At the middle level of the DAB, FTU, NTAS, and KFA, overlapping memberships can also be identified. For example, Wong Mo-tai of the DAB is also chair of the Shatin Women Society, which is affiliated with the NTAS. Wen Choy-bon is not only the director of the FTU's District Services Center but also the chair of the DAB's party branch at Kowloon City district. These overlapping memberships constitute an informal and a lateral channel of communications between the DAB and its various supportive organizations.

The Liaison Office is a hidden but crucial chess player overseeing the entire campaign strategies of the patriotic front (see Figure 5.1). According to our informant, the Liaison Office serves as "babysitter" for the DAB in the DC elections and its deputy director Zhang Guoxiong is responsible for managing the DAB.[56] There is no concrete evidence to prove that some key figures of the DAB's supportive organizations are members of the local underground Chinese Communist Party (CCP), which is managed by the Hong Kong Work Committee (HKWC).[57] Officials of the Liaison Office, however, have frequent interactions with the leaders of the DAB's supportive organizations.[58] It is likely that the Liaison Office functioned as a behind-the-scenes commander, orchestrating the coordination of patriotic candidates and mobilizing united front organizations in the 1999 DCs elections.[59]

According to an insider of the patriotic front, the underground CCP was very active in the 1999 DC elections.[60] It sent "pro-Communist" candidates to prepare for the DC elections two or three years in advance.[61] The underground CCP reportedly mobilized residents to register as voters long before the elections and held various district activities, such as snake soup dinners, tours, and services for the elderly, to win the hearts and minds of the voters. It also served as a electoral commander, coordinating candidates, providing information to members of the patriotic front, formulating campaign strategies, and sending "cadres" to supervise each of the five geographical constituencies in the Legislative Council elections.[62] Obviously, the underground CCP viewed the 1999 DC elections as a critical battle prior to the 2000 Legislative Council elections. According to another informant, it is usual for the patriotic forces to establish "standing points" in various districts.[63] All the activities conducted by the underground CCP and the patriotic front can be seen as indispensable steps toward the process of entrenching the foundation of such "standing points."

Overall, the patriotic front was well organized, skillfully coordinated, and fully mobilized. The interrelationships can be seen in Figure 5.1, in which the DAB, FTU, and the major united front organizations (NTAS and KTA) are like an iron triangle cooperating with each other. These organizations shared information about candidates in elections, political intelligence, and district

Figure 5.1 **Interrelationships Between the DAB, FTU, NTAS, KFA, and NCNA**

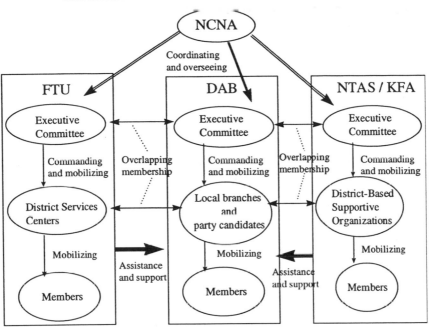

circumstances.[64] Through the exchange of information and intelligence, patriotic candidates came to understand who would compete in each constituency, which enabled them to try to avoid mutual competition but to simultaneously target their common enemy, namely the pro-democracy candidates. The triple alliance between the DAB, FTU, and united front organizations was very likely under hidden coordination and invisible supervision by the Liaison Office and the underground CCP. Consequently, the entire patriotic front constituted a formidable threat to the pro-democracy forces in the 1999 DC elections.

The Choices of Voters

Why did the voters choose the patriotic forces or the pro-democracy camp? The Hong Kong Transition project conducted a postelection telephone survey in mid-December 1999. There were 784 successful responses in which 549 respondents were registered voters. Among the 549 registered voters, 310 of them cast their ballots in the DC elections on November 28, 1999. The most significant reason for the respondents casting their ballots was that voting was the responsibility of citizens (77.2 percent, see Table 5.7). Other

Table 5.7

Reasons Given by Registered Voters for Voting in District Councils Elections, 1999

	Respondents	
	Number	Percent
It is the responsibility of citizens.	196	77.2
To exercise the right of citizens.	81	31.9
DC and DC members reveal my point of view.	31	12.2
DC and DC members work for my interest.	31	12.2
To support a particular candidate.	29	11.4
DC and DC members help to improve affairs in the district.	21	8.3
To support democratization.	9	3.5
Invited by some person or groups campaign workers.	9	3.5
The polling station was nearby.	6	2.4
Dissatisfaction with a group/party.	5	2.0
Motivated by promotional activities about elections.	4	1.6
Dissatisfaction with a candidate.	4	1.6
To support a particular group.	3	1.2
Other	36	14.2

Note: The respondents were those who were registered voters and who voted in the 1999 District Councils elections. They were asked to indicate which factors they considered in casting their ballots.

reasons included exercising the right of citizens and having district councilors represent their views as well as work for them.

With regard to the voters' choices, 36.4 percent of them voted for the candidates from the pro-democracy, 25 percent cast their ballots for the patriotic forces, and 38.6 percent supported the independents (Table 5.8).[65] The major reason for voters making their choices was the candidate's past performance in serving the public (51.6 percent, see Table 5.9). Other reasons included the candidate's electoral platform and political views (17.7 percent) and whether the candidate lived and worked in the district (6.7 percent).

The preference of voters was directly related to their attitude toward democracy. We find that the voters who supported a more democratic polity tend to vote for the pro-democracy forces. When the respondents' voting preferences are tabulated with their political stances on particular issues, there is a significant variation between the supporters of the pro-democracy and the patriotic forces. For instance, 68.6 percent of the respondents who voted for pro-democracy parties opposed and strongly opposed the DC's appointment system (see Table 5.10). But only 38.9 percent of the respondents who voted for patriotic parties opposed and strongly opposed the appointment system. Moreover, only 40.7 percent of the respondents who supported the independents also opposed and strongly opposed the appoint-

Table 5.8

Respondents' Choices in District Councils Elections, 1999

	Respondents	
	Number	Percent
Prodemocracy parties	86	36.4
Patriotic parties	59	25.0
Independents	91	38.6

Table 5.9

Major Reasons for Registered Voters' Choices in District Councils Elections, 1999

	Respondents	
	Number	Percent
Candidate's performance record in serving the public	131	51.6
Election platform or political viewpoint of the candidate	45	17.7
Candidates living or working in the district	17	6.7
Endorsement of the candidate by political party or pressure group	9	3.5
Candidate's affiliation with political party	9	3.5
Candidate's occupation and educational background	6	2.4
Candidate's character and personality	6	2.4
Candidate's desire for good relations with China	6	2.4
Wish to reflect my opinions to the authorities	6	2.4
Endorsement of the candidate by political figures	5	2.0
Candidate's appearance	4	1.6
Candidate's fame	2	0.8
Independence of candidate	2	0.8
Candidate recommended by relative, friend, neighbor, colleague, or schoolmate	1	0.4
Candidate's patriotism	1	0.4
Candidate's reputation	1	0.4
Attracted by the publicity and activity of candidate	1	0.4
Candidate's status as an incumbent	1	0.4
Candidate's support of a relatively fast-paced change to democratic rule	1	0.4
Total	254	100.0

ing system. On the issue of the abolition of the two municipal councils, the Urban Council and the Regional Council, 49.1 percent of pro-democracy supporters opposed and strongly opposed it, while only 17.3 percent of the respondents who voted for patriotic parties and 23.5 percent of those supporting independents opposed and strongly opposed the abolition (see Table 5.11). Obviously, the respondents who favored a more democratic polity with greater public participation in government institutions would more likely support pro-democracy parties.

Table 5.10

Cross-Tabulation of Respondents' Choices in District Councils Elections with Their Attitudes Toward the Appointment System for District Councils, 1999*

	Respondents' Choices in Elections					
	Prodemocracy Parties		Patriotic Parties		Independents	
	Number	Percent	Number	Percent	Number	Percent
Strongly oppose	34	39.5	10	16.9	16	17.6
Oppose	25	29.1	13	22.0	21	23.1
Neutral	11	12.8	13	22.0	18	19.8
Support	8	9.3	16	27.1	21	23.1
Strongly support	2	2.3	6	10.2	3	3.3
Don't know	6	7.0	1	1.7	12	13.2
Total	86	100.0	59	100.0	91	100.0

$*\chi^2 = 74.2$, d.f. $= 6$, p $< = 0.001$

Table 5.11

Cross-Tabulation of Respondents' Choices in District Councils Elections with Their Attitudes Toward the Abolition of the Two Municipal Councils, 1999*

	Respondents' Choices in Elections					
	Prodemocracy Parties		Patriotic Parties		Independents	
	Number	Percent	Number	Percent	Number	Percent
Strongly oppose	13	19.1	2	4.3	6	8.8
Oppose	21	30.9	6	13.0	10	14.7
Neutral	11	16.2	9	19.6	17	25.0
Support	11	16.2	15	32.6	20	29.4
Strongly support	8	11.8	12	26.1	11	16.2
Don't know	4	5.9	2	4.3	4	5.9
Total	68	100.0	46	100.0	68	100.0

$*\chi^2 = 40.0$, d.f. $= 6$, p $< = 0.05$

Besides, the identity of voters has significant correlation with their choices; 63.4 percent of supporters of pro-democracy parties identified themselves as Hong Kong persons and other identities with less Chineseness (Hong Kong British, Overseas Chinese, and others). Also, 36.6 percent of them identified themselves as Hong Kong Chinese and Chinese (see Table 5.12). On the contrary, only 35.2 percent of the supporters of patriotic parties identified themselves as Hong Kong persons, while 64.8 percent of them said they were Hong Kong Chinese and Chinese. There is no prominent

Table 5.12

Cross-Tabulation of Respondents' Choices in District Councils Elections with Their Self-Identity, 1999*

	Respondents' Choices in Elections					
	Pro-democracy Parties		Patriotic Parties		Independents	
	Number	Percent	Number	Percent	Number	Percent
Hong Kong Chinese	15	18.3	19	35.2	26	29.5
Chinese	15	18.3	16	29.6	16	18.2
Hong Kong person	45	54.9	19	35.2	46	52.3
Hong Kong British	5	6.1				
Overseas Chinese	1	1.2				
Others	1	1.2				
Total	82	100.0	54	100.0	88	100.0

*$\chi^2 = 28.8$, d.f. $= 6$, p $< = 0.05$

self-identification among respondents who voted for independents; 52.3 percent of them identified themselves as Hong Kong persons while 47.7 percent labeled themselves as Hong Kong Chinese and Chinese. In a nutshell, those who identified themselves as Hong Kong persons and other identities with less Chineseness would more likely support the pro-democracy parties. Those who identified themselves as having strong Chinese characteristics would more likely vote for the patriotic parties.

Conclusion

The 1999 DC elections signaled the formidable mobilization, coordination, and organization of the patriotic front in the HKSAR—an unprecedented phenomenon in Hong Kong politics. Not only did the DAB improve its overall performance in elections, but also it represented an electoral machinery having close linkages with united front organizations, the pro-Beijing FTU, and perhaps the Liaison Office as well as the underground CCP. The triple alliance between the DAB, FTU, and united front organizations constituted a powerful force in elections. Its intention was to prevent the pro-democracy forces from dominating the District Councils. The patriotic front succeeded in not only curbing the influence of the pro-democracy forces but also winning the hearts and minds of the voters who identified themselves more as Chinese than as Hong Kong persons. The patriotic front led by the DAB, FTU, and pro-Beijing united front organizations worked very hard at the district level, offering various welfare services to ordinary citizens. By trying to win the hearts and minds of the voters, the patriotic front has already accepted in the rules of the game in democratic elections. If democratization entails the electoral participation of political forces, the patriotic front's determination to grasp more elected seats in District Councils has the unintended consequence of consolidating democratization at the district level.

On the contrary, the pro-democracy forces failed to demonstrate their coordinating, mobilizational and organizational ability. The decentralized style of election campaign of the DP candidates was a testimony to the party's lack of leadership and planning. Even worse, a minority of DP candidates antagonized some voters, thus directly tarnishing the image of the pro-democracy flagship. Other pro-democracy forces also failed to demonstrate political leadership. The unsatisfactory performance of the Frontier is case in point. On the whole, if the pro-democracy forces cannot learn a bitter lesson from the results of the 1999 DC elections, not only will their future be at stake but also they will run the risk of being politically replaced by the patriotic front in the 2004 DC elections.

The political implications for democratization in the People's Republic of China (PRC) and the HKSAR are obvious. First, if the HKSAR continues to democratize its political system gradually, the patriotic forces will likely be the dominant forces. In other words, in the event that the HKSAR's legislature and District Councils were composed of all directly elected members, the triple alliance will very likely become the ruling coalition. Second, if democratization in the PRC takes place, the Hong Kong case illustrates that the CCP will very likely be the most powerful mobilizational and organizational force in local elections.[66] To put it simply, the CCP will likely remain politically preponderant over other forces in the mainland, especially when the opposition forces there remain relatively much weaker than their counterparts in the HKSAR.

Notes

1. For the background of political parties in Hong Kong, see Norman Miners, *The Government and Politics of Hong Kong* (Hong Kong: Oxford University Press, 1998), pp. 196–203; and Lo Shiu-hing, *The Politics of Democratization in Hong Kong* (London: Macmillan, 1997), pp. 137–76.

2. For the results of the previous DB elections in Hong Kong under the British rule, see Lau Siu-kai and Kuan Hsin-chi, "District Board Elections in Hong Kong," *Journal of Commonwealth and Comparative Politics* 22, no. 3 (November 1984): 303–17; Lau Siu-kai and Kuan Hsin-chi, "The 1985 District Board Election in Hong Kong: The Limits of Political Mobilization in a Dependent Polity," *Journal of Commonwealth and Comparative Politics* 25, no. 1 (March 1987): 82–102; Joseph Y.S. Cheng, "The 1985 District Board Elections in Hong Kong," in *Hong Kong in Transition,* Joseph Y.S. Cheng, ed. (Hong Kong: Oxford University Press, 1986), pp. 67–87; and Joseph Y.S. Cheng, "The 1988 District Board Elections: A Study of Political

Participation in the Transitional Period," in *Hong Kong: The Challenge of Transformation*, Kathleen Cheek-Milby and Miron Mushkat, ed. (Hong Kong: Centre of Asian Studies, University of Hong Kong, 1989), pp. 116–52.

3. For a critique of the DP's performance, including district work and campaign strategies, see Chan Wai-yip's submission to the DP's Central Committee, "Review of the 1999 District Councils elections," January 6, 2000, provided by Chan to the authors.

4. Furthermore, we observed that most of Ng's posters were damaged by a stamp saying that he was a "traitor." Wong Sing-chi of the DP admitted that his colleagues in Shatin did not perform well and he even said that one DP member, Wai Hing-cheung (who was defeated by a rising DAB star named Cheung Shui-fung) was "lazy." Personal interview with Wong Sing-chi, November 22, 2000.

5. Ng's opponent was Wong Che-ming, who was endorsed by the KFA. See *Wen Hui Pao*, November 15, 1999, p. A-7.

6. Our participant observation of an election forum in Mei Foo Sun Chuen, Lai Wan constituency, November 5, 1999.

7. Some leaders of the OTTA were invited by the PRC authorities to visit China, prompting an internal struggle within the OTTA's Executive Committee. The hard-liners in the OTTA's Executive Committee decided to disband the party. See *Apple Daily*, November 27, 2000.

8. Wong Chung-ki, for example, defected to the DP after his disagreement with the ADPL leaders over the Provisional Legislative Council. Wong and some defected ADPL members formed a group called the Social Democratic Front prior to their participation in the DP.

9. Ideologically, the DAB and the HKPA seem to be more pro-China than the LP. See Lo Shiu-hing, "Political Parties in a Democratizing Polity: The Role of the 'Pro-China' Democratic Alliance for the Betterment of Hong Kong," *Asian Journal of Political Science* 4, no. 1 (June 1996): 102–9.

10. The Neighborhood and Workers' Association is composed of district councilors such as Leung Yiu-chung and Leung Chi-shing. Personal interview with Leung Yiu-chung, November 22, 2000.

11. There were some examples. Hau Shui-pui told us that he did not want to abide by any party discipline and therefore he did not join any political party. He is a patriotic independent who defeated So Koon-chung of the DP in the Upper Ngau Tau Kok constituency. Personal interview with Hau Shui-pui, December 8, 1999. Chan Ping-woon, who was automatically elected in the 1999 DC elections in the Eastern district, did not join the LP or the DAB, which had approached him. Personal interview with Chan Ping-woon, November 26, 1999. Ng Chung-tak, a pro-democracy independent, left the DP because of family and personal considerations. Personal discussion with Ng, October 16, 1999.

12. For example, Lee Ling in Kwun Tong district got the support and endorsement of DP leader Szeto Wah. The former was also the chief coordinator of the latter's Kwun Tong district office. The authors went to the Kwun Tong District Office to study the political background and endorsement of candidates from mid-October to November 1999. It must be noted that in other districts, there were lots of candidates similar to Lee's situation. Another example is Chan Yuen-sum in Tsuen Wan district and he worked as an assistant to a DP candidate, Choy Tsz-man. Campaign materials of Chan available in the Tsuen Wan District Office, November 1999.

13. Examples include Hau Shui-pui and Law Lai-kuen, who were members of the

Kwun Tong Residents Association, a long-established patriotic group. See their campaign materials, available in the Kwun Tong District Office in November 1999. Another example is Lee Tat-yan, who was a leader of the Eastern Kowloon District Residents Committee, a patriotic group. See campaign materials of Lee Tat-yan, available in the Wong Tai Sin District Office in November 1999.

14. One example is Chu Yun-lam in Shatin district, and he did not have any party support in his campaign materials. Our study of candidates' campaign materials in Shatin District Office from October to November 1999.

15. It must be noted that in Sai Kung DC, the pro-democracy forces interestingly cooperated with the HKPA to select Ng Sze-fuk as the chair. See *Oriental Daily News*, January 8, 2000, p. A-19.

16. See *Ming Pao*, December 31, 1999, p. A-10. It must be noted that the rural leaders of the Heung Yee Kuk have varying political inclinations, ranging from pro-Taiwan to pro-Beijing. Therefore, they are not necessarily wholehearted supporters of the patriotic front. Personal interview with DP member Wong Sing-chi, November 22, 2000. Personal interview with Choy Kan-pui, November 6, 2000.

17. Before 2000, the District Management Committees did not have deputy chairs of District Boards. After the chairs and deputy chairs were allowed to participate in the committees in 2000, however, their influence has remained minimal as there is no need for members of the Committees (which have other government department officials) to vote on district issues. Personal interview with Lam Man-fai, the chair of the Wong Tai Sin District Council, November 13, 1999.

18. Chan joined the New Century Forum in 2000, helping a former government official Lan Hong-tsung participate in the Legislative Council's direct elections, held in September 2000 on Hong Kong Island. In a meeting of the Central and Western District Council in November 2000, Chan argued with Wu over the way in which the latter handled a question raised by the former. This might be an indication that their opinion difference stemmed partly from varying political support. Chan is supported by the patriotic force whereas Wu is backed up by the DP. Participant observation of the meeting in November 2000.

19. For more details, see *Oriental Daily News*, January 7, 2000, p. A-19. Also our participant observation of the meeting of the Central and Western District Council on January 6, 2000.

20. Personal interview with Fung King-man, November 19, 1999.

21. Ibid.

22. Chan Wai-yip of the DP said that Tsang did not know how to manage the election campaign and that he had to give advice to Tsang. Personal interview with Chan Wai-yip, January 18, 2000.

23. Tsang withdrew from the DP to compete in the Legislative Council elections.

24. Chan alienated lots of residents in Mei Foo Sun Chuen. Participant observation of the candidates' election forum (Lai Wan constituency) held by the Shumshuipo City District Office, November 5, 1999.

25. Personal interview with Wong Sing-chi, November 22, 2000. As early as 1998, the DAB succeeded in penetrating many Mutual Aid Committees in the New Territories East geographical constituency, see Lo Shiu-hing and Yu Wing-yat, "Politicization of the Mutual Aid Committees," in *Power Transfer and Electoral Politics: The First Legislative Election in the HKSAR*, Kuan Hsin-chi et al., ed. (Hong Kong: Chinese University Press, 1999), pp. 155–84.

26. The survey was conducted by the Hong Kong Transition Project in October 1999, and we sent 798 questionnaires to all the candidates participating in the District Councils elections. There were 170 respondents.

27. Personal interview with Chun Fei-pang, November 24, 1999.

28. For the election result, see *South China Morning Post*, November 30, 1999, pp. 8–9. Also personal interview with Mak Ip-sing, December 15, 1999.

29. Personal interview with King Cheng King-hung, November 11, 1999. Personal interview with Wong Mo-tai, January 18, 2000.

30. This point was admitted by Cheng himself to the authors, after his electoral defeat.

31. Au Wai-kwan was not supported by TF to compete in the Northern district. One Frontier member expressed her dissatisfaction with this decision. Personal discussion with the Frontier member, November 5, 1999.

32. According to our informant, this was a patriotic independent. Personal interview with the informant, November 12, 1999.

33. Personal discussion with a campaign manager in Sai Kung, November 1, 1999.

34. Personal interview with a DAB candidate who preferred to remain anonymous, November 17, 1999.

35. Personal interview with Ki Lai-mei of the DAB, October 22, 1999.

36. Personal interview with a patriotic independent Lee Tat-yan, December 9, 1999. Personal interview with a DAB candidate Ngan Chun-lim, January 21, 2000.

37. The letter sent by the FTU to its members in the Hing Fong constituency, "Please Cast Your Sacred Ballot to Candidate Number Two Peter Cheung," November 19, 1999 (30 copies). This letter was available for public inspection in Kwai Tsing District Office, January 2000.

38. One DP candidate, Danny Chin, in the Kwun Tong district told us that the DP made a strategic error by using Lee to try to unseat Kwok. Personal discussion with Chin, October 30, 1999.

39. Personal discussion with a FTU worker who volunteered to help Law, November 16, 1999.

40. Personal interview with Law Lai-kuen, November 4, 2000.

41. Personal interview with Hung Chung-fun, January 20, 2000.

42. Personal interview with FTU's legal advisor Kwong Chi-kin, who admitted that the FTU had "contradictions" with the DAB because some FTU members who joined the DAB made use of the union's resources. Personal interview with Kwong, January 21, 2000.

43. The corresponding organization in the Hong Kong Island is the Hong Kong Island Federation (HKIF), which did not exist until it was inaugurated in 1999. However, its role in the 1999 DC elections was not as significant as the KFA and the NTAS. The HKIF has four major affiliated organizations, namely the Unified Associations of Central and Western District, the Unified Associations of Wanchai District, the Unified Associations of Eastern District, and the Unified Associations of Southern District. These four organizations played an active role in mobilizing other affiliated groups and their members to vote for patriotic candidates. See "Hong Kong Island Federation Constitution," 1999; provided by an organizer of patriotic district groups in the Hong Kong Island on January 27, 2000. Also our personal interview with Chan Sze-chung of the DAB, November 3, 2000.

44. See *The Fourteenth Anniversary of the New Territories Association of Societies*

(Tai Po: New Territories Association of Societies, July 1999). Also see *Wen Hui Pao*, June 19, 1997, p. A-12.

45. Personal interview with Hau Shui-pui, December 8, 1999.

46. Personal interview with Lee Tat-yan, December 9, 1999. Personal interview with Chan Chung-kit, December 9, 1999.

47. Our observation of Kong's campaign posters in Mong Kok North constituency, November 1999.

48. Lee denied that he received the support of the NCNA during our interview with him, December 9, 1999. During the election forum of Lee Tat-yan and Lau San-ching, the former received the full support of some residents who were mobilized to question the latter. We observed that the residents were provided with two sheets of paper, one containing seven questions targeted on Lau, and the other having eight questions directed at Lee. This political mobilization was very well organized.

49. Personal interview with Lee Tat-yan, December 9, 1999.

50. See the campaign pamphlet of Chan Chung-kit. Also see *The Tenth Anniversary of the Tai Kok Tsui District Concern Group* (no publisher, September 1998). It must be noted that Tsang Yok-shing and Yip Kwok-chung of the DAB are the honorary presidents of the Group (p. 5).

51. Personal interview with Lee Tat-yan, December 9, 1999.

52. Personal interview with Chan Wan-sang, November 17, 2000.

53. Ibid.

54. See *Special Issue of the Second Anniversary of the Kowloon Federation of Associations* (Kowloon: Kowloon Federation of Associations, July 1999), p. 23.

55. Personal interview with Chau Chuen-heung, November 24, 2000. Personal interview with Choy Kan-pui, November 6, 2000.

56. Personal interview with an informant who preferred to remain anonymous, January 3, 2000.

57. The HKWC remains active in the HKSAR; see "The Activities of the Chinese Communists in Hong Kong and Macau Still Maintain an Underground Situation," *World Journal* (a North American Chinese daily), January 4, 2000, p. A-17. Before 1991, the HKWC was combined with the Macau Work Committee as the Hong Kong and Macau Work Committee (HKMWC). For a historical background of the HKMWC, see John P. Burns, "The Structure of Communist Party Control in Hong Kong," *Asian Survey* 30, no. 8 (August 1990): 749–63.

58. See the daily reports on the activities of social groups in *Wen Hui Pao*.

59. The HKWC exists inside the Liaison Office; see "The Activities of the Chinese Communists in Hong Kong and Macau Still Maintain an Underground Situation," *World Journal*, January 4, 2000, p. A-17. For the historical development of the former NCNA, see Li Gucheng, "The Functions and Role of the Hong Kong NCNA," *Asian Studies* (Hong Kong), no. 18 (June 10, 1996): 18–112. Also see John P. Burns, "The Role of the New China News Agency and China's Policy Toward Hong Kong." In *Hong Kong and China in Transition*, John Burns, Victor C. Falkenheim and David M. Lampton, ed. (Toronto: Joint Center for Asia Pacific Studies, University of Toronto-York University, 1994), pp. 17–60.

60. Lam Cheung-mei, "The Secret Weapon of the Pro-Communist Camp in the Election Battle," *Cheng Ming* (January 2000), pp. 61–63.

61. Ibid., p. 62.

62. Ibid., p. 61.

63. The term "standing points" also coincidentally appears in Lam's article, see ibid., p. 62. Personal interview with the informant who worked in the patriotic camp for many years, December 16, 1999.

64. Personal interview with Chan Chung-kit, December 9, 1999.

65. We grouped the political parties in the survey into two categories in accordance with our classification in this chapter: the pro-democracy camp and the patriotic forces.

66. For democratization in China, see Robert A. Pastor, "The Possibility of Democracy in China and its Feasible Paths," *American Asian Review* 18, no. 4 (winter 2000): 143–69.

Transformation of the Civil Service System

Anthony B.L. Cheung

Introduction

The Setting for Minimum Change

The civil service system had always been treasured in the run-up to Hong Kong's transition to becoming China's special administrative region (SAR) in July 1997 as one of the territory's major legacies, inherited from its previous British colonial masters. Indeed, even during the heated days of Sino-British row over political reforms in the final years prior to the handover, the smooth transition of the civil service, together with the continuity of the judiciary, was seen as the remaining pillars of political stability given the abolition of the "through-train" arrangements for the legislature and the selection by China of a person of her own choice as SAR chief executive, precluding any British participation.[1]

The smooth transition of the civil service had both administrative and political implications. Administratively, as in other respects, the civil service provided a permanent administration responsible for the day-to-day delivery of public services, ranging from the maintenance of law and order to the provision of education, welfare, and health care. Since the 1970s, when the British colonial administration began to clean up the corruption-afflicted civil service and to modernize its management and organization, the Hong Kong civil service had gradually evolved into a symbol of efficiency and integrity, something in which the local population could take pride, even though the territory was governed as a colony. With localization, a process much speeded up after the signing of the Sino-British Joint Declaration on the future of Hong Kong in 1984, the civil service had also increasingly become the embodiment of local self-administration—an institution that local residents now had the right to join on the basis of merit even though they were not given the political right to elect their own government.

Politically, the Hong Kong colonial state was essentially an "administrative state,"[2] with government by the bureaucrats under the leadership of the British governor, supported by business and professional elites in society. In the absence of electoral politics and political parties until the early 1990s,[3] the senior civil servants—mainly those who staffed the strategic "administrative class"—formed the political cadres of the government. Following the McKinsey reforms of 1973,[4] administrative officers underwent a process of "quasi ministerialization," assuming strengthened policymaking and political functions. The arrival of Chris Patten as the last governor in 1992 and his initiatives to open up the government, saw those top civil servants occupying policy portfolios as "secretaries," behaving in much the same way as ministers in other governments, busy in defending government policies, lobbying legislators, and answering questions before the Legislative Council. On the eve of the handover, with the exception of the governor and the attorney general (retitled secretary of justice, in SAR parlance) who were non-Chinese, all the top posts in the government were taken up by local Chinese who constituted in effect the governing party.

During the drafting of the Basic Law for the SAR in the late 1980s, much importance was attached by both sovereign governments in Beijing and London to retaining Hong Kong's long tradition of "executive-led" government. Thus the political design under the Basic Law tips the balance of power between the executive and legislative branches clearly to the side of the executive authorities.[5] The Basic Law drafters had clearly rejected a Westminster model of government whereby the government is to be formed by the majority party in the elected legislature; neither had they opted for a full version of separation of powers as in the U.S. system, which allows both the executive and legislative branches to initiate policies, budgets, and legislation.

Tensions in Continuity

Assuming the continuity of a partyless system of governance beyond 1997, Beijing leaders had contemplated Hong Kong's political transition as simply a removal of British governorship and its replacement by a local chief executive appointed by the central government in Beijing, with the rest of the administration being run by career bureaucrats as in the past. Some local academics had for a while subscribed to a scenario of a British-centered "ruling coalition" of administrative and business elites transiting to a China-centered "ruling coalition."[6] Under such a scenario, the governing role of senior civil servants would be reinforced rather than diluted in the new SAR governance. To them, an "executive-led" government was a government led by civil servants.

Despite the Sino-British political conflict during the final years of transition, China had honored its pledge to the civil service. Repeatedly, Beijing leaders had reassured civil servants of their important role in the future stability of Hong Kong. The new chief executive Tung Chee-hwa, allegedly on Beijing's good advice, had retained all British-appointed principal officials in their original positions when he formed the SAR government. The only appointment from outside the civil service was that of Elsie Leung, then a local delegate to China's National People's Congress, as secretary of justice. It can therefore be argued that the new SAR began on July 1, 1997 with a civil service system much the same as that of the previous administration.

Four years into Tung's leadership, however, there are clear signs that the civil service system inherited from the days of British rule is heading for some fundamental transformation. First, a consultation document on *Civil Service Reform* published in March 1999 sought to overhaul the permanent and pensionable civil service, turning it into an organization with a more flexible structure, making use of more contract staff.[7] Then, in his annual policy address to the Legislative Council on October 11, 2000, Tung Chee-hwa announced the intention to introduce a new system of accountability for principal officials at the secretary level, in effect turning them into political appointees employed on non–civil service terms.[8] Both of these measures, one managerially motivated and the other clearly politically driven, would create a great impact on the future of Hong Kong's civil service system.

Civil Service Reforms

Despite the claim on continuity and stability, the civil service system that the new SAR inherited was not an institution that had never undergone any changes. On the contrary, the civil service as the major politico-administrative system of British rule was from time to time the subject of reorganization and reform. Indeed, as this author has argued elsewhere, Hong Kong's colonial administrative history was marked with abundant examples of administrative reforms pursued to cope, directly or partially, with political problems and challenges to the power of the bureaucracy.[9] Most often, because of the reality that political solutions in the form of more fundamental constitutional reconfigurations or power readjustments were infeasible, managerial reforms became the only available means to take some pressure off the administration.

Reforms of the Administration and the Civil Service During the 1970s

Civil service reforms in Hong Kong should be understood in terms of both their managerial content and their wider political impact. The first major revamping of the colonial civil service took place in the early 1970s, in the aftermath of the 1966 and 1967 riots. Until then, Hong Kong had more or less followed the standard practice of any British crown colony, with government by civil servants under a constitutionally autocratic governor answerable only to the secretary of state in London. There was some limited political participation by British hongs and local Chinese elites through appointment to the two major councils of the governor—namely the Executive Council and the Legislative Council—as well as to various advisory committees. This system of "administrative absorption" characterized the nature of colonial governance.[10]

The riots of the late 1960s were instigated by both external influence from China's cultural revolution, as well as domestic restlessness from the young generation who yearned for political participation. Such challenges to colonial rule had not resulted in any constitutional reforms. Quite the reverse, the discussions on reforming local administration through delegation of some executive powers to the Urban Council or proposed new district authorities were halted.[11] However, there were clear attempts to open up the administrative system, through a quicker pace of localization in civil service appointments at recruitment-rank level and a new political strategy to nurture an outreaching government which, though nonelected, would still be able to impress the governed that it was a government for the people.

To achieve this new strategy, city district offices (later renamed "district offices" in line with similar setups in the New Territories) with the key functions of explaining government policies and assessing the moods of the local population were set up at the district level. Major government departments (such as education, social welfare, urban services, and police) were similarly "districtized." Instead of maintaining a hands-off policy toward local Chinese as in the past, the government began to take an active role in organizing community campaigns such as the Hong Kong Festival, the Clean Hong Kong Campaign, and the Fight Crime Campaign, so as to instigate a sense of community. By the late 1970s, community building was an essential element of the government's political agenda, supported by a configuration of district-based area committees and tenement block–based mutual aid committees and owners' corporations, organized and coordinated by district offices.

These organizations helped to provide a source of district community leaders, who were subsequently coopted into the government's advisory machinery as it was gradually extended to the grassroots level.[12] They also constituted important webs of local support to the government, replacing previous voluntary Chinese community organizations (such as the Kaifong [neighborhood] associations) and countervailing procommunist trade unions and residents associations. Eventually these district networks were further institutionalized when the government introduced the "district administration scheme" in 1981 with the formation of partially elected district boards as local representative assemblies and the establishment of interdepartmental district management committees to better coordinate policy and service delivery at the local level. District officers (who were administrative officers) became the government's local "political" representatives.

The 1970s also saw some drastic changes to the internal structure of the bureaucracy. Apart from the localization of recruitment, a major review of the central government machinery was conducted by the international management consultants McKinsey & Company. The McKinsey recommendations in 1973 resulted in the reorganization of the colonial secretariat, since renamed the "Government Secretariat," into several policy and resource branches headed by super-secretaries who were tasked to coordinate departments within specified policy areas.[13] New management methods were also introduced for program planning and resource management. These reforms helped to bring a modernized face to a hitherto rigid and inward-looking colonial administration and were compared to the 1968 Fulton Report in the United Kingdom (U.K.) which also sought to take the British civil service into the modern era.[14] The concurrent stepping up of anticorruption efforts, with the establishment of the Independent Commission Against Corruption in 1974, confronted a chronic problem of the colonial bureaucracy which had caused so much public resentment. By the early 1980s, when the future of Hong Kong was negotiated between China and Britain, the civil service system had changed so much that it was generally seen as a clean and efficient institution that should be kept intact after 1997.

The political significance of the reorganization of the Government Secretariat lay in the emergence of quasi ministerial policy secretaries, who provided policy coordination, and subsequently leadership, to their groups of government departments, in effect sharing governmental power with the governor, the chief secretary, and the financial secretary, to whom department heads had previously been directly subordinate. The top echelons of the civil service, made up mostly of officers of the administrative class, became politicized and ministerialized. At the same time, the chief secretary, together with the financial secretary and other secretaries, formed the de facto "cabinet" of the governor.

Public-Sector Reforms in the 1980s and 1990s

The 1980s were a decade of political negotiation on the future of Hong Kong, first in the Sino-British negotiations on the 1997 question and then in the drafting of the Basic Law as a miniconstitution for post-1997 Hong Kong. They were also a decade of attempted constitutional reforms, starting with the 1984 Green Paper on Representative Government advocating an elected Legislative Council and eventually an Executive Council to be elected by the legislature somewhat along Westminster lines.[15] Such reforms were only partially successful, as China quickly saw them as part of the British strategy for preempting the Basic Law and called for their halt. Direct elections to the legislature, originally hinted in 1984, were postponed to 1991 after the Basic Law was promulgated.[16]

The rhetoric on representative government, accompanied by a partial democratization of the political system, opened the gate to heated political debates in society and spurred the rise of political groups and quasi parties. Political pressure on government administration was on the increase, while its constitutional capacity to accommodate or to contain such pressure for participation was limited. Government-society relations remained tense. Only in management reforms could meaningful initiatives still be launched, to respond to rising public expectations. While public attention was mostly focused on the politics of the time, the government had quietly set foot on a different reform path—that of "public sector reform"—to improve its responsiveness to the community.

Following trends in Europe and North America toward privatization and efficiency drives,[17] the government began to explore the scope for privatization of some kind, resulting in more contracting out of service production (such as public car-park management and street cleaning), as well as the corporatization of public hospital services (in the form of the Hospital Authority established in 1991) and an attempt to corporatize Radio Television Hong Kong. The latter corporatization would have been accomplished if not for the political opposition of China and a managerial move to streamline the station's finances, which dampened staff enthusiasm for the organizational change.[18]

The most significant change came with the publication of *Public Sector Reform* in February 1989.[19] As far as the impact of this document on the civil service system was concerned, the public-sector reform program sought to replace the civil service administrative culture with a new managerial culture more oriented toward cost awareness, resource management, and customer satisfaction. Public-sector reform also envisaged a new organizational framework, with policy secretaries assuming both policy and resource management roles and entering into contractual relationships with service delivery agents, which could take the form of traditional department, self-accounting trading fund, nondepartmental public body, or public corporation. The *managerialization* of "ministerial" policy secretaries was in line with similar trends in Britain and other Organization for Economic Cooperation and Development (OECD) countries, notably Canada, Australia, and New Zealand. When Chris Patten became governor in 1992, he also transplanted the British citizen's charter onto the Hong Kong public sector in the form of "performance pledges." By 1995, public-sector reform in Hong Kong was modified to better suit the home turf, resulting in the *Serving the Community* program, which embraced four core principles:[20]

- Living within the means
- Managing for performance
- Developing a culture of service
- Being accountable

The emphasis is placed on customer service, managing for results, and improving productivity.

The launch of public sector reform in Hong Kong, though it was in tandem with the global trends of new public management (NPM),[21] also served a domestic political agenda. As this author has argued elsewhere,[22] Hong Kong did not venture into public-sector reforms in the 1980s and early 1990s because of an efficiency crisis or government overload similar to that suffered by OECD countries. There was neither a strong popular nor a powerful ideological demand in favor of reorganizing the public sector, causing the rise of NPM in other countries.[23] Quite on the contrary, Hong Kong's civil service had all along been praised for its cleanliness, efficiency, and effectiveness. Public expenditure had always been prudently kept at a relatively low level—under 20 percent of gross domestic product (GDP)—although in the final years of the transition, the government, under the pressure of legislative politics, was forced to grant various kinds of tax concessions in light of a sound fiscal surplus brought about by a booming economy. Public-sector reform in the Hong Kong context had actually underpinned a process of relegitimating public bureaucratic power and helped the politically hard-pressed senior civil service to regain its autonomy and legitimacy through the new "empowering the manager" ethos of NPM and promoting service responsiveness in lieu of political accountability.[24] By redefining government-citizenry relationship in market terms, civil servants as public-service managers could secure a new basis of legitimacy vis-à-vis citizens as customers through public consumerism and the efficiency paradigm.[25]

On the eve of the handover, despite the intact outer appearance of the civil service, it was already being gradually transformed into a management- and service-driven organization whose performance would be judged more by management and service standards than by political criteria. The principle of political neutrality was being emphasized, even though civil servants at principal official and deputy levels were increasingly behaving as ministers and junior ministers, and were also rendered more politicized by Sino-British conflicts on the transition arrangements, very often forced to take sides between the two sovereign powers. Even so, professionalism and meritocracy remained the defining features of the system, so much so that Chris Patten, in his last policy address in October 1996, put the continuity of the system at the top of his proposed list of benchmarks for appraising the success of Hong Kong as an SAR under China's "one country, two systems" framework: "Is Hong Kong's civil service still professional and meritocratic? Are its key positions filled by individuals who command the confidence of their colleagues and the community and owe their appointments only to their own abilities?"[26]

Post-1997 Civil Service Reform

In March 1999 the Civil Service Bureau of the new SAR government published a consultation document on civil service reform, titled *Civil Service into the 21st Century*. The need for reform was set in the following terms:

> [T]he public have not been happy with the handling of a number of specific incidents by the Government. There are also criticisms that the efficiency of certain departments has to be improved. We take public opinions seriously and are determined to look for ways to further improve the Civil Service.[27]

Three main directions of structural change were identified, namely:

- An open, flexible, equitable, and structured civil service framework, with more flexible entry and exit mechanisms to take in talent and remove nonperformers at all levels;
- An enabling and motivating environment for civil servants, with a competitive but performance-based reward system for attracting, retaining, and motivating civil servants.
- A proactive, accountable, and responsible culture, enhancing efficiency and quality of service and nurturing a performance-based and service-oriented management culture.

On the face of it, the SAR government can be seen as simply following the latest world trends in transforming an overly rigid permanent civil service system into a more market-competitive and flexible workforce in line with prevailing private-sector practices. The reform can be justified by making reference to Britain, to which Hong Kong owed its civil service model, where both the previous Conservative government and the present Labour government have been undertaking major changes to the civil service during the past decade.[28]

For good domestic reasons, despite the great concern for the continuity of the system and for upholding staff morale, the SAR government decided to introduce some fundamental changes to the civil service system as one of the major reform initiatives of Chief Executive Tung Chee-hwa's new administration. In a nutshell, the civil service had suffered crises of efficiency, efficacy, and probity ever since the 1997 handover.

The efficiency crisis was partly triggered by the Asian financial turmoil which led to the worst economic recession in Hong Kong in thirty years. Against such a gloomy scene, well-paid civil servants enjoying lifelong job security and pension protection became targets of the public's and the media's efficiency scrutiny. The fact that private-sector employees' wages were quickly cut back in response to market conditions while civil service pay could at most be frozen (except for the starting pay for new recruits which were lowered) meant that wage disparity between public- and private-sector employees was widened.

Several incidents of crisis mismanagement also revealed the incompetence and sleaziness of some civil servants. The messy way in which government departments handled the outbreak of the infectious "bird flu" and the subsequent slaughter of over 1.2 million chickens in December 1997 put the image of the new government in jeopardy. This was then followed by chaos during the initial opening of the new and highly expensive international airport at Chek Lap Kok in July 1998, resulting in great economic loss in addition to adverse international publicity. By then, the public was persuaded to believe that the civil service was no longer as competent or invincible as it was portrayed to be during the final years of the transition.

Since November 1998, the Director of Audit had published a series of "value-for-money" audit reports accusing junior civil servants, particularly outdoor staff, of sleaziness and laziness, and pointing to the lack of proper middle-management supervision. Not only that, top civil servants who committed improprieties were also exposed by the media—such as a former director of social welfare who traveled first-class to an international conference in Israel and made an unnecessary stopover in Britain for private matters, all paid for by the government; a former commissioner of Inland Revenue who failed to report his wife's business as a tax consultant; a former director of buildings who misused his authority by ordering his staff to take immediate action on an illegal structure attached to a private apartment that he was in the process of purchasing as a retirement home; and a former deputy director of urban services who rented out his government-provided apartment.

These reports and the subsequent public uproar led to demands by legislators and the community at large for more drastic actions to shape up the civil service. A window of opportunity was thus opened for those within the Civil Service Bureau who had already drawn up proposals for reform since the 1993 Human Resources Management Review but were prevented from pushing them ahead in the prehandover years because of Sino-British concerns about civil service morale and stability. By this time, the changes in the domestic political environment, coupled with the public's loss of faith in the hitherto sacrosanct civil service, had convinced the SAR government that reform of the service was unavoidable. As then Secretary for the Civil Service Lam Woon-kwong remarked at a public forum: "If we don't initiate the change ourselves, change will be imposed on us!"[29]

So, despite the rhetoric about facing challenges of the twenty-first century (on which little was in fact said in the March 1999 civil service reform document), the reform blueprint simply aimed at making civil service employment less permanent and secure. The main proposals related to the introduction of more contract appointments, the replacement of retirement pensions by a contributory provident fund, the strengthening of disciplinary mechanisms, and the provision for induced voluntary retirement (namely a voluntary retirement scheme for selected grades and departments where redundancy is expected, and a management-initiated retirement scheme for directorate officers deemed to be no longer promotable or transferable). There was also an attempt to implement schemes to link pay to performance, in order to impress the public that civil servants were worth the better pay and conditions they enjoyed.

Staff reaction to civil service reform was, to say the least, negative. The reform had created not only anxieties about job security, but also ill feelings, after the handover, among the rank and file, who saw it as an attempt by top officials to blame them for failures caused by their own poor leadership and performance. Staff opposition to the reform measures was based on the suspicion that the government was keen on downsizing the civil service and contracting out a whole range of public services to the private sector. Such suspicion was not without ground. Since the launch of the public-sector reform program in 1989, greater involvement of the private sector in the delivery of public services had always been on the government's reform agenda. In addition, senior policy officials had continually given lip service to making the civil service more flexible and more customer oriented. However, nothing too drastic—whether in terms of privatization or in terms of civil service reform—had been contemplated prior to the handover, mainly because the British administration had realized how sensitive and divisive large-scale reforms within the public sector might be. Thus public-sector reforms had taken only the limited shape of performance benchmarks and "pledges," the setting up of "trading funds" for a few selected commercialized services, and budgeting and resource management devolution. The essential terms and conditions of civil servants had remained untouched.

The post-1997 rhetoric of public sector reform was almost of a reverse order. For example, former Financial Secretary Donald Tsang said in his 1999–2000 budget speech that "the public sector should take full advantage of the recession to strengthen its fundamentals. This will help sharpen Hong Kong's competitiveness."[30] Tsang pushed for an "enhanced productivity program" among government departments and subvented agencies, aiming at reducing operating expenditure by 5 percent by 2002–03. He also instigated privatization of public corporations and more contracting out of public services. As a result, in 1999 the Housing Department adopted an ambitious policy of "private-sector involvement" through the phased service transfer of estate management and maintenance services to private firms or staff-initiated "management buyout" companies. Forty-nine per cent of the shares of the government-owned Mass Transit Railway Corporation were floated for sale on the market in September 2000. In his 2000–01 budget speech, Tsang further set the target of reducing the civil service establishment by 10,000 posts or 5 percent over two years.[31]

These measures for scaling down civil service and public-sector involvement, when viewed together, conveyed a message to civil servants quite opposite to the official rhetoric of civil service reform, which was to transform the service so as to make it more efficient and worthy of retention. For the first time in over two decades, there were mass demonstrations organized by civil service unions in the summers of 1999 and 2000, calling upon the government to put a stop to reform. Poor staff morale triggered by the reform also caused resentment and frustration among middle and senior managers of departments. Some legislators now came around to blame the reform for making civil servants restless and unstable.

With the replacement of Lam Woon-kwong by Joseph Wong as secretary for the civil service in February 2000, civil service reform had been quietly toned down in order not to agitate civil servants further. The government has given up the previous proposal to eventually turn all basic ranks, representing two-thirds of the civil service, into contract posts. It has also conceded that a full-fledged performance-related pay system is difficult to develop, if not practically impossible. Instead, attention is now focused on reforming the system of annual salary progression so that "increments" will no longer be taken for granted but will be clearly linked to performance appraisal. On the other hand, the government has succeeded in impressing upon most civil servants that their days of permanent tenure are gone. Voluntary retirement schemes that are now in place give the government greater flexibility in dealing with redundant staff in putting privatization or downsizing plans into effect.

The price for this partial success in civil service reform is a political one. Job security and steady pay progression, supplemented by generous job-related welfare and fringe benefits, had been instrumental in making the colonial civil service one of the most loyal workforces in the world, able to attract the best talent at the point of recruitment because new recruits could look forward to protected and promising careers. With the latest reform, the traditional edge of civil service over private employment is being gradually eroded. In future there will be more movements out of the service, particularly including those induced by voluntary exit schemes. Civil servants will also tend to become less loyal in terms of career commitment, and motivated more by material gains than by a sense of lifelong vocation.

Accountability of Principal Officials

In his 2000 policy address, in confronting the question of governance, Chief Executive Tung Chee-hwa discussed executive accountability as one of the major issues of public concern. He referred to those "principal officials" (numbering more than twenty) who play "an important role in the formulation and implementation of policies pivotal to the effectiveness of the administration."[32] These include the chief secretary for administration, the financial secretary, the secretary for justice, and other secretaries. The rationale for some change to be made to the system of accountability of these top officials was set out as follows:

> At present, most of the principal officials' posts are held by pensionable civil servants. The advantages of having civil servants appointed as principal officials are that they focus on objective analysis, establish internal consensus, maintain the continuity of our policies and ensure a high degree of administrative efficiency. The civil service places special emphasis on discipline, follows very strict codes of conduct and disciplinary procedures, and has maintained a very high standard of integrity. . . . I have noted that the previous Legislative Council and the community have expressed the view that as senior officials are involved in policy making and playing a leading role in public affairs, they should be held accountable for the outcome of their policies.[33]

Tung proposed to review the existing system at two levels:

- The principal officials at secretary rank assume an important role in policy formulation and implementation, which is different from that of other civil servants. Therefore, their accountability for their respective policy portfolios should be enhanced, together with a compatible system of appointment setting out their powers and responsibilities and at the same time defining clearly their role in formulating and implementing government policies under the new system.[34]
- As for the rest of the civil service, the existing principles of permanence and neutrality of the civil service will be preserved.[35]

What these considerations amount to is the introduction of some kind of "ministerial" system based on political appointments, to head the policy portfolios, which until now have been regarded as almost exclusively civil service appointments.[36] Tung's desire for change, despite being clearly a deviation from the Basic Law drafters' original intention to keep Hong Kong as a bureaucratic polity, reflects a result of the tensions at the center of the SAR government between the Executive Council and top civil servants in the few years since the handover. If implemented, the change is likely to open the way to the "presidentialization" of his own office.

"Ministerialization" of Top Civil Servants During British Rule

In contrast to development in Western democracies, as identified by Aberbach, Putnam, and Rockman,[37] whereby top bureaucrats were seen to have grown in influence and power, not only in the formulation of policy but increasingly in the brokerage and articulation of interests, functions conventionally reserved for elected politicians, the case of Hong Kong points to a reverse process. Here the bureaucrats had monopolized such political functions until the 1990s when newly emerging local politicians and political parties began to demand a share of governmental powers. A persistent dilemma facing senior civil servants within an increasingly politicized environment has been how far they should act as a "political officer."

Colonial "cadet officers," later renamed "administrative class officers," had always been expected to act as political officers in British colonies in the past, keeping full control over the indigenous population with the assistance of locally coopted community and tribal leaders, under a regime of indirect rule.[38] In Hong Kong, after the McKinsey reforms, some form of "ministerialization" was clearly in place,[39] with newly created secretaries heading branches of the Government Secretariat in effect playing the role of ministers over heads of departments and agencies. Indeed, such an evolutionary process toward ministerialization was also observed in ex-colonies becoming independent, with former secretariat divisions simply turned into new ministries or ministerial secretariats.[40] In line with such change, administrative class civil servants had become more political in their role orientation. During the days when professional politicians were absent from the scene, administrative officers took up the role of political officers representing the government and seeking support for the government. They formed, de facto, a "government party."

The arrival of a politician-governor, Chris Patten, in 1992 took the ministerialization process further. Patten set an example of political accountability by introducing Governor's Question Time in the Legislative Council and expecting his secretaries to explain and defend government policies in open meetings of the Legislative Council and its panels. Secretaries were also required to engage in active lobbying of political parties, legislators, and various interest groups, and to influence the media, so as to shore up the political legitimacy of government actions. As Patten's governorship focused mostly on relations and negotiations with China over Hong Kong's transition, he had left domestic policies largely to the stewardship of his chief secretary, Anson Chan, and the other secretaries, rendering their political and policy roles even more prominent in the final years of British rule.

Tung Chee-hwa's Paradox: Who to "Executive-Lead"?

One basic mutual understanding between the Chinese and British governments when negotiating Hong Kong's future was that the features of its bureaucratic polity would be preserved, in the name of retaining an "executive-led" system. Hence the Basic Law has imposed various constitutional constraints on the power of the Legislative Council and provided for the principal officials to remain civil servants.

When Tung Chee-hwa was elected chief executive in December 1996,[41] he expressed the wish to exercise "strong leadership" and expected the non–civil service members of his Executive Council to play a prominent policy role. His appointment in March 1997 of three of his executive councilors to lead policy teams to formulate policy proposals on housing, education, and elderly welfare, in preparation for his inauguration, sounded the first alarm to the senior civil servants. In face of bureaucratic opposition and a media uproar over the potential role conflict, Tung backed down by emphasizing that those three executive councilors would perform only a research role and would not convene formal policy teams.

Relations between the Executive Council and the senior civil service headed by Chief Secretary for Administration Anson Chan have remained tense since the handover.[42] Whereas previous members of the governor's Executive Council owed their appointment to the senior civil servants who groomed and nominated them, and were thus willing to work with the latter as loyal partners rather than political rivals, Tung's non–civil service executive councilors owed their political allegiance to him and Beijing leaders instead of the local bureaucracy. To them, an executive-led regime should be one in which the chief executive, together with his closest advisors, constitutes the executive authority, taking charge of policymaking and directing the civil service in policy implementation.

Two Models of Political Accountability

Two executive-led models have been in competition: the mandarins favoring a civil service–dominated ministerial system, and Tung Chee-hwa's supporters preferring a more presidential style of executive government, with more "outsiders" recruited into the SAR government as ministers. These two models fit into the present political tug of war between rival elites within the SAR establishment. On the one hand, the administrative elite of the civil service was keen to retain its policy formulation powers. Many voices in society that were critical of the undemocratically elected chief executive, including pro-democracy parties and legislators, were also skeptical of a political appointment system. To them, given the lack of constitutional checks through popular election and a more empowered legislature, an internal check on Tung's authority by meritocratic mandarins seems an acceptable strategy of expediency. On the other hand, Tung's supporters and other ambitious political actors in the pro-Beijing camp criticized the top civil servants under the leadership of Anson Chan for not giving him sufficient support and loyalty. They put the blame for the posthandover failure in government on the lack of cooperation by the senior civil servants and their incompetence. A political appointment system, in their view, would enable the top echelons of the administration to be filled by Tung loyalists who could make sure that his political agenda be implemented without distortion or delay.

Tung's latest intention to change the system of accountability for principal officials signals a change of heart on the part of the central government in Beijing, which had all along preferred government by bureaucrats. The latter might have been sufficiently persuaded by the advocates of political appointment that Tung's leadership is in danger of dissipation if the existing system continues and the tussle between his supporters and the mandarins persists. The change is also being facilitated by a window of opportunity opened by Tung's adversaries in the pro-democracy camp. In early July 2000, as the term of the first SAR Legislative Council came to an end, the democrats tabled a motion of nonconfidence in Housing Authority Chair Rosanna Wong and Director of Housing Tony Miller over the "short piles" scandal in public housing construction. In the heat of preelection campaign and media criticisms of the Housing Authority, that motion was passed by a majority of the legislature. Rosanna Wong (a non-civil servant) had resigned a few days before the vote, but Tony Miller stayed put on grounds of being a career civil servant. Meanwhile it was clear that the government's credibility had suffered seriously. The political message was that the public could no longer tolerate policy failure by top officials simply because they were of civil service status. This concern was subsequently referred to in Tung's policy address when justifying the need for reform.[43]

Realizing that the status quo is no longer sustainable, the counterproposal from within the civil service, as for example articulated by Secretary for the Civil Service Joseph Wong in a newspaper interview in November 2000,[44] is that any change should still be premised on a system with the civil service continuing to be the main source of supply of politically appointed ministers, rather than recruiting large-scale from the private sector. What the mandarins would prefer is the introduction of a new "political contract" for the secretaries who form a clear political layer, with existing senior civil servants invited to leave their civil service terms to accept appointments on new ministerial terms—that is, walking in full tandem with the chief executive in both political and policy agenda, and being prepared to step down to take political responsibility for policy blunders or if found in political disagreement with him. This is an approach to protect the power interests of the administrative class civil servants.

A more far-reaching blueprint for a ministerial system was offered by the Business and Professionals Federation, a conglomerate of pro-Tung business and professional leaders who are also close to Beijing. In its proposal submitted to Tung in November 2000, the Federation envisaged that future members of the Executive Council would become "policy councilors," who would have clear policy responsibility and would work closely with principal officials. Those principal officials would have to relinquish their position as career civil servants and be offered contract terms if they themselves were appointed executive councilors.[45] "Policy councilors" would be appointed full-time, would be remunerated adequately, and would be expected to be spokespersons for their policy areas and to explain and defend policies before the legislature. They would work closely with policy bureaus and would chair the relevant policy advisory committees. They would be accountable and answerable for any shortcomings in their policy area and could, in serious circumstances, be asked to resign by the chief executive. These executive councilors, in practical terms, would become full-time ministers, over-seeing senior mandarins who would still head bureaus and departments. The Executive Council would in effect become the real cabinet of the chief executive. If implemented, this model will likely see more "exchange of talent among the government, business, academia, think-tanks, public and semi-public bodies, and media organizations,"[46] rendering major nongovernment organizations more intermingled with the government.

Eventually Tung seems to have opted for a tidier ministerial system based on non–civil service (read "political") appointment. In his October 2001 policy address, he expressed his latest thinking as follows:

> Our idea is to introduce a new system of appointing principal officials, applicable to the top three Secretaries . . . and most Directors of Bureaus [i.e., Bureau Secretaries]. . . . The Chief Executive could nominate suitable candidates for all these positions from within or outside the civil service. These officials would be appointed on terms different to [sic] those in the civil service, including remuneration and conditions of service. The appointment contract would clearly state their rights and obligations. Their term of office would not exceed that of the Chief Executive who nominated them. . . . [Their] responsibilities would include formulating and explaining policies, defending policies, canvassing support from the Legislative Council and the public, and be[ing] answerable to the Chief Executive for the success or failure of their policies.[47]

In other words, future principal officials serve at the pleasure of the chief executive. As for existing top civil servants, they will become "permanent secretaries" of bureaus, operating as similar counterparts in the British system. Tung also indicated his intention to appoint all principal officials under the proposed new accountability system to the Executive Council, in addition to the top three secretaries who are members ex-officio.[48] This will mean the shoring up of the authority of the Executive Council as his powerful cabinet, which will exercise coordinated policy leadership over the rest of government. The bitter rivalry for policy domination between the Executive Council and top civil servants that has been witnessed in the last few years will then come to an end.

The optimistic view is that if Tung is able to demonstrate better governance with the recruitment of new talent and a stronger and more coherent policy leadership through political appointment, "popular demand for democratic reform, which is currently mild at best, would become even weaker as the people of Hong Kong become more satisfied with their executive-led government and more disappointed with their legislative representatives."[49] However, an opposite outcome may also arise if the chief executive is seen to be appointing close supporters who are unable to impress the public of their policy expertise and political abilities, thus feeding into further suspicions of a "political spoils" system and inducing even more sustained calls for the top office to be elected by universal franchise rather than by the present narrowly based election committee.

Conclusion

Nearly five years after the handover, it can be seen that the Hong Kong civil service is facing increasing difficulties in retaining its power as the most predominant political institution. Its performance has been seriously questioned both in terms of operational efficiency and crisis management, as well as policy leadership and competence. For senior civil servants who in the colonial past were able to enjoy almost unchallenged power, learning to become politically accountable and to subject themselves to democratic checks and balances is not easy. However, given the present executive power of the civil service, the institution is being appraised by the public in terms of both its administrative and its political performance. In a word, administrative domination in the post-1997 environment now carries both political power and political risk.[50] Senior civil servants cannot have one without the other. Either they take the doctrine of neutrality seriously and accept subservience to politically appointed ministers as their counterparts in all democracies do, or they would have to see their institutional integrity being subjected to prolonged challenge and gradual erosion by a politically more competitive environment, where elected politicians across the political spectrum as well as the newly emerging elites surrounding the chief executive are keen to share their power. The latter prospect is certainly not conducive to maintaining a stable civil service system.

The former colonial civil service legacy, which combined political power and administrative power within a single institution, is likely to witness a gradual separation between the two powers, with the chief executive's appointed ministers and elected legislators constituting a new *political regime* of the SAR, vis-à-vis the *administrative regime* as represented by the senior civil service. As civil service reform evolves, the ethos of bureaucratic culture will also change. Future civil servants, including administrative class officers, may see their jobs less as a lifelong vocation and more as work for reward, as the civil service employment context is gradually transformed to match the private sector. Whereas "managerialization" and "ministerization" started within the pre-1997 civil service following the same institutional logic of bureaucratic governance, these two processes, though continuing in the new SAR era, are now embarking upon divergent routes, so that ultimately two complementary but differently oriented regimes may emerge on the scene.

Notes

1. Before the collapse of Sino-British consensus over the transitional arrangements, the pre-1997 Legislative Council was to be allowed to automatically serve as the first Legislative Council of the new SAR under the so-called through-train model, involving only a nominal confirmation by the SAR Preparatory Committee. See Decision of the National People's Congress (of the People's Republic of China) on the Method for the Formation of the First Government and the First Legislative Council of the Hong Kong Special Administrative Region, April 4, 1990.

2. P. Harris, *Hong Kong: A Study in Bureaucratic Politics* (Hong Kong: Heinemann Asia, 1997), pp. 53–61.

3. Although direct elections, on universal franchise, were introduced to new District Boards in 1981, these boards were only advisory in nature. The first direct election of eighteen out of sixty seats on the Legislative Council took place in 1991.

4. McKinsey & Company, *The Machinery of Government: A New Framework for Expanding Services* (Hong Kong: Government Printer, 1973).

5. The chief executive controls the introduction of public bills, which can be passed by a simple majority of the Legislative Council, whereas in the case of private member's bills a double-majority vote in two "split sections" of the Legislative Council (that is, members elected by geographical direct election and the election committee on the one hand, and members elected by functional constituencies on the other) is required (Appendix 2, Section 2, of the Basic Law). Article 74 of the Basic Law only allows legislators to introduce bills that do not relate to public expenditure or political structure or the operation of the government. The written consent of the chief executive is required before bills relating to government policies can be introduced.

6. S.K. Lau, "Decolonization Without Independence: The Unfinished Political Reforms of the Hong Kong Government," Occasional Paper No. 19 (Hong Kong: Center for Hong Kong Studies, Chinese University of Hong Kong, May 1987), p. 36.

7. Civil Service Bureau, *Civil Service into the 21st Century: Civil Service Reform Consultation Document* (Hong Kong: Printing Department, March 1999).

8. C.H. Tung, *Serving the Community, Sharing Common Goals*, Address at the Legislative Council meeting, October 11, 2000 (Hong Kong: Printing Department), paras. 109–13.

9. A.B.L. Cheung, "Administrative Development in Hong Kong: Political Questions, Administrative Answers." In *Handbook of Comparative Public Administration in the Asia-Pacific Basin*, H.K. Wong and H.S. Chan, ed. (New York: Marcel Dekker, 1999), pp. 219–52.

10. A.Y.C. King, "Administrative Absorption of Politics in Hong Kong: Emphasis on the Grass Roots Level." In *Social Life and Development in Hong Kong*, A.Y.C. King and R.P.L. Lee, ed. (Hong Kong: Chinese University Press, 1981), p. 130.

11. N. Miners, *The Government and Politics of Hong Kong*, 1st ed. (Hong Kong: Oxford University Press, 1975), chap. 15.

12. King, "Administrative Absorption of Politics."

13. McKinsey, *Machinery of Government*.

14. P. Harris, *Hong Kong: A Study in Bureaucracy and Politics* (Hong Kong: Macmillan, 1988), pp. 135–41.

15. Hong Kong government, *Green Paper: The Further Development of Representative Government in Hong Kong* (Hong Kong: Government Printer, July 1984). See also Hong Kong government, *White Paper: The Further Development of Representative Government in Hong Kong* (Hong Kong: Government Printer, November 1984).

16. Hong Kong government, *White Paper: The Development of Representative Government—The Way Ahead* (Hong Kong: Government Printer, February 1988).

17. A.B.L. Cheung, "The Rise of Privatization Policies: Similar Faces, Diverse Motives," *International Journal of Public Administration* 20, no. 12 (December 1997): 2213–45. See also A.B.L. Cheung, "Understanding Public-Sector Reforms: Global Trends and Diverse Agenda," *International Review of Administrative Sciences* 63, no. 4 (December 1997): 435–57.

18. For a detailed account, see A.B.L. Cheung, "Reform in Search of Politics: The Case of Hong Kong's Aborted Attempt to Corporatize Public Broadcasting," *Asian Journal of Public Administration* 19, no. 2 (December 1997): 276–302.

19. Finance Branch, *Public Sector Reform* (Hong Kong, February 1989). See also A.B.L. Cheung, "Public Sector Reform in Hong Kong: Perspectives and Problems," *Asian Journal of Public Administration* 14, no. 2 (December 1992): 115–48.

20. Efficiency Unit, *Serving the Community* (Hong Kong: Government Printer, 1995). See also C. Sankey, "An Overview of Public Sector Reform Initiatives in the Hong Kong Government since 1989." In *Public Sector Reform in Hong Kong: Towards the 21st Century*, A.B.L. Cheung and J.C.Y. Lee, ed. (Hong Kong: Chinese University Press, 2001), pp. 3–30.

21. See, for example, C. Hood, "A Public Management for All Seasons?" *Public Administration* 69, no. 1 (spring 1991): 3–19. See also Organization for Economic Cooperation and Development, *Governance in Transition: Public Management Reforms in OECD Countries* (Paris: OECD, 1995).

22. Cheung, "Public Sector Reform in Hong Kong." See also A.B.L. Cheung, "Efficiency as the Rhetoric? Public-Sector Reform in Hong Kong Explained," *International Review of Administrative Sciences* 62, no. 1 (March 1996): 31–47.

23. C. Hood, "Exploring Variations in Public Management Reforms of the 1980s." In *Civil Service Systems in Comparative Perspective*, H. Bekke, J.L. Perry and T.A.J. Toonen, ed. (Bloomington: Indiana University Press, 1996), pp. 268–87.

24. Cheung, "Efficiency as the Rhetoric?" A.B.L. Cheung, "Public Sector Reform and the Re-legitimation of Public Bureaucratic Power: The Case of Hong Kong," *International Journal of Public Sector Management*, vol. 9, no. 5–6 (1996): 37–50.

25. A.B.L. Cheung, "Performance Pledges—Power to the Consumer or a Quagmire in Public Service Legitimation," *International Journal of Public Administration* 19, no. 2 (February 1996): 233–59.

26. C. Patten, *Hong Kong: Transition*. Address by the governor at the opening of the 1996–97 session of the Legislative Council, October 2 (Hong Kong: Government Printer, 1996), para. 89.

27. Civil Service Bureau, *Civil Service into the 21st Century*, para. 1.2.

28. British government, *The Civil Service: Continuity and Change*, Cmd. 2627 (London: HMSO, July 1994). See also British government, *Modernizing Government*, Cmd. 4310 (London: HMSO, March 1999).

29. Public forum entitled "Civil Service Reform: A Balance Between Stability and Flexibility?" jointly organized by the Center for Comparative Public Management and Social Policy, City University of Hong Kong, and the Hong Kong Policy Research Institute. City University of Hong Kong, May 13, 1999.

30. D. Tsang, *The 1999–2000 Budget: Onward with New Strengths.* Speech by the financial secretary moving the second·reading of Appropriation Bill 1999 at the Legislative Council. (Hong Kong: Printing Department, March 3, 1999), p. 71.

31. D. Tsang, *The 2000–01 Budget: Scaling New Heights.* Speech by the financial secretary, moving the second reading of Appropriation Bill 2000 at the Legislative Council. (Hong Kong: Printing Department (March 8, 2000), p. 119.

32. C.H. Tung, *Serving the Community*, para. 109.

33. Ibid., para. 100–11.

34. Ibid., para. 112.

35. Ibid., para. 113.

36. The only exceptions are Elsie Leung, Secretary of Justice; E.K. Yeoh, Secretary for Health and Welfare; and most recently Antony Leung, Financial Secretary (succeeding Donald Tsang in May 2001). But these secretaries are all still nominally appointed on a civil service contract.

37. J.D. Aberbach, R.D. Putnam, and B.A. Rockman, *Bureaucrats and Politicians in Western Democracies* (Cambridge, MA: Harvard University Press, 1981).

38. F.J.D. Lugard, *Political Memoranda: Revision of the Instructions to Political Officers on Subjects Chiefly Political and Administrative, 1913–1918*, 3rd ed. (London: International Specialized Book Service, 1998).

39. A.S. Huque, G.O.M. Lee, and A.B.L. Cheung, *The Civil Service in Hong Kong: Continuity and Change* (Hong Kong: Hong Kong University Press, 1998), pp. 146–49.

40. R.L. Wettenhall, "Modes of Ministerialization Part I: Towards a Typology— The Australian Experience," *Public Administration* 54, no. 1 (spring 1976): 1–20. See also R.L. Wettenhall, "Modes of Ministerialization, Part II: From Colony to State in the Twentieth Century," *Public Administration* 54, no. 4 (winter 1976): 425–51.

41. Tung was selected by the four-hundred-member Selection Committee formed by the Chinese government–appointed Preparatory Committee for the Hong Kong SAR.

42. Anson Chan retired in May 2001, one year ahead of the expiry of her extended term of office. She was succeeded by former Financial Secretary Donald Tsang.

43. Tung, *Serving the Community*, para. 111.

44. "Special Interview of Mr. Wong Wing-ping," *Hong Kong Economic Journal* 6 (November 2000): 6 [in Chinese].

45. Business and Professionals Federation of Hong Kong, "The Executive Authorities of the HKSAR" (Hong Kong: Business and Professionals Federation of Hong Kong, November 2000).

46. S.K. Lau, "The Revolving-Door Civil Service," *South China Morning Post* (Hong Kong, October 19, 2000).

47. C.H. Tung, *Building on Our Strength, Investing in Our Future.* Address at the Legislative Council meeting (Hong Kong: Printer Department, October 10, 2001), paras. 133–35.

48. Ibid., para. 138.

49. Lau, "Revolving-Door Civil Service."

50. A.B.L. Cheung, "Between Autonomy and Accountability: Hong Kong's Senior Civil Servants in Search of an Identity," in *Ethics in Public Service for the New Millennium*, R. Chapman, ed. (Aldershot, UK: Ashgate, 2000), pp. 185–202.

Bibliography

Aberbach, J.D., R.D. Putnam, and B.A. Rockman. *Bureaucrats and Politicians in Western Democracies.* Cambridge, MA: Harvard University Press, 1981.

The Basic Law of the Hong Kong Special Administrative Region of the People's Republic of China, April 4, 1990.

British Government. *The Civil Service: Continuity and Change*, Cmd. 2627, London: HMSO, July 1994.

―――. *Modernizing Government*, Cmd. 4310, London: HMSO, March 1999.

Business and Professionals Federation of Hong Kong. "The Executive Authorities of the HKSAR," Hong Kong, November 2000.

Cheung, A.B.L. "Public Sector Reform in Hong Kong: Perspectives and Problems." *Asian Journal of Public Administration* 14, no. 2 (December 1992): 115–48.

―――. "Performance Pledges—Power to the Consumer or a Quagmire in Public Service Legitimation." *International Journal of Public Administration* 19, no. 2 (February 1996): 233–59.

―――. "Efficiency as the Rhetoric? Public-Sector Reform in Hong Kong Explained." *International Review of Administrative Sciences* 62, no. 1 (March 1996): 31–47.

―――. "Public Sector Reform and the Re-legitimation of Public Bureaucratic Power: The Case of Hong Kong." *International Journal of Public Sector Management* 9, nos. 5–6 (1996): 37–50.

―――. "The Rise of Privatization Policies: Similar Faces, Diverse Motives." *International Journal of Public Administration* 20, no. 12 (December 1997): 2213–45.

―――. "Understanding Public-Sector Reforms: Global Trends and Diverse Agendas." *International Review of Administrative Sciences* 63, no. 4 (December 1997): 435–57.

―――. "Reform in Search of Politics: The Case of Hong Kong's Aborted Attempt to Corporatize Public Broadcasting." *Asian Journal of Public Administration* 19, no.2 (December 1997): 276–302.

―――. "Administrative Development in Hong Kong: Political Questions, Administrative Answers." In *Handbook of Comparative Public Administration in the Asia-Pacific Basin*, H. K. Wong and H.S. Chan, ed. New York: Marcel Dekker, 1999, pp. 219–52.

―――. "Between Autonomy and Accountability: Hong Kong's Senior Civil Servants in Search of an Identity." In *Ethics in Public Service for the New Millennium*, R. Chapman, ed. Aldershot, UK: Ashgate, 2000, pp. 185–202.

Civil Service Bureau, Hong Kong Government. *Civil Service into the 21st Century: Civil Service Reform Consultation Document.* Hong Kong: Printing Department, 1999.

Efficiency Unit, Hong Kong Government. *Serving the Community.* Hong Kong: Government Printer, 1995.

Finance Branch, Hong Kong Government. *Public Sector Reform.* Hong Kong: Government Printer, 1989.

Harris, P. *Hong Kong: A Study in Bureaucratic Politics.* Hong Kong: Heinemann Asia, 1978.

―――. *Hong Kong: A Study in Bureaucracy and Politics.* Hong Kong: Macmillan, 1988.

"Special Interview of Mr. Wong Wing-ping." *Hong Kong Economic Journal* (November 6, 2000): 6 [in Chinese].

Hong Kong Government. *Green Paper: The Further Development of Representative Government in Hong Kong*. Hong Kong: Government Printer, July 1984.

———. *White Paper: The Further Development of Representative Government in Hong Kong*. Hong Kong: Government Printer, November 1984.

———. *White Paper: The Development of Representative Government—The Way Ahead*. Hong Kong: Government Printer, February 1988.

Hood, C. "A Public Management for All Seasons?" *Public Administration* 69, no. 1 (spring 1991): 3–19.

———. "Exploring Variations in Public Management Reform of the 1980s," In *Civil Service Systems in Comparative Perspective*, H. Bekke, J.L. Perry, and T.A.J. Toonen, ed. Bloomington: Indiana University Press, 1996, pp. 268–87.

Huque, A.S., G.O.M. Lee., and A.B.L. Cheung. *The Civil Service in Hong Kong: Continuity and Change*. Hong Kong: Hong Kong University Press, 1998.

King, A.Y.C. "Administrative Absorption of Politics in Hong Kong: Emphasis on the Grass Roots Level," In *Social Life and Development in Hong Kong*, A.Y.C. King and R.P.L. Lee, ed. Hong Kong: Chinese University Press, 1981, pp. 127–46.

Lau, S.K. "Decolonization Without Independence: The Unfinished Political Reforms of the Hong Kong Government," *Occasional Papers No. 19*. Hong Kong: Center for Hong Kong Studies, Chinese University of Hong Kong, 1987.

———. "The Revolving-Door Civil Service." *South China Morning Post*, October 19, 2000.

Lugard, F.J.D. *Political Memoranda: Revision of the Instructions to Political Officers on Subjects Chiefly Political and Administrative, 1913–1918*, 3d ed. (London: International Specialized Book Service, 1970).

McKinsey & Company. *The Machinery of Government: A New Framework for Expanding Services*. Hong Kong: Government Printer, 1973.

Miners, N. *The Government and Politics of Hong Kong*, 1st ed. Hong Kong: Oxford University Press, 1975.

Organization for Economic Cooperation and Development (OECD). *Governance in Transition: Public Management Reforms in OECD Countries*. Paris: OECD, 1995.

Patten, C. *Hong Kong: Transition*, Address by the governor at the opening of the 1996–97 session of the Legislative Council. Hong Kong: Government Printer, 1996.

Sankey, C. "An Overview of Public Sector Reform Initiatives in the Hong Kong Government Since 1989," In *Public Sector Reform in Hong Kong: Towards the 21st Century*, A.B.L. Cheung and J.C.Y. Lee, ed. Hong Kong: Chinese University Press, 2001, pp. 3–30.

Tsang, D. *The 1999–2000 Budget: Onward with New Strengths*. Speech by the financial secretary, moving the second reading of the Appropriation Bill 1999 at the Legislative Council. Hong Kong: Printing Department, March 3, 1999.

———. *The 2000–01 Budget: Scaling New Heights*. Speech by the financial secretary, moving the second reading of the Appropriation Bill 2000 at the Legislative Council. Hong Kong: Printer Department, March 8, 2000.

Tung, C.H. *Serving the Community, Sharing Common Goals*. Address at the Legislative Council meeting on October 11. Hong Kong: Printing Department, 2000.

———. *Building on Our Strengths, Investing in Our Future*, Address at the Legislative Council meeting, October 10. Hong Kong: Printing Department, 2001.

Wettenhall, R.L. "Modes of Ministerialization, Part I: Towards a Typology—The Australian Experience," *Public Administration* 54, no. 1 (spring 1976): 1–20.

———. "Modes of Ministerialization, Part II: From Colony to State in the Twentieth Century," *Public Administration* 54, no. 4 (winter 1976): 425–51.

——— 7 ———

Chapter 1 of Hong Kong's New Constitution

Constitutional Positioning and Repositioning

Benny Y.T. Tai

On July 1, 1997, the Hong Kong Special Administrative Region (HKSAR) was established. The People's Republic of China (PRC) resumed exercise of its sovereignty over Hong Kong. The Basic Law of the HKSAR is Hong Kong's new constitution. This is a new constitutional order. However, it is not that new. The new constitutional order has inherited many features from the previous order under colonial rule.

Laws previously in force in Hong Kong are basically maintained.[1] The judicial system previously practiced in Hong Kong is maintained except the establishment of the Court of Final Appeal (CFA).[2] The political system of the HKSAR is to a certain extent very similar to that of the colonial system.[3] In addition, many parties that had participated in the constitutional process under the colonial rule reentered into this new constitutional order though some might be in another capacity.[4]

Every participant in the constitutional process, such as the CFA, the Central Government, the chief executive, the principal officials, the legislative council (Legco), and the political parties represented in the Legco, has to position itself under the new constitutional order. Each participant may have its own belief about what should be its role in the new constitutional order. We call the process of identifying and implementing such a role "constitutional positioning." Though the Basic Law has already provided guidelines on what constitutional position the parties should take, they still have room to fine-tune its constitutional position within the imposed constitutional limits.

In this article, we will examine how the different parties in Hong Kong's new constitutional process positioned themselves at the time Hong Kong's new constitutional order was established. We will also look at whether they have repositioned themselves as the new constitutional order has been stretching out it roots in the last three years.

The Court of Final Appeal's Original Constitutional Position

There would be no surprise on what constitutional positions the Central Government, the chief executive, the principal officials, the Legco, and the political parties would take. What was most uncertain immediately after the establishment of the HKSAR was the constitutional position of the newly formed CFA.

Before the transfer of sovereignty, final appeals in Hong Kong went to the Judicial Committee of the Privy Council in London. According to the Basic Law, the HKSAR shall be vested with the power of final adjudication.[5] The CFA exercises the power of final adjudication on behalf of the HKSAR.[6] The establishment of the CFA itself was a constitutional controversy. Because final appeals have to be heard in Hong Kong after the transfer of sovereignty, there was a need to establish the CFA in Hong Kong before the transfer of sovereignty to facilitate transition. However, there were different opinions on the composition of the CFA. The Chinese government insisted that the number of judges from other jurisdictions should be limited to one. Both the Joint Declaration[7] and the Basic Law[8] provide that the CFA "may as required invite judges from other common law jurisdictions" to sit on the CFA. It seems that there could be more than one judge from other common law jurisdictions. After a long negotiation with the Chinese government and internal debates within Hong Kong, the British government finally conceded. After a long delay, the Hong Kong Courts of Final Appeal Ordinance was finally enacted in 1995 but did not take effect until July 1, 1997.[9] The ordinance states that the number of judges from other common law jurisdictions cannot exceed one.[10] At the end, there was not sufficient time to establish the CFA before the transfer of sovereignty. This politicized background caused everyone to wait and see how the CFA would exercise its authority to deal with difficult political questions in constitutional disputes.

However, it was not until early 1999, sixteen months after the establishment of the HKSAR, that the CFA had the opportunity to spell out its constitutional position clearly. The opportunity was provided by the controversial decision concerning the right of abode of mainland children. In *Ng Ka Ling v. Director of Immigration*,[11] the CFA positioned itself as the guardian of Hong Kong's high degree of autonomy, rule of law, and the human rights.

The main dispute of this case was about whether the children of some Hong Kong permanent residents (HKPR) enjoy the right of abode of the newly established HKSAR. According to Article 24(2)(3) of the Basic Law, the children of HKPR[12] born outside Hong Kong enjoy the right of abode in the HKSAR. Before the transfer of sovereignty, these children did not have the right of abode in Hong Kong. Anticipating that they could have the right of abode in the HKSAR after the coming into effect of the Basic Law, many of these children illegally entered Hong Kong or overstayed in Hong Kong. Immediately after the transfer of sovereignty, they approached the Immigration Department seeking for recognition of their status as HKPR. There was no accurate estimation on the number of these children, but the HKSAR government feared that the sudden inrush of these children into the HKSAR might have an impact on social services that would be extremely difficult for the HKSAR to bear. Nine days after the transfer of sovereignty, the Provisional Legislative Council (PLC) enacted amendments to the Immigration Ordinance[13] limiting the rights of these mainland children to exercise their alleged right of abode. The legality of the amendments to the Immigration Ordinance were challenged in the courts of the HKSAR and finally heard by the CFA in *Ng Ka Ling*.

Logically, before the CFA could consider the substantial issues of the case, it had to first consider the constitutionality of the PLC, the body that enacted the amendments. The Preparatory Committee of the HKSAR,[14] in accordance with some decisions and resolutions of the National People's Congress (NPC) and its standing committee (SCNPC), set up the PLC.[15] However, nowhere in the Basic Law is any institution like the PLC mentioned.[16] Was there any contradiction between the decisions and resolutions of the national legislatures and the Basic Law? Would such contradiction deprive the constitutionality of the PLC?

There was an even more fundamental question: Do the courts of the HKSAR, as regional courts in an autonomous entity, have the jurisdiction to make ruling on these questions? The Court of Appeal of the HKSAR in *HKSAR v. Ma Wai-kwan David and others*[17] had already considered this question and decided that the courts of the HKSAR have no such jurisdiction. The CFA in *Ng Ka Ling* chose to deal with the question on the constitutionality of the PLC after it had dealt with the substantial issues. However, the CFA was keen to assert the jurisdiction and the judicial authority of the courts of the HKSAR clearly and boldly even before it touched on the substantial issues of the case.

The CFA overruled the decision of the Court of Appeal on the following grounds. First, the CFA disagreed with the general constitutional principle that there is no legal basis for regional courts to have jurisdiction to query the validity of any legislation or acts passed by the sovereign so relied on by the Court of Appeal.[18] The CFA, instead, put forward another general constitutional principle. Every constitution needs an independent judicial body to enforce it so that no other laws can contradict it. If inconsistency is established, the independent judicial body is bound to hold the law invalid. The CFA emphasized the constitutional status of the Basic Law, as it described the Basic Law as a constitution. Like other constitutions, the Basic Law distributes and delimits power. The courts of the HKSAR as the bodies exercising independent judicial power in the HKSAR must then be the bodies that enforce the Basic Law. Therefore, the courts of the HKSAR must have the power to review and invalidate a law enacted by the legislature of the HKSAR or executive act of the government of the HKSAR that is inconsistent with the Basic Law.[19] This reasoning is a typical "rule-of-law" analysis.

As against the legislative acts of the NPC and the SCNPC, the CFA relied further on the high degree of autonomy enjoyed by Hong Kong. The power of the courts of the HKSAR to review the compatibility of the legislative acts of the NPC or the SCNPC with the Basic Law was derived from the sovereign. To the CFA, this was a power that was necessary for Hong Kong to enjoy the high degree of autonomy that was granted to the HKSAR by the NPC in accordance with Article 31 of the Constitution of the PRC and the Basic Law.[20]

The CFA also rejected the Court of Appeal's analogy of the jurisdiction of colonial courts. The Court of Appeal decided that as the colonial courts of Hong Kong had no power to review the constitutionality of Acts of Parliament before the transfer of sovereignty, the courts of the HKSAR should also not have such power after the transfer of sovereignty. The main ground relied on was Article 19(2) of the Basic Law. It provides that "the courts of the HKSAR shall have jurisdiction over all cases in the HKSAR, except that the restrictions on their jurisdiction imposed by the legal system and principles previously in force in Hong Kong shall be maintained." The CFA decided that Article 19(2) of the Basic Law could not transplant a restriction of the previous constitutional order to the new constitutional order that is not compatible with the high degree of autonomy enjoyed by the HKSAR under the new order. Limiting the jurisdiction of the courts' power to review legislative acts of the NPC and the SCNPC on the basis of the doctrine of Parliamentary Supremacy was such restriction that cannot survive the transfer of sovereignty.[21]

After considering the jurisdiction of the courts of the HKSAR and before it touched on the substantial issues of the case, the CFA further developed its approach to interpretation of the Basic Law. The CFA suggested that a generous approach should be adopted in interpreting Chapter III of the Basic Law, which sets out the constitutional guarantees for the freedoms of the residents of the HKSAR. This will give Hong Kong residents the full measure of constitutionally guaranteed fundamental rights and freedoms. In interpreting other provisions of the Basic law, including the provision that defines the class of Hong Kong residents, the courts should simply consider the language in the light of any ascertainable purpose and the context. The context includes the provisions of the International Covenant on Civil and Political Rights (ICCPR) as applied to Hong Kong, which remain in force by virtue of Article 39 of the Basic Law.[22] No matter that, in interpreting the provisions that directly provide guarantee to fundamental rights and freedoms and all the other provisions, the protection of human rights in Hong Kong is a primary consideration. The CFA believed that human rights protection lies at the heart of Hong Kong's system and is one of the ultimate purposes of the Basic Law.[23]

Another question was about the mechanism of interpretation. According to the Basic Law, the courts of the HKSAR have the power to interpret on their own, in adjudicating cases, the provisions of the Basic Law that are within the limits of the autonomy of the region (nonexcluded provisions). The courts of the HKSAR also have the power to interpret other provisions of the Basic Law in adjudicating cases. However, if the CFA, in adjudicating cases, needs to interpret the provisions of the Basic Law concerning affairs that are the responsibility of the Central Government, or concerning the relationship between the Central Authorities and the HKSAR (excluded provisions), it has to seek an interpretation of the relevant provisions from the SCNPC if such interpretation will affect the judgment on the case. In *Ng Ka Ling*, the concrete question was whether the CFA is under a duty to refer both provisions to the SCNPC for interpretation under Article 158(3) of the Basic Law if the CFA has to interpret a nonexcluded provision and an excluded provision together in adjudicating a case.[24]

The CFA developed the "predominant provision test" to answer this question. According to this test, the CFA will look at the provisions and see, as a matter of substance, which provision is the predominant provision that has to be interpreted in the adjudication of the case. If the predominant provision is an excluded provision, the CFA is then obliged to refer. If the predominant provision is a nonexcluded provision, then no reference has to be made, although an excluded provision of the Basic Law is arguably relevant to the construction of this provision even to the extent of qualifying it. The CFA again relied on the principle of rule of law and the high degree of autonomy enjoyed by the Hong Kong as justifications for the test.

The test allowed the courts of the HKSAR to interpret the provisions of the Basic Law independently especially those provisions that are assigned to the courts of the HKSAR to interpret on its own in adjudicating cases. The CFA also found that if it were to be required to refer a nonexcluded provision to the SCNPC for interpretation whenever an excluded provision is only relevant to the previous article, it would take away the jurisdiction of the CFA the power to interpret nonexcluded provisions of the Basic Law, which are within the limits of the autonomy of the region. This would be a substantial derogation from the high degree of autonomy enjoyed by the HKSAR. Only the "predominant test" can prevent this.[25]

Finally, the CFA considered the substantial issues of the case and similar constitutional positioning could be found in the reasoning. There were three main issues concerning the right of abode of the mainland children. Firstly, one of the amendments added some procedural requirements that all claimants of the HKSAR permanent resident status under Article 24(2)(3) of the Basic Law[26] must satisfy before they could exercise their status as HKPR. They must hold a valid certificate of entitlement affixed to an one-way exit permit.[27] The application for a certificate of entitlement must be made through the Exit-Entry Administration of the Public Security Bureau in mainland China.[28] The Public Security Bureau is also responsible for issuing the one-way permits. In effect, it would be officials in the mainland but not the HKSAR government who would grant the permission for the mainland children to exercise their HKPR status and decide their order of arrival into the HKSAR. Though Article 24(2)(3) of the Basic Law does not include procedural requirement, it was argued that Article 22(4) of the Basic Law could supply the constitutional authority to support such an amendment. Article 22(4) provides that "people from other parts of China" must apply for approval from mainland Chinese authorities for entry into the HKSAR.

The CFA held that this amendment contradicted the Basic Law and was invalid. Article 22(4) was held to be irrelevant, as people from other parts of China could not include the mainland children. They are HKPR upon whom the Basic Law confers the right of abode in the HKSAR and Article 22(4) could not be used to qualify their right of abode. Article 24(2)(3) also could not qualify the high degree of autonomy of the HKSAR. The HKSAR, exercising a high degree of autonomy, is obliged to admit people who under its constitution are its permanent residents with the constitutional right of abode. This should not be subject to the discretionary control of mainland authorities, which have the power to determine both the quota and the allocation within the quota under the one-way permits system.[29]

The amendments also aimed to limit the number of person eligible for the right of abode under Article 24(2)(3) of the Basic Law. The amendments excluded illegitimate children[30] and those who were born to their parents before they became HKPR.[31] In another words, the amendments added more requirements to the express provision of Article 24(2)(3). The CFA decided that these amendments contradicted Article 24(2)(3) of the Basic Law by applying its approach of interpreting the Basic Law, which is very much human rights oriented. The CFA relied on the principle of equality as enshrined by Article 25 of the Basic Law and Articles 3 and 26 of the ICCPR and the right to family life, including the right to family union, so recognized by Article 23(1) of the ICCPR to invalidate the amendment that excluded illegitimate children.[32] Similarly, the CFA invalidated the amendment that excluded those who were born to their parents before they became HKPR by referring to the right to family life protected by Article 23(1) of the ICCPR.[33]

These are still indirect references to the ICCPR and the values and principles of human rights contained therein. The CFA further relied on Article 15(1) of the ICCPR to directly strike down the retrospectivity of the amendments,[34] as they were stated to have retrospective effect from July 1, 1997.[35] Article 15(1) of the ICCPR provides that no one shall be held guilty of any criminal offense on account of any act or omission which did not constitute a criminal offense, under national or international law, at the time when it was committed. By such direct reference, the CFA had also clarified the constitutional status of the ICCPR in the HKSAR. The CFA made it very clear that Article 39 of the Basic Law gives the ICCPR constitutional force in Hong Kong. However, there was no discussion of the legal effect of the repeal of the section 2(3)[36] 3[37] and 4[38] of the Hong Kong Bill of Rights Ordinance (HKBORO)[39] by the SCNPC.[40] The intention of the SCNPC of this decision, made in 1997 before the establishment of the HKSAR, was clearly to take away any superior legal status enjoyed by the HKBORO (if any) and the ICCPR before the transfer of sovereignty in Hong Kong.[41] The CFA just assumed that the ICCPR enjoys such constitutional status. This indeed provided the foundation for human rights protection in the new constitutional order of Hong Kong.

Though the CFA has positioned itself as the guardian of Hong Kong's high degree of autonomy, the guardian of Hong Kong's rule of law and the guardian of human rights in Hong Kong, it had not ignored the interest and concern of Hong Kong's sovereign. Though the CFA had unequivocally asserted the constitutional jurisdiction to review the legislative acts of the NPC and the SCNPC, in the review itself the CFA accepted the legality of the PLC without much questioning.[42] Knowing the political and practical significance of the PLC, the CFA dared not question its legality.

Court of Final Appeal Under Challenge

Though the CFA finally endorsed the legality of the PLC, serious criticisms, clearly with the endorsement of the Central Government, were fired at the CFA by four mainland legal experts, all of whom had been involved in the drafting of the Basic Law.[43] They criticized the CFA for putting itself above the NPC and the SCNPC. The jurisdiction of the CFA could not be extended to Beijing and the Basic Law has not granted such authority to the CFA. Such power of review asserted by the CFA is sovereign in nature and it is ridiculous that the CFA could have such power. The most serious criticism was that the judgment would have transformed Hong Kong into an independent political entity.[44]

After the Central Government expressed reservations,[45] the secretary for justice representing the government of the HKSAR made an application to the CFA requesting for a clarification concerning the constitutional jurisdiction of the courts of the HKSAR. The CFA accepted the application and exercised what it considered to be the inherent jurisdiction of the court to make a clarification.[46] In the clarification, the CFA just restated its original principle from another perspective. In the original judgment, the CFA stated that the courts of the HKSAR have the jurisdiction to review and invalidate legislative acts of the NPC and the SCNPC if those acts are inconsistent with the Basic Law. In the clarification, the CFA stated that the courts have no power to question the authority of the NPC and the SCNPC to do any act, which is in accordance with the Basic Law and the procedure therein. At this stage, the CFA was still very reluctant to reposition itself even in face of such serious criticisms from the Central Government. However, the Central Government seemed to be satisfied with such clarification and the first wave of challenge against the CFA was settled.

The second wave of challenge came not from outside but from within Hong Kong. This time it was against the substantive decisions of the case. The secretary for security announced the number of persons eligible for the right of abode in the HKSAR if the CFA judgments were to be enforced.[47] It would be around 1.7 million. This figure was compiled on the basis of a reestimation after a survey conducted by the HKSAR government. Using these data, the HKSAR government fanned the public opinion against the decisions of the CFA. It got support from the public to overturn the decisions of the CFA. A motion was moved in the Legco to support the chief executive's decision to request the State Council to invite the SCNPC to interpret Article 22(4) and Article 24(2)(3) of the Basic Law. Such motion was passed[48] and a report by the chief executive was sent to the Central People's Government asking for its assistance in seeking to have the SCNPC reinterpret Articles 22(4) and 24(2)(3) of the Basic Law.[49] As a result, the SCNPC re-interpreted the two provisions.[50] The interpretation in effect overruled the decisions of the CFA.

Faced with such challenges to the authority of the courts of the HKSAR, the CFA found that it must reposition itself to avoid any such challenge to happen again. Before we look at how the CFA handled such challenges, we will first examine the constitutional positions of the other parties in the constitutional process. It is interesting to see how the constitutional positions of other parties in the constitutional process may affect the repositioning of the CFA.

The Central Government's Constitutional Position

The Central Government has already reserved for itself much power in the Basic Law. First, the Central Government retains the power to enact and[51] amend the Basic Law[52] and is responsible for the defense[53] and foreign affairs[54] of the HKSAR. These are quite legitimate powers retained by the mother-state in an autonomous arrangement. The Central Government further retains the power to review local legislation[55] and the power to apply national laws to the HKSAR in limited situations.[56] They are also quite legitimate, as the HKSAR is not an independent state and can only exercise powers granted to her by the mother-state. There must be a certain mechanism that will enable the Central Government to ensure that the autonomous entity will not exceed its scope of autonomy. According to the Basic Law, the Central Government can only exercise these powers under certain conditions. This seems to be guarantees to protect the autonomy of the HKSAR from unnecessary intervention from the Central Government. However, the Central Government also enjoys the power to interpret the Basic Law and this may be its most important power.[57] It can then also determine whether the conditions for exercising the above-mentioned powers are satisfied or not. In other words, all such constitutional limits can only be self-imposed.

Through these constitutional arrangements, it has all the necessary powers to influence or even decide affairs within the HKSAR. However, since the transfer of sovereignty, the Central Government is keen to give an impression to the outside world that Hong Kong, under "one country, two systems," is able to decide its own affairs. It will respect the high degree of autonomy enjoyed by the HKSAR and restrict itself from committing any act that may cause people to suspect any interference. The constitutional position taken by the Central Government is an open-minded sovereign.

There might be another reason to explain such constitutional positioning. The Central Government allows the HKSAR to have the maximum degree of freedom because there is no need to interfere. By ensuring the selection of a loyal chief executive and granting him vast powers, it can more or less assure that the HKSAR would be in safe and trusted hands. The first chief executive was selected under the close supervision of the Central Government.

The several incidents during this period that might arouse concern about intervention from the Central Government in the internal affairs of the HKSAR were all not initiated by the Central Government. These included the attack of the four mainland legal experts on the CFA's decision in *Ng Ka Ling* concerning the constitutional jurisdiction of the courts of the HKSAR and the re-interpretation of Articles 22(4) and 24(2)(3) of the Basic Law by the SCNPC in response to a request from the first chief executive via the Central Government. Even when members of the Falun Gong in Hong Kong have taken a strong stand against the Central Government,[58] the Central Government still left the matter to the first chief executive.

Constitutional Positions of the First Chief Executive

The Basic Law has already assigned a difficult balancing task to the chief executive of the HKSAR. The chief executive is to be accountable to both the Central Government and the HKSAR. If there is a conflict between the interest of the Central Government and the HKSAR, he will have to make a choice. No matter what his choice, he will be in a constitutional position that cannot please everyone. The first chief executive, Tung Chee Hwa, knows very well the kind of constitutional position he takes. He is extremely careful in handling this delicate balance between the Central Government and the HKSAR. In order to fulfill his dual accountability, the best way is to avoid any such conflict of interests to arise.

This consideration caused the first chief executive, on many occasions in the last three years, to try to predict what the Central Government liked or disliked, and then to act accordingly so as not to antagonize it. The first example came even before the transfer of sovereignty. The Central Government had already voiced its objection to the Hong Kong Bill of Rights (HKBORO) at the time of its enactment. The colonial government was also criticized for having amended a lot of Hong Kong laws, including the Public Order ordinance[59] and the Societies Ordinance,[60] on the basis of the HKBORO. As it is stated in the Joint Declaration that the laws in Hong Kong should remain basically unchanged,[61] the Central Government considered such amendments were against the Joint Declaration. The first chief executive, a designate at that time, proposed Public Order (Amendment) Bill 1997 and the Societies (Amendment) Bill 1997, and these were passed by the PLC. The Reunification Ordinance enacted by the PLC immediately after the transfer of sovereignty confirmed these bills.[62] The amendments to the Public Order Ordinance repeal the notification system and revive a licensing system for public processions. A public procession may take place only if a notification is made to the commissioner of police and there is a notice of no objection issued by the commissioner of police.[63] The amendments to the Societies Ordinance repeal the notification system and revive a licensing system for the formation of societies.[64] There are also additional restrictions on the formation of societies in the HKSAR. A political body[65] that has a connection with a foreign political organization[66] or a political organization of Taiwan[67] may be refused registration in the HKSAR. These additional restrictions were intended to implement part of the provision of Article 23 of the Basic Law. During the last four and a half years, these laws, especially the Public Order Ordinance, were enforced in general in a liberal manner. However, the police authority in some occasions had used its power in some ways that severely restricted the rights of demonstrators to freely and effectively exercise their freedom of expression and freedom of peaceful assembly.[68]

Another example concerned the conflict of jurisdiction between the courts of the mainland and the HKSAR. Cheung Tze-keung, nicknamed "Big Spender," and his gangsters were suspected to have committed a series of criminal acts in Hong Kong and on the mainland. Cheung and some of his cohorts are Hong Kong residents. They were arrested in mainland China and prosecuted on various offenses. What had aroused public concern was that some of the charges were concerned with acts committed purely in Hong Kong. The lawyer representing Cheung wrote a letter to the secretary for justice requesting her to take action to have the trial of Cheung transferred to Hong Kong, as some of the offenses were allegedly committed in Hong Kong.[69] The secretary for justice rejected this request on the ground that the courts in the mainland had the jurisdiction to try Cheung's case, as he and his cohorts had committed offenses that occurred purely in the mainland.[70] At the trial it was revealed that the courts of the mainland had not just considered the acts committed in the mainland by Cheung and his gangsters but also the acts committed by them in Hong Kong. Nonetheless, the secretary for justice still refused to assert the jurisdiction of the HKSAR over Cheung's case as against the courts in the mainland. Another reason for the refusal was that there was yet no rendition agreement between Hong Kong and the mainland over the transfer of fugitives.[71]

In another case, a mainland resident was suspected to have murdered five Hong Kong residents. He escaped back to mainland China and was arrested there. The secretary for justice again refused to make a request to the Chinese authorities to have the suspect be transferred to the HKSAR for trial here. Similar reasons were given to explain the inaction.[72] Such refusals were seriously criticized in Hong Kong.[73] Article 18 of the Basic Law provides that only national laws listed in Annex III will be applicable to Hong Kong. The inaction of the HKSAR government actually allowed the indirect application of the Criminal Law of the PRC to the HKSAR, though it is not within the list of national laws applicable to Hong Kong. The HKSAR government also failed to assert the jurisdiction of the courts of the HKSAR, though the

Basic Law provides that the courts of the HKSAR have jurisdiction over all cases in the HKSAR.

When the four mainland legal experts criticized the CFA in *Ng Ka Ling* on behalf of the Central Government, the application by the secretary for justice to the CFA requesting for a clarification was another such incident. These incidents showed that the first chief executive was prepared to give up a certain degree of autonomy of the HKSAR even when there was no expressed request from the Central Government in order to avoid conflict. One may doubt whether this has gone too far.

Another major concern of the first chief executive is to maintain order in the HKSAR, and this also affects his constitutional positioning. This is also closely linked with his avoid-any-conflict position. As the Central Government believes that stability and prosperity in Hong Kong are of utmost importance to the implementation of "one country, two systems" in the HKSAR, it is natural that the first chief executive takes such a constitutional position. In addition, it is important to demonstrate his ability to rule Hong Kong. This factor was the most important force that caused the first chief executive to seek a reinterpretation by the SCNPC after the CFA's decision in *Ng Ka Ling*.

Aw Sian, the chair of a newspaper group in Hong Kong, was not prosecuted together with three current and former senior executives of the company. They were charged of conspiracy to defraud, and Aw Sian was also named as one of the parties of the conspiracies stated. There was worry that the pro–Central Government background of Aw Sian (who was close to Tung Chee Hwa) might have saved her from prosecution.[74]

The Secretary for Justice stated that her decision not to prosecute Aw Sian had a twofold basis.[75] One reason was insufficient evidence; the other was public interest. The secretary for justice's decision not to prosecute Aw Sian seemed to have been affected also by such "order" consideration. Her explanation of what constituted public interest in this case attracted fierce criticism. She stated that if Aw Sian were to be prosecuted, it would seriously affect the restructuring of the Sing Tao Group, of which Aw Sian was the chair, and that the group was facing serious financial difficulties. The secretary for justice further explained that if the group should collapse, its newspapers (which include one of only two local English-language dailies in Hong Kong) would, in all likelihood, be compelled to cease operation. The result was considered to be damaging, as it would push up the unemployment rate in Hong Kong. Very negative messages would have been sent to the international community, to the effect that a well-established and important media group could not survive. This interpretation of public interest was criticized as being against the general principle of equality before the law and the rule of law. Rich people, if they employed many people and their businesses were considered to be important, could be exempted from the punishment imposed by law.[76] However, what has been considered may only be "order" in the short run. Sacrificing the final adjudicative power of the CFA and the rule of law may affect "order" within Hong Kong in the long run.

There is one more matter that has affected the constitutional positioning of the first chief executive: his relationship with the civil service of Hong Kong. Though Tung himself was a member of the Executive Council under colonial rule, he did not have any actual experience in running a government. He has to rely on the expertise and support of the civil service in order to rule the HKSAR. However, also owing to his concern to maintain order, continuity, and stability, he chose not to appoint his own team as the first batch of principal officials. Instead, he reappointed almost all the secretaries under the colonial rule to be the corresponding principal officials in the new HKSAR government (except the secretary of justice).[77] This indeed has planted seeds of conflict within the HKSAR government. Some senior officials within the HKSAR government did not share the same view as the first chief executive on how the HKSAR government should position itself under the new constitutional order. The premature retirement in April 2001 of the chief secretary for administration, Anson Chan, raised serious suspicions about conflict between her and the first chief executive. The last public speech given by Anson Chan in her capacity as chief secretary for administration may give us some hints.[78]

Another constitutional position of the first chief executive is concerned with the internal affairs of Hong Kong. In many local policies, the first chief executive has danced between "maintain" and "develop" without any consistent pattern. The housing policies and education policies of the HKSAR government in the last three years were subject to serious criticisms. The first chief executive has exerted much effort to show that he is a reformer as well as a conservative. This balance like the previous balance is not easy to strike.

Constitutional Positions of the Principal Officials

A feature of the political system of the HKSAR that is very similar to the colonial government is the role of the senior civil servants.[79] As mentioned, the first chief executive nominated only senior civil servants as his principal officials at the time of the establishment of the HKSAR, though the Basic Law does not require him to do so.[80]

Principal officials of the HKSAR under the Basic Law are responsible for not only implementing the policies but also formulating the policies. However, principal officials inherited the tradition of senior civil servants under the colonial order to position themselves as neutral administrators. Though they are policymakers, as civil servants, principal officials need not be politically accountable for their decisions. They claim that they are not making political decisions in the sense that the decisions should not reflect the interest of a particular political party, person, or class of people in Hong Kong but are decisions made in the long-term interest of Hong Kong as a whole.[81]

Some recent events might demythologize this constitutional position of the principal officials. One of the principal officials recently openly stated that senior civil servants always have their political stance and are never politically neutral.[82]Another incident was the appointment of Anthony Leung as the new financial secretary. Leung was a banker before he took up this senior post in the HKSAR government. The first chief executive might have already started a new convention by breaking away from the long tradition of appointing noncivil servants to senior posts in the government.[83] He may want to build up his own team of officials and look to the business world for his pool of leadership rather than to the civil servants.

In his policy address 2000, the first chief executive stated that there would be a thorough review on the system of accountability of the principal officials, including the appointment of principal officials, their powers and responsibilities, and their role in formulating and implementing government policies. It is very likely that the principal officials will have to reposition themselves away from this role of neutral administrators. Another thing can be certain is that the review will not change the constitutional position of the executive authority as a whole vis-à-vis the Legislative Council as the dominating partner in their relationship.

Constitutional Positions of the Legislative Council and the Political Parties

The Basic Law has already assumed that the Legco will not be a very influential figure in the constitutional process. One reason is its composition, and the other is its scope of power.

The design of the composition of the Legco prevents a formation of majority party in the Legco. The objective is to divide and rule. The different election methods of the members of the Legco—geographical direct election, functional constituencies election, and the electoral committee election—make it extremely difficult for a single party to control the majority in the Legco. Different sectors elect their own representatives to the Legco through the functional constituencies election and the electoral committee election, and different interests are represented in the Legco. A proportional representation system replaces the single-vote, single-seat system used in the 1995 election in the geographical direct elections. This method makes it easier for small political parties to win a seat in the election. With such a divided Legco, the chief executive may easily evade all possible checks on his powers from the Legco.

Even a united front could be formed in the Legco if its powers are limited. According to the Basic Law, the executive authority is accountable to the Legco.[84] However, it only needs to implement laws passed by the Legco, present regular policy addresses, answer questions raised by members of the Council, and obtain approval from the Council for taxation and public expenditure. Government officials need not be politically accountable for their decisions.

There are also strict limitations on the ability of Legco members to initiate any policy change under the Basic Law.[85] The executive authority managed to utilize the friendlier PLC to freeze[86] and repeal[87] some policy changes caused by the passage of a number of private member bills[88] in the last days of the last Legco under the colonial rule. The limitations have two levels and are even harsher than during British colonial rule. Firstly, members of the Legco cannot introduce bills that are related to public expenditure or political structure or the operation of the government. For bills that are not related to these items, members may still have to get the written consent of the chief executive if government policies are involved. In other words, there is nothing significant that members of the Legco can introduce. There is also a different set of procedure for the passage of private members bills. The passage of motions, bills, or amendments to government bills introduced by individual members of the Legco requires a simple majority vote of each of the two groups of members present. The first group includes members returned by functional constituencies, and the second group includes those returned by geographical constituencies through direct elections and by the Election Committee.[89] Practically, it will be very difficult for the Legco to pass any bill that is against the interest of the business class in Hong Kong.

As no political party represented in the Legco could control the majority, the political parties have to cooperate among themselves before they can have some slight impact on the policies of the Government of the HKSAR. However, sometimes such cooperation is not easy. Political parties in Hong Kong cannot be classified as left-wing and right-wing parties, as is done in many Western states. If Hong Kong political parties were so classified, the resulting political grouping would be very different from groupings formed in classification according to their relationships with the Central Government and the first chief executive. Another method of classification is based on how the parties look at the democratic development of Hong Kong. As a result, it is rather difficult for the political parties to form a united front against the executive authority. In addition, there are quite a number of independent members not associated with any political parties, and this makes it even more difficult to form a united front.

As a result, the Legco does not have a capacity to position itself in any significant way, other than by putting up a weak or feeble opposition to the government.

Repositioning of the Court of Final Appeal

There was no major change in the constitutional positions of the other parties in the constitutional process. The parties acted in accordance with their own constitutional positions only after the CFA's controversial judgment in *Na Ka Ling*, but actions they had taken or decisions made forced the CFA to reposition itself.

After the interpretation made by the SCNPC, the CFA finally had to consider how it should reposition itself in *Lau Kong Yong v. Director of Immigration*.[90] *Lau Kong Yong* was another mainland children case. The applicants in the case were mainland residents who were physically present in Hong Kong without the permission of the director of immigration. They claimed that they had the right of abode in Hong Kong by descent on the basis that at least one of their parents was a HKPR according to Article 24(2)(3) of the Basic Law. After the decision of the CFA in *Ng Ka Ling*, the original scheme allowing mainland children to apply to come to the HKSAR was modified. However, the modified scheme was not able to operate, as the HKSAR government had not yet reached any agreement with the mainland authorities on how to implement the modified scheme. The director issued a removal order against the applicants, and they sought judicial review of the decisions of the director.

The judgments of the Court of First Instance and the Court of Appeal were made before the interpretation by the SCNPC, and they decided the questions on very different grounds from those of the CFA. The case reached the CFA after the interpretation, and the CFA had to face three questions: First, does the SCNPC have the power to make the interpretation? Second, what is the effect of the interpretation? Third, from what date is the interpretation applicable?

The CFA accepted the freestanding power of the SCNPC to interpret the Basic Law on the basis of Article 67(4) of the Chinese Constitution and Article 158(1) of the Basic Law. The SCNPC may interpret the Basic Law even without a referral from the CFA, under Article 158(3) of the Basic Law. Like an interpretation made by the SCNPC upon a referral from the CFA, the CFA is required to apply the Interpretation in adjudication. The effect of the interpretation is dated backed to July 1, 1997, when the Basic Law came into effect. It declared what the law has always been.

On the basis of such conclusions on the interpretation, the CFA decided against the applicants. In addition, the CFA noted that the SCNPC had, in the preamble to the Interpretation, expressed the view that the CFA in *Ng Ka Ling* had wrongly not sought an interpretation of the relevant provisions of the Basic Law from the SCNPC, in compliance with the requirement of Article 158(3). In light of such a view, the CFA admitted that it might need to revisit the predominant test in an appropriate case in the future.

Some criticized the CFA for making too much compromise in accepting unconditionally the freestanding power of the SCNPC to interpret the Basic Law. However, the CFA did not have much choice. The situation in *Lau Kong Yong* was different from the situation in which the clarification after *Ng Ka Ling* was issued. The SCNPC had already issued an interpretation that, in effect, overruled the CFA's interpretation in *Ng Ka Ling*. The CFA could not play with words to avoid direct conflict with the Central Government without changing its own stance.

Though the CFA could argue that the Interpretation was not binding on the CFA, as it was not delivered out of a referral from the CFA under Article 158(3), it would put the CFA into an even more difficult situation. If the CFA refused to accept the authority of the SCNPC to issue such interpretation, this would be a direct challenge against the authority of the Central Government. Such an act would just invite the Central Government to interfere further into the affairs of the HKSAR. There is a real risk that the Central Government would further limit the judicial authority of the CFA and the courts of the HKSAR, which the CFA had built up with much effort after the transfer of sovereignty. Grounds gained, such as the power of the CFA to decide whether there is a need to refer a provision for interpretation by the SCNPC under Article 158(3) of the Basic Law and the constitutional status of the ICCPR, might lose.

Among the different constitutional positions of the CFA (i.e., as the guardian of Hong Kong's high degree of autonomy, the guardian of Hong Kong's rule of law, and the guardian of human rights in Hong Kong), the CFA found these constitutional positions conflict among themselves and it had to make a choice. The CFA had decided that its constitutional position as the guardian of the rule of law to be more important at the price of the other two roles. By accepting the freestanding power of the SCNPC to interpret, the CFA had avoided further ingress on the judicial authority by the courts of the HKSAR, which is significant to the maintenance of rule of law in the HKSAR.

If *Lau Kong Yong* evidenced a reluctant compromise made by the CFA, *HKSAR v. Ng Kung-Siu and Lee Kin-Yun*[91] demonstrated how the CFA further repositioned itself to avoid possible conflict with the Central Government so as to prevent any challenge or interference from Beijing. In *Ng Kung-Siu*, the defendants were alleged to have damaged a national flag and an HKSAR flag contravening section 7 of the National Flag and National Emblem Ordinance[92] and section 7 of the Regional Flag and Regional Emblem Ordinance.[93] The defense was purely on questions of law that the two sections were inconsistent with Article 19 of the ICCPR and Article 39 of the Basic Law.

The CFA decided this case as a typical analysis of human rights cases. The CFA first recognized freedom of expression as protected under Article 19 of the ICCPR and applied to the HKSAR via Article 39 of the Basic Law. The CFA also accepted that the sections do impose some limits on the freedom of expression. The court then examined the extent of the restriction. It was stated that the prohibition of desecration of the national and regional flags by the statutory provisions is not a wide restriction of the freedom of expression but a limited one. It bans only one mode of expression but not the message expressed.

The CFA then considered whether such restriction is justified. Concerning this question, the CFA first established the special societal and community interests in the protection of the flags. A national flag is considered to be the symbol of the state and of the sovereignty of the state. It represents the PRC, with her dignity, unity, and territorial integrity. The manner in which the national flag was raised in the handover ceremony in Hong Kong to mark the PRC's resumption of sovereignty over Hong Kong at midnight on July 1, 1997, was used to illustrate the intrinsic importance of the national flag to the HKSAR. The CFA then considered whether such societal and community interests of the national flag fall within any legitimate ground to restrict the freedom of expression protected by Article 19 of the ICCPR.

The CFA found that it is within the scope of "public order (order public)." The meaning of public order adopted by the CFA was not the limited meaning of civil disturbance but a very wide meaning representing what is necessary for the protection of the general welfare or for the interests of the collectivity as a whole. The concept must remain a function of time, place, and circumstances.

Finally, the CFA considered whether it is necessary to restrict the freedom on such ground. By playing down the extent of restriction and giving great value to the national flag, it was not difficult for the CFA to conclude that the test of necessity is satisfied. The limited restriction was said to be proportionate to the aim sought to be achieved and has not gone beyond what is proportionate.

By relying on this human rights analysis, the CFA managed to avoid a sensitive constitutional question which, if decided wrongly, might invite any interpretation of the SCNPC to correct any such mistake. The question is whether the CFA has the power to invalidate section 7 of the National Flag and National Emblem Ordinance. The National Flag and National Emblem Ordinance is not purely a local legislation. It was enacted in accordance with Article 18 and Annex III of the Basic Law.

According to Article 18, national laws in general are not applicable in the HKSAR except for those listed in Annex III of the Basic Law. The laws listed in Annex III are to be applied locally by way of promulgation or legislation by the HKSAR.[94] The Law of the PRC on the National Flag[95] and the Law of the PRC on the National Emblem were not included in the original Annex III when the Basic Law was passed by NPC in 1990. They were added to Annex III immediately after the transfer of sovereignty.[96] Almost all the laws listed in Annex III are applied only by way of promulgation,[97] except the Law of the PRC on the National Flag and the Law of the PRC on the National Emblem. The National Flag and National Emblem Ordinance is specially enacted to apply and adapt these two national laws.[98] Section 7 of the ordinance is enacted to apply and adapt Section 19 of the Law of the PRC on the National Flag and Section 13 of the Law of the PRC on the National Emblem. These two provisions are worded very similarly to Section 7. The provisions of the national laws do not specify the criminal penalty for the offenses, which is provided in the Decision of the SCNPC on the Punishment for Desecrating the National Flag and the National Emblem of the PRC.[99] The penalty is imprisonment, criminal detention, control or deprivation of political rights for three years or less. This decision is not applicable to the HKSAR, as it is not included in the Annex III of the Basic Law.

As the two national laws do not provide the criminal penalty for the offenses, and as the national law that provides the criminal penalty is not applicable to the HKSAR, these two national laws have to be localized. Therefore, one very important function of the National Flag and National Emblem Ordinance is to provide the criminal punishment for the offenses and the highest penalty is a fine at level 5 and imprisonment for three years.

If the CFA declared that Section 7 of the National Flag and National Emblem is not compatible with the ICCPR, the same will be Section 19 of the Law of the PRC on the National Flag. Section 19, as a section in the Law of the PRC on the National Flag, is part of the laws of the HKSAR. However, by itself, it cannot establish an offense in the HKSAR, as the criminal penalty for the offense is not provided in the law. It needs Section 7 of the National Flag and National Emblem Ordinance to supplement it. If Section 7 is invalidated, then Section 19 also becomes unenforceable in the HKSAR. Such a decision would have the effect of indirectly invalidating Section 19 also. The sensitive question of whether the courts of the HKSAR have the power to invalidate a national law that is listed in Annex III and is made applicable to the HKSAR by promulgation will then come up.

Fine-Tuning of the New Constitutional Position
of the Court of Final Appeal

The CFA did manage to avoid any possible interference from the Central Government at a price that the human rights of Hong Kong have to pay for. However, that does mean that the CFA has given up its constitutional position as the guardian of human rights if there is no conflict with its more important constitutional position as the guardian of Hong Kong's rule of law. A good demonstration is the case *Albert Cheng and Lam Yuk Wah v. Tse Wai Chun.*[100]

Albert Cheng is not directly a bill of rights case but a defamation case. Albert Cheng and Lam Yuk Wah are cohosts of a popular phone-in radio talk show program on political and social affairs broadcasts on the Chinese channel of a local commercial radio station. They very often make very harsh comments against the Central Government and the officials of the HKSAR including the first chief executive. The case concerned some statements made by Cheng and Lam in the program concerning a lawyer named Tse Wai Chun.[101] Tse started a defamation action against Cheng and Lam for such statements. Cheng and Lam's defense was that the statements made were fair comments. The CFA decided in favor of Cheng and Lam.

The legal question before the CFA was whether the defense of fair comment was still available to Cheng and Lam if they had made those comments actuated with malice. By limiting the meaning of "malice," the CFA decided that if a defendant stated an honestly held opinion even if his purpose was to inflict injury, it might not deprive him of the protection of the defense of fair comment. The CFA emphasized that the purpose for which the defense of fair comment exists is to facilitate freedom of expression by commenting on matters of public interest and this accords with the constitutional guarantee of freedom of expression. The CFA found that especially in the social and political fields, those who make public comments usually have some objective of their own in mind, even if it is only to publicize and advance themselves. They often have what may be described as an "ulterior" object, such as promoting one cause or defeating another, or elevating one person or denigrating another. The presence of these motives is not a reason for excluding the defense of fair comment. The existence of motives such as these when expressing an opinion, does not mean that the defense of fair comment is being misused. On the contrary, this defense is intended to protect and promote comments such as these. Commentators, of all shades of opinion, are entitled to "have their own agenda." Politicians, social reformers, busybodies, those with political or other ambitions, and those with none, all can express their viewpoints freely on the condition they honestly believe what they have expressed.

This is a very good case for the CFA to show to the world that it has not given up its constitutional position as the guardian of human rights in Hong Kong. It has extended or clarified the defense of fair comments in defamation actions on the basis of the special concern given to the freedom of expression. The facts of the case might also be relevant. Though Hong Kong does not have effective institutional checks against the government, the media plays a very important supervisory role over the government. In these few years, this kind of phone-in talk show radio programs became very important channels through which the public could address their grievances against the government, and through which government officials could answer public concerns directly. The program hosted by the defendants in this case is the most popular radio program in Hong Kong, and even government officials have to pay close attention to what has been discussed in the program. Albert Cheng, one of the defendants of the case, is also a very outspoken critic against the government of the HKSAR and the PRC Central Government. By confirming the commentators' right to make comments on social and political affairs freely, the CFA indicates clearly that free speech will still be well protected in Hong Kong after *Ng Kung-Siu*. It may also explain the reasoning of the CFA in *Ng Kung-Siu* itself: that it only limits the mode of expression but not the content of the expression.

Further support can be found in another case, *Secretary for Justice and others v. Chan Wah and others*.[102] The applicants in the case have lived in their respective villages in Hong Kong all their lives and can plainly and properly be regarded as villagers of their villages. The electoral arrangements of village representatives excluded them from voting and from standing as candidates on the ground that they were not indigenous villagers, that is, they were not descendants by patrilineal descent of ancestors who in 1898 were residents of villages in the New Territories. The CFA relied on the political right of every HKPR to take part in the conduct of public affairs directly or through freely chosen representatives,[103] and decided that the electoral arrangements were invalid. As a village representative by statute represents the village as a whole (comprising both indigenous and nonindigenous villagers) and further has a role to play beyond the village level, the restrictions on the ground of not being indigenous are unreasonable and inconsistent with their constitutional rights.[104]

The CFA further decided that the lawful traditional rights and interests of the indigenous inhabitants of the New Territories protected by Article 40 of the Basic Law cannot justify the electoral arrangements. The indigenous inhabitants have long been loyal supporters of the Central Government. Article 40 was incorporated into the Basic Law to indicate the intention of the Central Government to continually protect their rights under the new constitutional order. The indigenous inhabitants criticised fiercely against the decision of the CFA and strongly demanded a reinterpretation of Article 40 by the SCNPC. However, the first chief executive and the Central Government took no action this time. The CFA might have rightly taken this strong stance against the indigenous inhabitants believing that such decision would not encounter any interference from the Central Government, as it might have to face in *Ng Kung-Siu*.

Conclusion: General Observations of Constitutional Positioning

Now that we have examined the constitutional positioning of the various parties of Hong Kong's new constitutional order, several general observations are in order. First, constitutional positions of the parties in the constitutional process are defined by the constitution itself. The maker of the constitution will spell out what is the intended position for each of the parties in the constitution according to its design. Therefore, the Basic Law has basically positioned all the parties of the constitutional process of Hong Kong. However, such constitutional positions cannot be 100 percent accurate. There will always be room for the party to fine-tune its position. The scope that each party has for further fine-tuning its position varies, depending on the clarity of the instructions that have already been incorporated into the constitution.

The maker of the constitution intentionally leaves a wide scope of discretion for some parties. Under the Basic Law, the Central Government has a much wider scope than the Legco. For some other parties, the maker of the constitution may have intentionally or unintentionally allowed some ambiguities in the constitution, and the parties may then make use of those ambiguities to have much freedom in their constitutional positioning. The CFA did make use of the ambiguities in the Basic Law to choose its constitutional positions, which might not be the intention of the maker of the constitution.

Second, the constitutional positions taken by each party interact with each other and such interactions may further affect how each party fine-tunes its own position. Such interaction may arise from the inherent conflicts of the constitutional positions taken by one party or it may arise from conflicts of the constitutional positions of different parties. The conflicting roles of the first chief executive caused him to make difficult political choices. The repositioning of the CFA demonstrated how other parties' constitutional positions interact with each other. If the first chief executive had not emphasized his constitutional position to maintain order in Hong Kong, the SCNPC would not have to reinterpret the relevant provisions of the Basic Law. As a result, the CFA was forced to reposition itself to avoid any situation that may invite another intervention from the Central Government. However, if the Central Government has not positioned itself as an open-minded sovereign, intervention might come even earlier when the CFA asserted its constitutional jurisdiction to review the compatibility of the legislative acts of the NPC or the SCNPC with the Basic Law. The CFA might also not be able to maintain a certain degree of human rights protection in Hong Kong if the Central Government were to pursue its original position against the direct application of the ICCPR in the HKSAR.

Third, constitutional positioning at the end reflects political choices of the parties in the constitutional process. Though the constitution may have already set certain limits on the positioning of the parties, most parties will still retain certain political room to fine-tune their positions and in some cases their freedom or discretion cannot be said to be little. The CFA is again a good example of this. It might be very legitimate for the CFA to have positioned itself as the guardian of Hong Kong's high degree of autonomy, the guardian of Hong Kong's rule of law, and the guardian of human rights in Hong Kong according to the Basic Law. Even after the first chief executive and the Central Government asserted their constitutional positions, the CFA might continue to maintain its constitutional positions in the following court decisions and the ball would then be back to their fields. The first chief executive and the Central Government would have to balance various political considerations on whether they would allow the judicial authority of the CFA be hurt again at any cost. However, the CFA has made the political decision to reposition itself so as to avoid any interference from the Central Government to happen again. This is the political choice of the CFA. Some may think that the CFA was too naïve in *Ng Ka Ling*, but became more politically mature in *Lau Kong Yong* and *Ng Kung-Siu*. However, some may consider that the CFA has sacrificed principles for real politics in the cases. Grounds gained in *Ng Ka Ling* were lost. No matter how one looks at the constitutional positioning of the CFA, one can safely conclude that even the CFA, a judicial body, cannot be exempted from making political decisions.

Fourth, constitutional positioning is closely linked to constitutional changes. We have already looked at the first few pages of the first chapter of Hong Kong's new constitution. The parties in the constitutional process under the new constitutional order have positioned and repositioned themselves accordingly. The first stage of constitutional positioning is now almost settled, after the CFA repositioned itself in *Lau Kong Yong* and *Ng Kung-Siu*. We may foresee that there will not be much change in the constitutional positions in the remaining pages of the first chapter as there will not be any major constitutional changes in the coming years until 2007.

According to the Basic Law,[105] the electoral arrangements of the chief executive and the Legco may all be changed to direct election after 2007. If the third chief executive and all members of the fourth Legco were to be directly elected in 2008, Hong Kong's constitution would turn to a new chapter. All the parties would then have to reposition themselves to adapt to any subsequent constitutional changes.

Notes

1. Articles 8 and 160 of the Basic Law.
2. Articles 19 and 81(2) of the Basic Law.
3. Chapter 4 of the Basic Law.
4. The first chief executive, Tung Chee Hwa, was a member of the Executive Council under the last colonial governor, Christopher Patten (1992–97).
5. Articles 2 and 19 of the Basic Law.
6. Articles 80 and 81 of the Basic Law.
7. Annex I, Section III.
8. Article 82.
9. Cap. 484, Laws of Hong Kong.
10. Section 5.
11. [1999] 1 HKLRD 315. As the issues were closely related, another judgment delivered by the CFA on the same day as Ng Ka Ling has to be considered together. The case is Chan Kam-Nga and others v. Director of Immigration [1999] 1 HKLRD 304.
12. They have to be either Chinese nationals born in Hong Kong [Article 24(2)(1) of the Basic Law] or Chinese nationals ordinarily resided in Hong Kong continuously for more than seven years [Article 24(2)(2) of the Basic Law].
13. Immigration (Amendment) (No. 3) Ordinance 1997 (Ord. No. 124 of 1997).
14. This was the body under the NPC responsible for the establishment of the HKSAR. It was established in 1996, and half of the members were from Hong Kong. See Decision of the NPC on the Method for the Formation of the First Government and the First Legco of the HKSAR of the PRC.
15. Decision on the Establishment of the PLC of the HKSAR approved in the Second Plenary Session of the Preparatory Committee on March 24, 1996.
16. The Chinese government refused to recognize the 1995 election of the Legco and insisted that such electoral reforms contravened the Joint Declaration, the Basic Law, and the understanding between the Chinese government and the British government in a series of correspondence between the two governments in the early nineties. The SCNPC decided that the Legco had to be terminated on June 30, 1997. The Selection Committee set up for the purpose of selecting the chief executive elected the PLC. As the 1995 Legco could not become the first Legco of the HKSAR, the Preparatory Committee of the HKSAR finally decided to set up the PLC to fill the constitutional vacuum. However, the authority of the Preparatory Committee to set up this PLC and the legality of the PLC were questioned.

First, it was not clear whether the Selection Committee had the authority to select PLC. This depended on the authority of its mother body, the Preparatory Committee. From the relevant decision of the NPC, it was not clear whether the Preparatory Committee had the authority to set up a body, which in turn would be responsible for selecting the PLC. The PLC was mentioned in neither the Basic Law nor the relevant decisions of the NPC. Second, the composition and the term of the PLC to a certain extent contradicted some provisions of the Basic Law but no amendment was made to the Basic Law. The Basic Law provides that the Legco of the HKSAR will be constituted by election. However, it would be stretching the meaning of "election" too much if the selection process of the members of the PLC could also be treated as a form of election. It is also provided that the term of the First Legco is two years, but the term of the PLC was not more than one year.

17. [1997] 2 HKC 315. The main issue in this case was whether the common law offense of conspiracy to pervert the course of justice is preserved after the transfer of sovereignty. The trial against the three respondents started before the transfer of sovereignty but was not finished before the transfer of sovereignty. Immediately after the transfer of sovereignty when the trial was resumed, the respondents raised the issue that the common law offense was no longer part of the laws of the HKSAR. They argued that Article 160 of the Basic Law requires a positive act of adoption of these laws either by the SCNPC or by the legislature of the HKSAR. They alleged that the SCNPC had made no such positive act. Also, the Reunification Ordinance failed to adopt the laws, though it was legislated to provide for the continuity of laws. It was argued that the establishment of the PLC contradicted the Basic Law and that all laws passed by this illegal body were therefore invalid. The judges decided that there was no need to have a positive act by the SCNPC in order to adopt the common law into the laws of the HKSAR. The provisions of the Basic Law are sufficient to achieve this purpose. The case actually could have stopped here as the legal issue before the court had already been resolved. However, the judges chose to continue to discuss the legality of the PLC, and also gave their comments on the jurisdiction of the courts of the HKSAR.

18. *Ma Wai-kwan* (note 17), per Chan CJHC, p. 335.

19. *Ng Ka Ling* (note 11), pp. 337–338.

20. Ibid.

21. *Ng Ka Ling* (note 11), pp. 338–39.

22. Article 39 provides that the provisions of the International Covenant on Civil and Political Rights; the International Covenant on Economic, Social and Cultural Rights; and international labor conventions as applied to Hong Kong shall remain in force and shall be implemented through the laws of the HKSAR.

23. *Ng Ka Ling* (note 11), pp. 339–340.

24. In this case, the two provisions were Article 22(4) and Article 24(2)(3).

25. *Ng Ka Ling* (note 11), pp. 341–45.

26. The provisions of the Basic Law were incorporated into the Immigration (Amendment) (No. 2) Ordinance 1997 (Ord. No. 122 of 1997) by adding a new schedule to the Immigration Ordinance defining the categories of persons who are permanent residents of the HKSAR. (See paragraph 2 (a), (b), and (c), Schedule 1, Immigration Ordinance, Cap. 115.)

27. Section 2AA of the Immigration Ordinance, Cap. 115.

28. Section 2AB(2)(a) of the Immigration Ordinance and G.N. (E) 21, of September 13, 1997.

29. *Ng Ka Ling* (note 11), pp. 345–48.

30. Paragraph 1(2)b of Schedule 1, Immigration Ordinance, Cap. 115. The amendments excluded illegitimate children only if they relied on a father-and-child relationship as their basis of claiming the right of abode under Article 24(3) of the Basic Law.

31. Paragraph 2(c) of Schedule 1, Immigration Ordinance, Cap. 115.

32. *Ng Ka Ling* (note 11), pp. 352–54.

33. *Chan Kam-Nga* (note 11).

34. *Ng Ka Ling* (note 11), pp. 350–52.

35. Section 1(2) of the Immigration (Amendment) (No. 3) Ordinance 1997 (Ord. No. 124 of 1997).

36. It provided that the purpose of the ordinance was to incorporate the provisions of the ICCPR as applied to Hong Kong into the laws of Hong Kong, and regard had to be given in interpreting and applying the HKBORO.

37. It provided that all preexisting legislation was to be construed as consistent with the HKBORO. All preexisting legislation that did not admit of a construction consistent with the ordinance was, to the extent of the inconsistency, repealed.

38. It provided that all subsequent legislation was to be construed so as to be consistent with the ICCPR as applied to Hong Kong.

39. Cap. 383, Laws of Hong Kong.

40. Decision of the SCNPC on the Treatment of the Laws Previously in Force in Hong Kong in accordance with Article 160 of the Basic Law of the HKSAR of the PRC adopted by the Standing Committee of the Eighth NPC at its 24th session on February 23, 1997.

41. Wu Jianfan, "Lawful Measures," *Window Magazine*, November 10, 1995; Shao Tianren, "Legal Vacuum Fears," *Window Magazine*, November 10, 1995.

42. *Ng Ka Ling* (note 11), pp. 355–57.

43. They included Professor Xiao Weiyun and Professor Shao Tianren of Beijing University, Professor Wu Jianfan of the Chinese Academy of Social Sciences, and Professor Xu Chungde of the People's University of China.

44. The full text of their opinions can be found in *Wen Hui Pao*, February 7, 1999 (in Chinese).

45. The next day after the opinions of the four legal experts were published, the director of the State Council Information Office, Zhao Qizhang, said the court rulings were wrong and should be reversed. A spokesman of the Hong Kong and Macau Affairs Office of the State Council also said the Chinese government was very concerned about the rulings and was seriously considering the views of mainland legal experts that the ruling contravened the Basic Law and the "one country, two systems" principle. See *Hong Kong Standard*, February 9 and 10, 1999.

46. *Ng Ka Ling v. The Director of Immigration (No. 2)* [1999] 1 HKC 425. Chief Justice Li admitted that it was exceptional for a court to clarify its own judgment after the judgment was given. However, as the case involved matters of great constitutional, public, and general importance, the CFA decided to exercise its inherent jurisdiction and to make a statement concerning the constitutional jurisdiction of the courts of the HKSAR.

47. The speech was delivered in the motion debate concerning the right of abode in the Legco on April 28, 1999. The full text of the speech can be found at http://www.info.gov.hk/gia/general/199904/28/sfs0428.htm.

48. Wednesday, May 19, 1999, Official Record of Proceedings of Legco.

49. Report on Seeking Assistance from the Central People's Government in Solving Problems Encountered in the Implementation of the Basic Law of the HKSAR of the PRC.

50. Interpretation of the Standing Committee of the National People's Congress on Article 22(4) and paragraph 3 of 24(2) of the Basic Law of the HKSAR.

51. Article 31 of the Constitution of the PRC.

52. Article 159 of the Basic Law.

53. Article 14 of the Basic Law

54. Article 13 of the Basic Law.

55. Article 17 of the Basic Law.

56. Article 18 of the Basic Law.

57. Article 67(4) of the Constitution of the PRC and Article 158 of the Basic Law.

58. Falun Gong is a sect in the mainland found by Li Hongzhi. Its members practice a certain form of *qi gong*, integrating Buddhist and Taoist principles. It is reported to have 100 million members on the mainland, and its membership has expanded to other countries and territories including Hong Kong. In 1999, after a silent protest outside Zhong Nan Hai, the headquarters of the Chinese government in Beijing, by around 10,000 members of the Falun Gong, the Chinese government decided to suppress Falun Gong as an evil cult. See Article 300, Criminal Law of the PRC; Resolution of the SCNPC on the Ban of Cults and Prevention and Punishment of Cult Activities (1999); Explanation of the Supreme People's Court and the Supreme People's Procuratorate on the Application of Law Concerning Crimes Involved in the Organization and Utilization of Cults (1999), and The Second Explanation of the Supreme People's Court and the Supreme People's Procuratorate on the Application of Law Concerning Crimes Involved in the Organization and Utilization of Cults (2001).

59. Cap. 245.

60. Cap. 151.

61. Paragraph 3(3).

62. Section 3, Schedule 1, Cap. 1556.

63. Section 13 and 14. In name, it is a notification system. However, as the applicants need to have a notice of no objection after he has notified the commissioner of police, it is in effect a licensing system.

64. Section 5.

65. Political body is defined as a political party or an organization that purports to be a political party; or an organization whose principal function or main object is to promote or prepare a candidate for an election.

66. Foreign political organization is defined as a government of a foreign country or a political subdivision of a government of a foreign country; an agent of a government of a foreign country or an agent of a political subdivision of the government of a foreign country; or a political party in a foreign country or its agent.

67. Political organization of Taiwan is defined as the administration of Taiwan or a political subdivision of the administration; an agent of the administration of Taiwan or an agent of a political subdivision of the administration; or a political party in Taiwan or its agent.

68. One good example was how the police handled the protest on June 30, 1997. A group of protesters gathered outside the Great Eagle Center to protest against the premier of the PRC, Li Peng, who came to Hong Kong to attend the handover ceremony. As the protesters shouted out their slogans, Lee Ming-kwai, Senior Assistant Commissioner of Police, who was the commander on the spot, ordered the broadcast of Beethoven symphonies over loudspeakers. The protesters alleged that the action was an abuse of power and had infringed their right to demonstrate. Lee's explained that he played the music just to let the police have some relaxation while they were on duty. The protesters lodged a complaint against Lee to the Complaints Against Police Office. The Independent Police Complaints Council ruled that there was an abuse of

power. However, Lee was not subject to any punishment and was even promoted. This kind of policing attitude was also found in the recent conflicts between protestors and the police during the Fortune Global Forum held in Hong Kong, May 8–10, 2001.

69. *Hong Kong Standard*, October 28, 1998.

70. Section 6 of the Criminal Law of the PRC provides that the law is applicable to all crimes committed within the territory of the PRC, except as specially stipulated by law. The law is also applicable to all crimes committed aboard a ship or an aircraft of the PRC. When either the act or the consequence of a crime takes place within PRC territory, a crime is deemed to have been committed within the territory of the PRC. As the courts of the mainland considered not only the acts that Cheung and his gangsters committed in the mainland but also the acts committed in Hong Kong, the only legal basis was the deeming provision, stated in Article 6, of treating those acts as committed in the PRC. However, in the judgment of Cheung's case, the court did not rely on Article 6 of the Criminal Law of the PRC but based its decision on Article 24 of the Criminal Procedural Law of the PRC. This section presumes that the courts of the mainland have jurisdiction and is only a provision on how to deal with cases in which two courts in the PRC have concurrent jurisdiction. The courts in the mainland have not clearly explained the legal basis of its jurisdiction.

71. Article 95 states that the HKSAR may, through consultations and in accordance with law, maintain juridical relations with the judicial organs of other parts of China, and that they may render assistance to each other.

72. In this case, the HKSAR government again asserted that the court of the mainland would have jurisdiction over the case. However, the alleged legal basis was Article 7 of the Criminal Law of the PRC, which provides that the law is applicable to PRC citizens who commit crimes outside the territory of the PRC. The HKSAR government used a rather strange interpretation of Article 7: that "the territory of the PRC" refers to the jurisdiction rather than to geographical territory. In this context, the HKSAR would not be within the "territory" of the PRC. It was also alleged that Article 7 would only apply to mainland residents but not to Hong Kong residents because Hong Kong residents are Chinese nationals only within the meaning of the Nationality Law but not within the meaning of the Criminal Law of the PRC. These interpretations, adopted by the HKSAR government, might be even against the spirit of the relevant Chinese law. The Chinese authorities have not yet clearly explained the legal basis of its jurisdiction over this case.

73. Gladys Li, "Alarmed by Top Officials' Lame Excuse," *South China Morning Post*, October 28 1998.

74. *Hong Kong Standard*, March 19, 1998.

75. The full text of the statement is available at: http://www.info.gov.hk/gia/general/199902/04/0204140.htm.

76. The Legco failed to pass a vote of no confidence in the secretary for justice after much lobbying by the HKSAR government in favor of the secretary for justice.

77. The only exception was the secretary for justice, Leung Oi Sie, who was a solicitor in private practice and a member of the Hong Kong Deputies to the NPC before her appointment. She was not the first attorney general (the name of the post of the secretary for justice during the colonial era) recruited from outside the civil service.

78. A speech given by the chief secretary for administration, Anson Chan, at the Asia Society luncheon, April 19, 2001. (See http://www.info.gov.hk/gia/general/200104/19/0419138.htm.)

79. The colonial government of Hong Kong was described as an "administrative state." An *administrative state* is a government in which political decisions are made by administrators but are still considered to be legitimate. See Peter Harris, *Hong Kong: A Study in Bureaucracy and Politics* (Hong Kong: Macmillan Publishers (HK), 1988), pp. 72–73.

80. Articles 48(5) and 61 of the Basic Law.

81. See http://www.info.gov.hk/gia/general/200105/02/0502239.htm.

82. See http://www.mingpaonews.com/20010501/__gba1h.htm. She is Regina Ip, the secretary for security.

83. Even before Anthony Leung's appointment, there were already two principal officials who were not civil servants before their appointments. They were Elise Leung, secretary for justice, and Dr. E.K. Yeoh, Secretary for Health and Welfare.

84. Article 64 of the Basic Law.

85. Article 74 of the Basic Law.

86. Legislative Provisions (Suspension of Operation) Ordinance 1997 (Cap. 538). There was no need to suspend the Interception of Communications Ordinance (Cap. 532), as the Ordinance will only come into operation on a day to be appointed by the chief executive by notice in the *Gazette*. No such notice has yet been issued.

87. See the Hong Kong Bill of Rights (Amendment) Ordinance 1998 (Ord. No. 2 of 1998) and the Employment and Labour Relations (Miscellaneous Amendments) Ordinance 1997 (Ord. No. 135 of 1997).

88. They included the Hong Kong Bill of Rights (Amendment) Ordinance 1997 (107 of 1997); the Trade Unions (Amendment) (No. 2) Ordinance 1997 (Ord. No. 102 of 1997); the Employee's Rights to Representation, Consultation and Collective Bargaining Ordinance (Ord. No. 101 of 1997); and the Employment (Amendment) (No. 4) Ordinance 1997 (Ord. No. 98 of 1997).

89. Annex II of the Basic Law.

90. [1999] 4 HKC 731.

91. [2000] 1 HKC 117. Chief Justice Li gave a judgment on behalf of the majority. Permanent Judge Bokhary only reluctantly accepted the analogy of the majority by saying, "these restrictions . . . are just within the outer limits of constitutionality."

92. Cap. 1557. Section 7 of the National Flag and National Emblem Ordinance provides that: "A person who desecrates the national flag or national emblem by publicly and willfully burning, mutilating, scrawling on, defiling or trampling on it commits an offence and is liable on conviction to a fine at level 5 and to imprisonment for 3 years."

93. Cap. 1558.

94. Article 18 of the Basic Law is unclear. It merely states that all the national laws listed in Annex III of the Basic Law have to be applied locally by way of promulgation or legislation by the HKSAR. There are some general points about national laws applicable in the HKSAR. First, national laws listed in Annex III have to be applied locally before they can enjoy any legal status in the HKSAR. Second, there are two methods for applying them locally: promulgation and legislation. Third, there is no guideline on how to determine which method should be used. We may assume that the HKSAR is to decide which method should be used. What is unclear is the status of the national laws applied locally by promulgation or by legislation. That is also the question in this case. There may be several possible interpretations. Article 11 only states that no law enacted by the legislature of the HKSAR shall contravene the Basic

Law. The power to invalidate any law that contradicts certain provisions of the Basic Law by the SCNPC under Article 17 of the Basic Law is also only related to laws enacted by the legislature of the HKSAR. A national law promulgated locally, strictly speaking, is not a law enacted by the legislature of the HKSAR. The chief executive of the HKSAR promulgated all these national laws by legal notices. It seems that the intention of the Basic Law is to presume that all national laws applicable in the HKSAR are compatible with the Basic Law. National laws may be applied locally by legislation, which means that the laws are to be enacted by the legislature of the HKSAR. However, it would be rather strange for a national law applied locally by legislation to have a different status than one applied by promulgation, especially if there is no substantial modification to the relevant provision. It is also not rational for the HKSAR government to be able to arbitrarily determine the status of a national law by just choosing the method of adoption. One may argue that all national laws, whether applied by promulgation or by legislation, should enjoy the same status. They should not be exempted from the courts' review power. Whether this argument is valid depends very much on the interpretation of Articles 11, 18, and 19 of the Basic Law. It again goes back to the purpose of Basic Law.

95. Enacted by the SCNPC at the Fourteenth Session of the Seventh SCNPC on June 28, 1990.

96. Decision of the Standing Committee of the NPC on the Addition and Deletion of National Laws listed in Annex III of the Basic Law of the HKSAR of the PRC adopted at the 26th Session of the Eighth SCNPC on July 1, 1997.

97. The chief executive declared in Promulgation of National Laws 1997 (Cap. 1554), Promulgation of National Laws (No. 2) 1997 (Cap. 1555), and Promulgation of National Laws 1998 (Cap. 1572) that national laws as set out in the schedules shall apply in the HKSAR.

98. Section 9 of the National Flag and National Emblem Ordinance.

99. Adopted at the Fourteenth Session of the Seventh SCNPC on June 28, 1990.

100. FACV No. 12 of 2000.

101. The case arose from the rescue of a man named Au Wing Cheung. Au was employed as a tour escort by the Select Tours. When a tour group lead by Au was going through the customs in the Manila Airport, Au was arrested for trafficking drug. Au was then prosecuted, convicted, and sentenced to life imprisonment by the court in the Philippines. Various groups in Hong Kong organized campaigns seeking his release. One of these groups was the Tourist Industry Rescue Group, of which the Select Tours was a member and Tse was its honorary legal advisor. Cheng had organized another group. As a result of the campaigns by these various groups, Au was finally released. After his return to Hong Kong a question arose on whether Au should claim compensation from his former employer, Select Tours, for the period of his imprisonment in the Philippines, on the ground that he was arrested and incarcerated while carrying out his duties as an employee. Cheng advised Au that he should make such a claim, while Tse advised him not to do so. Part of the program in question consisted of a conversational dialogue in Cantonese between the two hosts, Cheng and Lam. Tse complained that they had used words that would be understood as meaning that Tse had improperly influenced Au into not pursuing a claim against the Select Tours; acted unethically and unprofessionally in advising Au; allowed himself to be put into a position of conflict of interest; given his advice without regard to Au's interests and with a view to protecting the interests of the travel industry; and had

threatened or intimidated Au in deciding not to pursue a compensation claim against the Select Tours. Tse started a defamation action against Cheng and Lam.

102. FACV Nos. 11 and 13 of 2000.

103. Article 21 of the Bill of Rights set out in Part II of the HKBORO and Article 25 of the ICCPR.

104. The CFA also relied on the Sex Discrimination Ordinance (Cap. 480, Laws of Hong Kong) to strike down the electoral arrangements.

105. Annex I and Annex II of the Basic Law.

—— 8 ——

Legal Facets of Hong Kong SAR Economic Development

Colonial Legacy and Constitutional Constraint

Berry Fong-Chung Hsu

Introduction

The government of the Hong Kong Special Administrative Region (the HKSAR) possesses a mandate pursuant to the *Basic Law of the HKSAR* (the Basic Law), part of the Laws of the People's Republic of China, to provide "an appropriate economic and legal environment for the maintenance of the status of Hong Kong as an international financial center."[1] For instance, under the new legal order of the Basic Law, the Legislative Council may exercise its power to impeach the chief executive if the Executive Government fails to make good this provision.[2] Historically adherent to a laissez-faire policy, colonial Hong Kong was slow to support any form of regulatory control. Even when laws were enacted to regulate the financial markets, the politic and administrative will to enforce the laws was absent. When the People's Republic of China (PRC) resumed the exercise of sovereignty over the HKSAR on July 1, 1997, it also assumed control over one of the least developed legal systems in the developed common law world.

The Asian financial crisis of 1997 demonstrated the domino effect of unsound banking and financial markets.[3] With the advent of the PRC's membership in the World Trade Organization (WTO), the HKSAR could become the PRC's liability if it fails to reform better its laws relating to banking and finance in meeting the global challenge. The first and foremost priority for the HKSAR should naturally be the development and implementation of international standards in the regulatory framework of banking and finance. Globalization and increased competition from neighboring countries and other major cities within the PRC have already reshaped the HKSAR as an international financial center. Not only would information technology facilitate the utilization of human resources (as well as marketing and transportation of products in the global market), but also it is indispensable to banking and financial services. After all, an international center of banking and finance is just a "network of information." Naturally, the free flow of information requires a sound legal system to protect the rights of the citizens.

In a previous paper, the major aspects of the legal infrastructure necessary and essential in providing stability in the banking and financial markets were discussed.[4] The first aspect is the constitutional framework, which provides an independent judiciary to arbitrate rights, protects private ownership of property, and maintains certainty in economic policies. In the HKSAR, it also sets out the relationship between itself and the Central People's Government and the rule of law in the HKSAR in strengthening investors' confidence and preventing the arbitrary power of the state in meddling with private affairs. The Basic Law has provided this framework in enabling the HKSAR as an international center of banking and finance.[5]

The second aspect is the legal framework, which should protect banking and financial institutions, as well as investors, creditors, and depositors. It deals with the common law and legislation, which support the operation of banking and financial laws. However, this framework has yet to be improved.[6] A weak corporate governance, disclosure, and company rescue will greatly endanger the quality of the assets and hinder the development of the banking and financial market. The Executive Government has put forward a number of proposals and introduced relevant bills for legislative reforms in enhancing the legal framework. The burden is now on the Legislative Council to enact legislation implementing these reforms as soon as is practicable.[7]

Another important aspect is the revenue framework, which should achieve equity and provide a reliable source of income, in avoiding budget deficits and social disorder. This framework should address the soundness of public finance and the incentives offered to the international community in locating in the HKSAR, as well as the allocation of wealth in achieving a just society. This framework has provided the HKSAR with fiscal stability and tax incentives, which have made the special administrative region one of the most competitive locations for international investors.[8] There are, however, some potential problems in public revenue, which this chapter will discuss.

In developing and implementing international standards in regulating banking and finance, the above aspects of the legal infrastructure should be complemented by other facets of legal tradition, practices, and public policy in supporting the economic development of the HKSAR. The first facet is the exercise of inherent common law prerogatives of the state in financial crisis. At common law, residual powers are exercised by the state as prerogative powers. After June 30, 1997, the residual executive powers are assumed by the Central People's Government, which invested them to the HKSAR government through the Basic Law.[9] It is ironic that the measures taken by the HKSAR government in defending the Hong Kong currency during the Asian financial crises are legally justified by these prerogative powers in the absence of a sound regulatory framework in banking and finance. The second facet is the regulatory framework of prudential accounting. Only a sound accounting system would provide transparency and a level playing field in the financial markets. The present accounting system has not fully met international standards. The last facet is the implementation of an equitable public revenue system under the constitutional constraint of the Basic Law. The present revenue system relies to a certain extent on income from sales of land. As a result, not only is equity distorted but also the revenue system contributes to the instability of the banking sector. These three facets are discussed in the following sections.

The Common Law Prerogatives

The attack on the Hong Kong currency during the Asian financial crises demonstrates the effective employment of the common law prerogatives in defending the HKSAR financial markets from a total meltdown. Although the measures taken by the HKSAR government were criticized for being arbitrary and without legal justification, the residual powers of the state at common law nevertheless provide the HKSAR government with ample legal authorities to intervene in the financial markets under these rare and unusual circumstances. The flexibility of common law was exemplified.

The Defense of the Hong Kong Currency

The global effects of the Asian financial crisis led to a major speculative attack on the Hong Kong dollar in August 1998.[10] In order to defend the Hong Kong dollar peg to the U.S. dollar and the financial markets, on August 15, 1998, the HKSAR government intervened in a counterattack. Official justification for the move cited pressure and persistent attack on the currency.[11] The HKSAR government claimed it had evidence that there were speculators double playing; on the currency market and the futures market.[12] This allegation was not difficult to prove; an attack on the currency market would force up interest rates, and this would be followed by profit taking through short selling of the futures index, as high interest rates would cause the stock market index to fall. Free market economies have no regulatory controls for the use by investment banks of hedge funds to attack the Hong Kong dollar. Accordingly, the logic of free trade simply could not be applied to currency convertibility.[13] The government alleged that there were clear signs that the aim of these speculative attacks was to make quick profits in the futures market.[14] Taking no action risked a 50 percent surge in interest rates and the substantial drop in the Hang Seng Index.[15] This would further lower property prices and impose enormous pressure on the banking system.

In order to restore investor confidence in the financial markets, the HKSAR government decided to deploy its Exchange Fund to deal with this very exceptional circumstance; to purchase shares of a selected number of companies.[16] As a result of its two-week intervention in the financial markets, speculative attacks were at last fading. The total cost of the share acquisition by the HKSAR government was U.S.$15.2 billion.[17] The consequence of such a colossal injection of funds enabled the government to become the largest shareholder in HSBC Holdings PLC, which owns the Hongkong and Shanghai Banking Corporation and Midland Bank, with 8.80 percent of issued shares.[18] The HKSAR government could demand a seat on the board of directors of HSBC Holdings PLC. A legal barrier also arose; this substantial shareholding was barely short of the 10 percent ownership threshold, which required regulatory approval in the United Kingdom. The British Financial Services Authority naturally would be most concerned about whether the HKSAR government was a desirable substantial shareholder in a major British banking institution.[19]

In addition to this unprecedented governmental intervention in the financial markets, the HKSAR government also adopted seven measures to strengthen the currency board arrangements.[20] It also proposed some thirty measures to strengthen the order and transparency of the securities and futures market.[21] Although belatedly, the government also tightened the rules on short selling and settlement, and streamlined the automatic trading systems that in the past had enabled speculators to take advantage of the delay in the settlement process.[22] However, it was concerned that, if too many restrictions were imposed, the market would be unduly disturbed.[23] Speculator tactics were difficult to predict, the HKSAR had one of the most open financial markets in the world, there were no hard-and-fast rules in place that could prevent attacks on the Hong Kong dollar.[24] Accordingly, the HKSAR government has to balance the need to grant the chief executive wide discretionary powers to direct the financial markets in emergency situation with the rule of law, on which the rule-based financial markets of the HKSAR pride themselves.[25]

The Exercise of State Prerogatives

The nature and the alacrity of the government's action took many by surprise.[26] Economists were divided about whether this move would effectively stabilize the Hong Kong dollar. The intervention drew the wrath of the financial sector; as most of the major investment bankers were counting on the success of the attack of the Hong Kong currency to make some quick money. While the HKSAR government argued that it had to maintain a level playing field, its intervention was roundly criticized as illegal manipulation of the stock market.[27] The subsequent refusal of the HKSAR government to disclose its shareholdings was considered by some a breach of the Securities (Disclosure of Interests) Ordinance and the Code on Takeovers and Mergers.[28] Critics suggested that the HKSAR government was obliged to abide by the Securities Ordinance by "necessary implication" of the Interpretation and General Clauses Ordinance.[29] Leading members of the Legislative Council attacked such intervention as lacking in transparency and conflict of interests.[30] However, their argument was more political than legal.

During the crisis, the HKSAR government alleged that share prices, interest levels and interest rates in the HKSAR were dictated wholly by manipulators,[31] yet it was unable to identify the manipulators, being disguised as they were by many different channels.[32] In reality, the HKSAR is struggling to keep up with the latest developments in financial technology, as is its currently financially challenged regulatory framework. The HKSAR government did not have the emergency powers to suspend the relevant laws while the markets were under attack. In an emergency situation, it could hardly be expected that the government would reveal its strategy in order to comply with legal provisions on transparency. Therefore, short of imposing martial law, the government had limited options while it faced a meltdown of the financial system in the HKSAR. Similarly, in ensuring that the financial markets would operate smoothly after the terrorist attack on September 11, 2001, the U.S. Federal Reserve said it would take appropriate measures, such as cutting interest rates and pumping money into the financial system, until the restoration of the normal market.[33]

Without addressing the financial merits of the intervention, the HKSAR government had a better legal position regarding the intervention than was ostensible at the time. For the first time in the history of common law, the inherent common law power of the state was exercised in defending its financial markets. From the outset, there is a statutory provision in the HKSAR, which codified the long-established common law doctrine, that the state is not bound by a legislative provision unless such is expressly stated.[34] More importantly, the intended purpose of the Securities Ordinance is primarily the protection of the investing public through the regulation of the stock markets, control of trading in securities and the investment advisory business, and protection of investors.[35] The intended purpose of the Securities (Disclosure of Interests) Ordinance is to provide a level playing field by requiring certain persons to disclose their shareholdings.[36] These two ordinances, however, had never been intended to deal with the mischief the hedge funds had caused in the financial markets. In any event, the secretary of justice could always exercise the prerogative power of *nolle prosequi* in the unlikely event that there would be a private prosecution, or a prosecution initiated by the SFC, when all these legally based justifications fail.

The HKSAR government has many other common law jurisprudences to support its action to intervene in the financial markets. First, the Hong Kong dollar would not have survived the speculative attack had the HKSAR government not intervened so quickly and decisively. The issue is whether breach of the law would avert a greater evil. Such a departure from legislative norms could be justified on common law grounds of necessity, which would render an unlawful act lawful.[37] Second, the HKSAR government was performing its public duty to protect the Hong Kong dollar under the Basic Law, which gives it the mandate to provide an appropriate economic and legal environment for maintaining the HKSAR as an international financial center,[38] and requires the issue of Hong Kong currency must be backed up by a 100 percent reserve fund.[39] It could have argued that the intervention was necessary to and essential in carrying out these provisions of the Basic Law. The common law doctrine that any legislation that is inconsistent with the constitutional document is invalid was incorporated into the Basic Law.[40] Third, the proper forum for addressing possible wrongdoing by the executive arm is the Legislative Council, which has the power to impeach the chief executive as the head of the executive government.[41] There is little doubt that the HKSAR government was acting in the public interest when it intervened in the financial markets. According to Blackstone, "no human laws are of any validity, if contrary to" the law of nature.[42] In the case of *Dr. Bonham*, Chief Justice Coke said that no legislation should contradict common right and reason.[43]

While the HKSAR government could legally and morally defend its intervention in the financial markets, there were doubts about the fairness and soundness of the intervention. The government may have extrajudicial grounds to justify its intervention to correct the failures and improve the efficiency of the financial markets.[44] However, the general consensus remains that this type of intervention could well have the effect of hindering the efficiency of the financial markets.[45] In December 1998, the WTO raised concerns about the preference shown toward companies listed on the Hang

Seng Index by the HKSAR government.[46] However, the government was forced to select these shares because the futures index, which the speculators were short selling, comprised mainly these securities. The WTO also expressed its concern about the holding of HSBC shares by the HKSAR government, as it perceived a conflict of interest between the government regulator and the bank it regulated.[47] The government has since established, and appointed the directors of, Exchange Fund Investments Ltd., to manage and dispose the shares at arm's length. In the event, this concern has yet to be justified.

In retrospect, the intervention proved an aversion of the greater evil; repelling the speculative attack on the Hong Kong dollar, which might have caused the total meltdown of the HKSAR's financial markets. On March 6, 2000, the International Monetary Fund (IMF) praised the HKSAR government for having successfully defended and even strengthened the linked exchange rate. It attributed this to its skilful economic management and credibility of policy making.[48] Three years after the intervention, George Soros, whose Quantum Fund took sizable positions against the Hong Kong currency and the stock markets in the speculative attack, admitted that the HKSAR government did a very good job when it intervened to prevent the collapse of the Hong Kong capital markets.[49]

The Accounting Framework

Although the HKSAR government is revamping its regulatory framework of banking and finance, the legal infrastructure supporting this framework must be enhanced in the long run. In evaluating the HKSAR's long-term economic fundamentals, banking institutions ought to make proper disclosure of their strengths and weaknesses. The weakness in the financial structures of most Asian countries during their own financial crises was a lack of transparency and accountability among the institutions involved and the financial system itself.[50] A transparent system will enable market participants to have sufficient information to identify the risks they assume.[51] On October 17, 2000, the Securities and Futures Legislation (Provision of False Information) Ordinance was enacted. This ordinance addressed the absence of statutory provisions on the providing of false or misleading information to the Securities and Futures Commission (SFC).[52] Transparency is essential to the strength of a country's economic fundamentals.

This is just the tip of the iceberg, however. The HKSAR's banking and financial markets are far from transparent, in that the majority of participants in these markets do not have the ability to process information, and the availability to them of information on which they make their investment decisions is very much restricted. According to a 1993 study by Capital

Information Services, on bank accounting disclosure, including nonquantitative information, banks in the HKSAR were ranked just above their counterparts in mainland China, and below those in most East Asian economies, including Thailand, Malaysia, Indonesia, Taiwan, the Philippines, and South Korea.[53] Since the report, one could claim that very little change has occurred in the HKSAR's accounting system.[54]

The effects of globalization mean that the HKSAR can be adversely affected by external factors beyond its regulatory control. According to a 1997 report by the IMF, the Asian financial crisis has significantly clouded the prospects for economic growth and financial stability in the HKSAR in the short term, and has left it with a degree of vulnerability.[55] As the HKSAR practices a free and open capital market with virtually instant liquidity, it is vulnerable to global shifts in investor mood.[56] However, it can minimize the risk by adopting internationally accepted accounting practices and disclosure rules as well as international banking standards. The IMF report subtly criticized the disclosure requirements of the HKSAR by suggesting that "a further broadening of disclosure requirements could help reduce market uncertainty and limit the risk of unwarranted contagion."[57] The full effects of the financial crisis on HKSAR banks cannot be fully analyzed unless more information is disclosed. Unlike the retail and manufacturing sectors where sales volume counts, banks can always amend their balance sheets to give a rosy picture. These disclosures should therefore be highly specific.[58]

In August 1999, the IMF published another report that credited the HKSAR with making substantial progress in a number of areas. It stated that the HKSAR had achieved a high degree of transparency in data dissemination, fiscal policy, monetary and financial policies, and banking supervision.[59] Nevertheless, it subtly mentioned that there was room to improve transparency.[60] In ensuring a level playing field, the financial markets must not be informationally impaired. In the HKSAR, poor accounting practices often conceal the weakness in the financial markets. Studies have shown that investors and creditors give issuers and borrowers the benefit of the doubt if they are not given adequate information about the firms' financial performance.[61] Without full, timely, and accurate information, market participants are left to make investment decisions by drawing inferences from the limited information received.[62] That banking institutions may adopt their own accounting practices and methodologies in collusion with auditors to provide a rosy outlook is entirely legitimate in the HKSAR.[63] Had the Hongkong and Shanghai Banking Corporation adopted the "benchmark treatment," as some banking institutions have adopted, instead of the "alternative treatment," where investments are carried at fair market value at the date of the balance sheet, then its two interim reports on profits would have been higher by 72 percent and 93 percent, respectively.[64]

In the HKSAR, auditors must conform to the auditing standards prescribed by the Hong Kong Society of Accountants (HKSA). The HKSA publishes auditing guidelines, such as, Statements of Standard Accounting Practice. It also endorses some of the guidelines of the International Auditing Practices Committee of the International Federation of Accountants. However, the guidelines published by the HKSA are few and fall short of the International Standards of Auditing (ISA).[65] The Companies Ordinance requires every company to keep proper books of account.[66] A company must present a "true and fair" view of the state of its affairs and explain its transactions;[67] it must also prepare a balance sheet and a profit and loss account in accordance with the Tenth Schedule of the ordinance.[68] According to the *Consultancy Report on the Review of the Hong Kong Companies Ordinance*,[69] the information required by the Ordinance is no longer consistent with accounting practices.[70] The report recommended the adoption of generally accepted accounting principles (GAAP), which are to be set by an independent accounting standards body.[71] An IMF report published in August 1999 noted the HKSAR's finalization of twenty-two new Statements of Auditing Standards, which are compatible with the ISA.[72] However, a 1999 practice directive issued by the HKSA has stated that most securities, originally classified as long-term investments, can be booked through the profit and loss statement as "benchmark treatment" or booked through balance sheet reserves as "alternative treatment."[73] The latter treatment follows the ISA standards.[74] This flexibility led to a jump in the interim profits of HKR International of some 33 percent.[75] In any event, banking institutions should adopt conservative accounting practices to show steady profits in accordance with international standards.

Although the GAAP normally meet the "true and fair view" requirement, there are always cases that escape coverage.[76] As a result, there is always the possibility that even compliance with the rules may not give a "true and fair view." In two cases, *Lloyd Cheyham and Co Ltd v. Littlejohn & Co Ltd*[77] and *Prudential Assurance v. Newman Industries plc (No. 2)*,[78] the courts have shown that they are in fact not prepared to accept the standards as conclusive, although they are willing to give credence to the standards, the effect being that the standards are only of persuasive force.[79] The GAAP permit a departure in cases where adopting them does not give a "true and fair view"; the auditor must, however, state the particulars and reasons for the departure.[80]

As the "true and fair view" requirement is a matter of law rather than accounting,[81] it is necessary to consider what elements its legal definition should cover. "True and fair view" implies that this definition should go further than compliance with accounting conventions, but accountants are unable to agree on what more it should involve. There has been much argument about the "true and fair view" of balance sheets. The requirement of comprehensiveness is debatable because it is difficult to decide how much information should be revealed in each particular case.[82] Academic studies have consistently shown that auditors rely on precedent in choosing accounting standards. There is also a problem of what "true and fair" is in a cultural context. The economic, historical, political, and sociological background of the HKSAR's Chinese subculture should be considered in the formulation of such a view. Complexities may also arise if the nature of the concerned entity's trade is taken into account. If there is a difference between a precedent and a position that a company, or a particular trade, follows in adopting a certain accounting standard, the auditor would tend to rely on the precedent.

It also has been suggested that the legal test should concentrate on the effect of the accounts on users, rather than looking at the matter from the position of the company or of the auditors. However, this argument cannot seriously be presented unless some view is taken as to who the users are, or are assumed to be.[83] These different opinions on what is a "true and fair view" mean that an investor may not be able to receive optimal information. Another difficulty concerning the "true and fair view" is that, in many cases, those responsible for the accounts have no interest in making them helpful and informative because companies do not want to give full details of their financial position in a publication which may be read by their competition. Consequently, there is often pressure on auditors to accept the bare minimum of disclosure.[84] It is therefore necessary for auditors to maintain their independence. The *Companies Ordinance*[85] only requires the auditor to be a professional qualified under the *Professional Accountants Ordinance*[86] and to operate at arm's length from the company. However, there are no provisions prohibiting the company from shopping around for the auditor that will produce the most favorable report. Companies are always free to "result-shop" for the most favorable report.

Moreover, there is no provision in the HKSAR requiring an auditor to state which accounting rules it has used, or to expressly note and explain any departure from the *Companies Ordinance* or from the accepted professional standards. However, even if there were such a provision, it would not be of great help to nonaccountants.[87] In *Caparo Industries plc v. Dickman*,[88] the House of Lords held that auditors owed no duty to the investing public who relied on audited accounts to purchase shares, applying it also to existing shareholders who purchase further shares. There is no special relationship between the auditor and the investing public who rely on the auditor's report.[89] The members of the House of Lords do not seem to have considered the economic effect of such a decision on the securities markets.

Some auditors may manipulate accounting rules to circumvent or undermine the purpose of a regulation. This is known as "creative compliance."[90] Moreover, guidelines on the application of broad rules made by the regulatory authorities—the Stock Exchange of Hong Kong Ltd. (SEHK), the courts and legal opinion, and so on—may lead to an even narrower application.[91] As a result, despite their purpose to thwart creative compliance, these regulations may themselves turn out to be a recipe for the creation of new avoidance devices—effectively, the tighter the controls, the more ways around them that can be created. The present accounting standards of the HKSA allow depreciation to be computed by the straight-line approach or declining-balance method. A company is free to change the rates and period of depreciation. In August 1995, Cathay Pacific reported a 22 percent interim growth in profit as a result of switching to a straight-line basis over twenty years.[92]

A company that wishes to list its shares on the SEHK must comply with the Rules Governing the Listing of Securities of the Stock Exchange of Hong Kong Ltd. The company applying to list must normally provide audited accounts for at least the three financial years immediately preceding the listing.[93] The audit report is required to include the specified basic information, including assets and liabilities.[94] The auditor must certify whether or not the relevant information given presents a "true and fair view" of the results for the period reported and the assets and liabilities at the end of that period.[95] However, a company can choose an auditing firm that comes up with figures acceptable to the listed company, as each firm may have its own acceptable method.[96] This is a perfectly legitimate practice in the HKSAR. The SEHK has special listing rules for the Growth Enterprise Market (GEM) companies and the disclosure requirements for these companies are more stringent than those for the main board companies.[97] However, the market capitalization of former companies is far much smaller than the later companies.[98] As a consequence, the investing public may be misled into believing that the information available to them in a prospectus is accurate and precise, since the prospectus has to be filed with the SFC and, for listed companies, the audit report with the SEHK, both reputable bodies. In any event, regulatory control alone may not be sufficient because by the time any wrongdoing is discovered, the company may have already gone into liquidation.

The fundamental problem is that auditing firms are reluctant to report on any negative findings they uncover.[99] It is immaterial whether these firms have an international reputation, as they play by the rules of the game in the HKSAR.[100] In ensuring leniency, some banking institutions have routinely bribed the senior management of these auditing firms after paying them a handsome service fee.[101] It is therefore desirable that legislation requiring auditors to report to the appropriate authority any illegal activities discovered in the course of their duties be enacted. However, some leading members of the accounting profession have actively resisted law reform that might compel auditors to report corporate misconduct to the authorities.[102] They argue, without acknowledging that an auditor owes his duty to the shareholders collectively and not to the corporate wrongdoers, that such a move is against the public interest.[103] On March 24, 1999, the HKSAR government announced the inclusion of legislative amendments in the composite Securities and Futures Bill to grant immunity to auditors who report suspected fraud or malpractice to the regulatory authorities.[104] This was made after the discovery of auditing irregularities and material misstatements in eleven cases over a six-month period.[105] Some leading members of the accounting profession naturally expressed their displeasure over this proposal.[106]

An Equitable Tax Base Under Constitutional Constraint

Among two of the four major features of the Basic Law regarding tax legislation are that no revenue from the HKSAR shall finance services provided by the Central People's Government and the low tax policy provided by the Basic Law.[107] In reinforcing the free market economy and minimal government intervention of the private sector in the reallocation of resources from the rich to the poor, the Basic Law provides that "the HKSAR shall practice an independent taxation system. The HKSAR shall, taking the low tax policy previously pursued in Hong Kong as reference, enact laws on its own concerning types of taxes, tax rates, tax reductions, allowances, and exemptions, and other matters of taxation."[108]

The HKSAR government is bound to practice a tax policy that favors the rich and the middle-income taxpayers because of the "low tax policy" as stipulated in the Basic Law. It continues to provide the same basic level of education, health, and welfare as provided by the colonial administration. This is reinforced by the Basic Law, which requires the government to "follow the principle of keeping expenditure within the limits of revenues" and "to achieve a fiscal balance and avoid deficits."[109] Table 8.1 illustrates the historical sources of revenue in the HKSAR.

The "low tax policy" may be feasible because the HKSAR is fully subsidized by the Central People's Government in expenditures relating to defense and foreign affairs. However, this has resulted in polarizing the society and the continuation of land sales as a source of public revenue. Land sales income is a very lucrative source of revenue if it is supported by a high land price policy.

Table 8.1

Percentage of Sources of Revenue

Years	Salaries tax	Profits tax	Land sales	Stamp duty	Betting duty	Other duty	Others
1991–92	15	22	8	9	6	6	34
1992–93	15	24	7	10	6	6	32
1993–94	14	24	11	11	6	4	30
1994–95	14	27	11	7	5	4	32
1995–96	15	26	11	6	6	4	32
1996–97	14	24	13	10	6	4	29
1997–98	11	20	23	11	5	3	27
1998–99	12	21	9	5	6	3	44
1999–2000	11	16	15	5	5	3	45

Sources: Hong Kong Annual Reports 1991–99 (Hong Kong: Hong Kong Government, 1992–99); and for the 1999–2000 figures, verbal report from the Treasury of the Government of Hong Kong Special Administrative Region dated November 3, 2000.

Distributive Justice

One leading jurist, John Rawls, pointed out that social cooperation will improve life more than will individual effort.[110] This leads to a conflict of interests, as people always want a bigger share in the distribution of benefits produced by social cooperation. A set of principles is therefore required for the distribution of these benefits.[111] These principles are called the principles of social justice. They suggest how rights and duties are best allocated, and define how such benefits are best distributed.[112] People are affected by the political, economic, and social circumstances of the area of global and local society into which they are born. According to Rawls, such inequalities should be addressed by the principles of social justice.[113]

In distributing the benefits from social cooperation, there should be a system of justice in allocating these benefits by means of taxation and necessary adjustments in property rights.[114] The purpose of these levies and laws is to make good the distribution of wealth and to prevent power from being too concentrated.[115] However, a taxation scheme should be implemented to raise revenues that justice requires.[116] The executive arm of a government requires funds to adjust inequalities. However, the choice of an ideal tax system is often more political than it is based on jurisprudence. Rawls acknowledged that, in practice, one has to find compromises even in the least unjust tax system. The ultimate choice is a tax system that is not bettered by any other tax system. It is a compromise that entails compensating for injustices.[117] Such a scheme may, however, not be in conformity with efficiency, as it may have to give way to a more ethical distribution of wealth.[118]

Rawls advocated that a progressive rate tax is necessary to discourage the accumulation of property and the concentration of power in the hands of a few.[119] In achieving vertical equity, the higher the income bracket, the higher the tax that should be imposed. The question is whether or not efficiency would be the result. The concern would be that talented taxpayers may leave the jurisdiction if a progressive rate is introduced, yet this may be a healthy solution for the HKSAR. The present standard rate of 15 percent is far too generous as the HKSAR enters this new millennium with the third successive year of budget deficits.[120] Table 8.1 clearly illustrates the risk of relying on land sales as a major source of revenue. Low land prices would adversely affect the sources of revenue from stamp duty and profits tax of real estate related businesses.

High Land Price Policy

Up until the Asian financial crisis, land sales income in the HKSAR had long been an important source of Hong Kong government revenue. As it is the end purchaser who has to carry the cost of the high value of the land, the de facto high land price policy is in effect an equivalent form of indirect taxation.[121] Historically, the colonial government followed a high land price policy, which it implemented by limiting the supply of land. In addressing the PRC government's concern about the future supply of land in the territory, Annex III (Land Leases) to the 1984 Sino-British Joint Declaration[122] provided that only fifty hectares of land could be granted by the then Hong Kong government each year until June 30, 1997. However, land granted to the Hong Kong Housing Authority for public rental housing was excluded in order to encourage the colonial administration at the time to release more land for public housing.

The high land price policy naturally resulted in a high book value for assets in the form of share prices and mortgages. This problem was aggravated by banking institutions in the HKSAR, which were lending up to 90 percent of real estate values for mortgages, until the Hong Kong Monetary Authority (HKMA) issued guidelines restricting the upper ceiling to 70 percent of the value of a piece of real estate.[123] During the period of transition in 1997, the inflow of capital assets from overseas, taking advantage of the Hong Kong currency link to the U.S. dollar, helped the economy of the HKSAR to develop into a bubble economy.

The banks had for a while been granting mortgage loans for purchases of real estate with no consideration of the territory's economic fundamentals. Banks simply evaluated property value from its technical aspect. Basing future performance on experience, bankers were able to count on such a practice. At the end of September 1997, the average outstanding principal for a property mortgage was HK$1.3 million and the average loan-to-property value ratio was 52 percent.[124] Property acquired for investment purposes accounted for only 7 percent and the delinquency ratio of all mortgage loans, that is, loans overdue for more than 90 days, was 0.1 percent.[125] These figures were compiled before the Asian financial crisis spread to the HKSAR and shortly after the government's apparent determination to reverse the high land price policy of the former administration was made known.[126] The long-term plan to provide adequate housing to all HKSAR residents was announced on the first day of the establishment of Hong Kong as a Special Administrative Region of China.[127]

The chief executive of the HKSAR, Tung Chee-hwa, acknowledged that the HKSAR had inherited an economy from the former colonial administration that was plagued by soaring real estate prices, high inflation, and negative interest rates.[128] He stated that these problems had to be addressed. For the HKSAR to be competitive in the global markets as a value-added, service-based economy, real estate prices must be adjusted and stabilized. As a result of the HKSAR government's stated desire to provide adequate housing to its residents, and the Asian financial crisis, real estate prices were expected to fall 55 percent from their peak in June 1997.[129] (This was a conservative forecast, as real estate prices had increased by 50 percent between February 1996 and September 1997.[130])

Tung admitted that any further abrupt drop in real estate prices might adversely affect the banking system.[131] However, he was short of correlating this abrupt drop with the successive budget deficits. In reality, the banks could count on the government to take measures to ensure their survival at the expense of the public interest. The HKSAR government has taken a series of measures which may cushion the steep fall of real estate prices, including designating certain prime land for government offices,[132] providing greater flexibility in the land sale program to provide 85,000 flats each year,[133] implementing mortgage relief in the tax system,[134] and introducing fixed-rate mortgages.[135] These measures were not intended to boost real estate prices; rather, they were designed as a means by which the government could monitor a possible collapse in real estate prices. In addition, the HKSAR government has taken measures to improve the liquidity of the banking system and relaxed antispeculation measures on real estate one day after the HKMA gave a negative outlook for asset quality of banking institutions.[136]

The prudential banking practice in the HKSAR has paid a price in support of this high land price policy, as the HKSAR was debating a wider tax base. On July 28, 1998, the HKMA revoked the 40 percent nonstatutory guideline on overall property exposure by banking institutions.[137] As a result, there is no policy restricting sectorial lending. Finally, in June 2000, Tung stated that the target of providing adequate housing had not existed in substance but in name only.[130] The "low tax policy" has not only resulted in lowering the quality of life of HKSAR residents, but it also jeopardized the economic fundamental of the special administrative region. This is aggravated by the absence of capital gains tax in the HKSAR, which infringes the doctrine of equity. Budget deficits have become a serious problem in the HKSAR as it is entering this new millennium. Therefore, the HKSAR should not rely on land sales as a major source of income as it is highly elastic; it very much depends on the economic climate.

Conclusion

Although pursuant to the Basic Law the HKSAR has the appropriate constitutional, legal, and revenue framework necessary and essential to maintain it as an international center of banking and finance, the legal tradition, practices, and public policy are important facets of the legal system. As financial technology is improving rapidly, new financial products come out at a speed that is beyond the expectation of the regulators. In this globalized world, this would indicate that these new products may hit the HKSAR financial markets without any form of regulatory control. The almost successful attack on the Hong Kong currency provides the HKSAR government with an opportunity to invoke its common law prerogative powers to prevent a total meltdown of the HKSAR financial markets. However, these powers should be invoked only sparingly as an emergency measure and as a last resort. This does not imply that the HKSAR government may rely on these powers to elude its responsibility from introducing legislation in enhancing the legal framework of banking and finance to international standards.

Without a sound accounting system, the HKSAR can hardly pride itself as a substantial center of banking and finance. Most of the investors in the HKSAR are informationally impaired, as they have to rely upon the limited information available in the financial markets. The HKSAR government has a responsibility, in enacting legislation, to reform the accounting practices in the SAR. The lack of transparency and accountability in the financial markets is not conducive to attracting international investors and prudent market participants. As there is a conflict between the interests of the accounting profession and the public, the HKSAR government should not rely on the former to enhance the accounting standards.

The "low tax policy" in the HKSAR has resulted in land sales as a major source of public revenue. Not only would it distort equity, it creates instability in the banking sector, as the real property value has been artificially manipulated. The HKSAR has paid a heavy price as it has also resulted in high opportunity cost, making international businesses reluctant to locate here. Not only would this adversely affect the economic growth of the SAR, the quality of life of the HKSAR residents suffer as they can hardly afford decent housing. In this globalized economy, it is more difficult for the tax authorities to ascertain where the businesses are located. Therefore, it is imperative for the HKSAR government to look for alternative tax policy. In lieu of relying on income from land sales, it should broaden the present tax base in conformity to the "low tax policy" and to achieve equity in making the HKSAR a just society. Unfortunately, the report of the government-appointed Advisory Committee on New Broad-Based Taxes, released in August 2001, has failed to consider most of these issues.[139] The continuing economic downturn and high unemployment in the HKSAR, as acknowledged by Financial Secretary Anthony Leung in February 2002, seemed to have precluded the introduction of a sales tax of any major tax reform in the foreseeable future.[140]

Notes

The author wishes to acknowledge Dr. Brian Semkow, Associate Professor in Law, Department of Accounting, Hong Kong University of Science and Technology, for his valuable comments.

1. Article 109, Basic Law.

2. Article 73(9), Basic Law.

3. See for example, P.F. Delhaise, *Asia in Crisis: The Implosion of the Banking and Finance System* (Singapore: John Wiley & Sons [Asia] Pte. Ltd., 1998).

4. Berry Hsu, "The Legal Infrastructure of the Hong Kong Special Administrative Region: A Global Challenge." In *China Review 2000*, Lau Chung-Ming and Jianfa Shen, ed. (Hong Kong: Chinese University Press, 2000), pp. 159–62.

5. Ibid.

6. Ibid., pp. 162–66.

7. According to the secretary-general of the Legislative Council: "The Bill (Securities and Futures Bill) has been introduced into the Legislative Council last year. A subcommittee on the Bill has been subsequently formed and held its first meeting on 10 September 1999. So far, 4 meetings have been held. However, the Bill is held in abeyance for the moment since the priority has been given to other Bills. Thus, we can't tell when the subcommittee will resume its meeting for the time being." (E-mail to the author from the Legislative Council, pi@legco.gov.hk dated February 14, 2000.) In December 2000, this bill was reintroduced in the Legislative Council.

8. Hsu, "The Legal Infrastructure," pp. 166–69.

9. Articles 8 and 18, Basic Law.

10. "Transcript of Financial Secretary's Press Briefing," Daily Information Bulletin, Hong Kong Government Information Services, August 14, 1998.

11. Ibid.

12. Ibid.; "LCQ13: Gov't Move Aims to Frustrate 'double play' Strategy," Press Release, Hong Kong Financial Services Bureau, October 14, 1998.

13. J. Bhagwati, "The Capital Myth," *Foreign Affairs* 77, no. 3 (May–June 1998): 7.

14. "Transcript of Financial Secretary's Press Briefing."

15. *LC Paper No. CB(1) 534/98–99* (Hong Kong: Legislative Council, September 7, 1998), p. 4.

16. Ibid.

17. "Statement by Mr. T.L. Yang, Chairman of Exchange Fund Investment Limited," Hong Kong Monetary Authority, October 26, 1998.

18. "Authority Has Most Shares in HSBC," *South China Morning Post*, Hong Kong, September 2, 1998; Statement by Mr. T.L. Yang, October 26, 1998.

19. "Monetary Authority's HSBC Holdings Approaches British Hurdles on Ownership," *South China Morning Post*, Hong Kong, September 3, 1998.

20. *LC Paper No. CB(1) 534/98–99* (Hong Kong: Legislative Council, September 7, 1998), p. 4.

21. Ibid.

22. Ibid.

23. Ibid.

24. "Measures to Strengthen the Currency Board System," Press Release, Hong Kong: Financial Services Bureau, October 21, 1988.

25. "Front Section," *Wall Street Journal*, New York, September 30, 1998.

26. "Hong Kong Investors Play Guessing Game," *Asian Wall Street*, Tokyo, August 19, 1998.

27. K. Lynch, "The Temptation to Intervene: Problems Created by the Government's Intervention in the Hong Kong Stock Market," in *Challenges for the New International Financial Architecture: Lessons from East Asia* (Hong Kong: Asian Institute of International Financial Law, June 1999), p. 13.

28. Ibid, pp.15–16.

29. Ibid, pp.13–14.

30. *LC Paper No. CB(1) 534/98–99*, p. 5; Lynch, "The Temptation to Intervene," pp. 16–18.

31. "Financial Secretary's Transcript," Daily Information Bulletin, Hong Kong Government Information Services, September 8, 1998.

32. *LC Paper No. CB(1) 534/98–99*, p. 6.

33. "Fed Cuts Rates and Says It Will Work to Stablilize Markets," *New York Times*, September 17, 2001.

34. Section 66, Interpretation and General Clauses Ordinance, Chapter 1, Laws of Hong Kong; *Bombay v. Bombay Municipal Corporation* [1974] A.C. 58.

35. Securities Ordinance, Chapter 333, Laws of Hong Kong.

36. Securities (Disclosure of Interests) Ordinance, Chapter 396, Laws of Hong Kong.

37. J.C. Smith, and B. Hogan, *Criminal Law* (London: Butterworths, 1992), pp. 245–52.

38. Article 109, Basic Law.

39. Article 111, Basic Law.

40. Article 11, Basic Law.

41. Article 73(9), Basic Law.

42. W. Blackstone, *Commentaries on the Laws of England*, vol. 1 (Chicago: University of Chicago Press, 1979), p. 41.

43. (1610) 8 Co. Rep. 114 at p. 118.

44. *World Economic Outlook: Financial Turbulence and the World Economy* (Washington, DC: International Monetary Fund, October 1998), p. 101.

45. Ibid.

46. "Hong Kong, China's Free Market System Will Help Facilitate Economy Recovery," *Press/TPRB/95* (Washington, DC: World Trade Organization, December 4, 1998), p. 6.

47. Ibid.

48. "IMF Concludes Article IV Consultation Discussions Held with People's Republic of China in Respect of the Hong Kong Special Administrative Region," Public Information Notice (PIN) No. 00/15, March 6, 2000, http://www.imf.org/external/np/sec/pn/2000/pn0015.htm).

49. "Three Years On, Soros Praises Government over Intervention," *South China Morning Post*, Hong Kong, September 23, 2001, p. N-3.

50. *Report of the Working Group on Transparency and Accountability* (Basel: Bank for International Settlements, October 1998), p. v.

51. Ibid.

52. "Bill to Criminalise Provision of False Information," Press Release, Hong Kong Financial Services Branch, March 2, 2000.

53. Delhaise, *Asia in Crisis*, p. 48.

54. The lack of change in the HKSAR's accounting system will be discussed later in this section.

55. "IMF Concludes Article IV Consultation Discussions Held in 1997." Press Information Notice No. 98/5, February 16, 1998 (http://www.imf.org/external/np/sec/pn/1998/pn9805.htm).

56. Ibid.

57. Ibid.

58. "HSBC's Growth of 10 Percent Is Lower Than Expected," *Wall Street Journal*, New York, February 24, 1998.

59. *Experimental IMF Report on Observance of Standards and Codes: People's Republic of China–Hong Kong Special Administrative Region* (Washington, DC: International Monetary Fund, August 1999).

60. Ibid.

61. *Report of the Working Group on Transparency and Accountability*, p. 5.

62. Ibid.

63. "The Hongkong and Shanghai Banking Corporation Limited 1999 Interim Consolidated Results—Highlights," Press Release, Hong Kong: Hongkong and Shanghai Banking Corporation Limited, August 2, 1999, note 16. "If adopted the same accounting treatment as the bank of East Asia, Hong Kong and Shanghai Banking Corporation's interim profits would have risen by 72 percent." This is a translation from the Chinese-language newspaper, *Ming Pao Daily*, Hong Kong, August 3, 1999.

64. Ibid.

65. For a comparison, see T. Chan and G. Chau, "The Internationalisation of Accounting Standards Major Benefits for Hong Kong," *International Accountant* 7 (1999): 24–25. The Companies Ordinance, Chapter 32, Laws of Hong Kong, provides a general framework for auditors' responsibility. About 98 percent of companies in the HKSAR are private companies. Sections 4.11 to 4.13 of the Rules Governing the Listing of Securities on the Stock Exchange of Hong Kong Ltd. requires that the appropriate standards be those that are approved by the Hong Kong Society of Accountants and laid down in the Statements of Standard Accounting Practices.

66. Section 121(1), Companies Ordinance, Chapter 32, Laws of Hong Kong.

67. Ibid., Section 121(2).

68. Ibid., Section 123(2).

69. *Consultancy Report on the Review of the Hong Kong Companies Ordinance.* Hong Kong: Government Printer, March 1997.

70. Ibid., p. 100–101.

71. Ibid., p. 100.

72. *Experimental IMF Report on Observance of Standards and Codes: People's Republic of China–Hong Kong Special Administrative Region.* (Washington, DC: International Monetary Fund, August 1999).

73. "HKR Profits from Change in Accounting," *South China Morning Post*, Hong Kong, December 18, 1999.

74. Hong Kong Statement of Standard Accounting Practice 2.124, conform with International Accounting Standards 39.

75. "HKR Profits from Change in Accounting."

76. G. Macdonald, "Substance, Form and Equity in Taxation and Accounting," *Modern Law Review* 54, no. 6 (1991): 841.

77. [1987] B.C.L.C. 303.

78. [1980] Ch. D. 257.

79. A. McGee, "The 'True and Fair View' Debate: A Study in the Legal Regulation of Accounting," *Modern Law Review* 56, no. 6 (1991): 876.

80. "Foreword," in *Statements of Standards Accounting Practice and Accounting Guidelines* (Hong Kong: Hong Kong Society of Accountants, 1997).

81. McGee, "The 'True and Fair View' Debate," p. 876.

82. Ibid., pp. 879–81.

83. Ibid., p. 882.

84. Ibid., p. 883.

85. Paragraph 43, Part III, Third Schedule, *Companies Ordinance*, Chapter 32, Laws of Hong Kong.

86. See section 140(1)(a), *Companies Ordinance*, Chapter 32, Laws of Hong Kong, and *Professional Accountants Ordinance*, Chapter 50, Laws of Hong Kong.

87. McGee, "The 'True and Fair' Debate," p. 883.

88. [1990] 1 All E.R. 568.

89. In the context of a private company, the degree of foreseeability and proximity of relationship may justify the court in holding that auditors do owe a duty of care to shareholders, creditors, and potential investors. See V. Stott, *Hong Kong Company Law* (Hong Kong: Financial Times, 1999), p. 313.

90. D. McBarnet and C. Whelan, "The Elusive Spirit of the Law: Formalism and the Struggle for Legal Control," *Modern Law Review* 65, no. 6 (1991): 848.

91. Ibid., pp. 860–64.

92. "Analysts the Wary on Cathay," *South China Morning Post*, Hong Kong, August 11, 1995.

93. Rules Governing the Listing of Securities on the Stock Exchange of Hong Kong Ltd., Rule 4.04(1).

94. Ibid., Rules 4.04 to 4.07.

95. Ibid., Rule 4.08(2).

96. Case No. D52/96, Board of Review Decisions 554 at pp. 569–70.

97. "Unified Disclosure Seen for Main and Second Boards," *South China Morning Post*, Hong Kong, January 23, 2001.

98. Ibid.

99. Delhaise, "Asia in Crisis," p. 51.

100. Ibid.

101. Ibid.

102. "Accountants Slam Graft-Buster Plan," *South China Morning Post*, Hong Kong, October 5, 1996.

103. Ibid.

104. "Audit of the Accounts of Listed Companies," Press Release, Hong Kong Financial Services Branch, March 24, 1999, p. 3.

105. Ibid., p. 2.

106. "Fraud Case Auditors Gain Immunity," *South China Morning Post*, Hong Kong, March 25, 1999.

107. Hsu, "The Legal Infrastructure of the Hong Kong Special Administrative Region," p. 167.

108. Article 108, Basic Law.

109. Article 107, Basic Law.

110. John Rawls, *A Theory of Justice* (Oxford: Clarendon Press, 1972), p. 4.

111. Ibid., p. 4.

112. Ibid.

113. Ibid., p. 7.

114. Ibid., p. 277.

115. Ibid.

116. Ibid., p. 278.

117. Ibid., p. 279.

118. C.G. Veljanovski, "The New Law-and-Economics: A Research Review." In *Readings in the Economics of Law and Regulations*, A.I. Ogus and C. G. Veljanovski, ed. (Oxford: Clarendon Press, 1984), pp. 22–23.

119. Rawls, *A Theory of Justice*, p. 279.

120. *The 2000–01 Budget* (Hong Kong: Government Information Services, March 8, 2000). <http://www.info.gov.hk/fb/budget2000–01/english/eindex.htm>

121. Officially, there is no "high land price policy."

122. "Joint Declaration of the Government of the United Kingdom of Great Britain and Northern Ireland and the Government of the People's Republic of China on the Question of Hong Kong," Sino-British Joint Declaration, December 19, 1984.

123. "HKMA Gives Stern Warning on Mortgage Rules," *South China Morning Post*, Hong Kong, July 29, 1997.

124. *Survey on Residential Mortgages in Hong Kong* (Hong Kong: Hong Kong Monetary Authority, February 25, 1998).

125. Ibid.

126. "Housing Blueprint Sets High Targets," *South China Morning Post*, Hong Kong, July 2, 1997.

127. "Speech by the Chief Executive," Daily Information Bulletin, Hong Kong Information Services Department, July 1, 1997.

128. "CE's Letter from Hong Kong," Daily Information Bulletin, Hong Kong Information Services Department, February 14, 1998.

129. "Hong Kong Property Issues Falling to Attractive Level," *Wall Street Journal*, New York, January 27, 1998.

130. *Survey on Residential Mortgages in Hong Kong* (Hong Kong: Hong Kong Monetary Authority, February 25, 1998).

131. "CE's Letter from Hong Kong."

132. "Tamar Selected for Government Offices Complex," *South China Morning Post*, Hong Kong, January 17, 1998.

133. "Exco Backs 'Flexible' Land Sale," *South China Morning Post*, Hong Kong, February 11, 1998.

134. *Budget 98* (Hong Kong: Government Printer, February 18, 1998).

135. "HK Mortgage Corp. to Proceed with Fixed-Rate Mortgage Plans," *Wall Street Journal*, New York, February 26, 1998.

136. "Financial Secretary's Transcript," *Daily Information Bulletin*, Hong Kong Information Services Department, May 29, 1998; D. Carse, *Review of the Banking Sector First Quarter 1998* (Hong Kong: Hong Kong Monetary Authority, May 28, 1998).

137. "Withdrawal of the HKMA's 40 Percent Guideline," Guideline No. 5.9.5, Hong Kong Monetary Authority, July 28, 1998.

138. "Tung Accused of Housing Cover-Up," *South China Morning Post*, Hong Kong, July 1, 2000.

139. Advisory Committee on New Broad-Based Taxes, *A Broader-Based Tax System for Hong Kong* (Hong Kong, 2001).

140. *Sing Tao Daily*, February 6, 2002. This was in response to a recent IMF report, which expresses concerns over the HKSAR government's growing budget deficits since the late 1990s.

9

Hong Kong's Economy Since 1997

Francis T. Lui

Forecasts on the prospects of Hong Kong's post-1997 economy have often been based on subjective political beliefs rather than rational factual analysis. In 1995, a cover story of *Fortune* magazine predicted "the death of Hong Kong" after the handover (Kraar 1995). This agitated some local businessmen so much that they donated a handsome sum to establish the Better Hong Kong Foundation, the aim of which was to convince the rest of the world that Hong Kong would remain vibrant and alive. In contrast to the bearish view generally held by foreign journalists, there was also a belief that the economic integration with China would bring about unlimited profit opportunities. This sentiment dominated the market before the handover. Both the stock and the property markets reached historical peaks in mid-1997, a phenomenon that shortly afterward would set the stage for a free downfall.

Nearly five years after the handover, the Hong Kong economy has not died, but there is no prospect of the creation of a new world of wealth that would readily convert noisy critics into happy citizens. The economy is still vigorous, but difficult problems abound. Rationality should reign again when we review what has already happened and when we reformulate our expectations of the future.

The first section of this chapter will identify and discuss several issues that have critically affected Hong Kong's economy in recent years. The next section will examine the events associated with the Asian financial crisis and its impact on the Hong Kong economy. The third section will discuss the implications of the ongoing economic structural changes. In the fourth section, I shall provide an economic analysis of the rent-seeking activities prevalent in Hong Kong, which may have significant effects on both the economy and the political scene. The fifth section will report on the current state of the economy and how it will likely be shaped in the future. Concluding remarks are in the last section.

The Asian Financial Crisis and Currency Attacks on the Hong Kong Dollar

Perhaps the single most important economic event in Hong Kong after the handover was the currency attacks in 1997 and 1998, which were generally regarded as Hong Kong's manifestation of the financial crisis that plagued much of East Asia at the time. The effects of the currency attacks were so colossal that we can hardly find any counterpart in Hong Kong's financial history. Stock prices plummeted by as much as 60 percent from the peak in August 1997 to the bottom twelve months later.[1] The property market was equally troubled. The decline in real estate prices also reached the 60 percent mark in many instances, effectively causing investors to revert their long-term conviction that the housing value in Hong Kong would only appreciate. On the income side, the real per capita gross domestic product (GDP) went down by 7.8 percent in 1998, a phenomenon totally unknown to Hong Kong, which had never experienced a year of declining GDP in its recorded economic history.

The initial reaction of the Hong Kong Special Administrative Region (SAR) government was one of indifference and misguided self-confidence. In the summer of 1997, when Hong Kong, at the request of the International Monetary Fund (IMF), contributed U.S.$1 billion in cheap loans to rescue Thailand, the government obviously felt that it was financially strong enough to avoid a crisis of its own. After the first major attack on the Hong Kong dollar on October 23, 1997, when the interbank interest rate went up to 280 percent, the financial secretary was convinced that the speculators had been defeated, and that the Asian financial crisis would die down by Christmas of that year. Later developments have shown that this was entirely not the case. The government was so confident of its performance that, despite the warning of a depression by some economists, it predicted at the time a real GDP growth of 4 percent for 1998. It turned out that the growth rate was minus 5.1 percent!

The government's optimism was not without reasons. Even though asset prices were very high, statistics indicated that the Hong Kong economy was robust and strong. Its foreign reserves, valued at over U.S.$80 billion, were the third largest in the world. Moreover, the government did have a successful record of fending off a minor currency attack after the Mexican currency crisis in early 1995. Where did things go wrong?

The basic tool of defense against currency attacks used by the Hong Kong

Monetary Authority (HKMA) was the interest rate arbitrage, sometimes also known as the *automatic adjustment mechanism*. In essence, this means that interest rate of the Hong Kong dollar would automatically go up when an outflow of capital caused a decline in the liquidity in the banks. This would make deposits in Hong Kong dollars more attractive and the money flowing in would strengthen the Hong Kong dollars again. More importantly, it was believed that speculators would be "punished" in the process. Speculators who wanted to short the Hong Kong dollar would have to acquire it through borrowing. The rising interest rate would impose a higher cost on them, according to the logic. If the currency did not devalue, it was thought that they could only pay for the interest costs without being able to derive any profits. To make the penalty more prohibitive, the HKMA resorted to discretionary measures to artificially push up the interest rate further on October 23.[2]

Historical hindsight tells us that this approach was a costly policy mistake. First, the high interest rate was not effective in discouraging the speculators, who had at their disposal a more advanced strategy of attack. They would first short the Hang Seng Index of the stock market, and/or the Hong Kong dollar in the forward market. Then they would short the Hong Kong dollar in the spot market, knowing well that the latter action would trigger a rise in the interest rate. This in turn would lead to the fall in the stock and forward currency markets. Since they had already positioned themselves in these markets, they could make profits that would exceed the interest costs in the spot market. Thus, speculators could benefit even more if the HKMA tried to push up the interest rate.

Second, the theory that higher interest rate would strengthen the Hong Kong dollar, the very foundation of the automatic adjustment mechanism, was no longer valid. For this mechanism to work, we need the additional assumption that people had the confidence that the linked exchange rate system of Hong Kong would not be abandoned. Under the linked exchange rate, if people have confidence, then the interest rates of the Hong Kong dollar and the U.S. dollar should be the same. If confidence is eroded, then holding Hong Kong dollar denominated assets would incur higher risks. A rise in the interest rate differential between the Hong Kong dollar and the U.S. dollar could simply represent a premium to compensate the risk of holding the Hong Kong dollar. Recent empirical research has shown that after 1992, when the HKMA began to deviate from the fixed and passive rules of Hong Kong's currency board, that is, the linked exchange rate system, by intervening extensively into the currency market, the interest rate arbitrage had already lost its effectiveness. A rise in the interest rate would be associated with a weakened, rather than stronger, Hong Kong dollar (see Kwan, Lui, and Cheng 2001). The artificial measures taken on October 23 to push up the interest rate could be interpreted by the market as a further piece of evidence that the HKMA would not always follow the rules of a currency board, which by nature is a system of simple and passive rules. There would be less reason for people to believe that the HKMA would not abandon the linked exchange rate altogether. Thus, we saw that the interest rate of the Hong Kong dollar had persistently been higher than that of the U.S. dollar during and after the crisis, but the Hong Kong dollar did not strengthen.

Third, the high interest rate could induce two additional effects on the real economy. On the one hand, it made investment and consumption more costly. This would cause a decline in the aggregate demand in the economy. On the other hand, as discussed above, the market could interpret the higher interest rate as a signal that it was risky to hold assets denominated in Hong Kong dollars. People therefore would again cut back their investment and consumption. Both effects would lower the level of output of the economy. It was not surprising that Hong Kong entered a period of credit crunch and economic depression from late 1997 to late 1998.

The high interest rate strategy of the HKMA was endorsed by the IMF, which for a long time had been preoccupied by financial turmoil in Latin American countries. These economies were often characterized by high inflation and insufficient discipline on fiscal expenditures. In such an environment, the restraint on aggregate demand induced by high interest rate would make sense. However, this was not the case for Hong Kong and many other Asian economies. A group of economists at the Hong Kong University of Science and Technology, supported by Nobel Laureate Merton Miller, had long been insisting that the high interest rate was the wrong medicine and could only aggravate the problem. The key to the solution, according to them, was how the precondition of the proper working of the automatic adjustment mechanism could be restored. As discussed above, the reason for the failure of the mechanism was that confidence in the HKMA's determination of maintaining the linked exchange rate was eroded. If the market believed that the Hong Kong dollar's fixed link with the U.S. dollar would not be abandoned, then a small increase in Hong Kong's interest rate relative to that of the United States would be enough to strengthen the currency. The room for strategic speculation would also be limited. To restore confidence, it was not sufficient for the HKMA to declare that it would not devalue the currency. It had to put its money where its mouth was. Thus, these economists proposed the issuance of Hong Kong dollar put options, which were essentially an insurance scheme for the currency. Holders of the put options could demand compensation from the HKMA in case the latter had decided to devalue the Hong Kong dollar. Since the HKMA would lose money when it devalued the Hong Kong dollar, the very issuance of the put options would send the signal to the market that it had no intention of doing so.

The proposal was not welcome by the HKMA in the beginning. In an official review of the financial crisis published by the government in April 1998, it sharply criticized the proposal.[3] It also solicited advices from the IMF, which at the time was under severe attack from a number of prominent economists on its mishandling of the financial crisis. Not surprisingly, the IMF maintained its "company position" and dismissed the proposal.

Economic reality did not help the Hong Kong government's position. In January, June, and August 1998, speculative attacks occurred again and again. It became plainly true that the high interest rate doctrine had failed and was causing serious damage to the economy. Unemployment went up, income went down, and asset prices declined sharply. The HKMA also officially admitted that the speculators could profit through the double- or triple-playing strategy described earlier. It was hard for the HKMA, or for that matter, any organization, to abandon a paradigm it had held for years. During the speculative attack in August 1998, the Hong Kong government suddenly decided to intervene massively in the stock market. Its intention presumably was to break the circuit of the attack by making it more difficult to profit from shorting the stock index. Discussing the implications of this departure from the free market practice that was known to be a hallmark of Hong Kong's economy would be outside the scope of this chapter. However, it is still appropriate to ask the question of whether the intervention was effective and necessary in ending the crisis.

There were indeed no more speculative attacks after the stock market intervention. However, to conclude that it had terminated the attacks would be an example of logical fallacy. To understand this, we have to know more about some events occurring subsequently.

On September 5, 1998, the HKMA announced the introduction of seven "technical" measures that in effect amounted to the reversion of the high interest strategy. These measures essentially did two things. First, more liquidity would be provided in the aggregate balance of the banking system when needed, thus reducing the chance of interest rate hikes in times of capital outflows. Second, as testified by Professor Merton Miller in the Legislative Council on November 14, 1998, the so-called convertibility undertaking that was part of the measures was nothing but Hong Kong dollar put options in another form. The effects of the put options, as noted earlier, were to reduce the perceived risks of holding Hong Kong dollars. This in turn would lower the interest rate differential between Hong Kong and the United States. Indeed, recent research using high-frequency data shows that the differential had gone down after the introduction of the seven measures. However, it should be pointed out that put options have well-specified periods of expiration, thus making them legally credible. In the case of the seven measures, no such time element was present. This incompleteness quickly induced a market test. A rapid outflow of capital exceeding by far those during the currency crisis occurred on September 14, 1998.[4] The earlier stock market intervention was not able to calm down the market. The HKMA was forced to clarify the time frame of the convertibility undertaking. This filled the missing condition of the put options, and interest rate differential then remained at a low level, which made speculative attacks much more difficult than before.

An unexpected, but important, external event also significantly helped to restore market confidence. The collapse of a hedge fund, the Long Term Capital Management fund, caused a sharp drop in the exchange rate of the U.S. dollar relative to the yen. This means that the Hong Kong dollar, which has been linked to the U.S. dollar, also depreciated relative to the yen. Much of the pressure on the exchange rate of the Hong Kong dollar therefore disappeared, making it harder to profit through shorting the Hong Kong dollar.

The narrowing of the interest rate differential was a necessary condition for economic recovery. Without this, the market would look at investment in Hong Kong dollars or in assets denominated in Hong Kong dollars apprehensively. By the time the technical measures were implemented, Hong Kong was already in a state of deep recession. It was not that people did not have money, but that they were not willing to spend or invest. It took time for people to make sure that the risks of holding Hong Kong dollar assets had diminished. Figure 9.1 shows that output gradually picked up again and Hong Kong began to move out of the recession in the first quarter of 1999. The Asian financial crisis was over in Hong Kong, at least for the time being.

Structural Changes

The second phenomenon that has had fundamental impact on Hong Kong's post-1997 economy is the structural changes. When many people leave from one industry and move to another, we say that some structural change occurs in the economy. If those leaving an industry can immediately get jobs in others, structural changes do not affect the unemployment rate. However, the transition is usually not smooth because searching for new jobs and developing the new skills necessary for the jobs require time. Hence, the faster the structural changes, the higher will be the unemployment rate. A study by Kwan, Lian, and Lui (1995) has shown that around 60 percent of the fluctuations in unemployment in Hong Kong can be explained by structural changes.

In fact, structural changes are not new to Hong Kong (Lui 2000). In the

Figure 9.1 **Index of Seasonally Adjusted Quarterly Real GDP**

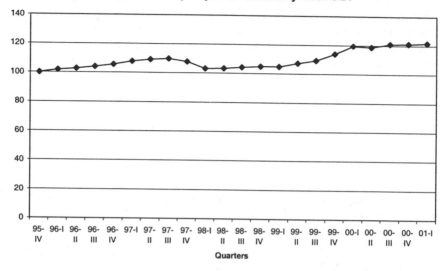

1950s, Hong Kong's economy depended on entrepôt trade, textiles, metal manufacturing, and other low-skill industries. A vigorous real estate sector began to develop in the 1960s. Some industries requiring a higher level of sophistication, such as electronics, toys, and watches, became more important. The most prominent structural changes affecting today's economy began later. First, Hong Kong has developed itself into a major international financial center since the early 1980s. This has created employment opportunities for a large number of well-educated professionals. Second, the open-door policy has made it possible for entrepreneurs in Hong Kong to take advantage of the abundance of cheap labor in China. Factories have moved to the north, causing a major shrinking of the manufacturing sector in Hong Kong. Employment in this sector has gone down from more than nine hundred thousand workers in the 1980s to fewer than three hundred thousand now. The service sector has expanded significantly, more than absorbing the people who have left manufacturing.

Several issues must be addressed about this transformation. The real prices of labor-intensive products in the world market have been declining since the 1980s. This may have been due to the fact that several labor-abundant countries, most notably China, have integrated into the world market. The new and large supply of labor-intensive products has pulled down their prices. Economic theory tells us that this would cause a dragging effect on the wage rate of low-skilled workers. In fact, from the 1980s to the time before the handover, the real wage rate of manufacturing workers had increased, but the magnitude of the rise was relatively small.[5]

Although workers' unions often complain about the low wages of the unskilled workers, what we really need to explain is not why they have low income, but rather, why their wage rate before the financial crisis was so resilient to the negative impact of declining product prices and competition of cheap labor from the Chinese mainland. A plausible explanation is the expansion of the domestic service sector. Examples of the services provided are retailing, food and restaurants, and transportation. Unlike manufactured goods, these services are often nontradables. Workers who have moved into this sector are therefore less affected by the process of factor price equalization under a free trade regime. However, the "protection" they have is fragile. Their wages are far from being immune to external shocks. So long as the residents of Hong Kong continue to be productive and enjoy rising income, the demand for domestically supplied services will remain robust. When there is an economic downturn, workers in this sector may be subject to double jeopardy. The reduced income will directly slow down consumer activities. Moreover, at lower income, many consumers will choose to purchase the much cheaper, though less convenient, services provided from across the border. After the onset of the Asian financial crisis, we have seen stagnancy or slow growth in the income of low-skilled workers.[6]

The stagnancy in wages and the rise in unemployment of low-skilled workers have been a major source of social tension after 1997. Since competition from the cheap labor in China will persist, these problems will likely remain. Are there measures to mitigate them? Two policies seem to be appropriate.

The first is to upgrade their skill level through training. So long as they are more efficient than their counterparts in neighboring economies, they may be able to maintain a higher income level. In reality, it is not always clear that low-skilled workers in Hong Kong are more capable than those in the Chinese mainland. The adult illiteracy rate for females in Hong Kong was as high as 11 percent in 1998, while that for males was 4 percent.[7] The task of training them could be difficult and inefficient for many workers, especially the more elderly ones. A second approach is to import a large number of highly educated professionals. If Hong Kong has enough of such people in the high-tech areas, the resulting cluster effect may be able to allow Hong Kong to develop some new profitable sectors.[8] As discussed above, this will raise the demand for domestic services and help to create employment opportunities for the less skilled.

The second approach is in fact a proclaimed policy of the government. In the budget speech for 2001–02, the financial secretary proposed a new scheme for importing talents from China. It does not limit the number of people who can come in, but they are restricted to the fields of financial services and information technology. Although still at a rudimentary stage, the primary objectives are targeted at strengthening these two sectors in Hong Kong. The implications for the financial sector may be less radical because a large number of expatriates have for a long time already been working in finance. However, the importation of Chinese professionals in information technology, if successful, will pave the way for another wave of major structural changes in Hong Kong. Is Hong Kong ready for high tech yet?

To understand the significance of this question, we have to realize that most of the previous attempts to develop high-tech industries in Hong Kong had led to losses in profits. Many industrialists have argued that without government support in the form of implicit subsidies, it would be difficult to build up these industries. However, if their long-term profits by themselves are not sufficient to attract investments, then why should other taxpayers pay money to either cover their losses or increase their profits? Industrial policy that involves picking the winners is not compatible with Hong Kong's own success story of free market economics. On the other hand, objecting to market intervention by the government does not imply that Hong Kong should not have high tech. If the market gives the signal that high tech is profitable, there is no reason Hong Kong should not develop it. In fact, in recent years, there has been a large increase in the number of scientists and engineers in Hong Kong, with many of them affiliated with universities. Their potential impact on society, however, has not been fully realized. This may be due to the particular nature of high-tech development, where economy of scale is important. When there are not enough talents around, high-tech companies will not be eager to invest in Hong Kong because production will be inefficient. They therefore will not hire these people. If Hong Kong has imported or produced enough talents, high-tech business will be more viable. The companies may find it profitable enough to invest in these industries and hire more talents. A necessary step to initiate the process is for the government to remove policies that obstruct the free movement of human capital into Hong Kong. Here I want to point out that importation and training of manpower in technology will help not only Hong Kong's industrial upgrading, but also alleviate the problem of declining wage rate for the less skilled people.

The Political Economy of Rent-Seeking Activities in Hong Kong

Although the attention of Hong Kong's people was largely captured by such devastating economic events as the Asian financial crisis and rising unemployment after the handover, we should not forget the fact that political contests were a hallmark of pre-1997 public affairs. Politics after 1997 continue to play an important role, but probably in other contexts. In a sense, economic and political interests have become so intertwined that it has become more difficult than before to draw a line between the two.

It is well known that during the colonial period before the 1970s, a few prominent companies, organizations and families were very influential in shaping government decision makings. Usually having some ties with Britain, they could share a significant portion of the economic and political interests available in Hong Kong. The emergence of a new generation of rich Chinese families, notably those in the business of real estate, was able to challenge the old elite. Such a historic event as the handover must inevitably come with further reshuffling of power and influences. With the receding of British interests, opportunities for new contenders arise. Since there is no established rule on who own the interests, essentially many newcomers can compete.

The theory of rent-seeking activities tells us that when benefits are allocated by nonmarket means, agents will spend time, and political and economic resources to compete for them. Examples include bribery, lobbying, exerting political pressure, organizing mass demonstrations, and maneuvering public opinions. At equilibrium, the value of the resources spent by an individual is almost as large as the expected benefits, or rents, he or she can get. The resources dissipated in the process are often "wasted," because they are not necessarily put into socially productive uses. However, from the individual's point of view, it is perfectly rational to engage in these activities because they may yield profitable returns. The theory also tells us that the bigger are the rents, the more will be the resources dissipated in the activities.

This theory can go a long way in explaining public affairs in Hong Kong in recent years. Political parties, labor unions, and business organizations often have to represent different interest groups to compete for benefits. The target of lobbying is usually the government, which controls a lot of resources that are not allocated by market means. If the government's allocation mechanism is such that it relies only on well-prescribed fixed rules, then probably the lobby groups cannot do much. However, if the government is perceived to be flexible when being pressured, then the expected returns of rent-seeking activities will be higher, and lobby groups will have greater incentives to engage in these.

Circumstantial evidence suggests that the government has indeed been flexible. For example, welfare expenditures relative to the GDP have been rising. The granting of land to build the Cyberport has often been viewed as a result of political influences. The temporary withholding of land sales in 1998 and the drastic and frequent changes in housing policies would not have happened without intensive lobbying. It is not the purpose of this chapter to evaluate the merit of these individual policies. What matters here is the perception that it is possible for some interest groups to gain by spending resources to influence the government.

These activities would amount to political pressure on the government. One easy way out is for the government to satisfy the wants of these interest groups as much as possible. However, this implies that greater public expenditures will have to be spent. After all, there is no compelling reason why an official should resist political pressure by refusing to spend public resources that he does not own. A vicious cycle could be created. When a pie gets bigger, people will make greater efforts to fight for a bigger slice of it. The government, feeling the pressure, may be induced to spend more and more. This partly explains why government expenditures as a share of GDP have been rising rapidly during the last decades or so.

In the long run, this will have its impact on the economy. First, as pointed out above, some resources will be dissipated in socially unproductive usages. Second, the rising government expenditures will likely reduce the long-term economic growth rate of Hong Kong.[9] Third, some sense of unfairness could be felt by those who have little means to compete for the rents. They may resort to engaging in political activities in which they have the comparative advantage, as for example, demonstrations on the street. This again is not an attraction for business investments. The negative impact, however, can be mitigated if the government tries hard to reduce public expenditures. When it is generally believed that not much can be gained by lobbying the government, then rent-seeking activities will diminish.

Prospects for Hong Kong's Economic Development

In this section, I will venture into the difficult issue of how Hong Kong's economy might develop in the future. To do this, I first provide a summary of where Hong Kong stands now.

Figure 9.1 is a good indicator of how Hong Kong's economy has been doing since the handover. We see that the quarterly real GDP began to decline in the last quarter of 1997, and it hit the bottom five quarters later. After that, it started to rebound. By the end of 2000, real GDP was at a level roughly 10 percent higher than that in 1996. However, since population also increased by about 10 percent during the same period, per capita real GDP remained unchanged. The decline during and after the financial crisis was largely due to the credit crunch induced by high interest rates. When the interest rates' differential diminished, investor and consumer confidence slowly recovered, and hence the bouncing back occurred in the year 2000. It is not clear how long this will continue. An econometric model constructed by Chow (1998) forecasts very slow or even negative growth for 2001 and possibly a certain period beyond that.[10] To put it in another perspective, a problem for Hong Kong is whether it can identify new engines of economic growth for the future.

There are two engines that are often mentioned in public policy discussions. The first is China's accession to the World Trade Organization (WTO) and the second is technological advances. Their policy implications are different.

How will Hong Kong be affected by China's accession to the WTO? Freer trade will enhance China's efficiency and growth, which will benefit Hong Kong both directly and indirectly. However, since there will be fewer trade barriers, other countries can trade with China without going through Hong Kong. Thus, there will be a process of deintermediation, which may hurt Hong Kong. It does not imply that Hong Kong will lose its role as an intermediary entirely. There may be certain intermediation in which Hong Kong has comparative advantage. When trade expands, it can gain more business in those areas that it has comparative advantage. For example, Hong Kong has acquired rich experience in being an international financial center. Its stock market is well suited to help China in privatizing many of its state-owned enterprises and provides access to vast amount of international capital. Probably no other stock market in China or elsewhere in the world enjoys the same combination of brand name, free market, rigorous system of monitoring and regulations, availability of a large pool of first-class financial talents, and cultural affinity as Hong Kong. Moreover, accession to the WTO requires China to allow foreign banks to operate in its land five years later. There are well-known difficulties plaguing Chinese banks. It is not clear whether Chinese banks can compete with foreign banks in providing financial services in a free market. Probably some of them will lose out. This is not necessarily bad for China, because better financial services will be available, and resources previously used by the local banks can be allocated for more efficient uses. It should be noted that some banks in Hong Kong are highly competitive, even in the world market. There is further potential for them to expand in China or to engage in joint ventures with other Chinese banks.

Technological advances will improve productive and management efficiency. This by itself can already be an engine of growth. More importantly, it provides new opportunities for Hong Kong to develop itself into a center in certain high-tech areas. The most important condition for this to happen is human capital. Without further training of its people and importation of talents from other places, especially from China, Hong Kong will not have the critical mass of people to succeed. Currently, educational and immigration policies are not yet conducive to developing high tech. If they are not re-formed, Hong Kong may lose the opportunities.

The importance of human capital should not be underestimated. Besides a wide array of well-known problems in the schooling system, the quality of labor in Hong Kong is plagued by another serious difficulty. Current economic structural changes in Hong Kong have the feature that low-skill jobs in manufacturing and local services are gradually abandoned. Hong Kong has for a long time been very efficient in these areas; that is, its people have acquired a lot of experience and expertise in labor-intensive products and services. Abandoning them means that the human capital of many people in Hong Kong will soon be obsolete. Moreover, the acquisition of new human capital necessary for the development of higher value-added industries is time consuming and costly. It is likely that during the long transition period that lies ahead, many workers will face difficulties in finding jobs.

Conclusion

Throughout history there have been prominent cities that have later receded into obscurity. For example, Venice was once the greatest commercial hub of the Western world, partly because of its geographical convenience in the Mediterranean. The historical accident of discovering the Cape of Good Hope changed the trade route away from the Mediterranean and led to the decline of Venice's relative economic importance.

Hong Kong has been a great commercial city. Will it lose its prominence because of some unexpected events, or will new opportunities lead it into even greater prosperity? Nobody can really be sure. The economic difficulties that Hong Kong has been facing after the handover may be a wake-up call for its people. Reflecting more carefully upon the strengths and weaknesses of Hong Kong, rather than immersing ourselves in misguided confidence, will improve the chance that Hong Kong will remain prominent.

Notes

1. The Hang Seng Index closed at 16,673 on August 7, 1997, and it reached 6,660 on August 13, 1998.

2. For more detailed discussions on how the HKMA attempted to defend the Hong Kong dollar during the currency attack, see Kwan, Lui, and Cheng (2001) and Lui, Cheng, and Kwan (1999).

3. See the *Report on the Review of the Financial Crisis* published by the Financial Services Bureau of the Hong Kong SAR government in April 1998.

4. See Kwan, Lui, and Cheng (2001) and Lui, Cheng, and Kwan (1999).

5. It is not correct to claim that real income of the less skilled workers had gone down during this period. Statistics from the census show that the number of low-

income people declined substantially before 1996, but the number of better-paid people had increased. See Lui (1997, chap. 29).

6. From September 1997 to March 2001, the real wage index of low-level workers actually had gone up by almost 9 percent, but the nominal wage index had increased only by 3 percent. Within this period, both the real and nominal wage indexes experienced declines in some instances. See the wage statistics at the website of the Census and Statistics Department of the Hong Kong SAR government (http://www.info.gov.hk/censtatd/eng/hkstat/fas/wages_index.html).

7. The average number of years of schooling of the workforce in Hong Kong is twelve years, which is four or five years less than in technologically advanced countries. This partly explains why Hong Kong finds it very hard to move into a knowledge-based economy. See World Bank (2000) for the relevant statistics.

8. In the financial sector, Hong Kong has already built up a sizable cluster. The income generated from this sector should have supported the demand for many domestically supplied services.

9. The empirical evidence in Barro (1990) shows that there is a negative relationship between government expenditures as a share of GDP and the long-term economic growth rate.

10. After the unexpected September 11, 2001, tragedy in New York City, the forecast for Hong Kong's economic growth has to be revised downward to a slightly negative value. Chow's model (1998) has been used to successfully forecast Hong Kong's economic performance for several years. The results are routinely reported at the website of the Center for Economic Development: http://www.bm.ust.hk/~ced/.

Bibliography

Barro, Robert J. "Government Spending in a Simple Model of Endogenous Growth," *Journal of Political Economy* 98, no. 5 (1990): S103–25.

Chow, Wai Yip William. "On Forecasting the Hong Kong Economy with Bayesian Vector Autoregression Model." Department of Economics, Hong Kong University of Science and Technology, Ph.D. diss., 1998.

Hong Kong SAR government. *Report on the Review of the Financial Crisis*. Financial Services Bureau. Hong Kong: April 1998.

———. *The 2001–02 Budget: Honing Our Strengths, Striving to Excel*. Speech by the financial secretary, March 7, 2001.

Imai, Hiroyuki. "Structural Transformation and Economic Growth in Hong Kong: Another Look at Young's Hong Kong Thesis," *Journal of Comparative Economics* 29, no. 2 (2001): 366–82.

Kraar, Louis. "The Death of Hong Kong," *Fortune* 131, no. 12 (June 26, 1995): 118–38.

Kwan, Yum K., Joseph Y. Lian, and Francis T. Lui. "Hong Kong's Unemployment and Imported Labor," Department of Economics, mimeograph, Hong Kong University of Science and Technology, 1995.

Kwan, Yum K., Francis T. Lui, and Leonard K. Cheng. "Credibility of Currency Boards Under Attacks: The Role of Institutional Arrangements." In *Regional and Global Capital Flows: Macroeconomic Causes and Consequences* (NBER–East Asia Seminar on Economics, vol. 10), Takatoshi Ito and Anne O. Krueger, ed. Chicago: University of Chicago Press, 2001.

Lui, Francis T. *Economics at the Eye of a Storm*. Hong Kong: Infowide Press (in Chinese), 1997.

——. "Hong Kong's Economic Structural Changes." In *Blueprint for the 21st Century Hong Kong*, Siu-kai Lau, ed. Hong Kong: Chinese University of Hong Kong Press (in Chinese), 2000.

Lui, Francis T., Leonard K. Cheng, and Yum K. Kwan. "Currency Board, Asian Financial Crisis, and the Case for Structured Notes." Center for Economic Development, Hong Kong University of Science and Technology (http://www.bm.ust.hk/~ced/), Research Papers, 1999.

World Bank. *World Development Report*. New York: Oxford University Press, 2000.

——— 10 ———

"Fifty Years No Change"?

Land-Use Planning and Development in Hong Kong Under Constitutional Capitalism

Lawrence Lai

> "The complexity of zoning law means more powers
> for regulators."
> (Siegan 1997: 189)

Hong Kong, as part of China, often captures attention in international politics in terms of human rights and free trade. While the issue of human rights[1] may be contentious, there is apparent universal acceptance that Hong Kong's economy has always been a good example of laissez-faire capitalism.[2] On the premise that the foundations of capitalism are the rule of law and private property rights,[3] this chapter will show that a number of land-use planning issues in Hong Kong involve not only human but also property rights problems. These property rights problems are pertinent to the operation of a market economy. These problems are also constitutional law problems under the Basic Law.[4]

On July 1, 1997, a Western democratic country "handed over" land and people under her administration to the last viable communist regime. Much has been said by local academics[5] about physical planning of the land uses of Hong Kong in the "transitional period" which ended on June 30, 1997. The literature generated focuses on specific town-planning issues (notably transport links with China, environmental protection); the uniqueness of Hong Kong among Chinese cities; and the internal consistency of the planning polices and strategies. However, there has been no attempt to evaluate the land-use planning system of Hong Kong within her constitutional law setting. This setting is provided by the Basic Law, which is stated to provide an overarching legal framework[6] for Hong Kong as a Special Administrative Region (SAR) of China for at least fifty years from July 1, 1997. This chapter attempts to fill the gap by discussing the key issues that pose as challenges to the government town planner in Hong Kong at the turn of the century within the context of the Basic Law.

As a result of the political origin of the Basic Law as a kind of guarantee of confidence for the future in the year of 1984,[7] the Basic Law was drafted to reflect three fundamental a priori presumptions. These presumptions are that (1) Hong Kong can take care of her own domestic affairs under the blessing of "a high degree of autonomy"; (2) the social and economic practices, notably "capitalism" and "private property," that evolved under colonial rule can be *preserved*; and (3) the fundamental guarantees under the Basic Law need not change for fifty years. These presumptions are expressed clearly in Articles 2 and 5 of the Basic Law.[8]

The key land-use planning issues in the official agenda or programs are:

1. Deepening of *statutory control of land uses* by extending the coverage of town plans and refining plans already in place;[9]
2. Speeding up *urban renewal* in the old urban areas of Hong Kong Island and Kowloon;[10]
3. Tightening *enforcement against unauthorized uses* on land on which agriculture has been abandoned;[11]
4. Accommodating the "*small-house policy*" for "indigenous villagers";[12]
5. Protecting *Victoria Harbor* from further reclamation;[13]
6. Protecting *Mai Po Marshes* from encroachment of suburban development;[14]
7. Developing a meaningful policy package of *sustainable development*;[15]
8. Creating new bases for *high-tech industries*, including a science park by Tolo Harbor and a "cyberport" at Pokfulam;[16]
9. Creating new *tourist attractions*, including a cable car route and a Disneyland on Lantau Island;[17] and
10. Creating model *smokeless townships* in the New Territories, where atmospheric pollution in Hong Kong has reached historically high levels.[18]

The first six issues have been carried forward from the colonial era, whereas the last four are innovations of the SAR government. Below, they are reduced to six sets of issues and are discussed in terms of the three fundamental presumptions of the Basic Law, namely protection of private property, a high degree of autonomy, and fifty years of no change.

Planning and Freedom Under Constitutional Capitalism

A meaningful discussion of the six issues can only be possible by reference to an unambiguous definition of "capitalism." This term is admittedly hard to define, as it is ultimately a matter of political theory and beliefs. However, we may, as a second best option, outline some fundamental features of capitalism that are well understood by the economist. This position is consistent with the overarching concern of the drafter of the Basic Law to embody one of the provisions of the Sino-British Agreement, namely the preservation of private property and economic freedom of the residents and investors of Hong Kong.

In this context, therefore, *capitalism* (or more specifically, *market economy*), as protected by the Basic Law, would mean the respect for and protection of private property as well as the rule of law. According to Thomas Sowell, private property rights are rigidities[19] that should not be altered unilaterally by government. This underlies the idea of James Buchanan that private property is a kind of self-production that allows the owner the liberty or freedom from the "blind forces of the market."[20] Such freedom constitutes the baseline of any social system that may be described as capitalist. Following Steven Cheung's thesis,[21] the term *private property rights* refers to the freedom to use, to derive income, and to alienate rights connected with a resource owned. Such freedom is exercisable by way of contract and includes the freedom, or the right, not to exercise any of these three rights. These dimensions constitute the baseline of any social system that may be described as capitalist. This baseline is the yardstick for assessing factual compliance of existing ordinances and policies subordinate and subsidiary to the Basic Law. Ideally, as advanced by the libertarian economist, the role of the government shall be confined to that of a laissez-faire minimalist state. The state would perform the role of adjudicators of contracts and would refrain from interfering with private contracts.[22]

Undoubtedly, one may contend that such idealized capitalism has never been in practice in Hong Kong, or indeed anywhere on earth, and that ideal capitalism is neither politically feasible nor correct. The fact is that Hong Kong has imported from the United Kingdom many salient features of the welfare state since the early 1970s. Public housing (for 50 percent of Hong Kong's population), subsidized education (from primary to university levels), and labor and social security legislation became part of Hong Kong law before the resumption of sovereign powers of China over Hong Kong. This chapter is not a political discourse on ideal capitalism. However, insofar as "capitalism" and one of its premises, "private property," are expressly stated to be preserved or protected in the Basic Law, we need to use the yardstick established above for interpreting the impacts of planning legislation and policies.

The Displacement of Contractual Planning by Statutory Planning

It has been said that the leasehold system of land in Hong Kong is inherently "socialist," and thus that statutory planning regulating private land rights conferred upon the lessee by the land lease is of no significance. This argument confuses two different issues, namely the nature of leasehold land tenure and the legitimacy of legislation overriding private rights. It may be arguable that the government has the *authority* to "socialize" private rights over land by legislation, say to impose certain uncompensated or compensated planning requirements. These requirements include those for uncompensated planning permission or downzoning (notably by lowering plot ratios); compensated resumption (the equivalent of compulsory acquisition, takings or eminent domain); and uncompensated nullification of common law rights to use agricultural land for open storage.[23] We shall discuss planning applications and downzoning here, and deal with resumption and planning enforcement in the following sections.

Two basic characteristics of the leasehold land system in Hong Kong have been neglected. First, it is a contractual system by which government allocates private rights and obligations over land to lessees for cash consideration.[24] Government stipulates in the land lease various controls over land use and building forms by express and implied covenants. Second, it is a means of private planning, as the development and management of land uses are matters of lessees. In other words, it is a means of private planning regulated by government by contract, the land lease.[25] These characteristics of the leasehold planning have been overwhelmed by the perception of town planning as a matter of statutory land use zoning introduced by the Town Planning Ordinance of 1939.[26]

By December 1999, almost all developable lands in Hong Kong had been covered by statutory town plans. This means that these plans cover all lands held privately under the leasehold system. When a piece of private land obtained by contract is zoned and the intended new land use for that land falls under Column 2 in the "Notes" of the statutory town plan or where there is another requirement for planning permission, the lessee must submit a planning application. This is so, notwithstanding that such intended use is permitted under the lease for which the lessee paid a market price. A planning application may be approved by the Town Planning Board only after repeated applications. The planning application system thus erodes private property rights of lessees to freely use land for its highest-value use and operates as an inefficient non–price allocation mechanism[27] that rations development rights. Rent-seeking activities are natural consequences of this institutional arrangement.[28] The grounds for zoning regulation of leasehold interests by planning application are often unsubstantiated, imaginary rather than objective.[29]

Where the private land of a lessee and that of others fall within the same "Comprehensive Development Area," each lessee would lose private property rights to use his or her own land without the consent of third parties. Lessees may only redevelop the zone jointly according to a master layout plan approved by the Town Planning Board. Though the results may be better physical development of the zone,[30] the transaction costs involved in reaching a joint agreement can be so prohibitively high that only compulsory resumption backed by government powers can get any redevelopment project off the ground. This outcome creates the problem of private property infringement of another kind, as discussed in the next section.

Sometimes the zoning plan may involve downzoning. One form of downzoning has the effect of restricting the choice of land uses open to the lessee. Another form of downzoning is the imposition of a plot ratio (tested in the *Crozet* case) smaller than that stipulated in the lease prevailing at the time the lease is purchased. In either case, the injured lessee is uncompensated. Downzoning therefore amounts to taxation in kind without benefiting the taxpayer financially. Presumably, the loss of the lessee is compensated by the benefits due to the improvement to the environment, an outcome that, above all, also benefits the public at large. Whether such benefits exist is an empirical question. However, uncompensated downzoning to the lessee affected is an infringement of private property rights to derive income according to the terms and expectation of a contract.

It is mentioned above that Hong Kong has imported welfare state legislation since the 1970s. In terms of planning legislation, an interventionist approach can be traced as far as the nineteenth century in the forms of various ordinances regulating building construction. Specific legislation known as town planning was introduced eventually by the Town Planning Ordinance of 1939. The legality of zoning that may override rights under the leasehold system was tested in the *Singway* case[31] in the early 1970s. Thereafter, effective introduction of statutory town plans has been speeded up cumulating in the almost complete coverage of land.

Under the interventionist mentality, statutory zoning has been taken for granted as a matter of "public interest."[32] However, the implication of the imposition of a statutory plan, which often attenuates private property rights over privately held land, has seldom been articulated in the politics of Hong Kong by reference to the Basic Law. This is notwithstanding the fact that academics and legal practitioners have been aware of the rather precarious nature of "private property" in "capitalist" Hong Kong.[33] The focus of this chapter is the conflict of the terms of land leases as contracts on the one hand and laws on the other. The peculiar nature of the conflict is that both leases and laws are products of the same executive-led government. That "public interest" is offered as a reason by government in unilaterally compromising or even extinguishing contractual land rights by planning legislation has seldom captured the attention of scholars. The application of the concept of "public interest" in handling planning matters can be so extreme that no private development is possible even where it is environmentally benign.[34]

The developer or the "market" is often viewed by officials and top judges with great contempt as threats to public interest[35] as they see fit for Hong Kong. This mindset is dramatically different from the international image of Hong Kong's economic order the SAR government seeks to maintain and promote.

It is definitely an erroneous view to construe a land contract entered into under the leasehold system, which patently establishes private rights and obligations, as a "socialist" entity. This is so notwithstanding the legal view that land and natural resources in Hong Kong "belonged to the Crown" before June 30, 1997, and "shall be State property" after.[36] The argument of this legal view is, as explained above, that the government has the authority to "socialize" land rights by edict, overriding contractual rights. The fact is that the lease is contractual, as affirmed in the *Tong Iu* case.[37] Even a socialist state can make and enforce a private contract. The issue posed by the statutory zoning plan imposed on land under preexisting leasehold interests is that government is in effect reneging on its contractual promises by legislation. While this is of course legal, the law is bad. Plainly, there is a breach of government promises. That such breach is explicable by the public interest it serves does not alter this fact. This state of affairs is above all problematic under Articles 6 and 8 of the Basic Law.[38]

Academic views about Articles 6 and 8 are that these provisions do protect private property better than colonial laws.[39] Gone are the days when the government was not bound by a higher law that expressly constrains her power vis-à-vis the lessee.[40] It has been argued that the leasehold system displaced the English property law concept of "real property" in its strict sense.[41] However, does the existing provisions of the Town Planning Ordinance, enacted before July 1997, contravene the Basic Law? The opinion of the author is that it does.

A counterargument advanced by a queen's (senior) counsel is that the "protection of private property" proviso is qualified by the expression "in accordance with the law." Thus, private property rights are always qualified by the "law" (namely ordinances, such as the Town Planning Ordinance, in force). Furthermore, Article 105 of the Basic Law expressly provides that property can be subject to "lawful deprivation" provided compensation "according to the real value of the property" is paid.

This counterargument is problematic in three respects. First, the overriding concern of Article 6 of the Basic Law should be the protection of private property. If the law affecting private property effectively deprives rights without compensation, such law obviously compromises and thus contravenes the Basic Law. The expression "according to the law" is a typical phraseology in Chinese national law, which is a continental law system. It denotes and emphasizes both *due process* (i.e. the opposite of arbitrary exercise of judicial power) and specific pieces of legislation. The point, however, is that the specific piece of legislation must not contradict the general spirit of the Basic Law. Second, the Basic Law stresses compensation, which is clearly absent from the Town Planning Ordinance where it deprives rights of the landowners. It may be contested that "deprivation" means *nullification of the entire property*, as in the case of resumption, while statutory planning merely attenuates certain rights. This is a dangerous suggestion as "attenuation" could be so strong that in effect the whole estate is devoid of its value and hence is equivalent to "deprivation." Third, the government taxes betterment of property in connection with lease modification that permits using land for a higher-value purpose, but it does not compensate for downzoning. This kind of asymmetry can hardly be said to be fair.

The view of the author is more "radical" than that of Hayek and Nozick, who have similarly made significant concessions to government planning overriding private land rights on the grounds of external effects.[42] However, it is consistent with any claim that the spirit of capitalism and the espoused laissez faire policy of the government of Hong Kong is well known to the world. Whether ideal capitalism or complete laissez faire is feasible or desirable is another issue. Nor is it asserted here that statutory town planning has no beneficial role to play even in a market economy, as the author has unambiguously argued elsewhere.[43] The fact is: The protection of property rights over land under the Basic Law as it stands has not been complete as far as the existing Town Planning Ordinance is concerned. Either the Basic Law or the Town Planning Ordinance needs to be amended, or both do.

At the conceptual level, statutory town planning in Hong Kong has displaced private planning based on the lease by planning by the bureaucrats whose judgment is deemed to represent "public interest." This is an interventionist approach to planning that has as its philosophical base market failure. This is inconsistent with the ideology of capitalist market economy that is supposed to be entrenched under the Basic Law.

The ideological radicalism of the author is in agreement with Lord Cooke's *ratio decidendi* in the Privy Council decision in the *Fok Lai Ying* case arising from the Crown Land Resumption Ordinance (Chan 2001). Lord Cooke remarked that the provisions of the ordinance are "singularly sweeping and on their face draconian." Then he went on to reject Justice Litton's view that compensation for land taken for public purposes renders the ordinance fair. Lord Cooke expressly disagreed with the view that "to take away for public purposes all or some of a person's home is neither arbitrary nor unlawful if compensation is furnished. Their Lordships are not to be taken as endorsing this approach. So far as it involves a kind of *expressio unis* argument—derived from the presence in the [Crown Land] Resumption Ordinance, the Town

Planning Ordinance and the Roads (Works, Use and Compensation) Ordinance of limited express rights to be heard—it may not be reconcilable with *Doody*, where a somewhat similar argument was rejected and the natural justice principle of supplementation applied." (Chan 2001: 142–43).

Unlike the U.S. Constitution, which uses the term "public use," the ordinances of Hong Kong employs the wording "public purpose." In the light of the Basic Law's express endorsement of capitalism, which requires a government that permits maximum economic freedom and protects private property, "public purpose" must mean "public use."[44] And public use, as argued by Professor Siegan, must be "limited to establish public ownership only when it is absolutely necessary to provide essential state services" (Siegan 1994: 56).

Land Resumption for Urban Renewal

Even where we may concede that the existing Town Planning Ordinance does not violate the fundamental premise of the Basic Law to protect private property, resumption of privately held land for the purpose of "urban renewal" in Hong Kong is obviously an infringement of private property rights over land. The counterargument is that all leases contain covenants or conditions that the land under lease can be resumed for "public purpose" provided "full and fair compensation is paid."

Two problems arise from the resort to "public purpose" in land resumption from time to time. The first problem is that such "public purpose" in some situations cannot be meaningfully justified. Where resumption is for the building of highways and community facilities, there is little problem with the concept of "public purpose." Problems do arise when private land is resumed for profit-making "urban renewal," which invariably means demolition for redevelopment rather than urban "rehabilitation," or "rejuvenation." The purpose is the creation of more floor space for sale to those who can pay for the new properties. These new owners may not be the displaced residents or shop owners. In one instance, the concept of "public purpose" is used to evict landlords for the purpose of accommodating "indigenous villagers" who had sold lands to these expropriated landlords. To call such purposes "public" is hardly intelligible in terms of social justice. Under the preexisting colonial laws, which were not subject to any entrenched protection of private property under the Letter Patents, "public purpose" meant whatever purpose the administration (acting through the governor in the appointed Executive Council) saw fit. "Public purpose" thus in effect meant any government purpose. One may use a political theory of paternal and benevolent colonial rule based on "discussion"[45] or "consent and consensus,"[46] to justify such purpose. However, it remained true that there was no legal constraint for construing "public purpose" for resumption as a matter of convenience or "administrative expedience for the public good," as exercised for urban renewal projects in Sheung Wan in the 1960s and those under the umbrella of the Land Development Ordinance[47] since the mid-1980s. The challenging question for the constitutional lawyer is whether the concept of "public purpose" should be given a restrictive interpretation under the Basic Law. The author would say yes, for otherwise the protection of private property as a constitutional principle is just propaganda. Without a more restrictive interpretation, government could continue selling to the lessee a piece of land at full market price for a terms of years, and then force the lessee to resell the same piece of land to the government before the natural expiry of the term. This could be justified by whatever purpose the government sees fit. The effect is the conversion of a land lease into a license determinable at will. The fact is that after June 30, 1997, there has been no amendment to restrict of the meaning of "public purpose" under the Lands Resumption Ordinance or the Land Development Corporation Ordinance. Indeed, a new ordinance, the Lands (Compulsory Sale for Redevelopment) Ordinance[48] has been passed to allow developers who acquire 90 percent shares of ownership in a multistory building to force the holders of the remaining 10 percent shares to sell property to them. Note that Article 29 of the Basic Law states: "The homes and other premises of Hong Kong shall be inviolable. Arbitrary or unlawful search of, intrusion into, a resident's home or other premises shall be prohibited." It is therefore arguable that the public purpose element of the Lands Resumption Ordinance and the Land Development Corporation Ordinance and the spirit and provisions of the Land (Compulsory Sale for Redevelopment) Ordinance are in breach of both Articles 6 and 29 of the Basic Law.

The second problem is that the contractual "full and fair compensation" provision in the lease is often restricted by the Lands Resumption Ordinance (previously Crown Land Resumption Ordinance) to exclude any gain on redevelopment. In the light of Lord Cooke's ratio in the *Fok Lai Ying* case, mentioned above, it is argued that the expropriated lessee should be entitled to at least a share of such extra gain in value, as it is part the opportunity cost of the land the lessee loses involuntarily. This interpretation follows naturally from the fundamental protection of private property under Article 6 of the Basic Law by reference to capitalism characterized above. The Swire Properties Limited was on the brink of applying for the exercise of the ordinance for assembling some remaining titles in Wan Chai. At the last minute, the matter was resolved by private settlement, a socially laudable though commercially less profitable move. In Hong Kong, there is little voice from various professional bodies against the encroachment of private property. These bodies seem to welcome more economic regulation than less.[49]

Criminalizing Economic Use of Land

As mentioned above, planning enforcement legislation erodes the private property rights of lessees to use land held under "agricultural lots" for the purpose of open storage, as affirmed in the *Melhado* case.[50] Other than "existing uses" that existed immediately before the publication in the gazette of applicable statutory zoning plans and have continued to exist from that time without "material change," any other use or development requires planning permission unless such use or development is permitted as of right under the applicable zoning plan. Unauthorized change in use or development is a criminal offense punishable by heavy fines. The justification for the imposition of the relevant plans, which effectively nullifies common law rights under the lease without any compensation, is land use control in the interest of the public: the lands controlled would remain scenic green fields and the externalities of container storage can be minimized in the interest of the public. Whereas planning enforcement legislation is a definite violation of private property rights, whether or not it delivers the espoused public benefits, which is an empirical question, is uncertain. The observed fact is that planning enforcement has not brought back active commercial agriculture to Hong Kong. Enforcement has not been overwhelmingly effective, as there seems to be no end to the actions of prosecution. However, even if enforcement is completely effective, farmland in Hong Kong will not revert to agriculture unless labor costs in Hong Kong fall to a level that is comparable to that prevailing in mainland China. The failure of the planning enforcement legislation reflects an inherent weakness of zoning regulation: it may restrict but cannot create the intended development. Simply, actual development still relies on the decision of the lessee. Where a lessee is prevented from achieving a use that can bring positive marginal benefits, the lessee would waste the land to minimize loss. The tool used by the Hong Kong planner is the same old zoning approach that was imported from prewar Britain and is an obvious misapplication of obsolete tools. Such misapplication is partly a result of the neglect of basic price theory. Indeed, local discussion of planning issues has seldom been informed by economic reasoning.

Planning Under a "High Degree of Autonomy"

Sustainable Development: Protection of Victoria Harbor; Mai Po Marshes; and Creation of Smokeless Towns

The protection of Victoria Harbor against further reclamation was one of the major political issues of town planning in Hong Kong before the reversion of sovereignty over Hong Kong.[51] The SAR government has conceded to lobbyists' demand to reduce the scale of planned reclamation in Victoria Harbor. The harbor protection campaign is conducted for a persuasive reason: to conserve the harbor for the benefit of residents, tourists, and marine life. There is no doubt that there are many individuals who have supported the campaign for these reasons. However, the most persuasive reason is that developers who possess rental properties along the waterfront do not want the sea view of their investment to be affected by prospective highrise development along the new artificial coastline. The reality is that, in planning terms, the cross-sectional profile of Victoria Harbor has been destroyed by postwar development, to the extent that a halt in further reclamation has little meaningful value in terms of harbor view protection. In any event, the battle for harbor view protection is a pointless one in the light of atmospheric pollution in the Pearl River Delta. Visibility in Hong Kong during months of winter monsoons has become so low that harbor views are lost.

The official account of the deterioration in visibility is air pollution generated by local vehicles. One environmental planning solution to this problem is to tighten regulations over local sources of pollution, with diesel vehicles as the target. While buses, lorries, and taxis run on diesel, taxis have been singled out for the compulsory adoption of natural gas as fuel.[52] Another environmental planning solution is the so-called innovative electrified, and thus smokeless, townships in the New Territories. The idea of smokeless townships, as exemplified by Ebenezer Howard's idea of the suburban garden city,[53] is in fact more than a century old.

While local combustion does contribute to air pollution, it is obvious that the severe degree of air pollution in recent years is due to industrial expansions in Chinese towns in the upwind direction of the Hong Kong SAR. Local air pollution should be rather insignificant, as the government has closed down all public incinerators and the bulk of Hong Kong's industries have been relocated to the affected Chinese towns. Despite denial of some mainland Chinese officials that air pollution in Hong Kong is created in their jurisdictions, even laypersons in Hong Kong appreciate the real cause of smog formation in Hong Kong. The most convincing proof is that in summertime, when the monsoons are onshore, during or in the immediate aftermath of typhoons and Chinese festivals, when factories close down, the air quality in Hong Kong is good.

If pollution cannot be reduced or bought out in these industrializing towns, which are simply repeating what happened in nineteenth-century Europe, neither harbor protection nor smokeless towns would achieve anything meaningful. Unfortunately, apparently the SAR government has very little to say about joint efforts with local authorities in mainland China to tackle the problem. Nor has any local political party or politician much to say on the issue, though it may have a lot to say on "saving the harbor."

The issue of air pollution in town planning reveals the fact that the planning of Hong Kong would depend on the support of local governments in mainland China. Where environmental issues cut across administrative boundaries, the notion of "autonomous government" becomes problematic. Indeed, air pollution is just one of the cross-border problems confronting the town planner of Hong Kong. The planner's approach to conserve Mai Po Marshes is another case in point.

Mai Po Marshes is an area owned by the government in Deep Bay, which is protected under an international treaty, the Ramsar Convention on Wetlands Conservation, entered into for Hong Kong by the United Kingdom. The area is basically manmade[54] and has since the 1940s been used for *gei wei* (intertidal pond) culture of shrimps. It is world famous for the number of migratory birds that converge on the area every year for food and shelter. The area is situated in the seaward side of a large privately owned fishpond area. As the land holdings of this area are huge, and hence the transaction costs of acquiring such properties for development are very low, developers have acquired substantial amounts of lands behind the marshes.

Using the same old zoning approach, the privately owned fishponds in the landward side of the marshes have been "protected" by buffer zoning. Planning applications for suburban development within the buffer zones have been turned down by a very restrictive policy. This policy led to the *Henderson* case,[55] in which the Privy Council issued a majority ruling in favor of the applicant. What the Hong Kong planner has attempted to do is to conserve all private lands near the marshes against any form of suburban development. Compensatory ecological measures proposed by the developer are discarded.

While the planner may succeed in withstanding local development pressures in the hinterland of marshes, he is completely helpless as regards the major threat to the survival of marshes from its sea front:[56] The quality of the sea water of Deep Bay that drains in and out of the marshes every day is not a pure Hong Kong variable. Into Deep Bay is discharged the ever-growing domestic and industrial sewage of Shenzhen Special Economic Zone and Shekou Special Economic Zone in the immediate vicinity of the marshes. While the SAR government has continued the policy of conserving the marshes, or more accurately the birds therein and around,[57] the Shenzhen zone has stepped up development in the mangrove marshes under its jurisdiction. Such development includes reclamation, construction of highways, flood drains, and high-rise buildings.

As Hong Kong is in the downstream location of the Pearl River estuary, Hong Kong has become subject to marine pollution created by effluents of new industries in the Pearl River Delta region. The threat confronting Mai Po Marshes is just a small fraction of a looming ecological disaster. If the environmental planning approach to conserving Mai Po Marshes appears to be myopic, the plan for "cleaning up the harbor" under the so-called Territorial Sewage Strategy commenced by the colonial administration is definitely ostrichlike. This strategy aims to improve harbor water quality by exporting local sewage through submarine outfalls in the continental shelves. It ignores completely the incoming polluted water from the Pearl River system upstream. Technical problems that have surfaced in the past two years suggest that it may become an abortive engineering project altogether.

In addition to atmospheric and marine pollution, contamination of fresh water supply to Hong Kong has also become a major challenge to the SAR government. Hong Kong has relied on the mainland for fresh water supply since the 1960s, for the construction of reservoirs cannot catch up with growth in demand for clean water and desalting seawater is considered too expensive. The once clean sources of supply in the mainland are now subject to the threat of increasing pollution. Again, the SAR government appears to have very little to say on the solution in her planning documents. Obviously, fundamental changes to the current myopic local planning approach needs to be adopted.

Planning for "Fifty Years No Change"?

The Future of the Small House Policy

The planning for "small houses" poses another Basic Law problem. *Small houses* are houses for which the male members of special categories of residents called "indigenous villagers" may, as a matter of government policy since 1972, apply to build on their private land or on government land. *Indigenous villagers* are descendants of the people of those villages found to exist in the New Territories after the British leased the territories from imperial China in 1898. These villages were designated by the colonial administration as "indigenous villages." As housing in Hong Kong is an expensive commodity, the policy has been criticized for violating a fundamental human rights principle of sex equality and involving unfair subsidy to a class of citizens based on blood. The author has elsewhere[58] addressed the historical context and problems of the small house policy comprehensively. Here the author shall only deal with the planning implications of the issue of sex discrimination, as it involves an examination of Article 40[59] of the Basic Law.

The small-house policy, which emerged in the early 1970s, can hardly be described a part of the traditional rights or interests of the indigenous villagers that can be traced back to 1897 or even earlier. However, one may argue that it is a derivative of their rights to use their private land holdings, once held at the pleasure of the Chinese emperors, for farming and housing purposes. Insofar as a small house is built on private land, the policy can arguably be said to be protected by the Basic Law. Politically, the SAR government has honored the policy. That being the case, the Basic Law would be running against the principle of sex equality, which is protected by Article 1 of the Bill of Rights Ordinance.[60] While the Bill of Rights Ordinance may be inferior and subject to the Basic Law, the latter should be read in conjunction with Article 48 of the Constitution of the People's Republic of China (the Chinese Constitution).[61] Plainly, sex discrimination is unconstitutional in China, unless the indigenous villagers can be regarded as belonging to a minority race of China. This possible argument from "ethnic minorities," however, has been rejected by the Court of Appeal in *Lau Wong Fat v. Attorney General*.[62] Thus some commentators have argued that the policy should be abandoned.

The argument for abolishing the small-house policy on the basis of sex discrimination in fact brings in more problems of its own. The reason is, assuming that the policy is not unfair to non–New Territories residents, that acceptance of sex equality would mean that government should allow female villagers to apply for small houses. This would double the size of the problem in terms of space demand. However, as there is not much private land zoned for small-house development, the policy is simply not sustainable for a life of fifty years, unless government is to sacrifice substantial amount of lands in the hilly country parks owned by government outside the villages. As forward planning takes time and the SAR has reached a critical point for making a definitive policy as regards the small-house policy, the planner must raise issue about the sustainability of the small house policy under the Basic Law. The saying "fifty years no change" may not hold for land-hungry Hong Kong.

High-Tech Industries and Tourist Attractions

Since the transformation of its status from a British Colony into a self-governing entity under Chinese sovereignty, Hong Kong has ceased to practice laissez faire in the same way as it was practiced in days of colonial rule. The *purchase by government of shares* in the stock market in its attempt to stabilize share prices during the "Asian financial crisis"[63] that emerged in October 1997; and the establishment of a policy of *subsidizing specific (high-tech) industries* by way of loans at below market interest[64] are cases in point. Though these specific policies are aspatial, the transition from free market capitalism to an interventionist approach to manage the economy is reflected in terms of land-use planning in the designation of three key packages of initiatives. They are (1) a "cyberport" at Pokfulam, tasked with a local company by grant,[65] (2) the government joint venture agreement with Disney to create a new theme park at Penny's Bay on terms highly favorable to the latter,[66] and (3) tourist facilities on Lantau Island.[67] Local and international investors have welcomed both the "cyberport" and Disney projects, as reflected in the short-term movement of stock prices after the announcement of each package of proposals. Hong Kong's economy is increasingly subject to the visible influence or control of the government.

Conclusion

This survey of the land use planning problems confronting the SAR government points to a couple of basic questions of jurisprudence. The first question is whether Hong Kong has a system of rule *of* law or, rather, rule *by* law. This question arises from the contradiction between Articles 6, 8, and 29 of the Basic Law and the provisions for uncompensated attenuation of property rights over lands in the Town Planning Ordinance and for resumption of lands under related legislation. The Basic Law in black print protects *private property*, whereas various planning and related ordinances point to other directions. Yet this conflict has been dismissed as a nonissue or ignored as purely "idealistic academic speculation." The conviction of the holder of this view is that government always arrives at unimpeachable *public purpose*. This leaves one wondering whether the argument that the Basic Law is sacrosanct in the legal system of Hong Kong is sustainable. There is no doubt that the Beijing rulers have allowed a high degree of autonomy enabling the people of Hong Kong to manage her domestic affairs, including the management of land on behalf of the state. Whether her land manager would honor contracts as contracts or treat them as mere licenses subject to determination at his pleasure is another question.[68] The second and more profound question is whether the strict application of the "fifty years no change" provision in the Basic Law is meaningful. As presented in this chapter, there is a host of environmentally sensitive planning issues that are cross-border in nature. Unless a Coasian approach by way of trading of pollution rights[69] can be established to internalize the externalities involved, the conventional interventionist approach to planning would call for a constitutionally difficult solution. This is the earlier if not immediate administrative integration of Hong Kong with the rest of China for more effective control, as physical segregation is impossible. One indeed could speculate that the Basic Law drafters might not have foreseen the property rights implications of this "miniconstitution" for the system and practice of planning inherited from the colonial administration. They had not anticipated the problems that led to the interpretation of the issue of Hong Kong SAR citizenship by the PRC People's Congress. While such solution and speculation are beyond the scope of this chapter, it must be stressed that in the context of the Basic Law, by virtue of its political and literal embodiment of capitalism, town planning as a matter of public affairs deserves no less attention in terms of property rights than the right of abode or freedom of expression and demonstration in terms of human rights. It follows that no apology for the town planning system today is legitimate on the basis of the legality of the system prior to July 1, 1997, as then the Basic Law had not yet been operative. On the other hand, while the drafters of the Basic Law envisage a "high degree of autonomy" for the governance of the SAR, no effective town planning today can be carried out in the absence of a better coordination with the neighboring planning authorities across the border.

Even if we may ignore the property protection provisions of the Basic Law from a jurisprudential perspective, we can hardly ignore the issue of private property rights as a matter of economic significance for Hong Kong. In a community where "privately owned lands" may soon house a smaller portion of the population than the vast and growing domain of public housing estates, concern about private property rights protection on private lands is not neurotic but sensible.

List of Cases Cited

Attorney General v. Tong Iu [1968] HKLR 603

Attorney General v. Melhado Investment Ltd. [1983] HKLR 327

Crozet Ltd. v. Attorney General HCMP 409/73 (1973)

Euclid v. Ambler Realty Co. 272 U.S. 365 (1926)

Fok Lai Ying v. Governor in Council (1997) 7 HKPLR 327 (PC)

First English Lutheran Church of Glendale v. County of Los Angeles 482 U.S. 304 (1987)

Hawaii Housing Authority v. Midkiff [1984] 467 US 229

Henderson Property Agency Limited v. Lo Chai Wan (for and on behalf of Town Planning Board) [1997] HKLRD 258

Lau Wong Fat v. Attorney General, Civil Appeal No. 247 of 1966 [1997] HKLR 533

Lochner v. New York 198 U.S. 45 (1905)

Lucas v. South Carolina Coastal Council 505 US, 112 S.Ct.2886, 120 L.Ed.2d 708 (1992)

Nollan v. California Coastal Commission 483 U.S. 825 (1987)

Poletown Neighborhood Council v. Detroit (1981)

Regina v. Secretary of State for the Home Department, ex parte Doody (1994) 1 AC 531

Singway Co Ltd. v. Attorney General [1974] HKLR 275

Tsei Kwai King & Cheung Kam v. Attorney General MP No. 1509 of 1993

Notes

The author wishes to thank the following individuals for their comments on an earlier version of this chapter as a conference paper: Dr. Frederik Pretorius and Dr. Tai-lok Lui. All faults are the author's.

"Fifty years no change" is political assurance made to the people of colonial Hong Kong and Macau for the idea of "one country, two systems" by the Chinese leader Deng Xiaoping on June 22 and 23, 1984 (Deng 1987), before the Sino-British Joint Declaration on Hong Kong, signed on December 19, 1984. The concept was reflected in Section I to Annex I to the Sino-British Agreement and Article 5 of the Basic Law, as discussed in the text. Some economists have even argued that the Basic Law as a written constitution provides a blueprint for further economic and political reforms in the rest of China (Rabushka 1989).

1. An example is the political debate ensuing from the Court of Final Appeal (CFA) case concerning immigration and citizenship matters, *Ng Ka Ling, Ng Tan Tan (infants suing by their father and next friend Ng Sek Nin) v. Director of Immigration*, FACV No.14/98; *Tsui Kuen Nang v. Director of Immigration*, FACV No.15/98; *Director of Immigration v. Cheung Lai Wah (infant suing by her father and next friend Cheung Miu Cheung)*, FACV No. 16/98 (1998). The PRC Central Government has severely criticized the CFA's decision for suggesting that the Hong Kong Court of Final Appeal is the ultimate authority on the Basic Law with the right of judicial review. The National People's Congress eventually reinterpreted the Basic Law's relevant provisions to the effect that the CFA decision was negated. This act led to criticism of the Hong Kong Bar and great controversies among jurists in Hong Kong. See Chan, Fu, and Ghai (2000).

2. For instance, according to scholars like Olson (1982), Vogel (1991), Woronoff (1992), Lau (1997), and MacEwan (1999), and jurists like Siegan (1994, 1997), consider Hong Kong a classic example of a laissez-faire economy. Hong Kong has been ranked as the most free economy according to the Heritage Foundation's "index of economic freedom" since 1996. Hong Kong maintains her top position in the 2001 assessment. However, the European Parliament has come to a different view. See http://www.heritage.org/news/2000/nr110100indexoverview.html, and note 65, post. See O'Driscoll, Holmes, and Kirkpatrick (2001).

3. See, for instance, Hayek (1944, 1960), Cheung (1974), and Sowell (1996).

4. The Basic Law of the Hong Kong Special Administrative Region of the People's Republic of China. It took effect on July 1, 1997. It is often said to be a "small" or "mini constitution" for Hong Kong as part of China.

5. For instance, Hammer (1997), Ng (1995), Yeh (1995), Yeung (1997), and Ng and Tang (1999).

6. Political theorists' interest in the Basic Law is largely confined to legalistic, administrative, and representative democracy issues. Rights referred to are political and human but seldom economic or property. See for instance Chang and Chuang (1999); Cheek-Milby and Mushkat (1989); Cohen and Zhao (1997); Davies and Roberts (1990); Miners (1998); and Overholt (1993).

7. See description located above note 1.

8. Article 2 of the Basic Law reads: "The National People's Congress authorizes the Hong Kong Special Administrative Region to exercise a high degree of autonomy and enjoy executive, legislative and independent judicial power, including that of final adjudication, in accordance with the provisions of this Law."

Article 5 of the Basic Law reads: "The socialist system and policies shall not be practiced in Hong Kong Special Administrative Region, and the previous capitalist system and way of life shall remain unchanged for 50 years."

In most industrialized countries, constitutions seldom prescribe or forbid any particular form of economic system. Some exceptions are the Spanish constitution of 1978, which guarantees "freedom of trade within the scope of a market economy" and the Swiss constitution of 1874, which guarantees the freedom of commerce and industry. The "previous capitalist system" provision" in Article 5 of the Basic Law of Hong Kong is therefore another important exception. It excludes Hong Kong from Article 15 of the Chinese constitution, amended in March 1993, which provides for "a socialist market economy." The qualification of "socialist" implies that the Chinese Communist Party retains ultimate control of the economy. For a discussion of the constitutional setting of competition laws, see So (1994).

9. See comments of Lai and Fong (2000) on the Town Planning Bill June 1996, and Town Planning Bill January 2000.

10. Lai (1993); Government of the Hong Kong Special Administrative Region (1999); "Urban Renewal Today" (http://www.plb.gov.hk/renewal/today.htm).

11. See note 9.

12. Lai (2000e).

13. Lai (1996); Lai and Fong (2000); links available at the website of the Hong Kong Special Administrative Region Environment and Food Bureau (http://www.info.gov.hk/efb/link/landquest/points.html); Planning, Environment and Lands Bureau, "Draft Vision Statement for the Victoria Harbor and Central Reclamation Phase III," for consideration on June 10, 1999, by Legislative Council Panel on Planning, Lands and Works (http://www.legco.gov.hk/yr98–99/english/panels/plw/papers/p11006_4.htm).

14. Yu, Shaw, Fu, and Lai (2000).

15. See Environment Resource Management (1998).

16. See Richard Li, Chairman and Chief Executive, "The Future of Hong Kong as an International Information Technology and Information Services Center," Pacific Century Group, press release, March 17, 1999. (http://www.info.gov.hk/itbb/english/cyberport/pr170399.htm); "Agreement on Residential Portion Land Value for Cyberport Reached," Hong Kong Special Administrative Region, press release dated August 3, 2000 (http://www.info.gov.hk/gia/general200008); (http://www.hksciencepark.com/hksp/HKHub/Hklocation.html).

The science park was first mentioned in para. 33 of the chief executive's policy address, 1997, and the cyberport was first mentioned in para. 33 of the chief executive's policy address, 1999. Another statement on the science park and the cyberport is given in para. 5 of the chief executive's policy address, 2000. The decision about the plans for the cyberport (and the Disney theme park) was described as an "exceptional step" taken in the budget of 1999–2000, by the financial secretary in his budget speech for the year 2000–01, paras. 6 and 13. See "Building Hong Kong for a New Era, Address by the Chief Executive of the Hong Kong Special Administrative Region, the Honorable Mr. Tung Chee Hwa on 8 October 1997"; "The 1999 Policy Address, Quality People, Quality Home, Positioning Hong Kong for the 21st Century by the Chief Executive of the Hong Kong Special Administrative Region, The Honorable Mr. Tung Chee Hwa on 6 October 1999"; and "The 1999–2000 Budget: Onward with New Strengths, Speech by the Financial Secretary the Honorable Donald Tsang, Moving the Second Reading of the Appropriation Bill 1999, Wednesday 3.3.1999," all publications of the HKSAR government.

17. http://www.info.gov.hk/planning/studies/wfm/wfm_public_forum/aiii.htm. See also para. 6 of the budget speech for the year 2000–01. The Disneyland and other tourism projects on Lantau were first mentioned in para. 32 of the chief executive's policy address of 1999. See "The 1999 Policy Address, Quality People, Quality Home, Positioning Hong Kong for the 21st Century by the Chief Executive of the Hong Kong Special Administrative Region, The Honorable Mr. Tung Chee Hwa on 6 October 1999."

18. Address by the Secretary for Planning, Environment and Lands to a Legislative Council Committee special session on the draft Estimates of Expenditure, 1999 to 2000, March 17, 2000.

19. Thomas Sowell (1996) cryptically describes such rights as "rigidities." He maintains that "people want [such rights] in some vital areas of their life, where they reject both the transaction costs and the indignity of having to submit to, or negotiate with, those who might challenge their possession of their home, their children, or their life." Such rigidities are also "boundaries limiting the exercise of government power and carving out areas within which individual discretion is free to shape decisions."

20. Buchanan (1993: 19).

21. Cheung (1974). Cheng's analysis is more general than that of Oestereich (2000).

22. This is subject to one exception, namely contracts that are endangering or are required for collective security. As Hong Kong has never been an autonomous political entity, this exception is not applicable.

23. The purpose of the enforcement provisions for "development permission areas" were introduced by the Town Planning (Amendment) Ordinance of 1990.

24. Roberts (1975).

25. Lai (1998).

26. Prior to 1939, several pieces of zoning legislation that were designed to exclude the Chinese from areas reserved for Europeans had been passed. These were repealed in 1946 after World War II. See Lai and Yu (2001).

27. Barzel (1974); Lai (1997).

28. Gifford (1987); Tullock (1994).

29. Lai (1998).

30. Lai (1997, 2000d).

31. *Singway Co Ltd. v. Attorney General* [1974] HKLR 275. Unlike the *Crozet* case, the issue is not whether plot ratio is a legitimate zoning matter but whether zoning is legitimate. In the United States, zoning has been regarded as "constitu-

tional" in the *Euclid* case in respect of the fourteenth amendment but Siegan (1989) points out that the *Lochner* case was a better interpretation of the amendment.

32. To appreciate the interventionist mentality of the planner, we may turn to the concluding passages of the Abercrombie Report, the first modern strategic plan for Colony Hong Kong, which has shaped the urban morphology of postwar Hong Kong. See Lai (1999a).

33. See, for instance, Willoughby (1978), Albert H.Y. Chan (1993), and Law (1999). For a discussion of the position of Singapore, see Christudason (2000).

34. In a planning appeal case concerning No.17 Bowen Road, the Appeal Board dismissed the appeal on the grounds that though the proposed development of a lessee would not create any social harm, it would not generate public benefits either. The logic of the Appeal Tribunal, which pays no respect to the concept of Paretian efficiency, is more interventionist than the Pigovian welfare economics. It implies that the lessee interest is ruled out as *part of* public interest. In other words, the human rights of an individual to pursue private happiness without violating the felicity of others are not guaranteed simply because he is a developer. See Lai (2000d).

35. See Lai (1999d).

36. Article 7 of the Basic Law.

37. *Attorney General v. Tong Iu* [1968] HKLR 603.

38. Article 6 of the Basic Law reads: "The Hong Kong Special Administrative Region shall protect the rights of private property in accordance with the law."

Article 8 reads: "The laws previously in force in Hong Kong . . . shall be maintained, except for any that contravene this Law. "

39. For instance, Hsu (1996).

40. Willoughby (1978).

41. Evans (1971).

42. Lai (1999c).

43. Lai (1996, 1997, 1998).

44. Lai (1993).

45. Endacott (1964).

46. Miners (1998). This had been used as a government expression before Hong Kong was allowed to develop democratic politics in the mid-1980s.

47. This ordinance established the Lands Development Corporation, which became the Urban Renewal Authority in 1999 established by the Urban Renewal Authority Ordinance.

48. The rationale for introducing this ordinance is the standard argument against "holding out," which stands in the way of redevelopment. Notwithstanding the efficient land resource allocation argument, it remains that this state of affairs violates private property rights. The SAR government should either respect the Basic Law and thus should have refrained from passing this ordinance; or it should ignore property rights under Article 6 altogether for "public purpose," entailing an amendment to the Basic Law.

In the United States, the power of eminent domain (the equivalent of resumption in Hong Kong) is limited to taking of land for a "public use." The term "use" rather than "purpose" is used. A public agency could not invoke its power of eminent domain to take a property from one individual for the sole benefit of another individual. However, as Eaton points out, "recent trends indicate that the courts interpret public use quite liberally" (Eaton 1995). In the case *Hawaii Housing Authority v. Midkiff*, the Supreme Court overturned the decision of the Federal Ninth Circuit Court that the

Hawaiian Land Reform Act was unconstitutional. The act in question is said to break a land oligopoly as a social and economic evil by allowing lessees living on freehold land of at least five acres to ask the state to condemn such land and sell it to them. The Circuit Court stated that this act is "a naked attempt on the part of the State of Hawaii to take the private property of A and transfer it to B solely for B's private use and benefit" (Eaton 1995). The author's view is that the Circuit Court's decision is correct. That the Supreme Court had decided to rule otherwise and hence established a binding authority for the time being should not preclude further inquiry as a matter of jurisprudence. Nor should it affect our analysis of the liberal use of the "public purpose" provision in Hong Kong. Suffice it to say that, as revealed in *Lucas v. South Carolina Coastal Council* (1992), the American court has in recent years returned to a more stringent view of the concept of public purpose and "constitutional theorists have argued for a return to some of the protections that property enjoyed before the revolution of 1937." (Murphy, Fleming, and Barber 1995). Another authoritative view affirming this trend is offered by Siegan (1994), referring to the *Lucas* case as well as two earlier cases: the *First English Lutheran Church of Glendale v. County of Los Angeles* and *Nollan v. California Coastal Commission* (Siegan 1994).

A unique difference between land allocation in the United States and in Hong Kong is that the former has often distributed land at zero premium whereas private land rights in Hong Kong have almost invariably been allocated by government contractually by auction or tender sale. Eaton (1995) has advanced the argument that eminent domain is an inherent right of the sovereign (the executive) and cannot be limited by the legislature. This argument, however, must be qualified where the polity has an entrenched constitution that stands above other laws. In the case of the Basic Law for the Hong Kong SAR, the key terms "capitalism" and "protection of private property" are express.

As regards the view that the interests of the lessee should be balanced against the public interest, one should note that laws under the American Constitution respect the private possession of guns notwithstanding arguable public interest to abolish such constitutional rights. This example serves to provide an analogy for Hong Kong jurists as regards the need to respect private property albeit persuasive arguments for more interventionist planning regulations.

49. The general lack of academic or professional criticism of the practice of Land Development Corporation (now Urban Renewal Authority) and Lands Resumption Ordinance can be easily explained by economics: Professional bodies derive status and income better by serving than by contesting these means of eroding private property. Some who were once politically vocal have been coopted by absorption into various kinds of appointed bodies. When those policy makers responsible for policies are challenged in respect of private property, they erect facade of "public interest," without mentioning Article 6. The problem is reduced to one of greedy property owners exhorting compensation as if the small proprietors were the land oligarchs (such as those targeted by the state of Hawaii) or squatters without rights. Sometimes, the success of urban renewal in Singapore is invoked to stop arguments. However, there is little inquiry as to the paternal treatment of affected landowners by the Singaporean government. Nor is there any sensitivity to the fact that the constitution of Singapore differs from that of Hong Kong. It is true that since July 1, 1997, the SAR government has committed to the rehousing of eligible tenants who have been displaced as a result of government urban renewal to public housing. However, respect for property owners has remained feeble. The most recent development in the

official argument for the need for stronger statutory power is that government-led rede-velopment projects are not necessarily commercially profitable or viable (http://www.plb.gov.hk/rebewal/today.htm). This argument begs the question of why redevel-opment rather than rehabilitation is imposed in the first place. The government, not the lessees, induces the risks. For a discussion of resumption or takings in the context of zoning and constitutional law, see Fischel (1985, 1995), Siegan (1989, 1994, 1997).

50. *Attorney General v. Melhado Investment Ltd.* [1983] HKLR 327.

51. Lai (1996).

52. A major complaint of taxi operators is that there are simply too few natural gas stations.

53. Fishman (1982). Colonial Hong Kong's version of a garden city, Kowloon Tong, today is an area of sex motels, kindergartens, and old-age homes rather than the ordinary residential precinct it once was.

54. See Irving and Morton (1988).

55. *Henderson Property Agency Limited v. Lo Chai Wan (for and on behalf of Town Planning Board)* [1997] HKLRD 258.

56. A government town planner said that government was "fighting a battle of ponds." This is true. The problem is that while this battle is conducted in the land-facing side of the marshes as a stronghold, government is leaving the sea-facing gate of the stronghold open (Lai 1999).

57. The government pays little attention to the complaints of commercial pond fish farmers of migratory birds predating on their fish.

58. Lai (1999d; 2000d).

59. Article 40 of the Basic Law reads: "The lawful traditional rights and interest of the indigenous inhabitants of the 'New Territories' shall be protected by the Hong Kong Special Administrative Region."

60. Article 1 of the Bill of Rights Ordinance reads: "(a) The rights recognized in this Bill of Rights shall be enjoyed without distinction of any kind, such as race, color, sex, language, religion, political or other opinion, national or social origin, property, birth or other status. (b) Men and women shall have equal right to the enjoy-ment of all civil and political rights set forth in this Bill of Rights."

61. Article 48 of the Chinese Constitution states: "Women in the People's Repub-lic of China enjoy equal rights with men in all spheres of life, political, economic, cultural, and social, including family life. The state protects the rights and interests of women, applies the principle of equal pay for equal work for men and women like and trains and selects cadres from among women."

62. *Lau Wong Fat v. Attorney General*, Civil Appeal No. 247 of 1966 [1997] HKLR 533.

63. This is officially said to be an "unprecedented incursion into the stock and futures markets to safeguard our (Hong Kong's) very economic survival." See paras 7 and 11 of the Budget Speech by the Financial Secretary for the financial year 2000–2001.

64. See note 16.

65. The land grant, inter alia, has been criticized by the European Parliament for favoritism and unfair competition. Many allegations against the tycoon Li Ka-shing are contentious. However, had the land for the cyberpot been allocated by auction or tender, this criticism would not have arisen. See report by Audrey Snee, "Li Family Firms Have Undue Influence, Says MPs' Report," *South China Morning Post,* Octo-ber 26, 2000, p.tt 2. See http://www.europarl.eu.int and note 2.

66. See note 17.
67. Ibid.
68. Being highly critical of government resumption of private land for profitmaking urban renewal projects, this chapter does not discuss practical means for overcoming property rights problems. The reason is that the author elsewhere suggested some such means as the establishment of an urban renewal trust fund (Lai 1993). Here, the author focuses on the ideological and jurisprudential dimensions of the problems.
69. Yu, Shaw, Fu, and Lai (2000).

Bibliography

Alderman, Ellen, and Caroline Kennedy. *In Our Defense: The Bill of Rights in Action.* New York: Avon Books, 1991.

Barzel, Y. "A Theory of Rationing by Waiting. *Journal of Law and Economics* 11, no. 1 (April 1974): 73–95.

The Basic Law of the Hong Kong Special Administrative Region of the People's Republic of China.

Bromley, Daniel W. "Property Regimes in Environmental Economics," In *The International Yearbook of Environmental and Resource Economics: a Survey of Current Issues: 1997–1998*, Henk Folmer and Tom Tietenberg, ed. Cheltenhem: Edward Elgar, 1997, pp. 1–27.

Buchanan, James M. *Property as a Guarantor of Liberty.* Aldershot, UK: Edward Elgar, 1993.

Chan, Albert H.Y. "The Basic Law and the Protection of Property Rights," *Hong Kong Law Journal* 23, no. 1 (1993): 31–78.

Chan, Johannes M.M. "Prospect for the Due Process Under Chinese Sovereignty." In *Judicial Independence and the Rule of Law in Hong Kong*, Steve Tang, ed. Chippenham, UK: Palgrave, 2001, pp. 132–56.

Chan, Johannes M.M., H.L. Fu, and Y. Ghai, eds. *Hong Kong's Constitutional Debate: Conflict Over Interpretation.* Hong Kong: Hong Kong University Press, 2000.

Chang, D.W.W., and R. Chuang. *The Politics of Hong Kong's Reversion to China.* London: Macmillan, 1999.

Cheek-Milby, Kathleen, and Miron Mushkat, eds. *Hong Kong: The Challenge of Transformation.* Hong Kong: Center of Asian Studies, University of Hong Kong, 1989.

Cheung, Steven N.S. "A Theory of Price Control." *Journal of Law and Economics* 17, no. 1 (April 1974): 53–71.

Christudason, Alice, "Insecurity of Tenure: Rights of Strata-Titled Property Owners in Singapore." Unpublished paper, Department of Real Estate, School of Design and Environment, National University of Singapore, 2000.

Cohen, W.I. and L. Zhao, eds. *Hong Kong Under Chinese Rule: The Economic and Political Implications Reversion.* Cambridge, MA: Cambridge University Press, 1997.

Davies, S.N.S., and E.V. Roberts. *Political Dictionary for Hong Kong.* Hong Kong: Macmillan, 1990.

Deng, Xiaoping. *Deng Xiaoping: The Construction of Socialism with Chinese Characteristics*, 2d ed. Hong Kong: Joint Publishing, 1987 (Chinese publication).

Eaton, J.D. *Real Estate Valuation in Litigation*, 2d ed. Chicago: Appraisal Institute, 1995.

Endacott, G.B. *Government and People in Hong Kong, 1841–1962*. Hong Kong: Hong Kong University Press, 1964.

Environment Resource Management. *Sustainable Development in Hong Kong for the 21st Century*. Hong Kong: Environment Resource Management, November 1998.

Evans, D.M.E. "Some Legal Aspects of Urbanization in Hong Kong." In *Asian Urbanization: A Hong Kong Case Book*, D.J. Dwyer, ed. Hong Kong: Hong Kong University Press, 1971, pp. 20–32.

Fischel, William A. *The Economics of Zoning Laws: A Property Rights Approach to American Land Use Controls*. Baltimore: John Hopkins University Press, 1985.

———. *Regulatory Takings: Law, Economics and Politics*. Cambridge, MA: Harvard University Press, 1995.

Fishman, Robert. *Urban Utopias in the Twentieth Century: Ebenezer Howard, Frank Lloyd Wright and Le Corbusier*. Cambridge, MA: MIT Press, 1982.

Gifford, Adam, Jr. "Rent Seeking and Non-Price Competition." *Quarterly Review of Economics and Management* 27, no. 2 (1987): 63–70.

Gleeson, Brendan, and Nicholas Low. "Revaluing Planning: Rolling Back Neo-Liberalism in Australia." *Progress in Planning* 53, no. 2 (2000): 83–164.

Hammer, A.M. "Planning Urban Development with a Change of Sovereignty in Mind— A Hong Kong Case Study." *Cities* 14, no. 5 (1997): 287–294.

Hayek, F.A. *The Road to Serfdom*. Chicago: University of Chicago Press, 1944.

———. *The Constitution of Liberty*. Chicago: University of Chicago Press, 1960.

Hobson, John, Stephen Hockman, and Paul Stinchcombe. "The Future of the Planning System," In *Law Reform for All*, David Bean, ed. London: Blackstone, 1996, pp. 214–22.

Hong, Yu-hung. "Transaction Cost of Allocating Increased Land Value Under Public Leasehold Systems: Hong Kong." *Urban Studies* 35, no. 9 (1998): 1577–95.

Hong Kong Special Administrative Region Government. *Consultation Paper on the Urban Renewal Bill*. Hong Kong, Planning, Environment and Lands Bureau, 1999.

Hsu, Berry F., "Judicial Development of Hong Kong on the Eve of 1 July 1997," in *The Hong Kong Reader: Passage to Chinese Sovereignty*, Ming K. Chan and Gerard A. Postiglione, ed. Armonk, NY: M.E. Sharpe, 1996, pp. 65–97.

Hu, Jichuang. *A Concise History of Chinese Economic Thought*. Beijing, Foreign Languages Press, 1984.

Irving, Richard, and Brian Morton. *A Geography of the Mai Po Marshes*. Hong Kong: World Wide Fund for Nature, 1988.

Kwan, Wai-ling, and Leung Ka-keung, "The Sources of Atmospheric Pollution in Hong Kong." *Next Magazine* 514 (January 13, 2000): 44–52.

Lai, Lawrence Wai-chung. "Urban Renewal and the Land Development Corporation," In *The Other Hong Kong Report*, Choi Po-king and Ho Lok-sang, ed. Hong Kong: Chinese University Press, 1993, pp. 175–91.

———. "The Harbor Reclamation Debate 1995–96." In *The Other Hong Kong Report*, Nyaw Mee-kau and Li Si-ming, ed. Hong Kong: Chinese University Press, 1996, pp. 349–66.

———. "The Property Rights Justifications for Planning and a Theory of Zoning." *Progress in Planning* 48, no. 3 (1997): 161–246.

———. "The Leasehold System as a Means of Planning by Contract: The Case of Hong Kong." *Town Planning Review* 69, no. 3 (1998): 249–75.

———. "Reflections on the Abercrombie Report 1948: A Strategic Plan for Colonial Hong Kong." *Town Planning Review* 70, no. 1 (1999a): 61–87.

————. *Town Planning in Hong Kong: A Review of Planning Appeal Decisions.* Hong Kong: Hong Kong University Press, 1999b.

————. "Hayek and Town Planning: A Note on Hayek's Views Towards Town Planning in the Constitution on Liberty." *Environment and Planning A* 31, no. 9 (1999c): 1567–82.

————. "Housing 'Indigenous Villagers' in a Modern Society: An Examination of the Hong Kong 'Small House' Policy." Research monograph presented to the CPD lectures for HKIS members, University of Hong Kong, September 11, 1999d.

————. *Town Planning in Hong Kong: A Critical Review.* Hong Kong: City University of Hong Kong Press, 1999e.

————. "Enforcement Against Alleged Breaches of Crown (Government) Leases in Hong Kong Industrial Premises." *Property Management* 18, no. 1 (2000a): 63–73.

————. Review of Consultation Paper on Sustainable Development. *Asian Journal of Public Administration,* 2000b, forthcoming.

————. *Zoning and Property Rights: A Hong Kong Case Study,* 2d ed. Hong Kong: Hong Kong University Press, 2000c.

————. *Town Planning in Hong Kong: A Review of Planning Appeal Decisions.* Hong Kong: Hong Kong University Press, 2000d.

————. "Housing 'Indigenous Villagers' in a Modern Society: An Examination of the Hong Kong 'Small House' Policy." *Third World Planning Review* 22, no. 2 (2000e): 207–30.

Lai, Lawrence Wai-chung, and Ki Fong. *Town Planning Practice: Context, Procedures and Statistics.* Hong Kong: Hong Kong University Press, 2000.

Lai, Lawrence Wai-Chung, and Marco Ka-Wai Yu. "The Rise and Fall of Discriminatory Zoning in Hong Kong." *Environment and Planning B: Planning and Design* 28, no. 2 (2001): 295–314.

Lau, C.K. *Hong Kong Colonial Legacy: A Hong Kong Chinese's Views of the British Heritage.* Hong Kong: Chinese University Press, 1997.

Law, Anthony M.W. "Judicial Review of Government Leases in the Hong Kong Special Administrative Region." *Hong Kong Law Journal* 29 (1999): 240–266.

MacEwan, Arthur. *Neo-Liberalism or Democracy: Economic Strategy, Markets, and Alternatives for the 21st Century.* London: Zed Books, 1999.

Miners, N., *Government and Politics of Hong Kong,* 5th ed. Hong Kong: Oxford University Press, 1998.

Murphy, Walter, James E. Fleming, and Sotirios A. Barber. *American Constitution Interpretation,* 2d ed. New York: New York Foundation Press, 1995.

Murphy, Walter F., James E. Fleming, and William F. Harris. *American Constitution Interpretation.* New York: Foundation Press, 1986.

Ng, Mee Kam. "Urban and Regional Planning." In *From Colony to SAR: Hong Kong's Challenges Ahead,* Joseph Y.S. Cheng and Sonny S.H. Lo, ed. Hong Kong: Chinese University Press, 1995, pp. 227–60.

Ng, Mee Kam, and Wing Shing Tang. "Land-Use Planning in 'One Country, Two Systems': Hong Kong, Guangzhou and Shenzhen." *International Planning Studies* 4, no. 1 (1999): 7–26.

O'Driscoll, Gerald P., Jr., K.R. Holmes, and Melanie Kirkpatrick. *2001 Index of Economic Freedom, Wall Street Journal,* 2001.

Oestereich, Jugen. "Land and Property Rights: Some Remarks on Basic Concepts and General Perspectives." *Habitat International* 24 (2000): 221–30.

Olson, Mancur. *The Rise and Decline of Nations: Economic Growth, Stagflation, and Social Rigidities*. New Haven, CT: Yale University Press, 1982.

Overholt, William H. *The Rise of China: How Economic Reform Is Creating a New Superpower*. New York: W.W. Norton, 1993.

Rabushka, Alvin. "A Free-Market Constitution for Hong Kong: A Blueprint for China." *Cato Journal* 8, no. 3 (1989): 641–52.

Roberts, P.J. *Valuation of Development Land in Hong Kong*. Hong Kong: Hong Kong University Press, 1975.

Siegan, Bernard H. *The Supreme Court's Constitution: An Inquiry into Judicial Review and Its Impact on Society*. London: Transaction, 1989.

———. *Drafting a Constitution for a Nation or Republic Emerging into Freedom*. Fairfax: George Mason University Press, 1994.

———. *Property and Freedom: The Constitution, The Courts and Land Use-Regulation*. London: Transaction, 1997.

So, W.Y. "Administered Competition." paper presented to the Symposium on International Harmonization of Competition Laws," Taipei, March 11–14, 1994.

Sowell, Thomas. *Knowledge and Decisions*. New York: New Books, 1996.

Tang, Bo-shing, and Hing-fung Leung. "Planning Enforcement in Hong Kong: Implementing New Planning Law Before the Change of Sovereignty." *Town Planning Review* 69, no. 2 (1998): 153–69.

Tang, Steve, ed. *Judicial Independence and the Rule of Law in Hong Kong*. Chippenham: Palgrave, 2001.

Tullock, Gordon. "Rent Seeking and Zoning." Unpublished research paper, 1994.

Vines, S. *Hong Kong: China's New Colony*. London: Aurum Press, 1998.

Vogel, E.F. *The Four Little Dragons: The Spread of Industrialization in East Asia*. Cambridge, MA: Harvard University Press, 1991.

Wesley-Smith, Peter. *An Introduction to the Hong Kong Legal System*. Hong Kong: Oxford University Press, 1998.

Willoughby, P.G. "Let the Land Owner Beware." *Hong Kong Law Lectures* (1978): 145–230.

Woronoff, Jon. *Asia's "Miracle" Economy*, 2d ed. Armonk, NY: M.E. Sharpe, 1992.

Yeh, Anthony K.O. "Planning and Management of Hong Kong's Border," In *From Colony to SAR: Hong Kong's Challenges Ahead*, Joseph Y.S. Cheng and Sonny S.H. Lo, ed. Hong Kong: Chinese University Press, 1995, pp. 261–92.

Yeung, Y.M. "Planning for Pearl City: Hong Kong's Future, 1997 and Beyond." *Cities* 14, no. 5 (1997): 249–56.

Yu, Ben T., Daigee Shaw, Tsu-tan Fu, and Lawrence Wai-chung Lai. "A Property Rights and Contractual Approach to Sustainable Development." *Environmental Economics and Policy Studies* 3, no. 3 (2000): 291–300.

11

Hong Kong's Language Policy in the Postcolonial Age

Social Justice and Globalization

Chao Fen Sun

After Hong Kong was placed under British rule, English was used as the only official language even though the absolute majority of people residing in the colony spoke nothing but Chinese. Chinese language began to be part of the government operation only in 1974, after two mass campaigns by a cross-section of Hong Kong society demanded an official status for the Chinese language (Fang 1993). However, Chinese remained secondary as all laws were still initially written, proposed, and interpreted in English. Chinese was then used only as a means of expediency. The primacy of English in Hong Kong followed from the linguistic attitude revealed in the Tianjin Treaty (see Article 50, below), which was signed between China and Great Britain in 1858 (T'sou 1997) and which extended Great Britain's rule of Hong Kong to include Kowloon peninsular. In the treaty Chinese was designated an expediency without legal effect.

Article 50
All official communications, addressed by the Diplomat and Consular Agents of Her Majesty the Queen to the Chinese authorities, shall, henceforth, be written in English. They will for the present be accompanied by a Chinese version, but it is understood that, in the event of there being any difference of meaning between the English and Chinese texts, the English Government will hold the sense as expressed in the English text to be the correct sense. This provision is to apply to the Treaty now negotiated, the Chinese text of which has been carefully corrected by the English original.

The dominance of English language can also be seen in Hong Kong's sec-

Figure 11.1 **Students in Chinese and English Schools**

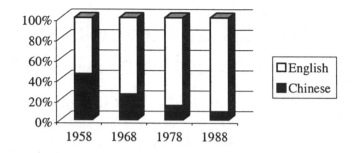

ondary schools before 1997, even though the Hong Kong government generally adopted a laissez-faire attitude toward schools' use of language in instruction (Poon 1999). Before 1949, when most of the secondary school graduates in Hong Kong went to mainland China for their tertiary education (Tung, Lam, and Tsang 1997), most students were naturally enrolled in the secondary schools where the medium of instruction was primarily in Chinese. However, this situation was drastically changed after the 1950s, when more and more Hong Kong students began to look to the West for opportunities in tertiary education. Students enrolled in English-medium secondary schools increased from about 55 percent (25,863 out of a total of 47,073) in 1958 to 92 percent (365,330 out of a total of 398,303) in 1988 (So 1992) (see Figure 11.1).

The secondary status of Chinese was legally ended by Article 9 of the Basic Law of the Hong Kong Special Administrative Region of the People's Republic of China, which was adopted at the Third Session of the Seventh National People's Congress in Beijing on April 4, 1990, and which designates the Chinese language as the primary language of the Special Administrative Region (SAR).

> Article 9
> In addition to the Chinese Language, English may also be used as an official language by the executive authorities, legislature and judiciary of the Hong Kong Special Administrative Region.

Even now, however, as a legacy from about a hundred and fifty years of colonial rule, English is still perceived by many locals, perhaps including the government itself, as extremely important. Hong Kong is now at a linguistic crossroads struggling to find a solution for itself. The chief executive, Tung Chee-hwa, said, in his first policy address in October 1997:

> We will press forward with mother tongue teaching, so that students can learn more effectively. (p. 29)

84. Confidence and competence in the use of Chinese and English are essential if we are to maintain our competitive edge in the world. The education commission Report No. 6 has already laid down a framework to achieve our goal for secondary school graduates to be proficient in writing English and Chinese and able to communicate confidently in Cantonese, English and Putonghua. Putonghua will become part of the curriculum in the next school year starting from Primary 1, Secondary 1 and Secondary 4, and a subject in the Hong Kong Certificate of Education Examinations by the year 2000.

85. Greater use of mother tongue teaching will help raise the standard of teaching in non-language subjects. It also allows more time to be given to specialised teaching of English and Chinese so that all language standards may be raised.

86. To make an immediate impact on improving the English language standard of our students, we will implement a new Native-speaking English Teachers Scheme, providing more than 700 additional native-speaking English teachers for secondary schools from next year.

87. We will also:

   - set language benchmarks for all teachers in 1998–99;
   - require all new teachers to meet the benchmarks before they join the profession in 2000;
   - provide training for in-service language teachers, so that within five years of the benchmarks being set, all will be able to reach them; and
   - provide more teachers to support school library services and the Chinese and English Reading Schemes in primary school.

88. In the longer term, we need to develop a centre of excellence in language teaching, and we will be looking into establishing a "Centre of Language Teaching" within the Institute of Education for the training and retraining of our language teachers. (pp. 29–30)

In the above paragraphs, Tung laid down the basis of the new government's language policy. As a matter of fact, this policy is commonly referred to as a policy of *liang wen san yu* (officially translated as biliterate trilingualism), meaning that the government is actively pursuing a language policy that would enable the Hong Kong public to "master written Chinese and English and . . . speak fluent Cantonese, Putonghua, and English" (Education Department home page, http://www.info.gov.hk/hkar99/eng/09/09–u.htm).

Before we continue the discussion, it is perhaps useful to take a look at the social statuses of the three languages in Hong Kong. As observed earlier, English was the language most highly regarded in the colony. Of the two Chinese languages, Cantonese and Putonghua, Cantonese was more commonly used on TV, on radio, and in daily life situations. Mainland China's standard dialect, Putonghua, was actually the one that had the lowest social prestige of the three, and most SAR residents cannot speak it at all. Arguably, of the three, English, as a language superimposed by the former colonial masters, still enjoys the highest prestige in the SAR. It remains the primary working language of the government and the all-powerful business sectors, as well as the medium of instruction in all of the local universities.

Ferguson (1972: 232) observed that "[i]n many speech communities two or more varieties of the same language are used by some speakers under different conditions . . . where many speakers speak their local dialect at home or among family or friends of the same dialect area but use the standard language in communicating with speakers of other dialects or on public occasions." However, in postcolonial Hong Kong the use of the standard language Putonghua is limited to the public occasions attended by officials representing the central government in Beijing. Moreover, Putonghua TV and radio programs are not most commonly watched by the SAR residents. On the contrary, the Common Law that is written in English language continues to govern the daily life and business practices of the SAR.

Nowadays, the Hong Kong people continue to speak Cantonese. Since July 1, 1997, the language most commonly used in legislative debates has changed from English to Cantonese, not to Putonghua. Otherwise, the social conditions for using the three languages in the SAR have not changed much since the change of sovereignty in 1997. Figure 11.2 shows that, as compared to the social conditions for the use of the three languages before the turnover, the status of English in SAR has fallen a little, the status of Putonghua has risen a little, and Cantonese remains the language with which the Hong Kong people identify themselves most closely. In discussing varieties of the language serving different functions in a society, Ferguson (1972: 247) also observes that "diglossia seems to be accepted and not regarded as a 'problem' by the community in which it is in force, until certain trends appear in the community. These include trends toward (1) more widespread literacy (whether for economic, ideological, or other reasons), (2) broader communication among different regional and social segments of the community (e.g., for economic, administrative, military, or ideological reason), (3) desire for a full-fledged standard 'national' language as an attribute of autonomy or of

Figure 11.2 **The Triglossic Situation in Hong Kong**

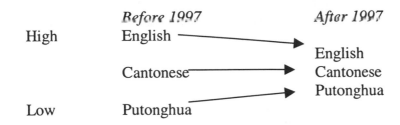

sovereignty." In light of Ferguson's observation, the lack of rapid change of the social conditions of the three languages follows from Beijing's allowance for Hong Kong to continue to practice British common law for fifty more years with a government of its own. With the pledge from Beijing not to interfere with the internal affairs of the SAR, the people of Hong Kong essentially need not change their lifestyle, including their choice of language. This may partially explain why Cantonese continues to be the most commonly used language in the SAR, whereas the national standard, Putonghua, remains the language least popular of the three.

In the context of little change with respect to the social perception of the three languages used in Hong Kong, the government's policy of biliterate trilingualism nevertheless marks a major departure from the laissez-faire practice of the colonial government. In particular, the promotion of mother-tongue education turns out to be very unpopular among the Hong Kong public. In 1997, the Hong Kong government decided to put into practice a streaming proposal originally put forth in the 1990 Education Commission Report, Number 4. The 1990 report observed that

> [T]here is pressure for children to learn English and to learn in English, since this is seen by parents as offering the best prospect for their children's future. Many children, however, have difficulty with learning in English; and conversely, Chinese is undervalued as a medium of instruction and the importance of the Chinese language skills is not sufficiently recognized.

The report also found that only about 30 percent of Hong Kong's secondary school students were deriving any benefit from the English-medium instruction, and proposed that primary school students be assessed for language ability and streamed into Chinese- or English-medium secondary schools based on these assessments.[1] In September 1997, the Hong Kong government for the first time firmly advised all local public-sector secondary schools to adopt Chinese as the medium of instruction, starting with their Secondary 1 intake in the 1998–99 school year and progressing each year to a higher level of secondary education. (At Secondary 4 of the Chinese-medium school, the medium of instruction can be changed to English at the discretion of the school authorities.) Only schools satisfying certain criteria regarding students' language ability, teacher capability, and support services were allowed to use, or continued to use, English as the medium of instruction. In the end, only about 30 percent of the secondary school students with the best scores (see note 1) could study in the schools that used English as the medium of instruction. To help parents choose the secondary schools best suited to their children's language ability, they were informed of their children's grouping and the medium of instruction adopted by individual schools.

This policy, when implemented in 1998, turned out to be wildly unpopular. Parents and teachers alike felt that the policy was unfair and divisive. Luke Yip Jing-ping, headmaster of St. Stephen's College, explained, "We don't oppose mother-tongue teaching. But we are very angry the Government is differentiating and labeling schools. And the judging is unfair." Some parents even suggested that their children should go on strike (*South China Morning Post*, December 9, 1997). Others worried that, since knowledge of English is necessary at the university level, "if their children do not have a sound grounding in [English] beforehand, they will be at a disadvantage when reading for a degree." There were also economic arguments against mother-tongue education: "Hong Kong . . . looks beyond its own horizons for career opportunities. Even for stay-at-homes, the job opportunities are in professions such as finance, where English proficiency is essential" (*South China Morning Post*, December 15, 1997).

In 2000, under the pressure and sponsorship from the business sectors, the government started a language campaign aiming at establishing benchmarks to reflect the standard of workplace English required of the employees in different occupations and sectors of the SAR. In addition, the government started to require all language teachers in primary and secondary schools to take benchmark tests. This practice resulted in split views from the general public. On the one hand, the parents and business sectors support the benchmark testing of the schoolteachers (*Sing Tao Daily*, May 26 and 27, 2000). In a survey reported in *World Journal* (October 9, 2000), 60 percent of the citizens investigated found the performance of the language teachers undesirable, and over 70 percent of the people investigated believe benchmark testing of schoolteachers is necessary. On the other hand, benchmark testing is extremely unpopular among the schoolteachers, who enjoy generous support from some high-profile politicians. Many of them refused to take tests (*Mingpao*, August 16, 2000), demonstrated in the streets (*Xing Bao*, June 12, 2000), and even challenged the chief executive to a public debate (*Sing Tao*, October 7, 2000).

Recently, it was also reported that the government might postpone the benchmark testing (*Mingpao*, September 15, 2000) and replace the test with a special training course for language teachers. In addition, it was also reported that the government had shown signs of backing down from its previous stand on mother-tongue education, as it was going to allow certain secondary schools designated for Chinese medium of instruction to use both English and Chinese as the medium of instruction (*Sing Tao*, September 2, 2000). The latest mixed signals from the government simply make the general public wonder whether the government is preparing to depart from its proclaimed policy on mother-tongue education.

The focus of this chapter is to show how, within Hong Kong's current culture and social structures, the new language policy proposed by the government has created additional social injustice by dividing the secondary schools into two groups, one with English as the medium of instruction and the other with Chinese as the medium of instruction. The second section examines the history and linguistic abilities of Hong Kong students, and the third section deals with the plausibility of the policy, given the power of English language in Hong Kong. The fourth section concludes the chapter, making a bilingual proposal that will jeopardize neither the children's education nor their creativity in learning, as it will avoid creating additional linguistic barriers.

The Linguistic History of Hong Kong

When Hong Kong was first taken over by the British Empire as its entrepôt into China a hundred and fifty years ago, it needed a large number of cheap laborers from the neighboring Guangdong province. Since then, Hong Kong has always been a safe haven for Chinese immigrants running away from either the political turmoil or the natural disasters that were ravaging their hometowns in different parts of China at various times. There were also many who came from China simply seeking economic advancement. However, as a British colony, it had never been considered as appropriate for any British settlement. Endacott (1964: v) observed, based on records of the Colonial Office and other sources:

> The Colony of Hong Kong was long regarded as different from all other colonies, as a phenomenon unique even in the many-sided story of British overseas expansion. . . . Lord Stanley said, "Methods of proceeding unknown in other British colonies must be followed in Hong Kong, . . . not with a view to colonization, but for diplomatic, commercial and military purposes." Sir Hercules Robinson, governor 1859–1865, remarked "Indeed, Hong Kong is totally unlike any other British dependency and its

position is in many respects so grotesquely anomalous." . . . Sir Richard Grave MacDonnell also observed, "There is however no parallel between this and any other British settlement. . . . Special, exceptional circumstances of this very peculiar place, its very peculiar inhabitants and most peculiar geographical position." . . . Phineas Ryrie, member of the Legislative Council from July 1867 until his death in February 1892, used to describe Hong Kong as sui generis.

As a result of this special venture of the British Empire without bringing in a large number of English immigrants, nowadays nearly 89 percent of the population of this former colony are Chinese, most of whom (89 percent; So 1998) speak Cantonese. Therefore, the Chinese language that is now used most commonly on Hong Kong TV and radio is Cantonese. Chinese students in the primary schools learn to read and write Chinese mostly through instruction given in Cantonese. Children (among them the author of this chapter) of non–Cantonese-speaking immigrants from mainland China, just like everybody else, all grow up speaking Cantonese as their mother tongue, if we define *mother tongue* as the main language that one grows up speaking.

Thousands of the local Chinese, particularly in the recent decades, who have acquired various degrees of English proficiency, have immigrated to countries like Australia, Canada, Britain, New Zealand, and the United States. Taking their place are thousands of Chinese-speaking immigrants from the north. Therefore, the population of Hong Kong is essentially composed of two monolingual communities, with 2 percent speaking English only and 98 percent speaking Chinese), including some Chinese who can function in both speech communities by using English in workplace environments. Given such a historical background, it is not surprising to see that the writer of an editorial in the local English-language newspaper *South China Morning Post* (March 22, 1997) observes that:

> One hundred and fifty years as a British colony have not made as great an impact as many might have expected on the English language skills of the Hong Kong public. A large proportion of the population can make a stab at speaking English, but the level of fluency varies. In many cases, it lags far behind Singapore and Malaysia, both of which are truly bilingual states.

In fact, throughout the history of the former colony, there had never been a time that had not been marked by criticism of the English-language abilities of the Hong Kong public. In 1878 Governor John Pope lamented, after a visit to the central school run by the government, that of the school's six hundred students, only about sixty could manage to speak English, and they spoke it poorly (Sweeting 1990). The title of the 1989 inaugural lecture of a professor of English language in the University of Hong Kong was "The Worst English in the World." The speech was highly critical of the English-language abilities of the Hong Kong public as well as his students in the best university of the colony (So 1998). About 71 percent of the students, after a diagnostic test of their English skills in the University of Hong Kong that regularly attracted the very best students, were required to receive remedial language assistance in order to function in the English-medium university (Lord 1974: 4). This situation persists and has perhaps worsened, as tertiary education in Hong Kong is no longer limited to the elitist few but is open to more and more secondary school graduates with various social backgrounds.

The absolute majority of the university students in Hong Kong are graduates of the secondary schools, with English as the medium of instruction. According to the new English syllabus for secondary schools proposed by the Education Department to be implemented in 2002 (see Figure 11.3), Key Stage 4 competence is expected of the students who finish Secondary 5. Sixth Form provides language preparation for further studies at tertiary level as well as work.

Therefore, the English-language competence of the Hong Kong secondary school students is expected to meet a very high standard, as Key Stage 4 is defined in terms of the following three highly demanding dimensions by the English syllabus for secondary schools:

Interpersonal Dimensions:
> To develop an ever-improving capability to use English
> - to establish and maintain relationships and routines in school, community and work situation;
> - to converse, compare, argue and justify points of view about feelings, interests, preferences, ideas, experiences and plans;
> - to produce or exchange a range of more complex messages both oral and written;
> - to participate with others in planning, organizing and carrying out more complex and extended events;
> - to obtain and provide objects, services and information in a wider and more complex range of real and simulated situations.

Knowledge Dimension:
> To develop an ever-improving capability to use English
> - to provide or find out, select, analyze, organize and present information on familiar and unfamiliar topics;
> - to interpret and use more extensive and complex information through processes or activities such as ordering, describing, classifying, comparing, explaining, justifying, predicting, inferring, summarizing, synthesizing and drawing conclusions;

Figure 11.3 **Proposed English Syllabus**

Key Stage 1	Key Stage 2	Key Stage 3	Key Stage 4	Sixth Form
Primary 1–3	Primary 2–6	Secondary 1–3	Secondary 4–5	Secondary 6–7

- to identify and discuss ideas in spoken and written texts, make connections, refine or generate ideas, express or apply them;
- to identify and define more complex problems from given information, consider related factors, explore options, solve the problems, explain and justify the solution;
- to develop and refine ideas by making appropriate revisions to own written texts independently and collaboratively;
- to understand how the English Language works in a wide range of contexts and how more complex texts are organized and expressed; and apply this understanding to one's learning and use of the language.

Experience Dimension:
  To develop an ever-improving capability to use English
- to develop as response to a wider range of imaginative literature through activities such as:
  –participating in the presentations of texts
  –identifying and interpreting themes
  –appreciating the use of language including rhythm and rhyme, other sound patterns and rhetorical devices;
- to respond to characters, events, issues, and themes in imaginative and other narrative texts through oral, written and performative means such as:
  –making predictions and inferences
  –analyzing the actions and motivations of characters and the significance of events relating to one's experiences
  –putting oneself in the imaginary roles and situations in the story
  –participating in dramatic presentations and reflecting on the way in which authors use language to create effects;
- to give expression to imaginative ideas through oral, written and performative means such as:
  –writing stories with a clear awareness of purpose and some development of plot and character
  –providing oral and written descriptions interpreting a situation, object or character

–creating poems and lyrics
–creating short dramatic episodes
* to give expression to one's experience through activities such as providing oral and written descriptions of feelings and events, incorporating where appropriate reflections on their significance.

With creating poems and lyrics and appreciation of literature as part of the expectation, in addition to competence in communicating one's ideas and feelings effectively in different domains of daily life situations and intellectual activities, this may look like an expectation for a highly cultured native speaker of English. But with a disclaimer like "to develop an ever improving capability to use English," this seemingly high expectation actually does not amount to much. In other words, never mind all the high-sounding criteria, the real expectation is "an ever improving capability to use English." If so, it may make better sense to set up the minimum standard that is expected to be met by most, if not all.

Do the best 30 percent of current secondary school graduates who are now studying in the universities, across the board, obtain Key Stage 4 English proficiency? Unfortunately, the best 30 percent of secondary school graduates have never attained such a level of sophistication in English. First of all, according to the government's own 1990 Education Commission Report Number 4, only 30 percent of students were deriving some benefit from English-medium instruction in Hong Kong's secondary schools. Furthermore, not every student among the 30 percent who enter a university would have such a high level of sophistication. Currently, universities in Hong Kong can enroll exactly about 30 percent of local secondary school graduates. A recent survey found that university students commonly do not have adequate English-language skills and have to rely on Chinese to complete their course work. In this survey (Walters and Balla 1998), 1,237 full-time students in seven degree programs at the City University of Hong Kong were investigated. The findings are summed up by the authors in one sentence: "Where possible, instruction is in Cantonese." They further observe that:

The move from a greater use of English in lectures towards a greater use of Cantonese in tutorials, which is evident in all courses except Law, suggests a situation where the material is presented largely in English to begin with, and then, when it comes to understanding it in detail, both staff and students switch to Cantonese. However, since Cantonese is not available to expatriate members of staff, it is worth examining the situation more closely . . . [As] a greater percentage of the senior positions is held by expatriate staff, a distinct pattern of lecture support develops. Material which may be delivered in English in the lectures is clarified in Cantonese, or by mixed Cantonese and English, in tutorials. (p. 378)

What emerges overall is a clear picture of face-to-face instruction which is heavily Cantonese-dependent and Cantonese-supported. . . . In these circumstances, it is extremely likely that students will be able to gain access in Cantonese to whatever information they need to know. Such access can be provided either directly through the Cantonese-speaking staff or indirectly through fellow students. . . . The prevailing attitude on the part of the Chinese lecturers and tutors is probably that, if the students are to fully understand, they should be addressed in Chinese. (p. 380)

It should be evident from the above paragraphs that the so-called English-medium instruction in Hong Kong's universities is not entirely in English. Without support, Chinese students might not be able to absorb anything that is completely presented in English. The mixed mode in learning may enable the students to pass, or even earn a decent grade, but it can never change the fact that even the best 30 percent of the secondary school graduates need not have the adequate English-language skills to succeed in a truly English-medium university education. Walters and Balla's (1998) investigation also tells us that the students have mastered a Cantonese-based linguistic hybrid that they use for learning almost any subject, perhaps with the law programs as the only exception. We can infer from all this that, had the students' imagination not been handicapped by the English-language instruction, they could have learned better and much more effectively with the Cantonese medium of instruction. In this regard, we do not see any evidence showing that, across the board, students after Form 7 in Hong Kong possess the level of English-language abilities that is expected of the Form 5 students by the proposed English syllabus of the Education Department. In addition, the 70 percent of secondary school students who are now enrolled in Chinese-medium schools are even less likely to attain the level expected of Form 5 students in the future.

The Cultural Background for the Hong Kong Language Policy

Why are Hong Kong parents not happy with the government's policy of promoting mother-tongue education? Strong opposition to the streaming policy implemented by the Education Department in 1998 came mostly from either English-medium secondary schools that had been designated by the government to change to Chinese-medium schools and from parents whose children could no longer study in an English-medium school. On the other hand, the principals and parents of children in the English-medium schools, which are now serving 30 percent of secondary school students, all seem happy and have no complaints. Furthermore, how can 70 percent of age-eleven children be deemed unfit to learn in English? Finally, why on earth do Hong Kong parents not want their children to learn in their mother tongue?

To find answers to these, we need to look at the cultural background and the power of the English language in Hong Kong. Although Cantonese is truly a means of identification among the people in Hong Kong, it has never been the language of social mobility. The data in Figure 11.4 are taken from the Appendix of the 1998 Almanac published by the Hong Kong government and from the 1998 master pay scale of the City University of Hong Kong.

Although the salaries of the university faculty are far from being the highest salaries in Hong Kong, they are, nevertheless, easily three to ten times higher than the average incomes of people from different walks of life in Hong Kong. Thus, a teaching position in the universities is considered to be a good job. As the medium of instruction in Hong Kong's universities is primarily English, a high level of English proficiency is a prerequisite for a teaching position in a Hong Kong university. The same can be said of almost all the jobs that pay better than the university lecturers in Hong Kong. The crux of the matter is that there is a correlation between a person's English-language ability and her or his career prospects in Hong Kong. In this light, it is quite understandable why so many parents are so angry about the government's streaming policy. The 70 percent of Hong Kong children who fail, at age eleven or twelve, to get into the top secondary schools with English curriculums are placed by government policy in a highly disadvantageous position at this early age, for their eventual levels of English-language proficiency, and in turn their career prospects, are not likely to be as good as those of the 30 percent of their peers who study in schools with English-medium curriculums. What kind of social justice is that? Schiffman (1996: 59) observes that

> Language policy is therefore not just a text, a sentence or two in the legal code, it is a belief system, a collection of ideas and decisions and attitudes about language. It is of course a cultural construct, but it is either in tune with the values of the linguistic culture or it is in serious trouble.

The power structure of the SAR, which has changed very little from its colonial form, makes the general public believe that the English language is the key to preparing the young people for a successful career. This cultural belief is deeply rooted in the soul of the people from all sectors of society. They even believe that the ability to use English makes them superior to their fellow Chinese in the north, as noted by Elaine Chan of the City University

Figure 11.4 **Average Incomes in Hong Kong, September 1998**

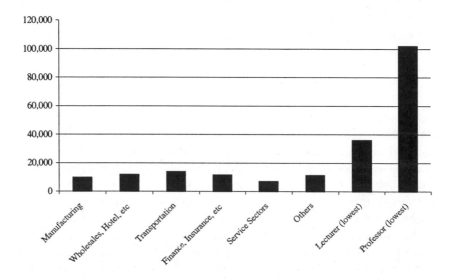

of Hong Kong (*Sunday Morning Post*, April 9, 2000), "People want to know English because they believe it confers superiority as it can lead to better jobs and in theory it differentiates them from other Chinese."A sense of superiority comes out in a different way in the chief executive's 2000 Annual Policy Address. In talking about Hong Kong's links to China and the rest of the world, the chief executive observes:

> [W]e need to train a critical mass of people with suitable talent as quickly as possible. These people should have a thorough understanding of the business environment of the Mainland, knowledge in international finance and commerce and proficiency in Putonghua and foreign languages, especially English. A good command of English is not only a tool for conducting business and trade with the world, but also a must in maintaining Hong Kong's status as an International financial centre.

Clearly, the chief executive is thinking that the English-language ability of the workforce is crucial in maintaining Hong Kong's competitive edge over other Asian cities, including those in the People's Republic of China (PRC). It is therefore fair to say that even though Article 9 of the Basic Law of the Hong Kong SAR of the PRC has given the Chinese language primary status, pertaining to the issue of success both at the individual level and in the SAR as a whole, English is still perceived as more important. Pertinent to this line of thinking, Schiffman (1996: 2) makes an interesting observation:

> For one thing, there is usually a difference between the policy as stated (the official, de jure or overt policy) and the policy as it actually works at the practical level (the covert, de facto or grass-roots policy).

From this point of view, we can see that the current policy of the government overtly promotes mother-tongue education (e.g., switching 70 percent of the secondary schools to Chinese-medium schools) but what really works at the grassroots level is that the de facto policy effectively preserves the colonial structure in which the most talented elite who could, among other things, speak English well, were heavily rewarded. This de facto policy, in a way, agrees with the belief system of the angry parents whose children were not placed in secondary schools with an English curriculum. Things actually can be worse for angry parents who have such a cultural belief. A "through-train" model has been proposed for primary and secondary schools after the abolition of the Academic Aptitude Test for primary school students. The current system, to a large extent, relies on Academic Aptitude Test scores to determine whether an eleven-year-old in the primary schools should study in an English-medium, or a Chinese-medium, school. In the newly proposed through-train model, the government planners state (from the website of the Education and Manpower Bureau):

> (i) Primary and secondary schools applying to form a "through-train" should have the same philosophy and aspiration for education; there should be genuine continuity in the curriculum, teaching methodology and students' personal development; and
>
> (ii) based on the principle of "not giving up on any student," the number of S1 places in a "through-train" must exceed the number of Primary 6 (P6) graduates, and the linked secondary school must admit all P6 graduates of its linked primary schools so that there will not be any unnecessary selection, and the students of other schools will still have the chance to be admitted to the linked secondary school. (September 2000: 85)

To view this model narrowly from the vantage point of social divisiveness pertaining to the issue of medium of instruction, one can easily find that it may give rise to another nightmarish situation for many already very angry parents, if such a proposal is put into practice. Suppose that all the secondary schools with an English curriculum are structurally linked to a number of primary schools, and the same is true for all the schools with a Chinese curriculum. Then, to make sure their children, at age five, get on a through-train leading to an English-medium school, what should Hong Kong parents do? Should they start to prepare their children appropriately as soon as they are born so as to enable them to enter a primary school with the appropriate links? How can schools screen applicants at age four, using fair criteria to determine whether a child is better suited to receive a Chinese or an English education? Is it wise to institutionalize such a divisive system and to place so much pressure upon children at such a young age? Do we really want to have such an unfair language policy, which will inevitably create additional social injustice in postcolonial Hong Kong? As a matter of fact, the government is aware that this system may bring in students who may not be able to survive an English-medium secondary curriculum. In an April 2001 briefing distributed to members of the legislature by the Education and Manpower Bureau, entitled "Study on Enrichment of Language Learning Environment," the government reported that "the diversity in Students' ability in a secondary school to learn effectively in English may widen as a result of the reform of the SSPA system. The study would explore effective support measures to help students adapt to English-medium learning environment." In other words, the government is now determined to implement the through-train system in spite of its foreseeable pitfalls. In the same briefing, the government also laid out its plan to allow more English instruction in the Chinese-medium secondary schools: "The Steering Committee recommended that an enrichment programme should be developed at Secondary 2 and 3 levels respectively to increase students' exposure to English learning. The main body of the programme would be a series of teaching modules (about 30 for each of the two levels) written and taught in English on cross-curricular themes or selected topics from some key learning areas." It appears that the through-train model will tolerate a more bilingual program in the Chinese-medium schools only. These measures do not change the fact that the proposed new model remains an unfair and rigid system for classifying children at an incredibly young age—a system that will have serious social consequences.

What Should the Future Policy Be?

To sum up, the majority of secondary school students cannot truly benefit from a curriculum with English as the medium of instruction. Researchers found that even most of the university students who are now supposedly studying in degree programs, in which English is the medium of instruction, cannot survive such a curriculum without systematic Chinese support. Furthermore, in order to maintain instruction in English for those who can truly learn in English in secondary schools and universities, the government's streaming policy, which places 70 percent of children in a disadvantaged position at age eleven, and possibly at age five a few years from now, is totally unfair and would only create social injustice. Then, in the postcolonial SAR in which 98 percent of the people are Chinese, would a monolingual policy, adopting Cantonese, which is the mother tongue of 89 percent of the local residents, work better for Hong Kong? After all, it is generally accepted that no language would work better than the mother tongue in children's education.

> It is axiomatic that the best medium for teaching a child is his mother tongue. Psychologically, it is the system of meaningful signs that in his mind works automatically for expression and understanding. Sociologically, it is a means of identification among members of the community to which he belongs. Educationally, he learns more quickly through it than through an unfamiliar linguistic medium. (UNESCO 1953: 11)

However, such a monolingual policy would go against the cultural belief of the majority of the people in Hong Kong. First of all, the current power structure in the SAR makes the general public believe that individual success begins with attaining a high degree of English proficiency (see the salary scale in Figure 11.4). Furthermore, the ability to speak English well is taken by the general public to be part of the local identity and to play an important role in maintaining SAR's competitive edge over other Chinese cities in the ever more globalized international economy. In a society in which the majority of parents want their children to learn in English, rather than in their mother tongue, the mother-tongue-only policy will never succeed.

It was mentioned above that, in talking about diglossia, in which different languages are used in different social settings, Ferguson (1972: 247) said that such a situation would "be accepted and not regarded as a 'problem' by the community in which it is in force, until certain trends appear in the community. These include trends toward (1) more widespread literacy (whether for economic, ideological, or other reasons), (2) broader communication among different regional and social segments of the community (e.g., for economic, administrative, military, or ideological reason), (3) desire for a full-fledged standard 'national' language as an attribute of autonomy or of sovereignty."

According to the Basic Law, which was adopted by the National People's Congress in Beijing for Hong Kong after 1997, the people in Hong Kong need not serve in the Chinese military and are not governed by the same laws as the rest of the PRC. Except for growing economic ties with mainland China, which began long before 1997, the people of Hong Kong are essentially living in a lifestyle that varies little from the colonial lifestyle of just a few years ago and that is distinctively different from the lifestyle of the rest of China. Therefore there is no new trend, in the senses cited by Ferguson, that calls for a drastic change of local identity in Hong Kong. However, this does not mean that the SAR government should continue the colonial system in which most secondary school students studied in a language that prevented them from learning effectively. This does not mean that the SAR government should prolong a system that corrected a problem by creating another problem in social injustice. Hong Kong needs a new bilingual system that is free from social injustice.

The current streaming policy for secondary school students has created a new classification system that institutionally places 70 percent of children in a less than advantageous position and that should be abolished immediately. Angel Lin (1997: 439) thoughtfully observes:

> These untenable models assume in the public discourses lead us nowhere and seem to only have effect of scapegoating teachers and students in disadvantaged schools. They will not lead to curricular practices that affirm and capitalize on children's L1 resources to help them to expand their linguistic and sociocultural repertoire to include Mandarin Chinese and English. We need to depart from these models and propose the alternative model of education as dialogue . . . and as interaction of different languages and cultures. . . . We need to put the child back into the center of our discussion to see what children need (and not merely what the labor market needs) and what kind of language education curriculum can be developed both to meet their intrinsic needs and to equip them with the necessary resources to survive and succeed in, as well as to contribute to, our society.

The proposed English syllabus for the secondary school, discussed in the second section of this chapter, should be revised to take into account the fact that the majority of the students probably will never reach the Key Stage 4 level of English sophistication typical of a well-educated native speaker of English. Instead, a more pragmatically oriented approach should be developed to identify more realistic goals for the Hong Kong students to attain as second language learners. For example, the proficiency levels of foreign language learners in the United States are commonly measured according to the proficiency guidelines developed by the American Council on Teaching Foreign Languages in terms of a set of interrelated, multidimensional criteria, including levels described as novice, intermediate, advanced, and superior. Each level is defined in terms of students' ability to use the target language accurately and effectively in different social settings. An "intermediate high" learner is someone who can, in most informal settings, handle a topic with discrete sentences in a manner that is somewhat difficult for a native speaker to understand. A "superior" learner is someone who can, in most formal and informal settings, communicate with virtually no error that would disturb a native speaker in actual communication (Hadley 1993: 15). Use of these levels implies recognition that the students are foreign language learners; not all of them are expected to become superior learners. Therefore, students who plan to go to college should aim to achieve at least an advanced status in English, so that they can, in most informal and some formal settings, communicate well enough to be understood without difficulty. In 1935, a British inspector of schools, Admund Burney, visited Hong Kong to report on the state of public education. He observes

> [T]he teaching of English in the schools of Hong Kong should be reformed on a frankly utilitarian basis, i.e., the pupils should be taught to understand, speak, read and write such and so much English as they are likely to need for their subsequent careers and no more. . . .
>
> Education policy in the colony should be gradually reoriented so as eventually to secure for the pupils, first, a command of their own language sufficient for all needs of thought and expression, and secondly, a command of English limited to the satisfaction of vocational demands. (Sweeting 1990: 356)

It, then, follows that Hong Kong secondary schools should not be divided into Chinese-medium and English-medium schools. Instead, certain subjects, such as Chinese history, social studies, and Putonghua, should be taught in Chinese in all schools. On the other hand, English lessons should naturally be conducted in English as much as possible. The medium of instruction in all other subjects can be decided on the basis of the students' linguistic competence by the school authorities, and in consultation with the students' parents. The government, specifically the Department of Education, should function to monitor how adequately consistent standards for various subjects taught in either language are met by students' performance. Schools failing to meet the standards should be subject to appropriate government regulations. Thus, the public will no longer think that only the English-medium schools are good schools. The society as a whole will be less divisive and more harmonious. The key is that, without being out of tune with the cultural belief of the local society, the medium of instruction will no longer constitute a linguistic barrier to learning for most students. Furthermore, all the secondary schools will be truly bilingual in the sense that, by using two or more languages for formal instruction (Hornberger 1990: 14), they will be preparing their students well to join a workforce that requires a high degree of competence in both English and Chinese.

This bilingual model should be extended to tertiary education as well. In his 2000 annual policy address, the chief executive observes that the HKSAR government is planning to double the current enrollment in Hong Kong's universities within ten years, to allow 60 percent of secondary school graduates to receive tertiary education locally. Pertaining to the issue of medium of instruction, if many of the top 30 percent of current secondary school graduates cannot survive the English curriculum without Chinese support, what would put the 60 percent of secondary school graduates of the future in a better position to cope with an English university curriculum? What is more, 70 percent of secondary school students nowadays are already studying with a Chinese curriculum. After the implementation of the streaming policy in the secondary schools, one principal says that

> his present students are less motivated to learn English because English is no longer that important to them and their proficiency in English will no longer affect the results of other subjects. Formerly his students wanted to improve their English because English was the medium of instruction. Poor English would result in poor performance in content-matter subjects. (Poon 1999: 140)

If this principal's observation accurately describes the current trend in the secondary schools, it becomes clear that to realize the chief executive's goal in doubling the current size of university students in ten years, planning to reform the tertiary education to become truly bilingual needs to begin immediately. Without a truly bilingual system in ten years, in which half of the course offerings are rendered in Chinese and half in English, it is predictable that the quality of education will be negatively affected. With a truly bilingual system, a student can work for a degree in a language of her or his choice or through a combination of courses taught in Chinese and courses taught in English.

In other words, the government should continue to promote mother-tongue education and to extend the vision of the SAR public by recognizing the flexibility that a truly bilingual educational system would add to Hong Kong. In the current social context, Cantonese, no doubt, should be treated as the primary Chinese language. However, in ten to twenty years, courses in the universities should be allowed to be taught in either Cantonese or Putonghua, as Putonghua is already being taught as a subject starting in Primary 1. Although current Hong Kong university students may find it difficult to study in Putonghua, the same may no longer be true in fifteen to twenty years. Evans and colleagues (1998) find that a cross-section of Hong Kong society already considers Putonghua important in areas such as government and law, as well as in business and commerce, even though they still give Cantonese the highest ranking, with Putonghua second and English third, in everyday life situations. Visionary scholars in Hong Kong already recognize that Cantonese is no use outside southern China and pockets of Chinese immigrant communities worldwide. Professor Cheng Kaiming of Hong Kong University says, "I'm not quite sure the majority is the choice, you also have to think of the utility of the language. Cantonese is leading us nowhere" (*Sunday Morning Post*, April 6, 2000).

The government should, therefore, continue to spare no effort in promoting the learning of Putonghua by the Hong Kong public. Putonghua and Cantonese are actually two cognate languages sharing the same writing systems. Although Cantonese speakers cannot immediately understand Putonghua, literate speakers of both Cantonese and Putonghua can readily communicate with each other in writing. As the grammar of Chinese writing is based on Putonghua, students may even be able to learn to write better in Chinese as a result of learning to speak Putonghua at a young age. Even though Hong Kong is not completely integrated into the state system of the People's Republic, it will be to the advantage of the SAR if its residents are adept in the language of their fellow Chinese. Admittedly, nobody can confidently predict what is likely to happen in China even during the next few months. However, it might be safe to say that China is not likely to adopt English as its national language, or as its official language. Therefore, Putonghua should be recognized as the official language in Hong Kong. Pertaining to the issue of Hong Kong's identity, Putonghua should be part of it too. As is now, globalization to most people in Hong Kong may mean trades and interactions with the West, and, therefore, English is of paramount importance. However, the numbers in Table 11.1 show that, according to statistics from the government's website (http://www.info.gov.hk/hkar99/eng/appendices/app_47.htm), nearly half of visitors to Hong Kong in 1998 were already Putonghua speakers.

With economic ties continuing to bring the SAR closer to the PRC, the SAR's future prosperity may become contingent upon the prosperity of China. Thus it should be self-evident that the future of Hong Kong will be much affected by how well the people of Hong Kong speak the official language of their own country.

Moreover, in monolingual countries like China and Japan, degree-granting foreign-language institutes have been turning out many much-needed workers who can perform their duties adequately in English-speaking workplace environments. For example, many of the clerks who staff the China offices of many international companies in Beijing and Shanghai are foreign-language degree holders from universities and foreign-language institutes.

In the next few years when Hong Kong is engaged in the reform of its

Table 11.1

Visitors to Hong Kong, 1998

Language	Number	Percent
Putonghua	4,410,076	46
English	1,649,769	17
Others	3,514,866	37
Total	9,574,711	100

tertiary education, it might be a good idea to consider establishing degree-granting, vocationally oriented institutes focusing on international trade and English, so that the graduates of these institutes will supply the local workforce with linguistically competent and professionally knowledgeable young workers. With a new bilingual educational system, Hong Kong will then be well positioned to add new components to the universities to meet the needs of the business sectors of the SAR.

In summary, maintaining the colonial-style, English-only curriculum in Hong Kong's secondary schools and universities need not be the best choice in the long run. Hong Kong students cannot learn well in English without the support of Chinese-speaking teachers. Furthermore, the kind of expectation set up in the English syllabus for nonnative Hong Kong students is unsuitable and unrealizable. The streaming policy in secondary schools only blatantly institutionalizes a practice that is socially unjust. Therefore, in the process of developing a language policy that is fair to all, the government should vigorously engage in building up a bilingual system for secondary schools and universities, whereby students will not face additional linguistic barriers or be placed in socially disadvantaged positions by the educational system. Addition of some vocationally oriented institutes that have a language training component at the tertiary level will create a new bilingual educational system—a solid foundation that will enable Hong Kong to continue to compete with a linguistically competent workforce in the ever-increasingly globalized economy. Hong Kong does need all three languages —Cantonese, Putonghua, and English. But the language skills of the three languages to be acquired in the secondary schools should be targeted at the levels that are truly needed and should be realistic.

Recent developments in Hong Kong suggest that language planning needs to be carried out more effectively with better coordination in the midst of various educational reform projects. It has been reported[2] that, in spite of the economic downturn and record unemployment rates in the SAR, within the three years since 1997, 60 percent more elementary and secondary school students have been sent by their Hong Kong parents to study in England.

With respect to issues relating to the medium of instruction, recent educational reforms in regrouping the secondary schools into three new categories, band-1, band-2, and band-3, have not produced desirable outcomes. For example, this new policy has made many English-medium schools admit a large number of students who are unable to learn in English, thus forcing many teachers in these schools to slow down the pace of instruction considerably. Consequently, many other students have complained of being unable to learn much from school. If educational reforms since 1997 had been better planned, these kinds of difficulties could have been avoided. The planning team for education reforms in the Education and Manpower Bureau should include language policy experts to think about all the possible impacts of various projects that might affect the government's proclaimed language policy, biliterate trilingualism. It should not only have clearly articulated long-term objectives but also contain concrete, specific measures and procedures that can be implemented in a step-by-step manner without giving rise to too many unexpected negative social impacts. The government's new language policy should enable Hong Kong, as a cosmopolitan Chinese city, to capitalize on its colonial past without creating additional social injustice.

Notes

This chapter grew out of a four-month sabbatical leave in the University of Hong Kong supported by a grant from the Stanford Center for the studies of Chinese Language and Culture in 1999. The research of the project was partially supported by a faculty grant from the Stanford Center for East Asian Studies. I must thank the two research assistants who help me collect many materials from different sources. I also want to thank my friends, Dr. Yin-bing Leung, Dr. K.K. Sin, Dr. Benjamin Ts'ou, and Dr. Eric Zee for sharing with me some of their own materials, and for giving me their valuable comments and assistance in many ways during my visit. Finally, I want to thank Professor Quadalupe Valdes of Stanford for allowing me to sit in on her class on language policy.

1. According to Administrative circular No. 49/93, Education Department, students in Primary 5 and Primary 6 are scaled into three groups on the basis of their test scores by the Academic Aptitude Test:

Group I: These pupils are within the top 40 percent in both Chinese and English subject groups. They should be able to learn effectively in either English or Chinese.

Group II: These pupils are either not within the top 40 percent in both Chinese and English subject groups, or are within the top 40 percent in one subject group (Chinese or English) but not within the top 50 percent in the other subject group. They should be able to learn more effectively through the Chinese medium.

Group III: These pupils are within the top 40 percent in one subject group (Chinese or English) and within the top 50 percent but not the top 40 percent in the other subject group. They should be able to learn better through the Chinese medium.

2. *Sing Tao Daily*, January 27, 2002.

Bibliography

Endacott, G.B. *Government and People in Hong Kong, 1842–1962*. Hong Kong: Hong Kong University Press. 1964.

Evans, Stephen, Rodney Jones, Ruru S. Rusmin, and Cheung Oi Ling. "Three Languages: One Future." In *Language in Hong Kong at the Century's End*, ed. Martha Pennington. Hong Kong: Hong Kong University Press, 1998, pp. 391–418.

Fang Bochao. "Xianggang di yici zhongwen yundong (1970–71)" (The first Chinese language movement in Hong Kong [1970–71]). Hong Kong Zhuhai University MA thesis (unpublished), 1993.

Ferguson, C.A. "Diglossia." In *Language and Social Context*, P.P. Giglioli, ed. Middlesex, England: Penguin, 1972, pp. 232–51.

Hadley, Alice Omaggio. *Teaching Language in Context*, 2d ed. Boston: Heinle & Heinle Publishers, 1993.

Hornberger, N. "Bilingual Education and English-Only: A Language-Planning Framework." In *English Plus: Issues in Bilingual Education*, C.B. Cazden and C.E. Snow, ed. Philadelphia: American Academy of Political and Social Science, 1990, pp. 12–26.

Lin, Angel Mei Yi. "Analyzing the 'Language Problem' Discourses in Hong Kong: How Official, Academic, and Media Discourses Construct and Perpetuate Dominant Models of Language Learning and Education." *Journal of Pragmatics* 28, no. 4 (October 1997): 427–40.

Lord, Robert. "English—How Serious a Problem for Students in Hong Kong." *English Bulletin* 6, no. 3 (1974): 1–10.

Poon, Anita. "Chinese Medium Instruction Policy and Its Impact on English Learning in Post-1977." *International Journal of Bilingual Education and Bilingualism* 2, no. 2 (1999): 131–46.

Schiffman, Harold. *Linguistic Culture and Language Policy*. London: Routledge, 1996.

So, Daniel. "Language-Based Bifurcation of Secondary Education in Hong Kong: Past, Present, and Future." In *Into the Twenty First Century: Issues of Language in Education in Hong Kong*, K.K. Luke, ed. Hong Kong: Linguistic Society of Hong Kong, 1992, pp. 69–95.

———. "One Country, Two Cultures and Three Languages: Sociolinguistic Conditions and Language Education in Hong Kong." In *Teaching Language and Culture: Building Hong Kong on Education*, David Asker, ed. Hong Kong: Longman, 1998, pp. 152–75.

Sweeting, Anthony. *Education in Hong Kong, Pre-1841 to 1841: Fact and Opinion*. Hong Kong: Hong Kong University Press, 1990.

T'sou, Benjamin. "'San yan' 'liang yu' shuo Xianggang" (A brief discourse on Hong Kong). *Journal of Chinese Linguistics* 25, no. 2 (1997): 290–307.

Tung, Peter, Raymond Lam, and Waiking Tsang. "English as a Medium of Instruction in Post-1997 Hong Kong: What Students, Teachers, and Parents Think." *Journal of Pragmatics* 28 (1997): 441–59.

UNESCO. *The Use of Vernacular Languages in Education: Monographs of Fundamental Education*, vol. 8. Paris: UNESCO, 1953.

Walters, Steve, and John Balla. "Medium of Instruction: Policy and Reality at One Hong Kong Tertiary Institution." In *Language in Hong Kong at Century's End*, Martha Pennington, ed. Hong Kong: Hong Kong University Press, 1998, pp. 365–90.

12

The Transformation of Academic Autonomy in Hong Kong

Gerard A. Postiglione

Academic Incidents

In the month following the return of sovereignty, the world watched and waited to see how Hong Kong was to be transformed from a free, open, albeit undemocratic society, to one under the banner of the People's Republic of China (PRC). At the time, it seemed significant that one of the first incidents occurred within a month of July 1, 1997, and involved the academic profession (Postiglione 1998b). A member of the Hong Kong Legislative Council aimed to remove two professors from their university posts for what he viewed as their unpatriotic views. The incident unfolded before the watchful public through front-page press coverage by Hong Kong's leading newspapers. Though the legislator wrote to the presidents of two universities demanding that these two professors be terminated for their views, the universities stood their ground and reaffirmed the principle of academic freedom. Within days, the legislator in question made a public apology to the two professors. A week later, the incident was gone without a trace. Hong Kong remained a society that protected academic freedom.

In the years that followed, however, and unknown to most of Hong Kong, another scholar was beginning to find himself under increased pressure to curtail his research. The powers that be were uncomfortable about the public opinion research being undertaken at Hong Kong's oldest university, which pointed to the declining popularity of the chief executive. An aide to the chief executive paid a visit to the office of the university vice chancellor, who chose not to enunciate the university's policy on academic freedom, and instead initiated action that eventually led to his own resignation. This second post-1997 incident involving the academic profession differed from the first. Rather than consisting of high-pitched argumentation before the press and public, this one occurred inside the walls of the academy, and was too subtle to be detected until the local media published an account by the professor in question. The incident, which took over a year to come to the attention of the local public and international media, was less important for what it was than for what it represented. It revealed a post-1997 brand of educational politics that threatened the morale of the academic profession. A part of higher education had acquiesced within a culture of consensus, and, whether intentionally or not, had colluded with government to curtail the right of professional autonomy. For the global academy, it was yet another affront to professional autonomy. Yet, this time it was not from the developing world, where there is a higher incidence of such events, but rather from a developed society with a reputation for freedom and openness. The mainland Chinese authorities remained quiet throughout the incident in accordance with the one country, two systems policy, though it was unlikely they appreciated those viewed as not supporting the Hong Kong SAR government line.

The irony of this incident was that it would not have come to the surface had it not been for Hong Kong's free press, one that fought many battles for its survival long before sovereignty was returned to China in 1997. The same was not true for the academy. For most of Hong Kong's history, its one or two universities were insulated from a society in which commercial interests towered high above those of academe.

This chapter begins by raising several questions: Why was autonomy for the academic profession never a major issue in Hong Kong? Why did it take so long to become one? How has academic autonomy been transformed? What is the state of the academic profession in the Hong Kong SAR? These questions are approached through a brief periodization of Hong Kong's academic history, followed by a look at various dimensions of the national and global contexts.

Academic Periods

Period 1

During the earlier colonial period, when Hong Kong was a one-university town, trade and commerce reigned supreme. The local university was an elite institution that was said to serve the key function of supporting the development of the Chinese mainland. By the 1950s, it had shifted its function locally to the preparation of the territory's civil servants.[1] It was staffed and run by British academics and fewer local Chinese, until after World War

II. The University of Hong Kong, to be joined in this endeavor in 1964 by the Chinese University of Hong Kong, remained a teaching institution with little research capacity until the 1980s. Its student body was increasingly working class, as the middle class sent its children overseas for their higher education. There is little evidence that university academics were muzzled in any way. With no threat to unseat the colonial government in Hong Kong, university academics were generally free to speak their own minds. Yet, their impact on the society of immigrants was not very significant. Overseas academics were less likely to receive coverage in the Chinese media. Their academic freedom was ensured by law, but also by lack of power, since their foreignness largely prevented them from being a potent organizing force in the society. Most overseas academics were British, and their aspirations for social change were funneled through the Foreign Office or through their compatriots in government during the days of small-town university life. In the 1970s and 1980s, Chinese academics became increasingly active, though mostly through small nongovernment activist groups and forums. Academic freedom was not a major issue in higher education during this period.

Period 2

As 1997 approached, Hong Kong found itself with an academic profession that was increasingly self-conscious, slightly more activist, and globally networked. The caliber of the academic staff increased by virtue of the expansion of postgraduate education and the ability to attract top academics through generous salary packages, as well as Hong Kong's global visibility. British academics became a minority within the overseas academic community for the first time, and the large number of Hong Kongese who had earned doctorates in the United States and elsewhere began to return in larger numbers. The Hong Kong University of Science and Technology, established in 1990, recruited heavily from the United States, and moved academic culture more toward the American higher education model. Two polytechnics and two colleges were also moving toward university status, a trend that would significantly strengthen academe in relation to business and commerce, and would give Hong Kong a greater global academic presence. Local academics took advantage of the increasing opportunities to turn their activism toward the society where education levels were increasing. Hong Kong cultural identity was becoming more salient, and opportunities to enter politics through district boards and legislative council elections were increasing. In this period, professional autonomy in the academy was discussed more than ever before, though it was never seriously tested (Postiglione and Tang 1997). The University Grants Commission issued a statement about academic freedom and professional autonomy that reflected the international status quo, which placed an increased emphasis on accountability. This pre-1997 period was largely one that anticipated, with increasing concern, what academic life under a one country, two systems framework would mean. It was a period in which Hong Kong journalists, more than academics, were being tested. Largely unnoticed, however, was a growing trend toward self-censorship in the Hong Kong academy.

Period 3

The post-1997 era found Hong Kong with seven publicly funded universities. The expansion of student numbers, greater interuniversity competition for funding, public demand for accountability, and the Asian economic crisis all weighed heavily on university life (Postiglione and Mak 1997). As the cult of managerialism engulfed the universities, the relationship with the new SAR government with its sovereignty having shifted from London to Beijing, began to change. The government's strong ties to the business community intensified the call for more market-oriented thinking on university development, something that many other countries were also experiencing to one degree or another (Green 1997). The academic profession became increasingly localized, while at the same time, both closer to academics in the mainland and more integrated into the global academy. The same was true of the university administration. Yet, while the university administration become more aligned with the government and business community, the academic profession remained pluralistic and liberal minded. Meanwhile politics in Hong Kong was becoming more polarized than ever before, largely on the basis of being for or against a closer relationship to Beijing. Self-censorship in the academy remained high; however, those who had views to express could do so without concern of loosing their posts. A culture of obedience fostered by the Hong Kong education system, and reinforced by government, was situated side by side with a globalized academic tradition that still valued critical thought and scholarship. Sooner or later these two forces would face off. Given the circumstances, the academic freedom incident of 2000 was almost inevitable. Hong Kong has entered the twenty-first century with a small victory for academic freedom and autonomy, and with more realistic expectations about future challenges facing the academic profession.

Academic Contexts

Hong Kong experienced major changes in higher education during the last decade of the twentieth century. Changes include institutional consolidation, a credit unit system, staff reviews, management reviews, recurrent funding assessment, teaching and learning quality process reviews, new admission standards, broadening courses, staff retitling, an increase of students from outside Hong Kong, and a "top-slicing" of department budgets for reallocation by university heads. These changes are part of a systematic effort to increase quality, after a large expansion that took place in the first half of the 1990s (University Grants Committee 1996). Very little of this change, so far, seems directly tied to Beijing's 1997 resumption of sovereignty over Hong Kong. As a result of the closer relationship with the rest of China, academics in Hong Kong began to ponder the possible new challenges to preserve academic freedom and institutional autonomy (Postiglione 1996). Also, the Asian economic slowdown tended to divert the higher aims of a university education to the vagaries of market forces (Postiglione 1998a). The economic climate changed at a time when a larger and more educated middle class in Hong Kong become more interventionist in matters pertaining to publicly funded higher education. The middle class, who sent their children overseas for higher education, viewed the cost of local higher education as less relevant but still exorbitant. Meanwhile, local employers were less than satisfied with the quality of local university graduates. Not surprisingly, this led to a call for market forces to play more of a role in covering and recovering the cost of higher education.

The knowledge economy also had a profound influence on the academic profession generally and in Hong Kong in particular (Altbach 1997; Task Force 2000). Hong Kong academics continue to be far more involved in the flow and control of knowledge than their academic counterparts on the mainland. For most of the 1990s, they wielded significant influence upon academic policies at the department, school, and institutional levels. Nevertheless, new forms of management, similar to those introduced globally, were implemented beginning in 1998, and have muted to some extent the clout of academic staff in university governance. Yet, the composition of Hong Kong's professoriate, with a high proportion of overseas-trained Hong Kong Chinese and foreign academics, ensured itself a central role in global academic discourse (Postiglione 1996: Table 5.1).

Information technology has strengthened global linkages in Hong Kong higher education (Blurton 1999). The early digital orientation of the universities in Hong Kong, for example, gave them a jump on their counterpart mainland institutions. The gap continues to shrink. Nonetheless, an increasingly vibrant electronic discourse takes place between universities in mainland China and Hong Kong, despite all the restrictions.

By the end of the twentieth century, the academic profession in Hong Kong had benefited much from global Internet access. Hong Kong received dividends in the form of research output by coupling its substantial research funding and information technology resources with mainland China's vast pool of academic talent so as to expand data bases and increase research publications across all fields of science. Massive amounts of data flow in either direction in a split second, and the organization of such research projects has strengthened the quality of research methodology and skills on both sides. The potential for this electronic interaction is almost limitless.

Academic Views

This section examines the profession and its views. The average age of Hong Kong faculty was forty-three in 1993 and forty-five in 1999. This was relatively young as compared to many countries (University Grants Committee 1996). Japan, Russia, and Israel, for example, averaged fifty-one years in 1993 (Boyer, Altbach, and Whitelaw 1994: 35). By the time of Hong Kong's sovereignty retrocession, most of mainland China's full professors were between fifty-six and sixty; however, almost 30 percent of mainland academic staff across equivalent ranks of assistant, associate, and full professor were between thirty-one and thirty-five, due largely to the rapid expansion of higher education in recent years (*China Education Statistical Yearbook* 1995: 28).

Regarding the proportion of staff at different academic ranks, Hong Kong's system is bottom heavy compared to counterparts overseas. For example, at the University of Hong Kong in 1995, fewer than 20 percent of staff members were full professors (including chair professor and reader categories) as compared to 42 percent at the University of British Columbia, 49 percent at the University of Montreal, 59 percent at Brown University, and 56 percent at Harvard University.[2] This situation has changed since a system of retitling from British to American systems was introduced to improve efforts to recruit internationally, as well as to provide incentives to longstanding lower-rank staff.

Hong Kong has been one of the most international cities in China, if not the most, and therefore, we might expect this to affect the view of academic staff about their degree of professional autonomy. Though it may be argued that there is more intellectual freedom in Shanghai than in Beijing, independent critiques of the system are risky in both cities. At Hong Kong universities, independent critiques of the system may sometimes be frowned upon; however, a critical tradition rooted in the Western university model survives quite well. The 2000 crisis at the University of Hong Kong elevated, for the first time in a major way, the issue of academic freedom in post-1997 Hong Kong higher education where a colonial university culture evolved within the context of a conservative Chinese society. In short, each academic system has its own limits of expression, and while Hong Kong universities have clearly been more open, that openness has not been without limitations.

Scholarship

The contemporary concept of scholarship has increasingly come to include the integration between activities of teaching, research, and service (Glassick, Huber, and Maeroff 1997). Academic units of universities in Hong Kong are allocated public resources on the basis of their student numbers, research productivity, procurement of outside research funds, and postgraduate student completion rates. In mainland China, universities relied on government for most of their funding, but are now being encouraged to raise more of their own funds (Min 1997). Low- and no-budget research is still the norm, and under these conditions, government funding still remains the largest source for research, and therefore has a major influence on the direction and scope of research. Most academic journals are based at universities or research institutes, rather than closely tied to professional associations as in the West. Nevertheless, there are more similarities with regard to views concerning research than in all other areas surveyed.

Over half of the staff from Hong Kong's three type 1 research universities (HKT1RU) say their interests lean toward or lie primarily in research rather than in teaching—a not unexpected result for research universities.[3] By 1999, however, the HKT1RU figure had increased to 70.2 percent, indicating that recruitment, incentives, and university culture had changed to reflect the new reforms in higher education. Over 50 percent of the academic staff from nine of the fourteen countries, including Hong Kong, in the international study also stated that their interests leaned toward or were primarily in research. Most HKT1RU faculty agree that a strong record of successful research was important in staff evaluation at their institution, and that it was difficult for a person to achieve tenure if he or she did not publish. By 1999, 95.5 percent of HKT1RU staff agreed or strongly agreed that a strong record of successful research was important in staff evaluation at their institutions. Moreover, 88.9 percent agreed or strongly agreed that it is difficult for a person to achieve tenure if he or she does not publish. When asked whether publications used for promotion are just counted and not qualitatively evaluated, 23 percent of HKT1RU staff disagreed with that statement in 1993. This increased to 33.6 percent by 1999, however, the 1993 figure was still lower compared to most countries in the international survey, except Russia. In Hong Kong, the issue of how to assess the quality of publications was prominent in the period leading up to the survey, and the Hong Kong University Grants Committee (UGC) responded with measures to make the process more objective; however, the issue remains heavily debated. Still, HKT1RU staff appear to have more faith in the system of research assessment than their counterparts, who largely view it as a counting exercise.

When it comes to the pressure to do research and how much is expected, only Chilean academics (38 percent) in 1993 felt under more pressure than those in Hong Kong (26 percent) (Altbach 1996). In 1993, 28 percent of HKT1RU faculty agreed that they frequently feel under pressure to do more research than they would actually like to do. The figure increased to 45.5 percent by 1999. In 1993, 85 percent of HKT1RU staff believed that regular research activity was expected of them, however, the HKT1RU figure increased to 97.2 percent by 1999. The reforms in higher education did much to account for the changes in the Hong Kong figure. In 1993, 38 percent of HKT1RU faculty agreed that research funding was easier to get than it had been five years before. This decreased to 31.5 percent in 1999, due to both the economic crisis and the increased competition for funds. Moreover, the rating given to research equipment and computer facilities contrasted sharply. Hong Kong academic staff were near or at the top of the international ratings, agreeing strongly that they were satisfied with the resources provided by their universities.

An authoritarian style of administration would seem to support restrictions on professional autonomy in conducting certain types of research. In fact, only about 38 percent of the academic staff from four type 1 research universities (T1RU) in Beijing and Shanghai agreed that they could focus their research on any topic of special interest to them, while the figure for Hong Kong higher education staff was over 80 percent (81.8 percent in 1999).[4] While this is a big difference, and has a good deal to do with the sensitivity of so many research topics, the differences also depend to some extent on access to research funding. In China, it is difficult to acquire research funds on topics that are outside the national five-year plan for research. Hong Kong research funds are not limited in the same way.

Over 60 percent for those surveyed in eleven of these countries and territories, including Hong Kong (77.8 percent in 1999) agreed it was an especially creative and productive time, much higher than on the mainland where most academics stay at one institution their entire career, including their graduate training. About 30 percent of HKT1RU staff have held regular academic appointments at more than two institutions. This dropped to 24.7 percent in 1999 due to the increased localization and little mobility between the three research universities in Hong Kong.

HKT1RU faculty had a more favorable view of the competency of top-level administrators than their mainland counterparts. Yet, compared to academic staff in other counties, Hong Kong academics had a less favorable view of their administrators. When we look at the survey ratings for Hong Kong's other institutions of higher education in Table 12.1, they appear remarkably similar to those in Beijing (BT1RU) and Shanghai (ST1RU). These institutions surveyed are more globally connected, which would seem to indicate that their staff-administrator relations are better than the national average. At the same time, however, they also have more academics who spend time at overseas universities, making them more willing to take a critical view of their own university governance system (Neave and Van Vugt 1994).

While Hong Kong's original universities were colonial in nature, almost all university staff had access to agendas, detailed minutes, and supporting documents of university senate meetings, something not done in mainland China. By the late 1990s, this administrative transparency in Hong Kong was extended even further. Another contextual consideration concerned the fact that most HKT1RU academics (over 90 percent) had received their doctorates in Western universities where the tradition was more open, less hierarchical, and more decentralized than in Hong Kong, which might account for certain aspects of their response patterns. The full effect of the current pattern of managerialism on Hong Kong institutions is not yet clear.

Academic Freedom

All universities in Hong Kong tout academic freedom as an important value embodied in their university traditions, yet only a minority of academic staff at HKT1RU agreed that the administration supports academic freedom. Even fewer faculty members at Hong Kong's four other institutions of higher education agreed in 1993 and 1999. To explain why Hong Kong's other institutions of higher education do not see their administration as very supportive of academic freedom, it should be pointed out that these institutions were only recently upgraded to university status and their academic and administrative cultures have taken more time to evolve. Yet, by contrast with HKT1RU, the agreement rate of Hong Kong's other four institutions rose significantly.

Table 12.1

Views of Academic Staff in Hong Kong, Shanghai, and Beijing

	HKT1RU	ST1RU	BT1RU	Hong Kong's other universities
Top-level administrators are providing competent leadership. (% disagree)	57 (1993) 55 (1999)	36	11	
The administration is often autocratic. (% disagree)	57 (1993) 76 (1999)	72	42	
Relations between faculty and administration are good to excellent. (% agree)	40 (1993) 39 (1999)	22	24	23 (1993) 39 (1999)
The administration supports academic freedom. (% agree)	65 (1993) 47 (1999)	69	55	34 (1993) 39 (1999)
I am generally free to determine the content of the courses I teach. (% agree)	78 (1993) 74 (1999)	42	51	44 (1993) 64 (1999)
I can focus my research on any topic that is of special interes to me. (% agree)	90 (1993) 82 (1999)	50	53	
Based on your experiences at this institution, how would you assess the intellectual atmosphere? (%)	Excellent 7 (1993) 6 (1999)	18	19	Excellent 0.8 (1993) 3 (1999)
	Good 44 (1993) 45 (1999)	64	57	Good 29 (1993) 40 (1999)

Sources: 1993 data, The Carnegie Foundation for the Advancement of Teaching, *The International Survey of the Academic Profession 1991–1993*, Princeton, NJ; 1999 data, The University of Hong Kong Research Grants Committee.

HKT1RU faculty indicated they were generally free to determine the content of the courses they teach. A very high number of HKT1RU faculty indicated that they were free to focus their research on any topic they choose.

Higher Education and Society

In Hong Kong, a place not noted for being an intellectual, scientific, or cultural center, fewer than 25 percent of HKT1RU staff members believe academics are the most influential opinion leaders. In mainland China, there is also a long tradition in which the state both expects and uses scholars to speak out in support of its policies. The figures for HKT1RU were that about 50 percent in 1993 and 72.9 in 1999 agreed that the status of academics is declining; so, while Hong Kong academics were becoming more influential opinion leaders, the respect they received from the public was declining. This is supported by research, which shows that Hong Kong residents, particularly in 1990, were distrustful of politicians and unwilling to give them high popularity ratings. In this case, the involvement of Hong Kong academics in politics has actually contributed little, if anything, to their status in society. More generally, this may also be linked to growing globalization as witnessed by the international academic crisis and the decline of the professoriate (Altbach 1997).

International Dimensions of Academic Activity

The global character of universities is tied to their aim of dealing with issues shared by most of humanity. Beyond this, there are many indicators of globally linked academic activity, and some universities excel more in this respect than others. Some excel only on one or two indicators, and fall far behind on others. Among some of the indications are the numbers of foreign students and scholars who flow back and forth between university systems, the global character of the curriculum, and cross-national scholarly publishing in other languages.

Hong Kong's T1RU would seem to be much more global in character than T1RUs in mainland China. This may be due to the links with Britain, a large number of tenured overseas staff, exposure to the West, English medium of instruction, and other such factors. Only 32 percent of HKT1RU academics stated that foreign students are enrolled frequently or occasionally at their institutions. However, this increased to 60.4 percent by 1999, as Hong Kong's institutions of higher education expanded graduate programs and began to reach out to other countries. The obstacle in Hong Kong higher education still has much to do with the high costs of living in Hong Kong for foreign students, the shortage of dormitory facilities for international students, the choice by international students of Mandarin language in Beijing and Shanghai, rather than Cantonese dialect in Hong Kong, and the more expansive outreach of universities in China to other countries (i.e., Japan, Korea, and Russia) because of state-to-state relations, while Hong Kong is more focused, for historical reasons, on English-speaking Western nations.

When we examine the flow of students and scholars in the other direction, however, the picture is quite different. More HKT1RU staff, for example, say that their students have studied abroad. In 1993, 19 percent said frequently and 30 percent said occasionally. In 1999, 30.2 percent said frequently and 45.2

percent said occasionally. When it comes to staff traveling abroad to study or do research, over 70 percent in 1993, and 65 percent in 1999 of HKT1RU academics indicated they had done so for one or more months over the last three years. The reason has much to do with the ease with which HKT1RU academics can travel in or out of Hong Kong without having to apply to the authorities for permission, as is the case in other parts of China. That most earned their doctorates overseas and a large proportion make their permanent home overseas is not a neutral factor. The drop of 5 percent may be accounted for by the increased number of local faculty and the ease of overseas content through the Internet, as well as by the tightening of funds for this purpose due to the economic crisis in the late 1990s. The same response pattern appears for service as a faculty member at an institution in another country. Fewer than one in four HKT1RU staff had been faculty members at such institutions, in 1993, and one in five in 1999.

Hong Kong has a reputation as an international city with a cosmopolitan outlook; however, this may not hold true for all aspects of Hong Kong life. In 1993 over 66 percent of academic staff in HKT1RU, and in 1999 77.6 percent, indicated that they thought the curriculum needed to be more international in focus. The curriculum in Hong Kong's top institutions may be more international than that in mainland China universities, but the expectations of HKT1RU staff are higher in this regard, as reflected in their response pattern.

Almost 45 percent of HKT1RU staff reported that international connections are important in faculty evaluations at their institutions. Finally, about 100 percent of HKT1RU academics, all of whom can read English, indicated that they must read books and journals published overseas in order to keep up with developments in their fields.

Conclusion

A key question remains whether Hong Kong academics will move more toward self-imposed censorship, or whether reforms on the mainland will bring academic culture more in line with that in Hong Kong, and with the mainstream culture of the global academy.

Unlike most universities on the mainland, the Hong Kong academy has maintained a global academic culture and a relatively international staff. If the economy begins to prosper again, there is every reason to expect a further expansion of higher education in early years of the new millennium, and a conversion from a three- to a four-year undergraduate system. There is also a potential for staff recruitment in Hong Kong to be more globally inclusive than in the past, when recruitment was from a small number of countries.

The same may not occur for some time in mainland universities, where the overseas academics are generally few and marginalized.

Changes affecting the academic profession in China's two systems have been very much a function of global trends in higher education, such as the devolution of financial responsibility, and the new managerialism (Scott 1998, Currie and Newsome 1998). Until the late 1980s, when Hong Kong was a two-university city, per-unit costs were higher, but the scale of higher education was small. Staff costs account for almost half of the expenditure, and the public is increasingly conscious of getting value for money. The total expenditure on education as a percentage of the gross domestic product (GDP) in 2000–01 was 4.1 percent (over HK$50 billion), of which higher education received 23 percent (HK$13 billion), excluding another 10 percent for postsecondary education. University staff are exposed to continuous assessment processes, and the pressure to produce has increased. Given staff salaries in mainland universities, the authorities there are finding it harder to place new demands on academic staff. This will change in the coming years, especially as student enrolments expand. For Hong Kong, staying abreast of global trends has helped it keep up with or ahead of most mainland universities. A remaining handicap for Hong Kong is a student recruitment network focused almost exclusively on local secondary school graduates, which will be expanded in years to come.

The integration of Hong Kong academics into the global academy has strengthened the values of academic autonomy and freedom. Increased engagement with academics in mainland China has caused some to acquiesce to the view of academic freedom as a privilege rather than a right. However, as academic freedom on the mainland has improved gradually in recent years, mainland China's universities have also come to take a more central place in global academic discourse. If academic traditions are preserved despite the new managerialism, the degree of academic integration of Hong Kong SAR faculty into the global academy will be maintained. While the mainland academic profession may become confined to a more restricted space for some time to come, especially in the social sciences and humanities, for the Hong Kong SAR system, the key issues will remain the maintenance of high academic standards, the preservation of academic freedom, and continued integration into the global academic discourse.

Notes

1. I thank Peter Cunich for his helpful comments on the brief historical section. According to Peter Cunich, the function of the university from 1912 until 1950 was basically to produce (1) doctors for private practice and hospitals in HK and British

Malaya, (2) engineers for HK and China's civil and mechanical engineering projects/ ventures, and (3) teachers for the HK and Malayan education systems.

2. Calculations by K.W. Ng, in "Comparison of Academic Staff Between UHK and North American Universities," Statistics Department, University of Hong Kong, February 2, 1996, draft, figure 1.

3. Since these three universities (the University of Hong Kong, the Chinese University of Hong Kong, and the Hong Kong University of Science and Technology) have the largest programs of postgraduate study, we refer to them as HKT1RU.

4. Type 1 research universities in Beijing and Shanghai refers to those institutions that are considered to have prestigious programs of research. The institution in Beijing is among the top-rated universities in the country. Those in Shanghai include Shanghai Jiaotong University, East China Normal University, and Shanghai University.

Bibliography

Altbach, Philip G. *Comparative Higher Education: Knowledge, the University, and Development.* Boston: Center of International Higher Education, 1997.

Altbach, Philip G., ed. *The International Academic Profession: Portraits of 14 Countries.* Princeton, NJ: Carnegie Foundation for the Advancement of Teaching, 1996.

Blurton, Craig. "Perspective on the Potential Impact of Information Technology on China's Universities." Paper presented before the Comparative and International Education Society, Toronto, April 18, 1999.

Boyer, Ernest L., Philip G. Altbach, and Mary Jean Whitelaw. *The Academic Profession: An International Perspective.* Princeton: Carnegie Foundation for the Advancement of Teaching, 1994.

China Education Statistical Yearbook 1995. Beijing: People's Education Press, 1995.

Clark, Burton. "Small Worlds, Different Worlds: The Uniqueness and Troubles of American Academic Professions." *Daedalus* (fall 1997): 21–42.

Currie, Jan, and Janice Newsome, eds. *Universities and Globalization: Critical Perspectives.* Thousand Oakes, CA: Sage Publications, 1998.

Glassick, Charles E., Mary Taylor Huber, and Gene I. Maeroff. *Scholarship Assessed: Evaluation of the Professoriate.* San Francisco: Jossey-Bass, 1997.

Green, Madeleine F., ed. *Transforming Higher Education: Views from Leaders Around the World.* Pheonix, AZ: Oryx Press, 1997.

Levine, Arthur. "How the Academic Profession Is Changing." *Daedalus* (fall 1997): 1–20.

Min Weifang. "China." In *Asian Higher Education*, Gerard A. Postiglione and Grace C.L. Mak, ed. Westport, CT: Greenwood Press, 1997, pp. 37–55.

Neave, Guy R., and Frans A. Van Vugt, eds. *Government and Higher Education Relationships Across Three Continents.* Oxford: Pergammon, 1994.

Pepper, Suzanne. *Radicalism and Educational Reform in 20th Century Education.* New York: Cambridge University Press, 1996.

Postiglione, Gerard A. "Maintaining Global Engagement in the Face of National Integration." *Comparative Education Review* 42, no. 1 (February 1998a): 30–45.

————. "Under Chinese Rule, Subtle Changes for Universities and a Sense of Unease." *Chronicle of Higher Education*, March 6, 1998b, B10.

————. "The Future of the Hong Kong Academic Profession." In *The International Academic Profession: Portraits of 14 Countries*, Philip G. Altbach, ed. Princeton, NJ: Carnegie Foundation for the Advancement of Teaching, 1996, pp. 191–227.

Postiglione, Gerard A, and Grace C.L. Mak, eds. *Asian Higher Education*. Westport, CT: Greenwood Press, 1997.

Postiglione, Gerard A., and James T.H. Tang, eds. *Hong Kong's Reunion with China: The Global Dimensions*. Armonk, NY: M.E. Sharpe, 1997.

Scott, Peter, ed. *The Globalization of Higher Education*. Buckingham, UK: Open University Press, 1998.

Task Force on Higher Education and Society. *Higher Education in Developing Countries: Peril and Promise*. Washington, DC: World Bank, 2000.

University Grants Committee. *Higher Education in Hong Kong*. Hong Kong: Government Printer, 1996.

——— 13 ———

Walking a Tight Rope

Hong Kong's Media Facing Political and Economic Challenges Since Sovereignty Transfer

Tuen-yu Lau and Yiu-ming To

Introduction

The media scene in Hong Kong since it became the Hong Kong Special Administration Region (HKSAR) under Chinese sovereignty in 1997 can be summarized in one word: eventful. The leading players, including the HKSAR government officials, Chinese leaders, media owners, and practicing journalists, all want to influence the role of the media. Their interplay, verbal attacks, and even confrontations suggest that they want to play a more active role in shaping Hong Kong's media developments. They differ, however, in their views on how to build responsible media.

Overall, the past four and a half years have witnessed a very tough time for media owners and practitioners in posthandover Hong Kong. Facing a grave economic crisis that translates into tighter advertising revenues and constant threats of layoffs and retrenchment, they have to focus their efforts on putting out the fires in their own backyards. In a bid for survival in a cutthroat market, some of them risk losing their professional credibility by resorting to sensationalism. Readers and media critics deplore such sensationalism and urge the establishment of a monitoring body. Finally, some newspapers collaborated to establish a voluntary press council in July 2000 to avoid a regulatory body imposed by the government.[1]

Despite such efforts, there are still severe criticisms at the political and the ideological levels. Many People's Republic of China (PRC) leaders in Beijing and officials in Hong Kong, including President Jiang Zemin, former Foreign Minister Qian Qichen, and Hong Kong Beijing Liaison Office's He Zhiming, publicly warned Hong Kong journalists not to use Hong Kong as a base to promote Taiwan separatism. HKSAR government officials also made more open criticisms of the media.

Therefore, in a way, Hong Kong media workers are sandwiched between the Beijing and HKSAR leaders, while also facing economic tough times and gradual staff layoffs.

To a significant extent, economic pressure is much stronger than political forces in shaping media developments in posthandover Hong Kong. This chapter seeks to examine changes in media practices and content in Hong Kong within the context of market capitalism, journalistic professionalism, and a multiparty political process that shows a diversified ideological patriotism. The chapter will first examine the political and ideological levels, followed by an examination of economic pressures. Many events of the five years since the sovereignty transfer in 1997 will be highlighted. Then the impact of those events on the role and performance of the media workers will be explored.

The Conflicts of Ideals and the Ideological Tensions

Events:[2]

- HKSAR Secretary for Justice Elsie Leung criticized Hong Kong intellectuals, October 2000.
- HKSAR Secretary for Security Regina Ip compared Hong Kong media to George Orwell's "Animal Farm," October 2000.
- PRC President Jiang Zemin commented on Hong Kong journalists' quality and experience, October 2000
- Hong Kong Beijing Liaison Office's He Zhiming warned Hong Kong businesspeople about supporting Taiwan separatism, June 2000.
- China's Hong Kong Office's official Wang Fengchao commented on Hong Kong media's coverage of Taiwan, April 2000.
- China Deputy Premier and former Foreign Minister Qian Qichen asked Hong Kong media not to back calls for Taiwan split, August 1999.
- Hong Kong Xinhua Assistant Director Lee Wai-ting warned against anti-Beijing forces in HKSAR, March 1998.

The expected ideological change in Hong Kong, as stipulated in the "one country, two systems" concept, has attracted global attention both before and after the handover. Debates, doubts, and concerns have been ongoing for more than a decade, since the late Deng Xiaoping disclosed the concept. Because of China's dubious records, notably the 1989 Tiananmen incident, many observers have serious reservations about whether China will keep its promise. As it turns out, China has implemented an almost "noninterference" policy. Even an outspoken critic, the Hong Kong Journalists Association, says, "the past year (1998–1999) has not seen any significant deterioration or improvement in freedom of expression in its most tangible sense. Individuals continue to express views at variance with the Hong Kong and Chinese governments, for example, and these views continue to be published and aired in the media."[3] The June 1999 Political and Economic Risk Consultancy Report also said there was no evidence of censorship pressure from Beijing.[4] The deputy U.S. secretary of state also testified before Congress that press freedom continues to exist in posthandover Hong Kong.[5] Ongoing public opinion polls on Hong Kong residents' satisfaction with the level of press freedom between September 1997 and March 1999 also showed almost 70 percent of the respondents expressing satisfaction[6] (see Figure 13.1).

The status quo of Hong Kong media, however, is constantly under challenge arising from the conflicts among competing visions of journalism by competing agents of change. The status quo, upheld by political and media establishments before 1997, is a regime of press freedom established and enacted by laws. Being a former British colony, though, Hong Kong is likened to Western democracies where the press enjoys freedom to publish whatever it wants, unless the contents published serve to undermine public order or harm individual's interests as protected by legislations. At first, the "rule of law," especially before the 1990s, was colonial authoritarianism in disguise. While the British sovereign state allowed the press to be ruled by laws, a host of colonial laws conferred unrestrained powers on government in both interpreting the laws and enforcing it to restore public order when it deems necessary. For instance, news media, when considered by government as publishing false information and causing public fear, could be prosecuted for criminal liability.[7] With a police warrant, law enforcement officers could search premises of media organizations and seize materials collected by reporters without the prior approval by court. Media organizations are treated as equals before the law; however, the colonial government is above it. It is only into the 1990s that the British administration began to liberalize its legal regulation of media. With the introduction of a bill of rights in 1991 and, more important, a new policy toward China since 1992, the British initiated a program of legal reforms in order to comply with canons of human rights provided for by the International Covenant on Civil and Political Rights. Before the expiry of the British rule in 1997, more than thirty legal provisions involving seventeen ordinances, deemed by the government to contravene human rights requirements, were either revised or repealed.[8] Though the legal reforms introduced by the British administration in the final days of

Figure 13.1 **Satisfaction of Press Freedom Opinion Polls, September 1997–March 1999**

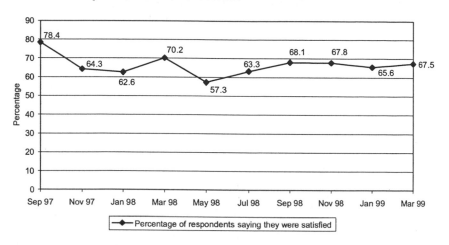

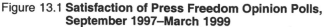

colonial rule cannot avoid criticism for being incomplete and therefore half-hearted, no doubt they promoted press freedom to an unprecedented status best protected by law in the 145 years of colonial history. Despite the short-comings of these reforms, they became the status quo of press freedom before the transfer of sovereignty, facing continuous challenges by competing visions of journalism after 1997.

One source of challenge comes from civic groups of liberal persuasion. While they acknowledged the achievement by the British administration in beefing up legal protections for press freedom, they doubt whether or not the reformed legal order, even if unchanged, would be adequate to maintain the status quo of press freedom after 1997. To safeguard freedom of the press after 1997, they argued, a more liberal legal and constitutional order is badly needed.[9] It should be aimed at keeping government power in line with international norms of human rights on three fronts. First, it involves legal reforms in three areas related to press freedom: (1) checking the unrestrained power of the chief executive, conferred by the Emergency Regulations Ordinance, in censoring the press; (2) preventing the administration from abusing its power when it enforces legal and constitutional provisions in securing national security and maintaining public order; and (3) protecting the rightful access of the press to government information by allowing "public interest" as a defense for leaking government secrets and asserting the right of access to government information by legislation, instead of an administrative code.[10] Second, civil liberties should be secured to provide a favorable environment in which press freedom can flourish.

Since its establishment, the SAR government enters a new age with obsolete laws. It imposes restrictions on freedom of assembly and association, allegedly infringing human rights, by reviving colonial provisions of the Public Order Ordinance and the Societies Ordinance that were repealed by the colonial government before 1997. Resembling its colonial version, the law stipulates, among other things, that demonstrations with more than thirty participants should seek the prior approval of the police; this police approval is disguised as a no-objection notice. A second stipulation is that an association must first register, with government approval, before it can become a legal organization. The concept of "national security" is also introduced as a criterion on which the police will decide whether or not to approve a demonstration or an association. Accordingly, police will ban activities viewed by them as advocating independence of Hong Kong, Taiwan, or Tibet.[11] The Hong Kong Journalists Association argues that these repressive measures, if not stopped, will not only undermine civil liberties generally but also curb the scope of freedom of speech and of the press.[12] Third, a democratic political system should be established to hold the government accountable and to safeguard press freedom. According to HKSAR Basic Law, the Electoral committee, which is composed of eight hundred members, selects the chief executive. The members are from business groups (25 percent), professional bodies (25 percent), grassroots organizations (25 percent), and political institutions (25 percent). With fewer than two hundred thousand people eligible to vote for members of the Electoral Committee, it is caricatured as exclusive games by small groups. The chief executive who is selected by it suffers greatly from severe lack of legitimacy.[13] For the legislature, though universal suffrage is practiced, only 40 percent of the legislative seats are returned by direct elections. The rest are composed by representatives from functional constituencies (50 percent) and the Electoral Committee (10 percent).[14]

The persistence of the present undemocratic political order, it is argued, poses perennial threats to freedom of speech and of the press. With its undemocratic alliance gaining a majority share in the legislature, an undemocratically formed government could easily push through legislations undermining civil liberties. Representatives of the people, returned by universal suffrage, on the other hand, find insurmountable difficulties winning majority support for their efforts to liberalize repressive legal restrictions. As the highly unsatisfactory regime of press freedom is protected by an undemocratic political system, the enhancement of press freedom requires, among others, democratic reforms of representative politics based on universal suffrage. Given the central concern for enhancing legal protection of the press, securing civil liberties, and democratizing the political system, these civic and political groups represent the liberal challenge against the status quo left behind by the British administration.[15]

At the other end of the ideological spectrum is the conservative challenge represented by Beijing and its local supporters. While Beijing takes no action to intervene to the internal affairs of Hong Kong, there is no lack of expressed concern by senior Chinese officials over how press freedom should be properly exercised or restrained in the Special Administrative Region. These officials never ask Hong Kong media to follow the communist model of the press, working as a mouthpiece for the ruling party and government. Rather, both before and after 1997, repeated messages by Beijing officials have served to forewarn or criticize Hong Kong media with the aim of establishing norms of political correctness without resorting to legislating repressive laws. They are always ready to set general guidelines for media practice as well as send out warnings on unacceptable performance by individual media, which they think has overstepped the proper boundary of press freedom. Of foremost concern is whether or not media coverage on Taiwan will be exploited as a public venue for promoting Taiwan independence or separatism. While press freedom is promised in the Basic Law, Beijing officials have been quick to draw the line, which excludes from the Basic Law's protection media perceived to be advocating the independence of Taiwan, Tibet, and Hong Kong. But what causes public alarm is what Beijing officials condemn, as political advocacy is a widely accepted practice of journalism in Hong Kong.[16] The interview of the then vice president–elect of Taiwan, Annette Lu Hsiu-lien, broadcast by the news channel of the Wharf Cable Television in March 2000, for instance, attracted strong criticisms by the deputy director of the Central Government Liaison Office in Hong Kong, Wang Fengchao. He argued that media should honor the duty and responsibility of safeguarding national unity and territorial integrity by refraining from reporting views for Taiwan independence. Against the common sense of Hong Kong journalists, he takes for granted that reporting on pro-independence views amounts to political advocacy and, by Beijing's standard, commits crimes of sedition and secession. To the mainstream press in Hong Kong, however, this is just a routine newsworthy story, a follow-up on the presidential elections in Taiwan. Their interview did not mean an endorsement of Annette Lu or Taiwan separatism.[17]

Certainly, Beijing's political sensitivity and grievances do not stop at issues of Taiwan or Tibet independence. Hong Kong media also feel the heat of dissatisfaction from the Chinese leadership when they were criticized for being aggressive in challenging the authority of Beijing officials. The criticisms by the head of the Chinese Communist Party, Jiang Zemin, in particular sent out a shock wave for Hong Kong media in October 2000.[18] Responding to a question by a television reporter on whether he supported Chief Executive Tung Chee-Hwa for the second term in 2002, Jiang criticized

Hong Kong journalists as "too simple(istic) and naïve" but without formally declaring his support for Tung. HKSAR journalists, however, find this question legitimate in addressing public concern over whether Beijing will continue its support of Tung to run his second term of office after his administration faced a summer of discontents in 2000, when an enormous number of individuals and groups, ranging from business tycoons to grassroots organizations, came out and aired their grievances against the government. Beijing officials took prompt action by meeting with several groups and showing their support of Tung. More than a pacifying act, this was widely seen as Beijing's initiative and a maneuver to secure Tung's continued rule after his first term of office expires in 2002.[19] Reporters took it as a common agenda to be followed up when Tung flew to Beijing to meet Jiang in person. Jiang's angry response not only was uncooperative with journalists, but also it questioned the propriety of the agenda and the method of news reporting of Hong Kong journalists. To Jiang, there is no question of Beijing's handpicking a candidate for the chief executive election even though no similar indication of support has been shown to other potential candidates. It is supposed that Hong Kong journalists by self-discipline should toe the unspoken line of reporting drawn by Beijing so as not to challenge the head of the state and give any impression that Beijing is interfering in Hong Kong politics by picking its favorite as candidate for the chief executive election.

Though the ideological tensions persist both before and after 1997, the agents of change have undergone realignment since the transfer of sovereignty. Before 1997, while liberal challengers asked for more changes than the British administration could offer, they joined hands to fight against resistance by conservative forces, the major camp being Beijing and its local supporters, pushing for legal reforms to strengthen protection of press freedom. After the political handover, however, the balance of power shifted to favor the conservative challengers, as the leading pressure group, Beijing, became the master of the SAR government. Though Beijing pledges not to intervene in Hong Kong politics, some observers wonder how the SAR government, formed by a largely undemocratic mechanism, could defend the liberal cause of press freedom while working to comply with measures of "political correctness" whenever it revises the legal status quo of freedom of speech and of the press. Given the changed balance of power, the status quo achieved in 1997 has been under constant pressure for change toward a less liberal regime, while liberal challengers in the past are now recast as the main defender of the status quo. In the absence of a system of democratic deliberation, the unavoidable clashes between these opposing ideological persuasions have resisted the formation of consensus and served to create uneasy tensions indefinitely.

Ideological tension aside, another source of challenge comes from the SAR government. For nearly five years since the political handover, the popularity of the SAR government and the chief executive in particular has been low. Some HKSAR government officials attribute the result of low popularity to inadequate public relations efforts by the government and negative reporting by the press. The remedy therefore lies not in government or policy reforms but in beefing up government publicity and seeking cooperation by the press. Unfortunately, the latter is sought by pursuing verbal attacks on media. The secretary for justice, Elsie Leung, for instance, condemns the press for being socially divisive. By her impression, without any documentation or evidence, the image of posthandover Hong Kong society portrayed by media is always seen as pregnant with conflicts, confrontations, and controversies.[20] The community is divided and the media are to blame. In stark contrast to the press nowadays, she said, the media in 1984 showed the ideal of solidarity when the media unanimously gave their blessing to the Sino-British Joint Declaration on the future of Hong Kong. On the other hand, HKSAR security secretary Regina Ip compared Hong Kong media to the "dictatorial leaders" portrayed in the political satire *Animal Farm*, written by George Orwell.[21] To her, government officials, among others, are on trial by media while the journalists themselves are above criticism. Another senior official also put the blame on media for adversely affecting the morale of the civil servants by its preoccupation with bad news of the civil service. Whether these HKSAR leaders are justified in their criticisms is debatable. Their remarks show that they want the media to paint a more favorable picture of the HKSAR, especially in view of the economic hardships the people of Hong Kong are going through. Instead of being critical in order to show their independence, the media should be sympathetic to the enormous difficulties encountered by the fledgling SAR government. They should work as a subordinate partner with the administration, promoting social consensus according to the dictates of the government. But government aspirations to have compliant media publishing only good news are doomed to fail.

Against the wishes of government officials, media executives remain adamant that bad news (e.g., poor economic performance and human-interest stories of social and economic hardship) is more attractive to an audience than good news (i.e., government publicity). Apart from market considerations, the media are interested in reporting negative news because it is an integral part of social reality, especially in times of economic difficulties and political conflicts. When frustrated by government policies, individuals, civic groups, politicians, and political parties take action to air their grievances and pressure the administration to address the problems in question. To drum up the impact of their actions, they will seek media coverage to amplify their voices of appeal. Bearing the impact of media in mind, politicians and pressure group leaders become keen to make effective choices of words and actions that will bring them the best publicity effects through media. As a result, the media becomes a venue, if not a battlefield, where competing groups of interests, including the government, rally for public support. This is especially so in Hong Kong, where the undemocratically formed government lacks legitimacy and support from the citizenry. Given the present political system, government can always push through unpopular policies, even when it fails to secure public support. On the other hand, citizens, who find government policies unacceptable but feel hopeless to seek redress from formal power structure, may appeal to the public by deploying informal power of influence such as public demonstration and assembly. Likewise, popularly elected legislators may find themselves powerless in a largely undemocratic legislature, and may use the media to make their cases heard publicly. As media attention on these actions determines how and how far the message of protest can reach out to the public, mobilization of media by citizen groups in mounting pubic pressure against the government becomes particularly important. Facing these challenges, the government also joins the competition for access to media to seek public support. Government officials use the media to state their cases in response to accusations, and they sometimes even go proactive to explain government position on issues of public concern. Sandwiched between accusations and clarifications, attacks and counterattacks, Hong Kong media, except those sponsored by Beijing, keep their doors open. As a channel for public information, media fulfill the duty of keeping the public informed about a diversity of views in society. It could only be done by keeping itself accessible to agents of different views while maintaining fairness in providing its audience with a balanced account of the issue concerned. Exclusive concern for good news, on the contrary, is one-sided and therefore partisan. It is meant to be a denial of reality as well as a denial of the audience's right to know.

The ideal of solidarity applauded by the secretary for justice, if practiced, would sing songs of praise to the administration and would, it is hoped, drum up support for government; but preoccupation with good news could only be done with deliberate neglect of bad news. Promotion of social solidarity must be based on a thorough understanding of social reality, however good or bad it is. It could never be achieved by whitewashing what the government has done wrong with good news. The official version of good press, however, is blind to the contributions made by criticism and negative news. It implies a weakened role of the press as a monitor of the administration. Deprived of the right to publish negative news and critical commentaries, the media are unable to draw public attention to problematic aspects of society that any responsible government must address. In other words, the urge by government official for a well-behaved press is a disguised call for the media to disarm its weapon. The result is growing distrust between government and the press.

Ideological tension and mutual distrust not only cause controversies and conflicts, but also become an obstacle to long-overdue media reform. Since the political handover, government and related bodies have published three consultation papers on media reforms, two of them on protecting privacy against media intrusion and the other on controlling publications of obscene and indecent articles. The first two papers are mainly concerned with the setting up of the Press Council on Privacy for adjudication of public complaints against media, and with the introduction of civil liability to journalistic activities that infringe upon privacy. The third aims to protect youth by strengthening the regulation of indecent and obscene materials. These moves represent legitimate concern about media malpractice over the years. Complaints are there that journalists collect information by unscrupulous means, infringing upon individuals' privacy, but no adjudication body of any kind has ever been set up to discipline malpractice. Complaints about the increasing extent of obscenity in the content of some newspapers have also become frequent. In addition to nude photos of women, they published a guide to prostitution. Ideally, problems connected with privacy rights and obscenity, unlike ideological and political issues, could be properly addressed without touching the nerve of political sensitivity; but the general distrust of the undemocratic nature of the SAR government by the journalism community, plus unreasonable proposals by consultation papers, throw reforms into doubt and defeat.[22] While the majority of journalists opt for creation of a nonstatutory body to oversee media, according to a survey, media organizations express concern over the potential danger of government intervention in media regulation. To preempt the forming of a statutory body, the Newspaper Association volunteered to organize the Press Council, to adjudicate public complaints on media intrusions into privacy. The council was formed in September 2000, but its jurisdiction is limited to handling complaints against its member organizations only. Two newspaper groups, together holding a lion's share (80 percent) of the total circulation of local daily newspapers, refused to join. Thus effective reforms have been delayed, if not denied.[23]

Given the present circumstances, as described above, Hong Kong media continue to face uncertain challenges in the years to come. Ideological tension will continue. Parties from both liberal and conservative camps, pushing for change of the status quo, show no sign of concession. Political conflicts will recur. Both government and the media are unlikely to seek reconciliation. Public concern about media reforms is justified, but a government that lacks legitimacy could hardly dare to go ahead with proposed regulations in the face of strong resistance from the media. And media reforms are destined to occur from time to time.

Hong Kong Media Owners and Workers During the Economic Hardships and Paradigm Shift:

Events:
- The overall economic performance of Hong Kong, especially the rise and fall of the Hong Kong stock market and real estate markets was tracked, 1997–2001
- Some newspapers, magazines, and Internet portals were closed, and newsworkers subsequently laid off, 1999–2001.
- Four new Pay TV licenses were issued, December 2000.
- *Sing Pao* changed ownership, October 2000.
- Jimmy Lai's Next Media Group was listed on the Hong Kong Stock Exchange, April 2000.
- China market–focused Phoenix TV was listed on Growth Enterprise Market, June 2000.
- I-Cable, the monopoly franchise owner of cable TV in Hong Kong, was listed on NASDAQ, 1999.
- Traditional media and new media formed strategic partnerships; for instance, *Ming Pao* sold 10 percent of its *Ming Pao* online news to HKNet for HK$100 million, May 2000.
- The *Sing Tao* newspaper group changed ownership, June 1999.
- One of two terrestrial TV networks, ATV, added new owners who are China-related, mid-1998.
- Chief Executive Tung Chee Hwa's popularity polling results were reported regularly, 1998–2001.
- PRC President Jiang Zeman commented on Hong Kong journalists' quality and experience, October 2000.
- Sensational news, such as the Chan Kin Hong incident in *Apple Daily* and the *Cyber Daily* online showing of a videotape of a reporter's actual sexual intercourse with a prostitute was reported, 1997–2001
- An *Oriental Daily* editor was jailed for sending reporters to monitor a judge's activities, 1999.
- The media played the role of a watchdog, as in *Apple Daily*'s exposé on legislator Gary Cheng Kai-nam (August 2000) and HKU Robert Chung's incident (August 2000), 1997–2001.

Amid the political changes, Hong Kong media owners are trying to stay out of the economic troubled water. Some media manage to keep their heads above water, but some sink. When the financial crisis struck across Asia in

Table 13.1

Hong Kong Economic Performance, 1995–2001

Year	Composite Consumer Price Index	Real GDP	Nominal GDP
1995	9.1	3.9	6.6
1996	6.3	4.5	10.7
1997	5.8	5.0	11.1
1998	2.8	−5.3	−4.9
1999	−4.0	3.0	−2.5
2000	−3.8	10.5	3.2

1997, Hong Kong was not an exception. As Table 13.1 shows, Hong Kong faced a sharp decline in its real and nominal GDP since 1997. The decline has given rise to an increased unemployment rate, whereas Hong Kong had previously enjoyed almost full employment status for many years. Also, now that mainland China's economy is on the rise, Hong Kong is facing a paradigm shift, which will involve preparing the workforce to enter the anticipated knowledge-based economy. Therefore, much unhappy news about the economy has dominated the news content.

A Hong Kong University opinion poll in May 1999 showed that about 68 percent of respondents were not satisfied with economic conditions.[24] An all-time high unemployment rate, resulting in further layoffs and retrenchment, and the continuous plunge of real estate property prices have dominated the news. The political party leaders and media find a convenient target to blame—the HKSAR government. Hong Kong University opinion polls between July 1997 to April 1999 show that fewer than one-quarter of Hong Kong residents were satisfied with the HKSAR government's performance.[25]

Since the 1980s, real estate advertisements had been a major source of advertising revenues. The "bubble" of the real estate boom burst just a few months after July 1997. Some of the media companies have seen a sharp drop in their real estate advertisements. Another source of advertising revenues, the job vacancies classified advertisements, also shrinks because of the high unemployment rate. The hot Internet expansion in the first quarter of 2000 was short lived.[26]

The battered Hong Kong economic environment makes it very difficult to manage the media. All media reported either loss or significant drop in revenues. It is often assumed that competing newspapers in the same market facilitate a marketplace of ideas. With the *Oriental Daily* and *Apple Daily* capturing almost 80 percent of the mass market and naturally creating a duopoly, there will be few contrasting voices.[27] The economic impact is politics-blind. The pro-China newspapers (*Ta Kung Pao*, *Wen Wei Po*, and *Hong Kong Commercial Daily*) also are affected. At one point, there were rumors that these three newspapers would be merged.[28]

The overall mood of the political scene in Hong Kong is affected by frequent debates between SAR government officials and elected legislative members. All parties concerned want to propose solutions to the economic crisis. For the media, such controversies are welcome because they will make good news stories. Therefore, media owners and practitioners play double roles acting as both agenda setters and "firefighters," who are trying to put out the fire in their backyards.

Because Hong Kong has always been a "business city" to media owners and practitioners, perhaps excluding those in pro-China media, economic conditions in posthandover Hong Kong have set the political inclinations of the newspapers. For example, the chief editor of *Apple Daily* once said in his daily column that it is a "profitable policy" to promote democracy and take an anti-Beijing stand, because this helps to sell more copies.[29] However, in taking such a stand, a newspaper has to be managed professionally. For example, a short-lived newspaper, *Mad Dog*, which even used the Nationalist flag of the Taipei regime as the cover of its first issue and was launched on the Taipei regime national day, Double Ten, in 1997, had to be closed.[30] Before it was closed, it changed its content to devote almost the entire coverage to Hong Kong's favorite sport—horse racing. Not even this effort could save *Mad Dog* from being closed.

Because of the economic crises, several media have changed hands. The saga of Sing Tao Group has attracted media attention. Sing Tao Group owns a Chinese-language daily, *Sing Tao Daily*, as well as the English-language *Hong Kong Standard,* and Culture Comm, which owns a popular Chinese daily, *Tin Tin Daily*. Finally, Sing Tao Group was sold for HK$524 million, which ended the Sally Aw family's sixty-year involvement in the Hong Kong media industry.[31]

In Hong Kong, there have been several well-respected media owners cum journalists. Louis Cha, who used to own *Ming Pao* and whose editorials were widely read, is no longer active in Hong Kong affairs. Lam San Mu, owner of the elite financial daily *Hong Kong Economic Journal* (*HKEJ*), has gradually transferred daily operation to his daughter, who withdraw *HKEJ*'s Audit Bureau of Circulation (ABC) membership in order to hide the shrinking circulation. Cha and Lam are the journalists turned owners because their editorials are the selling points of their newspapers respectively. At present, no other editorial writers command similar stature in Hong Kong's contemporary journalism history.

In fact, many nonjournalists have now entered into media ownership in

Hong Kong. A recent case is the purchase of *Sing Tao Daily* by an investment group, Lazard Asia, which was sold later to another listed company, Global China Technology, in 2001. Because the Sing Tao Group, the Oriental Daily Group, and the Culture Comm are all listed companies, theoretically they may have to answer to the shareholders and make profits their primary goal, just as some publicly listed media groups in the United States are under similar pressure.

Another "legendary success story" is that of the former garment factory owner turned "Hong Kong democracy fighter" (a term conferred by the Western media before the handover), Jimmy Lai, owner of the largest circulation popular magazine, *Next Magazine*, and a daily newspaper, *Apple Daily*. One media critic credited Lai with using new market-oriented strategies to establish two highly popular publications in a short time. Another criticizes Lai for sensationalistic practices in news treatment and contents. Having celebrated its seventh anniversary in June 2001, *Apple Daily* is here to stay and will continue to take a market-oriented approach, meaning giving the readers what they want by adding more "salt and spices" to its contents.

Another businessman turned media owner is Chan Kwok-keung. Chan bought a family-owned daily newspaper, *Sing Pao*, from its former owner, Ho Man-fat. Chan, considered a financial strategist, is reknown for his use of publicly listed companies as vehicles to acquire various companies and turn their shares into high prices. His purchases of media properties, include newspapers (*Sing Pao*), and Internet companies (Stareast).

In terms of electronic media, a PRC-related group became the major shareholder of Asian Television (ATV). This PRC group is chaired by Liu Changle, who is the major shareholder of Phoenix Satellite television channel with which Rupert Murdoch's STAR TV wants to team up so as to enter the lucrative mainland China market. Liu also managed to list Phoenix TV on the Hong Kong Growth Enterprise Market in June 2000.

Two significant phenomena stand out in terms of ownership and structural change on the Hong Kong media scene. The first phenomenon is that many media companies jumped on the bandwagon to become listed. They included the I-Cable, Next Media Group, and Phoenix TV. By changing their companies to listed companies, they will have to become more transparent in their business operations. Additionally, the purpose of listing, in theory, is to raise capital for expansions. As listed companies answerable to shareholders, they will have to be more concerned about their bottom lines and about share prices.

The second phenomenon is the media convergence trend. The convergence first goes through the stage of traditional media expansion into the online delivery mode. So far, the most "successful" in using this model to raise funds is *Ming Pao*, which sold 10 percent of its on-line news portal to HKNet for HK$100 million in May 2000. In the second stage, the so-called new media companies go back and buy into traditional media companies to strengthen their content and get immediate revenues to boost their financial outlook. A recent case in point is Tom.com's purchase of 50 percent of *Asia Weekly* (*Yazhou Zhoukan*), and also its purchase of outdoor media companies in China.

As shown above, the ownership of media companies in Hong Kong has undergone significant changes—in terms of the rise of group ownership, taking the companies public on the stock market, the withdrawal of former journalist cum owners, and the rise of former businesspersons turned media owners. Some of these changes happened in the four years after the handover. The changes may be due to casualties of the economic crises or the planned withdrawal of the media owners. The lack of a clear answer to this speculation highlights the need to study in greater depth the philosophies and missions of these owners. Do these owners simply want to make money or do they want to do some good for society? Or, can these two goals coexist? The findings will offer more insight into the impact of the handover and contribute to the thin body of literature on this aspect of Hong Kong's journalistic development.

The economic conditions also impact on organizational-level changes within the media. The past two years have also seen an intensified competition between the two major groups, namely, *Oriental Daily* and *Apple Daily*. Oriental Daily Group launched another popular newspaper, the *Sun*, on March 18, 1999, to try to lure away some readers from *Apple Daily*. The *Sun*, when newly launched, used a price-cutting strategy—lowering its newsstand price from HK$5 to HK$2 per copy, plus offering many freebies. *Apple Daily* responded by lowering its newsstand price from HK$5 to HK$3 per copy. When *Apple Daily* employed the price-cutting tactic to break into the already crowded Hong Kong daily newspaper market, it caused several newspapers to close, for example, *Express Daily*.

Only media groups with deep pockets can survive a price war. The former publisher of *Apple Daily*, Loh Chan, said in May 1999 that *Apple Daily* lost HK$20 million in the month after the price war broke out in 1999. The Oriental Daily Group reported an operating loss of HK$13.3 million in 1998, compared with a profit of HK$145.6 million for the same period in 1997. Other publicly listed media groups also reported losses during the same period. The Sing Tao Group lost HK$62.2 million, Hong Kong Daily News HK$37.1 million, Tin Tin Daily News HK$28.5 million, and Ming Pao Enterprise HK$5.9 million.[32]

Amid this economic atmosphere, media owners' journalistic practices are affected. As Hong Kong is a relatively transparent society, there are many interactions among sources, journalists, and audiences. Audiences are out-spoken in the many live phone-in programs on radio and television. They also write to the newspapers to express their opinions. Further, academics, who usually represent the interests of audiences, play a significant role in the public opinion formation process. The most significant group is political leaders, who need votes to keep their seats in the legislature. Also, many pressure groups, together with the politicians, have accumulated more knowledge on how to manipulate the media in getting across their views. When one of the authors was a television reporter for the leading television network in Hong Kong in 1977, he did a half-hour documentary on how the pressure groups resorted to various gimmicks to get their issues reported in the media. Today, after more than twenty years, some of these former social movement activists have become elected legislators and are veterans of media manipulation.

Writing in the *South China Morning Post*, its former editor Jonathan Fenby said that the media were an integral part of democratization and progress of society, particularly in a place like Hong Kong, whose sophistication and international character live side by side with a fledgling political culture.[33] Therefore, the multiparty political process has given rise to more negative coverage of the HKSAR government. The reasons are that those issues usually have direct impact on people's daily living, and controversies are high in market-oriented news value. In an interview with *Apple Daily* in August 1998, the director of HKSAR Information Services Department, Thomas Chan, said that it was understandable that reporters were now more sensitive about press freedom than they had been before and that their criticisms of the government would be harsher.[34]

"Conflicts and controversies" are two good news values for the news media to work on. However, one traditional news value has drawn heavy criticism from many quarters in Hong Kong. The first news value defined in a journalism textbook is: People, especially prominent people, make news. Another classical news value is "unusualness"; for instance, "Man bites dog" is a good news story. The mass circulated newspapers—*Oriental Daily*, *Apple Daily*, *Sun*, and other copycats—all employ similar journalistic techniques to report news. Tabloid journalism also becomes a norm on evening prime-time news magazines on the two leading networks' Chinese-language channels. The media assign paparazzi teams (in Hong Kong these are called "puppy teams") to spy and eavesdrop on celebrities, government officials, business tycoons, and even people on the street. Therefore, stories such as "Buddhist Nun by Day and Party Girl by Night" (*Apple Daily*, June 25, 1999) and "Special Hidden Camera Disguised in a Walking Shoe to Take Pictures of Women Under Skirt" (*Sun*, June 11, 1999) are abundant.

The most controversial story was about a Hong Kong man, Chan Kin Hong, who was unemployed when his wife and children committed suicide by jumping off a high-rise building. Showing no sign of sorrow or remorse, Chan was pictured by the media, notably *Apple Daily*, entertaining himself with his mistress in Shenzhen, a city known for prostitution, just one hour from Hong Kong. Later an *Apple Daily* reporter admitted that she gave HK$5000 to Chan as a "loan" in exchange for permission to take pictures of him with his mistress in a hotel. Confronted with stern public criticism, *Apple Daily* issued a public apology in the front page.[35]

This was not the end of the so-called Chan Kin Hong incident. Many critics of the media took the opportunity to propose establishment of a monitoring body similar to the media council. The HKJA representatives said that their survey of members showed that 77 percent of the respondents considered that media ethics were worse or much worse than twelve months ago. The chairman of HKJA, Liu Kin-ming, pledged to take the lead in setting up a media-monitoring forum, and to consult the public in creating a plan.[36]

Finally a voluntary press council was established in July 2000. The press council includes two media workers associations and eleven newspapers, but three major newspapers, *Oriental Daily, Apple Daily,* and *Hong Kong Economic Journal,* are not members. The press council has mandate only to handle complaints about its members, and is confined to privacy issues. However, the first report released in November 2000 by the chair, Professor Edward Chen, who is president of Lingnan University, showed that only two cases were about privacy violation and the other eleven cases were about sensational news coverage. Whether the existing press council should expand its jurisdiction beyond the issue of privacy violation, as proposed by Chen, is subject to further debate.[37]

Meanwhile, the sensationalistic practices of some journalists and media continue. For example, in early December 2000, an on-line newspaper, *Cyber Daily*, showed a videotape of a reporter "investigating" a brothel and having sex with a prostitute. The sexual intercourse was shown in great detail. It is not surprising to find that Hong Kong University opinion polls between September 1997 and March 1999 on whether the news media could be considered to conduct themselves responsibly showed an all-time low (Figure 13.2). It has dropped to less than 17 percent in March 1999, with the lowest point of 12.8 percent in November 1998, when the Legislative Council special meeting was held.[38]

There are also cases of legal consequences the journalists have to bear because of their violations. In June 1999, the Court of Appeals ruled that a former editor of *Oriental Daily,* Thomas Wong, was guilty of criminal contempt of court when he waged a campaign against the judiciary and pub-

Figure 13.2 **Opinion Polls on Whether News Media Are Responsible, September 1997–March 1999**

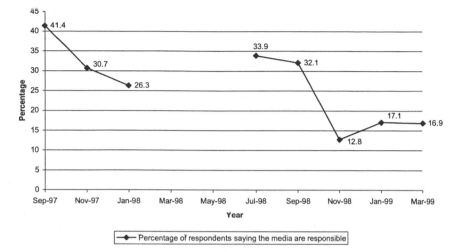

lished scurrilous and racist attacks. Wong served his jail term and returned to *Oriental Daily* as its online news service editor. The HKJA said *Oriental Daily's* actions had breached professional ethics and would not affect freedom of speech.[39] An *Apple Daily* reporter was found guilty of bribing a communications officer in the police headquarters for access to police calls. The chief editor of *Apple Daily*, Yip Yat Kin, was found guilty of contempt of court because of the way the newspaper reported a sexual assault case.

Yellow journalism is an age-old issue almost everywhere; there are no immediate solutions. As long as the Hong Kong media are engaging in a cutthroat survival war, unacceptable reporting practices are bound to happen. The pro-China media, because their source of funding does not depend on circulation, are exempt from such problems.

Hong Kong journalists are faced with double pressures: one from the overall economic crises, and the other from the impact on their personal careers. In 1989 in the aftermath of the Tiananmen Incident, there was an exodus of professionals, including journalists, from Hong Kong. During the 1980s, when the Hong Kong economy was booming, many journalists changed jobs and got promotions. Today, many journalists do not want to take the risk of leaving their jobs. They may not have received tempting offers to switch, and they know it is quite difficult to get a good-paying job in Hong Kong's current economic situation. The Internet boom soon turned to bust. Therefore, some journalists may tend to preserve the status quo and be comparatively unconcerned about fighting for professional or societal well-being.

Pro-Beijing journalists are not exempt from economic pressures. Their future also is up in the air because of the persistent rumor about merging the number of newspapers from three to one. On the posthandover Hong Kong journalistic scene, pro-Beijing journalists also have to face the challenges of professionalism, market pressures, and their patriotism toward mainland China.

On the other hand, the HKSAR government officials often publicly challenge the journalists. A recent example is Secretary for Security Regina Ip's comparison of Hong Kong media to the leaders in *Animal Farm,* by English author George Orwell. In another example, Hong Kong secretary for the civil service James Wong Wing-ping attributed the low morale of his workforce to constant negative news converge on the government. This open challenge to Hong Kong government officials could be interpreted as a healthy sign of a transparent process.

Before blaming the journalists for using sex and sensationalism to get the audiences, we should also examine the prevailing behaviors of the audiences. In a worldwide comparative study of the lifestyles of peoples in thirty-five cities, Roper Starch Worldwide found that about 34 percent of people in Hong Kong belonged to the so-called money hungry group, one of six lifestyle groups. The other lifestyle groups were the family-oriented, party-type, innovative-type, academic-type, and religious-type groups. Hong Kong's 34 percent in the money-hungry group is higher than the world average of 23 percent.[40] If journalists are eager to please audiences by dishing out what they like, it is no wonder that stories on how to get rich by either hard work or speculation have dominated the news. Even some media observers say this formula contributed to the success of the popular *Next Magazine,* which filled its pages with get rich and entrepreneur stories.

Conclusion

As times change, Hong Kong faces a paradigm shift both ideologically and economically. Many issues, such as housing, education, transportation, and employment, have yet to find solutions. In a way, the media are the outlets and agenda setters of these issues. If the leaders and people (including the media workers) of Hong Kong, as well as the PRC leaders, cannot find a solution, the HKSAR media scene will continue to be controversial and eventful.

Notes

1. Jimmy Cheung and Ng Kwai-Yan, "Media Watchdog Expands Its Role," *South China Morning Post*, July 27, 2000.

2. These events are listed in chronological order, with the latest first. The same event may be cross-listed on various levels.

3. Ying Ting Mak and Malcolm Smart, "The Ground Rules Change: Freedom of Expression in Hong Kong Two Years After the Handover to China, 1999 Annual Report," Joint Report of the Hong Kong Journalists Association and Article 19, June 1999. http://www.freeway.org.hk/hkja/whatnew/whatnew.html.

4. "Political and Economic Risks Consultancy Report: Hong Kong Media Are Not Subject to Censorship by the Party Central," *Ming Pao*, June 4, 1999, p. A-12.

5. "Foreign Corruption Causes U.S. to Lose International Contracts Worth 18 Billion," *Sing Tao Daily*, July 2, 1999, p. A-5.

6. *Pop Express*, Social Sciences Research Center, University of Hong Kong, no. 32 (April 1999): 15.

7. In 1987, the Hong Kong government amended the Public Order Ordinance to prohibit the dissemination of false news; the amendment was repealed in 1989. See Hong Kong Ordinance, chapter 245, section 27.

8. Hong Kong Journalists Association and Article 19, *Annual Report on Freedom of Expression 1997*, June 1997, p. 33.

9. This concern has been repeated again and again in annual reports on freedom of expression jointly presented by the Hong Kong Journalists Association and Article 19 since 1993. See also Frances D'Souza, Introduction to *Urgent Business: Hong Kong, Freedom of Expression and 1997*, Joint Report of Article 19 and the Hong Kong Journalists Association, January 1993, p. v.

10. Hong Kong Journalists Association and Article 19, *Annual Report on Freedom of Expression 2001*, pp. 18–22.

11. Hong Kong Journalists Association and Article 19, *Annual Report on Freedom of Expression 1998*, section 1, p. 16.

12. Ibid., pp. 16–17.

13. Joint Report of Article 19 and the Hong Kong Journalists Association, January 1993, p. 13.

14. The Basic Law of the Special Administrative Region of Hong Kong, People's Republic of China, Joint Publishing, Annex 2, pp. 43–44.

15. To keep Hong Kong under international limelight, both the Hong Kong Journalists Association and Article 19 have committed to publication of an annual report to monitor the status of freedom of expression in the years to come. The former is also active in commenting on press freedom issues from the said perspective. See also press freedom on the website of the Hong Kong Journalists Association, www.hkja.org.hk.

16. Hong Kong Journalists Association and Article 19, *Annual Report on Freedom of Expression 2000*, June 2000, p. 6.

17. Ibid., p. 6.

18. Hong Kong Journalists Association and Article 19, *Annual Report . . . 2001*, p. 9. See also To Yiu-Ming, "From Curse to Blessing: Towards Investigative Reporting on Jiang Zemin's Handpicking of the Chief Executive," *Media Digest* (November 2000): 2–3.

19. Ibid., pp. 9–11.

20. To Yiu-Ming, "Officials Should Produce Evidence When They Criticize Media," *Ming Pao*, November 21, 2000, p. A-28

21. Lee Huay Leng (Singapore's *Lianhe Zaobao* Hong Kong correspondent, who interviewed Regina Ip for this story), "What Was Really Said in the Regina Ip Interview," *Hong Kong Economic Journal* (October 11, 2000): 12.

22. Hong Kong Journalists Association and Article 19, *Annual Report . . . 2001*, pp. 27–29.

23. Ibid.

24. *Apple Daily*, June 26, 1999.

25. *Pop Express*, Social Sciences Research Center, University of Hong Kong, no. 32 (April 1999): 11.

26. During the period 1995–2001, there were layoffs even by major media companies in Hong Kong, including, tvb.com, ichannel, applydaily.com, and Metro Broadcast; there were also closures of media publications, including *Internet Magazine*, March 2001; *Hong Kong Globe*, January 2001; *Fruit Magazine*, November 2000; *Champion*, October 2000; *Joyce Magazine*, January 2000; *Tin Tin Daily News*, 2000; *M Magazine*, May 1998; *Surprise Weekly*, January 1998; *Sing Tao Evening News*, December 1996; and *Eastern Express*, June 1996.

27. Mak and Smart, "The Ground Rules Change."

28. Ibid.

29. *Apple Daily*, June 18, 1999.

30. *Press Freedom and Self-Censorship Sixth Report*, Media Research Sub-Division of the HKSAR Information Services Department, December 4, 1997.

31. Mak and Smart, "The Ground Rules Change."

32. Ibid.

33. *Press Freedom and Self-Censorship Tenth Report*, Media Research Sub-Division of the HKSAR Information Services Department, August 4, 1998.

34. Ibid.

35. Hong Kong Journalists Association and Article 19, *Annual Report on Freedom of Expression 1999*, June 1999, p. 22.

36. Minutes of the Legislative Council Panel on Home Affairs Special Meeting, November 25, 1998. Chamber of the Legislative Council Building, Wednesday, LC Paper No. CB(2)1400/98–99.

37. Hong Kong Journalists Association and Article 19, *Annual Report on Freedom of Expression 2001*, p. 22.

38. *Pop Express*, Social Sciences Research Center, University of Hong Kong, no. 32 (April 1999): 16.

39. *Press Freedom and Self-Censorship Tenth Report*.

40. *Hong Kong Economic Times*, "One-Third of Hong Kong Are 'Workaholics' and Only Interested in Materialistic Life, Wealth and Power," June 28, 1999, p. A-18.

14

Postcolonial Cultural Trends in Hong Kong

Imagining the Local, the National, and the Global

Agnes S. Ku

In Hong Kong, on July 1, 1997, the handover simultaneously signified a break from colonial rule and marked the historic beginning of national re-unification. In theory, there can be a few different cultural strategies vis-à-vis colonialism. They range from a simple return to precolonial heritage (nativism), or a revival of nationalism which seeks to uproot anything colonial, to a more complicated process of reordering and restructuring different old and new ideological elements for a renegotiated identity in changing times. The Hong Kong Special Administrative Region (HKSAR) government has mobilized its cultural apparatus in the task of imagining a distinctive political community with a common purpose under the grandiose principle of "one country, two systems." What we find is an attempt to evolve a cultural consciousness in society through mixed appeals to localism, nationalism, and globalism.

The purpose of this chapter is to analyze the hegemonic structure as well as contested character of culture in Hong Kong in the postcolonial context. More specifically, it attempts to unpack the structure of ideologies and myths that the government (or governing coalition) has been constructing for Hong Kong in the post-1997 era. As we shall see, the SAR government draws on a narrative of economic and governing success which has become hegemonic since colonial times to project a vision of world city, while incorporating certain elements about Chineseness into the narrative. Apparently, the government resorts to all the cultural imaginings of the local, the national, and the global; however, it has not clearly explained the logic of each as well as the relationship among them, especially the possible tensions within and among them. From a postcolonial point of view, we are particularly concerned about how far such hegemonic ideologies and myths by the local state embody a continuation of colonialism or how far they are transposed onto a plane of postcolonial consciousness.[1] If it is an indisputable fact that Hong Kong has entered a postcolonial era in the temporal sense since July 1, 1997, on a deeper level, the question nonetheless remains as to whether it has already superseded colonialism culturally or ideologically.

Imagining the Local, the National, and the Global

In hegemonic discourse, the imagination of a shared communal identity is often represented through myth or narrative, which not only delivers over the past but also mediates our concerns and aspirations, imaginatively expressing a possible future with its attendant hopes or fears. In Ricoeur's metaphor, narrative is a thread that unites otherwise disparate happenings into the significance of a development, a directionality, or a destiny.[2] Since the early 1980s, in the context of the "1997" issue, there has been a growing self-consciousness of Hong Kong identity in society, as manifested in the continuing vogue for narrating, exhibiting, and preserving the changing faces of the city in museums, memoirs, movies, archives, architecture, political speeches, and also academic conferences. Local cultural analysts find in these prevailing discourses and representations a hegemonic myth of "a miraculous economic success without political instability," as forged by the governing coalition.[3] In particular, the myth entails imagining the rise of a modern metropolis—of barren rock or fishing village turned into a modern city.[4] While the narrative is centered around economic transformation as its main plot, it has at the same time incorporated other elements as its constituent parts such as rule of law, free market, and efficient administration. Through discursive articulation, such elements become integrated into an apparently coherent whole, when in fact their relationship is subject to interpretation and reinterpretation. Before 1997, the colonial state had successfully established the hegemonic status of such a narrative so much so that the prospects of reunification with communist China once engendered a feeling of anxiety in society over the possible loss of the glamor of the city.

Since 1997, like any other state, the newly formed SAR government has engineered certain kinds of cultural projects—campaigns, programs, statements, and policies—to legitimate its power in meaningful terms and to unify the people through specific symbolic appeals. Basically, the government draws and further expands on the preexisting narrative of economic success with all the more vigor to boost its political status at local, national, and international levels. An archetypal example of the way the government grounds its governance through such a cultural imagining is seen in the continual invocation of the "success formula" in its annual policy speeches. For instance:

> It is essential that we all re-affirm our commitment to preserving these fundamentals, which are the basis of our success. I would like to state clearly that the Government will uphold the rule of law and protect the independence of the Judiciary; guarantee freedom of speech and of the press, and facilitate access to information; continue to manage our economy on a free-market basis within a regulatory framework which creates a "level playing-field" for investors; maintain a strong stance against corruption; emphasize the importance of law and order; and preserve the international character of Hong Kong.[5]

In society there has existed a more or less consensual understanding that attributes such fundamentals for success as the rule of law and free market to Hong Kong's being part of the British colonial legacy. In reiterating the same tale of success, the chief executive of the SAR government is implicitly subscribing to this view. Clearly he has not used any kind of simple binary, dichotomous frame of nativism versus colonialism to replace everything colonial with a precolonial heritage. He nonetheless pronounces the fundamentals for success as already rooted in society, without making explicit reference to the British legacy. In this way, the colonial becomes absorbed or dissolved into the local.

Regarding the relationship between the colonial and the local, it is indeed often the case that the colonial legacy of values, institutions, and identities is too deeply intertwined with the local culture that it becomes impossible to reject the former without rejecting parts of oneself.[6] However, by means of a simple absorption of the colonial into the local, the government fails to seriously engage in public discussion about what legacies are, and on what grounds they are to be preserved, enhanced, discarded, or changed. In other words, it does not develop a critical consciousness of the colonial legacy. As a result, it even fails to face squarely the fact of colonial history. The decision over the name and function of the ex–Governor's House is an example. Although the architecture itself is integrally preserved, it is renamed and its function is redefined in a way that neutralizes or hides the colonial past. Such an attempt to hide history would demonstrate what Abbas[7] calls "a culture of disappearance" whereby history is emptied of its critical potentials. The issues at stake concern not only the question of what for but also the question of who has the power to make the decision despite resistance and counterproposals from the public. The problem is manifested in a number of other ways, which will be discussed in later sections.

On one level, the colonial becomes absorbed or dissolved into the local. On another level, the colonial is transfigured as part of the global. King argues that colonial city can prefigure the global city: "[C]olonial cities can be viewed as the forerunners of what the contemporary capitalist world city would eventually become."[8] Indeed globalization is very much a product of the history of colonialism and neoimperialism, which is itself largely a product of capitalist expansion. This perhaps explains the high degree of ease with which the colonial and the postcolonial governments transmute the city into a vision of world city or global city through appeals to a cosmopolitan imagination. In public discourse, there are attempts to subsume the British legacy under the larger context of a cosmopolitan culture:

> Britain has established in Hong Kong a rational, modern system. . . . These institutions were not invented by the British, but are what the world's peoples have invented through trial and error over the past two centuries. They are the world's peoples' common property.[9]

Contrary to the above quotation, the government's strategy is not to make such an explicit metaphorical stretch between colonialism and cosmopolitanism. Rather, without suggesting any link with the British, the government simply appropriates the colonial formula of success for use in the formula of success for the development of a world city:

> [W]orld cities have a distinctive economic structure. . . . World cities are also underpinned by less tangible features such as the rule of law, freedom of expression and association, free flow of information, openness and diversity.[10]

Clearly the smooth transition to a vision of world city is made possible through an appropriation of the discourses of liberalism and capitalist growth that have prevailed since colonial times.

The idea of Hong Kong's attaining an increasingly prominent international status in the world is in fact not new. Under British colonial rule, there were constant references to Hong Kong's role as one of the major trading economies, one of the busiest ports in the world, and so on. The most remarkable one was registered in the policy address of 1989, which, in the wake of the Tiananmen Square incident in Beijing, deliberated on the theme "Hong Kong's Place in the World." What distinguishes the postcolonial talk from the colonial talk of global city perhaps lies in the former's conscious articulation of a long-term development plan that aims to develop a distinctive strategic position within the nation and within the region. This is prompted by a growing consciousness about an imminent possibility of the city itself being overshadowed, in the context of increasing global competition and China's rapid economic development, by other neighboring cities, especially Shanghai and Singapore.[11]

The vision of global city is spelled out most distinctly in an official document entitled *Bringing Vision to Life—Hong Kong's Long-Term Development Needs and Goals*, which was published in February 2000 in conjunction with the formation of the Commission on Strategic Development in early 1998. The whole idea is to consolidate Hong Kong's position as a great international metropolis both in the nation and within the Asian region, comparable to that of New York and London:

> [T]he Commission has been aware of the need for Hong Kong to establish a distinct position for itself following reunification. We have studied the roles of New York and London, which are not only the most cosmopolitan cities in America and Europe respectively, but are also international financial centers, tourist destinations, homes for the headquarters of multinational corporations and international communication and transportation centers. I believe that Hong Kong too has the potential to become, not only a major city within one country, but also the most cosmopolitan city in Asia, enjoying a status similar to that of New York in America and London in Europe. We must devote our efforts to consolidating our position and at the same time give renewed impetus to our economic development.

Given such a vision, the government constructs Hong Kong as a world city (or as carrying the potentials to be one) not only by drawing on and extending the preexisting narrative of success. It also turns to Chinese culture as the cultural resource or ingredients to bring about success. From a constructivist point of view, Chineseness is not a set of given attributes about Chinese personality or Chinese culture. Rather, any tradition is always an invention that has to be created or recreated through discursive and symbolic processes.[12] In this light, the definition of Chineseness is always subject to selective interpretation by specific people or institutions, which usually serves particular political ends. The question then is: To what extent is the definition of Chineseness by the SAR government a critical rejuvenation of Chinese culture that may supersede colonialism? We can find an answer by turning to another formulation of the discourse of success.

In colonial times, the government had often drawn on the vague and simplistic metaphor "East meets West" to spell out a magic formula for success in Hong Kong. For example, in 1996, under the heading "Hong Kong's Success Story," Governor Patten explained:

> Success in Hong Kong is the result of a combination of factors. This is a Chinese city. Its success is the result of the hard work and skill of its Chinese

men and women. Its is also a city over which, for a century and a half, Britain has held stewardship. We have tried to exercise that stewardship in a way which has been true to our political values. Those values have been institutionalised in the rule of law and a meritocratic, politically neutral Civil Service.[13]

Such a narrative attributed the colony's success to the "smooth combination of British administration and Chinese entrepreneurship."[14] Representating the imperialist and colonialist encounter as a moment of harmonious blend between two cultures without tracing the instances of aggression and domination in the narrative concealed the unequal relationship embedded in colonialism. In post-1997 Hong Kong, the SAR government draws on the same abstract metaphor, "East meets West," but twists it with a different cultural interpretation of Chineseness. In his first policy speech, the chief executive conjures up the imagery of a "melting pot" for Chinese and Western cultures as a symbol of cosmopolitanism:

We are a melting pot for Chinese and Western cultures. . . . Ours is a cosmopolitan city. Our ability to embrace the cultures of east and west is one of the secrets of our success, shaping a unique social culture of our own. While we deepen our understanding of Chinese history and culture, we will continue to develop our own diverse cultural characteristics. China's culture, like every other culture, is growing and changing as we journey forward into the twenty-first century. Hong Kong stands in a unique position in this process, able to act as the center of exchange for China to learn about western cultures and the world to learn about Chinese culture.[15]

In formulating the dual goal of having Hong Kong be both Asia's world city and a major city in China, the chief executive stresses the need to nurture certain qualities among the citizenry as cultural ingredients to both bring about the status of world city and strengthen the link between Hong Kong and the mainland. Such qualities consist in a set of traditional Chinese values including "such things as trust, respect for families and elders, a commitment to self-improvement, a sense of obligation to the community and a focus on consultation rather than confrontation . . . diversity, openness, individual creativity, competitiveness and volunteerism."[16]

Tensions in the Dual Identity as Chinese City and as Global City

The above quotation by the chief executive echoes part of the description of the Chinese residents during earlier colonial times as being "industrious, peaceful and law-abiding."[17] Indeed in the early period of colonial rule, from the government's point of view, an affirmation of the "peaceful and law-abiding" qualities of the people was necessary to safeguard and reproduce a depoliticized citizenry whose energy, with their industrious character, would be most usefully diverted to economic activities. In later years, such a description formed part and parcel of the hegemonic narrative of economic success which discouraged political participation and which justified the absence of democracy. In this light, it is perhaps interesting to note that, toward the final stage of colonial rule, and given the increasing politicization of society, the qualities of peace lovingness and law abidingness began to disappear from official discourse. This is apparent in Chris Patten's policy address, as quoted above. Nevertheless, such themes reappeared after 1997. In particular, what strikes us as signifying a revival of early colonial discourse is its attempt to essentialize Chinese culture as preferring "consultation rather than confrontation."[18] To a significant extent, such a selective reinvention of Chinese culture is feeding itself on a discourse of stability—order, harmony, and consensus—which has served to maintain the status quo of authoritarian governance since colonial times. It may be argued that such themes reflect, albeit not exclusively, a Euro-Western–centric view on the colonized "other," to justify paternalistic rule in colonial times. In the postcolonial context, the SAR government appropriates the same themes in order to justify its own authoritarian rule. In his most recent policy address, the chief executive reiterates an association between such essentialized cultural qualities of Chineseness and the vision of world city:

> Most want a society with greater harmony, less hostility, less unnecessary quarrelling, but more rational discussion. . . . Instead of indulging in negativism, let us join hands and direct our efforts at making Hong Kong the world city in Asia.[19]

Instead of reflecting on the cultural infrastructure that sustains the institution of the rule of law and protects civic liberty, the SAR government simply reverts to Chinese culture without explaining why and how those highlighted qualities are essential to the achievement of a world city.

Within society, quite contrary to the government's rhetorical appeals, there is a lurking fear that Hong Kong will become just another Chinese city rather than a truly global city. The following two quotations from public critics underline a tension between the identities as a global city and as a Chinese city, which the government fails to acknowledge or resolve by simply drawing on the conventionalized imagery of "East meets West."

> On the surface [the Committee] emphasizes time and again the vision of Hong Kong being a world city, but when it comes to the specifics, it is

> oriented inwardly towards the Mainland rather than outwardly to Asia and the whole world. . . . [T]he Committee stresses how Hong Kong is to become a major city in China much more than how Hong Kong may help propel China forward to face the world and to confront new changes and challenges under globalization.[20]

> Hong Kong has been a metropolis with a global horizon, but within a short period of just a few months, it becomes a Chinese city which orients itself to the north and looks to Beijing for positive reinforcement on every matter without itself making any progress forward.[21]

Literally speaking, given the geopolitical fact of Chinese sovereignty, Hong Kong is indeed a Chinese city, though it is more precisely a special administrative zone within the Chinese state. Yet the more pertinent issue here concerns the subjective identification or deidentification of the people: What specific symbolic meanings does the image "Chinese city" connote, which many Hong Kong people feel so uneasy or repugnant about? Likewise, how does the image "global city" appeal to popular imagination? In fact, neither idea is clearly and directly articulated among the public. Still, as far as the notion of Chinese city is concerned, we may detect two levels of meaning prevailing in public discourse. First, politically, it underlines a tendency for the SAR government to look up to Beijing for positive reinforcement on its policies, as a result of which Hong Kong may lose the high degree of autonomy that should distinguish from all the other Chinese cities under the "one country, two systems" principle. Second, on the cultural level, it embodies values and norms that are not in tune with the international standard or outlook, including respect for rule of law, human rights, and democratic principles. These two levels are closely intertwined. During the past three years, there have been quite a few instances in which the SAR government may have undermined the institutions of civil society by subordinating the principles of freedom, rule of law, and democratic value to the concerns of order, stability, and control.

In principle, the Basic Law lays down, among others things, the basic civil rights of Hong Kong people, such as freedom of speech; freedom of association; the right to a fair trial; and, most important of all, the power of final adjudication. To this extent, the Basic Law delineates the normative and institutional boundary of a local civil society in legal and formal terms. However, under the overarching principle of state sovereignty and under an undemocratic political structure, the Basic Law vests final interpretive authority over laws pertaining to Hong Kong in the National People's Congress. In this way, notwithstanding the constitutional safeguard of the common law tradition on local matters in Hong Kong, the Basic Law has subjected itself to an interpretive community "committed to the discourse of democratic centralism."[22] For example, in the right of abode controversy, the difference between the local and the national legal systems generated two competing legal discourses—Chinese law versus common law—in the process of struggles which, due to the principle of state sovereignty, resulted in the former subordinating the latter in the event of unresolved tension.[23] To a significant portion of the local public, including legal professionals, academics, democrats, and human rights activists, the outcome of the event conjured up the negative imagery of Hong Kong as basically a Chinese city with very limited autonomy, at least with regard to politically sensitive issues.

In some instances, the power of Chinese sovereignty becomes the overriding principle in the final moment of local political and civil struggle. In other instances, the conventionalized imagery of Chineseness is called forth with a view to discouraging democratic participation, antigovernment type of action, and expression of more radical opinions, just as the colonial government once did. In this light, the cultural strategy of invoking the imaginary Chinese city does not hold out the promise of overcoming colonialism but would, on the contrary, reinforce it. For the long-term development of Hong Kong, if the vision of a Chinese city is not a satisfactory option, is the present local-colonial-global formation the answer? Perhaps not quite. The phrase "local-colonial-global formation" refers to the absorption by the postcolonial government of the colonial discourse of success into a discourse of local identity, and to its extension into a discourse of world city. However, the glossiness of such an easy articulation of the local, the colonial, and the global, by means of the symbolic strategies of absorption and extension, can be deceptive.

Tensions Within the Local-Colonial-Global Formation

While there exists a perceived tension between the trajectories of development as Chinese city and as global city, a binary or dichotomous framework that puts them in simple contrasting terms would nonetheless overlook the contested nature of the cultural construction of global city. As we have seen, the image of a world city builds on a fairly straightforward extension of the logic of success from the local level to the global level. Such a linear projection reflects a pattern of development that is by and large governed by the logic of capitalism, which has a propensity for translocal and transnational expansion. However, in uncritically adhering to the logic of global capitalism, the government fails to conceive the multiplicity of the vision of global city on the one hand, and to confront the possible tensions between global interests and local interests on the other.

The hegemonic construction by the government reflects a predominant concern with big corporate interests or a glamorous international image. For instance, thus far the government has tried hard to bid successfully for such projects as a Disney theme park and the 2006 Asian Games, which are believed to carry an international trademark or help boost Hong Kong's international status. More important, it turns increasingly to the hegemonic international community, which is dominated by transnational corporate interests, for informal endorsement or reinforcement over a number of policies such as environmental policy and financial policy. In many instances, it is the interests of the big corporations and expatriates that it appeals to:

> The expatriate community contributes greatly to our economy and to our unique culture. We are determined to make this community more welcome in Hong Kong, and to remain the city of choice for multi-national companies wishing to establish a base in the Asia Pacific region.[24]

It is not difficult to see that the ultimate goal is to ensure an environment that is conducive to economic development and foreign investment in Hong Kong. However, how much costly projects and economically skewed policies can help enrich local culture, preserve local history, and improve the well-being of the majority of the local people remains rather unclear, if not doubtful. Moreover, given its preoccupation with economic considerations, the government has given little thought to the question of establishing the necessary cultural as well as institutional infrastructure to facilitate the emergence of a global city in its multiple manifestations.

What constitutes a global city? There is perhaps no definite answer to this question, yet there are at least two issues that should concern us. First, "global city" is itself a highly contested idea which carries with it different economic, political, social, environmental, and cultural agenda. An overriding concern with economic development, as in the case of postcolonial Hong Kong, will result in the subordination of other agenda as having secondary or, at best, instrumental values. The government's recent appeal to green consciousness as an adjunct of an economically friendly environment is a case in point. Its vision of educational reform as primarily a springboard to enhance economic competitiveness of the city reflects the same kind of mindset.[25] In this light, comparison of Hong Kong to the global cities of London and New York becomes only superficially grounded. Second, there has been a growing international literature on the issue of globalization which the government should have consulted so as to bring forth the complexity of the subject matter for open discussion, public education, and consideration in policy formulation.[26] Just to give one example: In 1995, to coincide with the fiftieth General Assembly of the United Nations, the Commission on Global Governance published a report that addressed, among other things, the issue of global responsibility or global civic ethic in the process of globalization. At issue is not so much how to rival other cities in a context of increasing global competition as how to develop international cooperation and enrich cosmopolitan cultural experience without denigrating the civil society of smaller groupings.[27] Competition versus cooperation, efficiency versus responsibility, and cosmopolitan culture versus local participation—these are but some of the issues raised in the literature on globalization. The government's failure to address all the pertinent issues on a broader horizon bespeaks a thin conception of global city in its hegemonic project.

In terms of cultural discourse, the metaphor of "East meets West" also shows limitations and inadequacies in the prevailing understanding of global city. The metaphor is made up of two elements, namely the East and the West, to represent the range and diversity of cultures present in society. However, the fact is, "West" refers primarily to the British (or the European in general) whereas "East" refers only to the Chinese. The metaphor has reduced into a structure of facile binarism what is or should be a complex space of cultural diversity in two senses. First, the metaphor has left out a whole range of ethnic minorities who have stayed in the society for quite a long period of time, such as the Indians, the Pakistanis, and the Filipinos. This does not just present a simple rhetorical oversight in the metaphor but perhaps reflects certain forms of racism in the mainstream culture. On the one hand, under the impact of Western imperialism, a sense of racial as well as cultural superiority has often been attached to the white population. On the other hand, the Chinese counterpart in the community manages to assert its own sense of cultural pride vis-à-vis the imperial West by striking a balance through the dichotomous framework. However, being circumscribed by the simple dichotomy, the government, as well as the whole community, has become quite unable to address the question of multiple ethnic cultures in Hong Kong, which should form a crucial dimension of many of the global cities today. This is not to mention that the metaphor has had the effect of making invisible the variety of national origins of the people under the umbrella category of the West, and also, perhaps more importantly, the fact of cultural diversity or pluralism within the Chinese community under the umbrella category of the East. It is beyond the scope of this chapter to delve into the issue of local cultural diversity, but it should be instructive to take note of, for example, some recent efforts by certain women's groups to document the history and experiences of women of different age groups as an alternative form of writing history.[28] Such efforts can be understood as conscious attempts to contest the master, singularizing, and homogenizing narrative about Hong Kong identity with a view to bringing into the light the fact of diversity in outlook and experiences within the local community, especially those of the marginalized people. Nonetheless, under the weight of the dominant narrative, such attempts remain barely recognized in our mainstream culture.

If the present projection of the global is skewed in that it overlooks the immediacy and complexity of the local, rather unfortunately, the current conception of the local by the government also falls short of cultivating respect for equality, pluralism, and democracy within the local community. For the deep problems remain within the historical colonial and local formation.

Historically, the twin forces of imperialism and global capitalist expansion had resulted in colonialism in Hong Kong. Despite instances of protest showing anticolonial sentiments, by and large colonial rule was being ideologically buttressed through the discourses of liberalism and capitalist growth, with a subtext of Chineseness as embodying certain cultural qualities. On the positive side, such discourses conjure up an identity imagery of a civilized state as well as an advanced modern city, which is founded on an unusual but beneficial historical encounter between the East and the West. This benign interpretation of colonialism nonetheless tells only half the truth. As Pieterse and Parekh succinctly point out, colonial rule usually introduces modern values to justify itself with the pretence of a civilizing mission but it does so only halfheartedly to ensure the continuity of colonial domination. This was indeed the situation in Hong Kong, where the colonial government neither consolidated a system of democratic governance nor helped build up a profound democratic and pluralistic cultural environment within the society. Thus, on the negative side, we may argue that the discourses of liberalism and capitalist growth ideologically served to conceal or sublimate the condition of colonial domination before 1997. In this light, after 1997, the SAR government's strategy of a simple absorption of the colonial into the local inevitably causes a failure to develop a critical and reflective consciousness of the colonial legacy. As a result, the government has demonstrated a certain degree of idiosyncrasy, inconsistency, and bias in its interpretation of the meanings of rule of law, individual freedom, and democracy without showing a genuine commitment to such principles. Very often, such an inclination is reinforced either through reference to the image of Chinese sovereignty or by means of some casual reference to Chinese culture within the one country, two systems framework. Moreover, the government tends to reproduce or even further reinforce the same kind of cultural biases that have developed within the colonial and local discursive formation. The following two short sections will offer an analysis of the wider and deeper political and cultural implications of the narrative of success with reference to specific events. We shall briefly explain how and how far the hegemonic culture in postcolonial Hong Kong shows a trend of cultural continuity of (or even regression from) colonial times.

Culture of Localism and Rationalization of Exclusion

The hegemonic discourse of success is never just a neutral, objective, and apolitical discourse about the success story of Hong Kong. Rather, it privileges the economic as the overriding way of defining success and accordingly presumes as given and necessary a particular set of socioeconomic and cultural parameters that are regarded as conducive to economic growth. Such a discourse of success would at the same time draw up a symbolic boundary, often with substantial institutional implications, between the desirable versus undesirable elements, profiles, and scenarios. This is most conspicuously manifested in the construction of certain inferior "others" who fail to meet up the standard of success or who may pose a threat to the condition of success. Within the colonial and local formation, a discriminatory culture of localism has taken root around the hegemonic discourse of success which lays the cultural basis for a politics of division or even exclusion vis-à-vis certain categories of "outsiders." Rather unfortunately, the SAR government has further deepened such cultural biases. The right of abode (ROA) is a case in point.

Since the 1970s, the hegemonic myth of a miraculous economic success has simultaneously constituted the Hong Kong identity. To a certain extent, this sense of Hong Kong identity turns on a negative juxtaposition against an internal "other" of economic and cultural backwardness—the new migrants from the mainland.[29] For some time, an awareness of the huge socioeconomic difference between Hong Kong and the mainland has developed into a sense of cultural distance from and even superiority to the mainland Chinese. In the process of identity formation in Hong Kong, locality has become a badge of identity distinguishing the local people from the mainlanders in China and, as in the right of abode case, distinguishing the local-born children of Hong Kong residents from the mainland-born children of Hong Kong residents.

Initially, the Basic Law guaranteed right of abode to all persons, among others, of Chinese nationality born to Hong Kong residents regardless of their place of birth. The curtain of the controversy was raised when, under the effective jurisdiction of the miniconstitution in July 1997, hundreds of mainland China–born children of Hong Kong residents who had either overstayed upon expiry of their temporary permits or entered the territory illegally made a public claim to their right of abode upon the local state. The episode soon escalated into deeper civil conflicts, as the government, finding itself pressed with the danger of an uncontrollable influx of migrants, made the rights of these people conditional upon an administrative procedure.[30] This then triggered off a process of intense legal and political struggle until the Court of Final Appeal's ruling was partially subjected to constitutional reinterpretation by the Standing Committee of the National People's Congress in June 1999.

In the ROA event, the absence of institutional democracy within the local state and the disjunction between the local and the national legal systems had allowed the government to assert its executive power vis-à-vis the local law. Such actions by the government nonetheless were given a certain degree of legitimacy through hegemonic discourse. In the public sphere, there developed in the process of struggles between two competing discourses, namely stable and prosperous governance versus judicial autonomy (rule of law). Despite strong resistance, the former was able to prevail through a discursive articulation that constructed a demographic, economic, and cultural crisis out of the myth of success on the one hand, and that reduced law to a political means of resolving the crisis on the other.[31]

On the cultural level, through a massive appeal to the hegemonic discourse of success, the event has ended up deepening a sense of prejudice against the mainlanders that is embedded within the culture of localism. How? According to Ku,[32] the government turned on the prevailing sense of Hong Kong identity and used its institutional and cultural resources to mobilize a public sentiment of discrimination against the mainland-born children in order that it could carry through the option of constitutional reinterpretation with popular support. Within the discourse of stable governance, it struck a raw nerve in the public by constructing a doomsday scenario of Hong Kong suffering from an uncontrollable influx of mainland migrants.[33] It drummed up a public sentiment of prejudice against them in negatively stereotyping them as poor, unemployable, and welfare-dependent through statistical presentation. In brief, the hegemonic discourse was mobilized to rationalize the discriminatory and exclusionary practices, which reflected a culture of narrow localism. Such a strategy worked effectively, especially at a time when the society was facing an economic downturn. Survey findings showed that the strategy succeeded in significantly swinging public opinion in the direction of discrimination against the mainland-born children and opposition to the court ruling.[34] This policy of restricted entry for those mainlanders who were initially entitled to the constitutional right of abode was contrasted to a later policy of importation of an unrestricted number of professional elite from the mainland. Obviously, the government's proposal for population control as well as immigration control embodies a hegemonic interpretation of local identity with exclusionary consequences based on economic considerations. Economic interests may be at stake, but the cultural implications are also far reaching. The event has served to reinforce the dominant discourse of success, which judges the worth of people in money terms, and which rationalizes exclusionary practices on economic grounds. A culture of localism that carries with it a strong consciousness of economic hierarchy will hamper the development of an ideal civil society of inclusion and solidarity in the long run.

Administrative Paternalism and Displacement of Democracy

The hegemonic narrative of success is political also in that it has served to displace the democratic agenda. According to Ku, the term "displacement of democracy" means that the democratic agenda is undermined not so much by direct opposition as by being made out of place, secondary, irrelevant, or peripheral in a narrative construction centered around a different set of codes such as "stability" and "prosperity." The claims of prosperity and stability are not in themselves counterdemocratic but have been articulated in a way that counteracts democratic development. For instance, in the public sphere, drawing on a discourse of stability, the more conservative groups express their concerns with order, harmony, and smooth transition as opposed to disorder, conflict, and unstable change whereby to justify a more conservative blueprint for political reform. In this connection, the hegemonic narrative of success displaces the democratic agenda by, more specifically, incorporating a paternalistic and administrative discourse that promotes the virtues and efficiency of the administrative machinery as part and parcel of the formula of success. Put in another way, the culture of colonial paternalism is translated into an administrative discourse of good performance that is articulated onto the hegemonic myth of success. This shows how, through the mechanism of discursive articulation, otherwise disparate ideological elements such as prosperity, stability, and administrative efficiency can become related to one another in a seemingly coherent, natural, and unquestionable narrative, which simultaneously displaces other ideological elements such as democracy. After the handover, the SAR government has been emphatically striving for a strong administration capable of steering a course for prosperity and stability as a stronghold for effective self-government. This reflects a strategy of narrative displacement of democracy.

At this point, of particular interest is the question of how, given the rise of a challenging discourse of democracy in the final colonial years, the existing set of discursive elements might allow for democratic change after 1997. It has been argued that, under hegemonic relations, democratic challenge initiated from below is most effective when the dominant narrative begins to crack through a process of demystification in the public sphere and also when a discourse of democracy is already in the making.[35] In postcolonial Hong Kong, a number of episodes such as the earlier bird flu saga and the more recent public housing piling scandal have exposed the inherent weaknesses of the administration. Through such moments of dramatic happenings and crises, the myth of administrative strength begins to crack through an ironic discourse against a spoiled culture of bureaucratism. Under the code of bureaucratism, the civil service is recharacterized as being incompetent, arrogant, inefficient, unresponsive to public sentiments, and lacking in a sense of public responsibility. In the process, the ironic distancing between the bureaucracy and the public further evolves into a reinvigorated democratic discourse of public accountability that focuses on the specific issue of ministerial system in lieu of the authoritarian state. It is in the context of such changing cultural climate, as most recently manifested in mounting public pressure against the government over the public housing piling scandal, that the first sign of breakthrough is seen in the stepping down of the Housing Authority chair, Rosanna Wong, ahead of a no-confidence vote by the legislators in June 2000.

In any case, discursive change is seldom an all or nothing matter which either effects profound political change overnight or remains a purely rhetorical construction with no short-term or long-term significance. In the case of Hong Kong, there have been signs of growing tensions between state paternalism and democratic consciousness. After all these crises and challenges, we find that the SAR government has appropriated the discourse of democracy and then incorporated it into the hegemonic discourse of governing success, giving rise to both changes and continuity on the cultural and institutional levels.[36] For instance, the government begins to actively mobilize its political machinery and ideological resources to maintain power by increasing publicity as well as strengthening its public relations skill. In one sense, such changes may bring about a higher degree of openness of the administration. Yet in a deeper sense, senior officials nonetheless stick to a paternalistic mode of thinking in that they see better media publicity as a redress against a deficiency in their public communications skills rather than an indispensable ingredient for the development of a publicly accountable system.[37] In this light, it has the effect of displacing democracy through a modified paternalistic and administrative discourse that includes the practice of media publicity in its expectation for a more favorable public relations outcome.[38] A tinge of deep-seated paternalism is clear for all to see when very recently the chief executive questioned the motives of his critics, whom he dismissed as having indulged in "negativism." His negative reception of open criticisms demonstrates a failure to appreciate that "differences in opinion are a healthy sign in a democracy."[39] This is not to mention that in actual practice the government has already shown signs of regression to a system of greater authoritarian control—by disbanding the elected municipal councils in a rush in the name of administrative effectiveness, by reintroducing a system of appointment in the district boards, and so on. The recently pronounced plan to introduce a quasi-ministerial system registers a halfhearted attempt to enhance accountability: The existing system of executive domination is to be preserved through a modified administrative discourse of efficiency and effectiveness. The battle between administrative paternalism and democracy is still going on.

Conclusion

In its cultural projection of the long-term development of Hong Kong, the SAR government has made mixed appeals to localism, nationalism, and globalism. To recapitulate, on the one hand, the government extends the narrative of economic and government success on the local level into a formula of success for the development of world city. More specifically, the smooth transition to a vision of world city is made possible through an appropriation of the discourses of liberalism and capitalist growth that have prevailed since colonial times. On the other hand, the government turns to Chinese culture as the necessary cultural resource to bring about success within the conventionalized framework of "East meets West." Further under the imperative of "one country," the invocation of a Chinese identity—in terms of certain essentialized cultural qualities of Chineseness and also the political principle of Chinese sovereignty—seems to become all the more natural and legitimate. However, as the chapter has shown, the tensions within and among the three levels of concern become dissolved, through certain discursive strategies, without being resolved. More important, such strategies do not hold out the promise of superseding colonialism on the cultural or ideological level.

From a postcolonial point of view, colonialism signifies a system of domination and authoritarianism, the nature of which is often concealed through certain discourses such as a civilizing mission, liberalism, capitalism, stability, and administrative efficiency. This has been the case in Hong Kong. The more successful the concealment, the deeper the impact on the collective psychic structure, and the more difficult it is to supplant colonialism. Chen points out, in a general remark:

> [T]he history of colonial identifications has set limits on the boundaries of the local cultural imaginary, consciously or unconsciously articulated by

and through the institutions of the nation-state, which in turn has shaped our psychic-political geography.[40]

In this light, the HKSAR government's cultural strategy of first absorbing the colonial into the local, and then extending the local into the global, reflects and necessarily results in a lack of critical consciousness of the colonial legacy. Therefore, as we have seen, the government reproduces and even reinforces the same kind of cultural biases—as generated by the discourse of economic success—that have developed within the colonial and local discursive formation. Moreover, it shows a certain degree of idiosyncrasy and conservatism in its interpretation of the meanings of rule of law, individual freedom, and democracy, which is often concealed in the name of political order and administrative effectiveness. Among other things, this paper singles out the narrow culture of localism and also the culture of administrative paternalism as two manifestations of the continuity of colonialism in post-1997 Hong Kong.

If the local and colonial formation is not supplanted, it follows that a simple extension from the local to the global based on the same logic of success will be inadequate as a strategy for transmuting Hong Kong into a multidimensional global city. As the chapter has pointed out, the SAR government fails both to conceive the multiplicity of the vision of global city and to confront the possible tensions between global interests and local interests. The question that remains is how we may progress toward a truly global city, through a critical engagement with the existing literature, while being able to draw on the rich tradition of Chinese culture without essentializing it; how we can acknowledge the principle of Chinese sovereignty without making it absolute; and, most important of all, how we can restore the immediacy and plurality of the local in a democratic way.

Notes

1. For more in-depth discussion of the notion of postcolonialism as a form of cultural critique, see Bill Ashcroft, Gareth Griffiths, and Helen Tiffin, eds., *The Post-Colonial Studies Reader* (London: Routledge, 1995); Chen Kuan-hsing "Introduction: The Decolonization Question," in *Trajectories: Inter-Asia Cultural Studies*, Chen Kuan-hsing, ed. (London: Routledge, 1998); Arif Dirlin, *The Postcolonial Aura: Third World Criticism in the Age of Global Capitalism* (Oxford: Westview Press, 1997); and Jan Nederveen Pieterse and Bhikhu Parekh, "Shifting Imaginaries: Decolonization, Internal Decolonization, Postcoloniality," in *The Decolonization of Imagination—Culture, Knowledge and Power*, Jan Nederveen Pieterse and Bhikhu Parekh, ed. (London: Zed Books, 1995), pp.1–19.

2. P. Ricoeur, *Time and Narrative*, vol. 1 (Chicago: University of Chicago Press, 1985).

3. Agnes S. Ku, "The 'Public' Up Against the State: Narrative Cracks and Credibility Crisis in Post-Colonial Hong Kong," *Theory, Culture and Society* 18, no. 1 (2001): 121–44.

4. Law Wing-seng, ed., *Whose City?* (Hong Kong: Oxford University Press, 1997) (in Chinese); Ren Hai, "The Dialectics of Seeing: Hong Kong on Display" (author's translation), in *Hong Kong in Transition: The Continued Search for Identity and Order*, Liu Qingfeng and Kwan Siu-chun, ed. (Hong Kong: Chinese University of Hong Kong, 1998) (translated from the Chinese).

5. Chief Executive, policy speech (1998).

6. Pieterse and Parekh, "Shifting Imaginaries."

7. Ackbar Abbas, *Culture and the Politics of Disappearance* (Hong Kong: Hong Kong University Press, 1997).

8. Anthony D. King, *Global Cities* (London: Routledge, 1990), p. 38.

9. *Ming Pao*, June 30, 1997.

10. Hong Kong government, *Bringing Vision to Life* (2000).

11. For example, there was a time in Toronto when Tung Chee-hwa, after delivering a speech, was asked whether Shanghai would one day replace Hong Kong as an economic powerhouse. He replied, "I want to make sure Hong Kong is always ahead of Shanghai" (*South China Morning Post*, April 6, 2000).

12. Eric Hobsbawm, and Terence Ranger, *The Invention of Tradition* (New York: Cambridge University Press, 1992); Paul Heelas, Scott Lash, and Paul Morris, *Detraditionalization* (Cambridge, MA: Blackwell, 1996).

13. Policy speech (1996).

14. Abbas, *Culture and the Politics of Disappearance*, pp. 71–72.

15. Policy speech (1997).

16. Hong Kong Government, *Bringing Vision to Life*, section 2.63–2.64.

17. *Hong Kong Hansard Reports of the Sittings of the Legislative Council of Hong Kong* (1897/98), p. 7.

18. In the same occasion in Toronto, Tung Chee-hwa added that what gave other Chinese cities a competitive edge was the "diligence and frugal habits of their inhabitants." In singling out such qualities among mainland Chinese people while overlooking all the others, he shows a very narrow and even limited understanding of the cultural qualities that should characterize the Chinese people, that help vitalize the life of a modern city, and that help develop a truly global city.

19. Policy address (2000).

20. T.L. Lui, "Hong Kong Not to Be Turned into a Local City," *Economic Journal*, February 29, 2000 (author's translation).

21. H.C. Lam, "Time Not Yet Ripe for 'Hong Kong People Ruling Hong Kong,'" *Economic Journal*, June 30, 2000 (author's translation).

22. W. MacNeil, "Righting and Difference," *Human Rights in Hong Kong*, R. Wacks, ed. (Hong Kong: Oxford University Press, 1992), p. 103.

23. For general discussion of the common law tradition in the context of Hong Kong, see Berry Hsu, *The Common Law: In Chinese Context* (Hong Kong: Hong Kong University Press, 1992). For specific discussion of the conflicting legal view points involved in the right-of-abode controversy, see Y.S. Kai, M.M. Chan, and W.L. Fu, *Right of Abode: The Constitutional Disputes* (Hong Kong: Hong Kong University Press, 2000) (in Chinese).

24. Hong Kong Government, *Bringing Vision to Life*.

25. See K.C. Tse, "Educational Reform," in Hong Kong *Social Policy 2000*, K.W.

Chan and C.T. Wong, ed. (Hong Kong: Joint Publishing, 2001) (in Chinese), pp. 17–44.

26. For reference, see Fredric Jameson and Masao Miyoshi, *The Cultures of Globalization* (Durham, NC: Duke University Press, 1998); John Tomlison, *Globalization and Culture* (Chicago: University of Chicago Press, 1998).

27. See Tomlison, *Globalization and Culture.*

28. See, for example, Ng Chun-hung and Tsang Ka-yin, eds., *Crying and Laughing: Ah Poh Narrating History* (Hong Kong: Association for the Advancement of Feminism, 1998).

29. Ma Kit-wai, *Television and Cultural Identification* (Hong Kong: Breakthrough, 1996) (in Chinese); Agnes S. Ku, "The Paradoxical Project of Colonialism: Politics of Local Belonging," speech presented at the Asia-Pacific Sociological Association meeting, Japan (2000).

30. A few days after the handover, the government proposed the Immigration Bill (Amendment No. 5), which requires that mainland-born persons claiming such abode right in Hong Kong prove their status with a certificate of entitlement affixed to a one-way permit that is exclusively available through the exit-entry administration on the mainland. However, at that time, the government had not yet introduced a scheme that would enable the migrant to claim a certificate of entitlement.

31. Agnes S. Ku, "Hegemonic Construction, Negotiation and Displacement: The Struggle over Right of Abode in Hong Kong," *International Journal of Cultural Studies* 4, no. 3 (2001): 259–78.

32. Ibid.

33. The secretary for security and the various policy bureaus released two sets of figures showing that, with the Court of Final Appeal ruling, an estimated 1.67 million people might cross the border, costing taxpayers HK$710 billion (approximately US$5,538 billion) in ten years in the areas of housing, education, medicine, and social welfare, and pushing the unemployment rate up to as high as 18 percent.

34. For discussion on public opinion in relation to the event, see Wong Wai-ho, "Right of Abode, Public Opinion Strategy and Political Development in Hong Kong" (author's translation), *Economic Journal Monthly* no. 269 (August 1999): 43–49 (in Chinese).

35. Ku, "The 'Public' Up Against the State."

36. Ibid.

37. As a newspaper columnist observes, "All that is at default, they (top officials) surmise, is the politicians' and the media's irresponsible behaviour in fanning mass discontent in pursuit of votes and readership. There is a strong sense of bitterness within government circles in the wake of the Wong incident. . . . They maintain that the issues have been unduly politicized. They are still under the illusion that public-office bearers should somehow be left alone to implement their policies in a manner that they see as in the best interests of the public" (A. Ho, *South China Morning Post*, June 27, 2000).

38. Ku, "The 'Public' Up Against the State."

39. A Ho, *South China Morning Post*, October 12, 2000.

40. Chen, "The Colonization Question," p. 2.

15

Conclusion: Crisis and Transformation in the Hong Kong SAR

Toward Soft Authoritarian Developmentalism?

Alvin Y. So and Ming K. Chan

The chapters in this volume have provided detailed analysis on the Democratic Party (DP), the District Council elections, political cleavages, mainland–Hong Kong political interactions, constitutional repositioning, economic performance, urban planning, reform in the education and civil service systems, cultural trends, media politics, and so on. They have greatly enhanced our understanding of the major changes in these areas since the handover. Still, in this conclusion it will be useful to bring their findings together in order to provide a broader perspective in which to examine the development of Hong Kong Special Administrative Region (HKSAR) as a whole.

What really has happened to Hong Kong since July 1, 1997? What are the distinctively new features of the HKSAR? What are the major factors determining the course of Hong Kong's development as a part of the People's Republic of China (PRC)? Finally, in which direction is the HKSAR heading? In order to answer these questions, a "crisis-transformation" framework will be used to highlight the findings in this volume. First, we will examine the five major crises facing the HKSAR, namely, the democracy crisis, the constitutional crisis, the governability crisis, the developmental crisis, and the legitimacy crisis. Then we will discuss the "blessings" that have empowered the various HKSAR actors to deal with these crises, resulting in such transformations as a weakening of democratic forces, constitutional compromise, executive accountability, developmental state, and soft authoritarianism. At the end, we will try to project the trajectory of Hong Kong's development into the future.

The Crises

The HKSAR has been a crisis-ridden city. No sooner did Hong Kong become a SAR of the PRC than various crises propped up. Some crises—such as the democracy crisis, the constitution crisis, and the legitimacy crisis—can be regarded as the legacies inherited from the British colonial era. But the other crises—including the governability crisis and the developmental crisis—are rather unexpected and came as very unpleasant surprises.

The Democracy Crisis

Since the mid-1990s, Hong Kong has seemed to be heading toward a contested democracy. Influenced by the 1989 Tiananmen Incident, the Democratic Party adopted a harshly critical stance toward Beijing. In response, Beijing denounced key DP leaders as "subversive," and PRC officials refused to communicate directly with the DP. Pro-Beijing forces labeled the DP as "pro-British, anti-Beijing, troublemakers in Hong Kong." There were even doubts about whether the DP could legally survive in Hong Kong after the retrocession.

Ming Chan's chapter highlights the fact that Beijing's decision to dismantle Governor Chris Patten's electoral reforms, especially the replacement of the Legislative Council (Legco, which was fully elected in 1995) with the appointed SAR Provisional Legislative Council (PLC), signaled an antidemocratic rollback and disenfranchisement. There was no firm legal basis to force the 1995 elected legislators to step down right after Beijing resumed sovereignty over Hong Kong on July 1, 1997. In protest, DP members chanting "Oppose the provisional legislature, oppose the rubber stamp" frequently demonstrated outside the Xinhua News Agency local office (the PRC's de facto consulate in Hong Kong) before the handover. Most democratic camp activists asserted that because the PLC had no clear legal or constitutional basis under the Basic Law, it was an unlawful and illegitimate body. Subsequently, the DP launched a court challenge to the PLC in early June 1997.

In addition, Chan also points out that the democratic camp as a matter of principal boycotted the proceedings of the Beijing-appointed SAR Selection Committee, which selected Tung Chee-hwa as the first SAR chief executive and also selected the sixty members of the PLC. In return, Tung accused DP chair Martin Lee of "badmouthing" Hong Kong in the international arena. As Lee's "patriotism" was already under hostile scrutiny, there were doubts about whether he would be allowed to play any political role in the HKSAR. It was also feared that the DP would be disallowed to participate in post-1997 local elections.

In early 1997, Lee revealed a plan: Some DP Legco members had threatened to chain themselves to pillars or chairs in the Legco building on the night of June 30, 1997. As many democrats were elected in 1995 to serve a four-year Legco term, they felt they had a right to remain in the Legco to prevent the PLC from taking over after the handover. If they had followed through with the plan by refusing to exit the Legco after June 30, 1997, midnight; if DP Legco members were to be arrested during a political protest; if the DP were barred from reentering electoral politics; or if the PLC was ruled unconstitutional by the courts, a serious democracy crisis that might result in political instability in the new HKSAR would have been triggered.

The Constitutional Crisis

Immediately after the 1997 transition, the PRC Central Government began to largely pursue a "hands-off" policy toward the HKSAR, except for maintaining control of foreign affairs and defense. The People's Liberation Army garrison has stayed nearly invisible. Chinese state leaders have paid only cursory visits to the HKSAR. Analysts have begun to praise Beijing for faithfully keeping its promise to yield Hong Kong a high degree of autonomy in internal affairs.

Still, Benny Tai's chapter provides a very interesting account of the emergence of a constitutional crisis in the SAR (see chapter 7). According to the Basic Law, the HKSAR shall be vested with the power of final adjudication. The Court of Final Appeal (CFA) exercises the power of final adjudication on behalf of the HKSAR. Since the establishment of the CFA itself was a matter of constitutional controversy, it was important to see how the CFA would exercise its authority to deal with the difficult political questions and constitutional disputes.

Not until early 1999 did the CFA have the opportunity to clearly spell out its own constitutional position, as manifested in its controversial decision on the right of abode of the mainland children of Hong Kong parents. According to Article 24 (2)(3) of the Basic Law, the children of Hong Kong permanent residents born outside Hong Kong shall enjoy the right of abode in the HKSAR. Before the sovereignty transfer, these children did not enjoy any legal right of abode in Hong Kong. Anticipating that they could have the right of abode in the HKSAR after the Basic Law came into effect on July 1, 1997, many of these children illegally entered or deliberately overstayed in Hong Kong. Since the HKSAR government feared that the sudden influx of these children might have a strong adverse effect on social services, the PLC enacted amendments to the Immigration Ordinance (such as they must hold a valid entitlement certificate affixed to a PRC one-way exit permit to prove that they did enter Hong Kong legally) limiting the rights of these mainland children to exercise their presumed right of abode. The legality of these Immigration Ordinance amendments was challenged in the HKSAR courts and finally reached the CFA.

According to Tai, after the CFA considered the substantive issues of the case, it held that the PLC's amendment contradicted the Basic Law and was thus invalid. The CFA ruled that the HKSAR exercises a high degree of autonomy and is obliged to admit people who under its constitution are its permanent residents with the legal right of abode, which should not be subject to the discretionary control of mainland authorities.

However, serious criticisms were fired at the CFA from four mainland legal experts. Tai points out that these four experts, who were all involved in the drafting of the Basic Law, criticized the CFA for placing itself above the National People's Congress (NPC) and the Standing Committee of the National People's Congress (SCNPC). They charged that the jurisdiction of the CFA could not be extended to the PRC Central Government in Beijing and the Basic Law has not granted such authority to the CFA. The power of constitutional review as asserted by the CFA is sovereign in nature, and it is thus ridiculous that the CFA should claim such power. Their most serious criticism was that the CFA's judgment would have transformed the Hong Kong SAR into an independent entity beyond Beijing's purview.

It was generally believed that these mainland legal experts could not possibly openly criticize the CFA judgment without Beijing's official blessing. This was soon confirmed, as right after their opinions were publicized, the director of the PRC State Council Information Office insisted that the HKSAR court rulings were wrong and should be reversed. As such, their criticisms could be regarded as a constitutional challenge to the CFA's duty and authority to exercise the power of final adjudication on behalf of the HKSAR. If the CFA and the SAR administration failed to meet this constitutional challenge, then the foundation for the "one country, two systems" formula and the autonomy of the SAR would be fatally undermined.

The Governability Crisis

Although the territory was governed as a British colony, Hong Kong's civic administration had enjoyed a high reputation for efficiency and integrity before 1997. However, as Anthony Cheung's chapter delineates, a "governability crisis" unfolded soon after the handover (see chapter 6).

First, Cheung points to the incompetence and sleaziness of some civil servants, as revealed in two incidents of crisis mismanagement. In December

1997, the confusion and ineptness with which government departments handled the outbreak of the "bird flu" epidemic, and the subsequent slaughter of over 1.2 million chickens and fowls, put the public image of the new SAR government in jeopardy. The chaos during the July 1998 opening of the new and very expensive Chek Lap Kok international airport resulted in huge economic losses in addition to adverse international publicity.

Second, Cheung shows that the SAR bureaucracy was plagued with scandals. Since November 1998, the director of audit has published a series of "value-for-money" audit reports accusing junior civil servants, particularly outdoor staff, of sleaziness and laziness. Not only that, but improprieties involving senior officials were also exposed by the mass media; these officials included a former commissioner of Inland Revenue who failed to report his wife's business as a tax consultant, a former deputy director of Urban Service who rented out his government-provided apartment, and a former director of building who ordered his staff to take immediate action on an illegal structure attached to a private apartment that he was in the process of purchasing as his retirement home. In July 2000, Legco passed a motion of nonconfidence in Housing Authority Chair Rosanna Wong and Director of Housing Tony Miller over the widespread "short-piling" scandals in public housing construction. These reports led to demands by legislators and the community for drastic actions to shape up the civil service.

Third, Cheung reviews the March 1999 Hong Kong government civil service reform plans that aimed to transform an overly rigid permanent system of civil servants into a more market-competitive and flexible workforce in line with prevailing private-sector practices. The main proposals include the introduction of more contract-term appointments, the replacement of retirement pensions by a contributory provident fund, the strengthening of disciplinary mechanisms, the provision for induced voluntary retirement, and the implementation of schemes to link pay with performance.

Staff reactions to civil service reform were highly negative. The reform had created not only anxieties about job security, but also ill feelings among the rank and file, who saw it as an attempt by top officials to score political points by making them scapegoats for the poor leadership and performance of the SAR regime after the handover. As Cheung reports, for the first time in two decades, there were mass demonstrations organized by civil service unions in the summers of 1999 and 2000. Politicians who were affiliated with labor unions unequivocally stood behind the civil servants and the collective labor interests. In sum, the new HKSAR faced a crisis of governability caused by crisis mismanagement, public scandals, poor staff morale, and civil service unrest.

The Developmental Crisis

Before the handover, most forecasts of Hong Kong's economic future were highly optimistic, as the colony had enjoyed a long period of rapid economic growth since the 1980s even while it was under the shadow of 1997. What was not predicted, however, was the damaging social and economic impact of the Asian financial crisis on Hong Kong after 1997.

Francis Lui's chapter confirms that, in just one year after the handover, stock prices plummeted by as much as 60 percent, from the peak in July 1997 to the bottom in August 1998 (see chapter 9). The property market has also been in deep trouble. The sharp decline in real estate value has exceeded the 50 percent mark in many instances, effectively causing investors to reverse their long-held belief that the property value in Hong Kong could only appreciate upward. On the income side, the real-term GDP per capita went down by 7.8 percent in 1998, a negative growth phenomenon almost unknown to Hong Kong, which had not experienced a year of declining GDP in its recent history.

Lui points out that, in January, June, and August 1998, speculative attacks on Hong Kong's currency occurred again and again. Yet the basic tool of defense by the HKSAR regime—a very high interest rate—not only failed to defend Hong Kong's currency but, rather counterproductively, also caused serious damage to the local economy. Unemployment went up sharply from 3 percent in the mid-1990s to more than 6 percent, income went down, and asset value declined sharply. As other Asian economies (such as Thailand, Indonesia, and South Korea) fell victim to the financial crisis, there were grave concerns that Hong Kong might be forced to follow in the footsteps of its distressed and devaluated Asian neighbors.

Although the negative impact of the Asian financial crisis is unmistakable, the economic recession in the post-1997 period also has much deeper structural roots. Starting in the mid-1980s, Hong Kong's robust economy was built upon two legs: its successful functioning as an international financial hub and as a global manufacturing center. However, by the mid-1990s, most of Hong Kong's manufacturing industries already had been relocated to the Pearl River Delta hinterland to take advantage of the much cheaper and more docile labor there. Lui delineates the massive shrinking of the manufacturing sector in Hong Kong, where employment declined from more than 900,000 workers in the 1980s to fewer than 400,000 in the late 1990s. Around 60 percent of the fluctuations in Hong Kong's unemployment can be attributed to this extensive deindustrialization of manufacturing relocation and production shrinkage.

The HKSAR, therefore, has faced a deepening crisis of development since the late 1990s. It must search for a new path of development, given that its industrial base was largely dissipated and its financial base was badly shaken by the Asian financial crisis. What then could the SAR administration do to stop the trend of closing factories and offices, rising unemployment, increasing poverty, and a fast-widening gap of income inequality? And what could the government do to prevent Hong Kong from being overshadowed not only by Singapore but also by other Chinese cities (like Shanghai and even Shenzhen)? The HKSAR's slow and painful economic recovery from the 1997 pan-Asian financial turmoils was again set back if not entirely derailed by the deepening American recession, especially in the aftermath of the September 11, 2001 terrorist attacks. The sharp global economic downturn triggered off by the New York tragedies has already jeopardized the much heralded official investment in and expansion of Hong Kong's tourist industry, global-linked transport networks, and related services, as major sources of earning and employment to replace losses from manufacturing declines in the short term. The vulnerability of Hong Kong's economy to external forces would make the SAR's ongoing economic restructuring an extremely difficult process and thus render very uncertain its government-projected vision of development for the twenty-first-century world city.

The Legitimacy Crisis

From the very beginning, the SAR government has suffered from a legitimacy crisis. There are several sources for this legitimacy crisis. First, the chief executive, the Provisional Legislative Council (PLC), and the Executive Council (Exco) are not popularly elected. Ming Chan's chapter points out that the SAR Exco and the PLC membership reflect the pro-Beijing and pro–big-business bias of the SAR polity (see chapter 3). Their composition as nonelected bodies only deepened their acute lack of public credibility and popular mandate.

Second, lacking electoral legitimacy, the Tung government has to rely upon economic growth and a high standard of living to gain the support of the Hong Kong populace. Unfortunately, Hong Kong's economy suffered a severe setback right after the handover and is still depressed, with neither much effective short-term relief effort nor many uplifting prospects for near-future improvement. Tuen-yu Lau and Yiu-ming To's chapter reports that an all-time high unemployment rate has resulted in further layoffs and retrenchment, while continual plunges in real estate prices have dominated the local news headlines (see chapter 13). Various public opinion surveys since mid-1999 have shown that over two-third of respondents were not satisfied with economic conditions. As in other matters, the SAR government was blamed—

this time, for the serious economic plight of Hong Kong. For instance, University of Hong Kong (HKU) opinion polls between July 1997 and April 1999 showed that fewer than one-quarter of respondents were satisfied with the HKSAR regime's performance. This is hardly an encouraging scorecard for its early performance.

Third, SAR Chief Executive Tung Chee-hwa, as Hong Kong's first home-groomed leader, has to take personal blame for the poor performance of his administration. Though Tung is a decent and honest person, his own dubious democratic legitimacy as the non–popularly elected SAR leader was further weakened by his overtly pro-Beijing slant on sensitive political matters and his narrow, pro–big-business sympathies on domestic socioeconomic policies. When people demanded decisive leadership during the 1997–98 Asian financial crisis, Tung failed to take charge decisively and did not respond with effective countermeasures to relieve the suffering populace, especially the grassroots. In the June 1998 HKU polls, 44 percent of respondents viewed Tung's performance in his first year in office as inferior to that of the last British colonial governor, Christopher Patten. Even today, Tung's public approval ratings remain low, hovering around 50 percent, much lower than the ratings of the two top officials under him.

Fourth, instead of acknowledging the narrow electoral basis of support and lackluster performance of the SAR government, especially on the economic front, various senior officials attributed the legitimacy crisis to negative reporting by the mass media. Lau and To amplify the series of verbal attacks on the mass media by senior officials: Secretary of Justice Elsie Leung condemned the press for being "socially divisive." She lamented that while the mass media in 1984 promoted the positive ideal of reunification with their blessings on the Sino-British Joint Declaration, the media has, since the late 1990s, mistakenly presented a negative image of a post-handover society by highlighting conflicts, confrontations, and controversies. In addition, HKSAR Security Secretary Regina Ip compared the local media with the "dictatorial leaders" portrayed in George Orwell's political satire *Animal Farm*. According to Ip, SAR officials are on trial by the mass media, while the mass media itself is above criticism. These verbal assaults by senior officials have only worsened the officialdom-media relationship, and were perceived as clear threats by the SAR regime to intimidate the mass media. Furthermore, Agnes Ku's chapter shows that the myth of administrative capacity of the Hong Kong government has become so badly shaken since the handover that the once highly praised civil service is now recharacterized and even publicly taunted as incompetent, arrogant, inefficient, unresponsive to popular sentiments, and lacking in real public accountability (see chapter 14). These are also the points vividly outlined by Anthony Cheung.

In sum, the narrow electoral basis of support, the economic recession, the poor public relations, and the worsening government-media relationships—together with the ongoing democracy crisis, the constitutional crisis, the governability crisis, and the developmental crisis—led to a serious legitimacy crisis in Hong Kong. Since the handover, the HKSAR has experienced an unprecedented tidal wave of social protests from the civil society. Government employees in the Housing Department protested against the subcontracting out of their services. Schoolteachers protested the imposition of an English proficiency examination to certify their language skills. Lawyers and overstayers from the mainland protested the SCNPC's restrictive reinterpretations on the right of abode. Students and human rights advocates protested the Public Order Ordinance's repressive clauses. Prodemocratic activists protested the regressive SAR electoral system. Middle-class home owners protested the SAR government's inaction to relieve their crushing negative equity burdens. In addition, there were numerous protests by workers and unionists against plant relocations, business closures, layoffs, worsening work conditions, wage freezes or salary reductions, and other dire threats to the already fast-shrinking rice-bowl bottom line.

The Blessings

Facing one crisis after another within such a short period, other territories might have already fallen into dire conditions such as economic collapse, political instability, social disintegration, and even regime breakdown. Hong Kong, however, has been truly blessed in the sense that several favorable external and internal forces as well as auspicious circumstances have buttressed the ability of key HKSAR actors to confront these crises and make use of the opportunities afforded by Hong Kong's new status as a part of China.

The first of these forces is the positive China factor. During the immediate 1997 transition period, the PRC had a stable national leadership, a relatively cordial relationship with the United States and the other world powers, and an almost uniquely strong growth economy despite the negative influence of the Asian financial crisis. A stable and confident PRC regime enabled its leaders to speak with one voice, to actualize the HKSAR's promised high degree of autonomy without being labeled as betraying Chinese national interests, and to be flexible and even generous when dealing with Hong Kong matters. Friendly ties with the United States and the other Western industrial democracies, as well as glaring attention from the global media, induce Beijing leaders to respond correctly and cautiously to overt attempts to interfere in Hong Kong affairs, let alone to repression of local democratic forces. The mainland's strong and continuous growth directly and significantly strengthens Hong Kong's economy, as the two economies have become even more closely integrated since the mid-1990s.

The second favorable force is the inverted Taiwan factor. In a curious sense, Hong Kong has indirectly benefited from the rising tension between mainland China and Taiwan over the issue of national reunification. After the hostilities of 1995–96, Beijing and Taipei seemed to be on friendlier terms until the Taipei regime's mid-1999 advocacy of the special "state to state" concept, which provoked stern reactions from Beijing, leading to the cancellation of scheduled cross-strait visits and bilateral talks. The victory of the Progressive Democratic Party's Chen Shui-bian in Taiwan's March 2000 presidential election further worsened cross-strait relations. Hong Kong has been the prime "one country, two systems" showcase in the PRC's top-priority drive for peaceful reunification with Taiwan; thus it might seem that the more intense the hostility between Beijing and Taipei, the greater the efforts Beijing would exert to ensure the effective functioning of the HKSAR system with its high degree of autonomy in internal affairs. The rapid souring of Taiwan's economy and the Chen regime's worsening maladministration have yielded various indicators pointing to a marked increase in ratings of Taiwan residents' receptiveness to the "one country, two systems" formula as being actualized in Hong Kong. The recent improvement in Hong Kong–Taiwan functional links (such as simplified HKSAR entry procedures for Taiwan visitors) underlines Hong Kong's continued usefulness and vitality in mainland–Taiwan interfaces for economic purposes and human traffic.

The third favorable force is the timing of the retrocession. Hong Kong was perhaps fortunate because the Asian financial crisis broke out only *after* the PRC had effectively resumed sovereignty over Hong Kong on July 1, 1997. Had this crisis broken out a year or even just a few months earlier, it might have triggered not only simply an economic recession but also a serious situation of social instability with widespread labor unrest and class conflicts, thus further complicating the preexisting crisis of confidence in Hong Kong's uncertain post-1997 prospects. This could be a most fortuitous case of historical timing when considering the very different consequences of the two contrasting scenarios. Although at its inauguration it escaped by only a few days a direct assault from the Asian financial meltdown, the new HKSAR is still engulfed by serious economic woes that have depressed the lives and work of many, as the unexpected growing pains of its infancy. Still, unlike the Macau SAR, which was established in December 1999 under economic dark clouds, the HKSAR was able to enjoy a celebration at its moment of birth.

Finally, Hong Kong could still be regarded as rather blessed because these crises impacted at a time when the territory had already built up a basically sound economic foundation to weather the pan-Asian financial turmoil. In

1997, the HKSAR government inherited from the earlier growth era with many fat years of budget surplus a very substantial pool of fiscal and foreign exchanges reserves. Such valuable and highly liquid resources should enable and equip it to respond creatively to the challenges of the Asian economic crisis, the developmental crisis, and the legitimacy crisis. The stock market intervention of August 1998 reflected, among other things, the impressive financial war chest at the SAR's direct command. In a technical sense, the HKSAR regime could, as proposed in Tung Chee-hwa's fifth policy speech on October 10, 2001, still afford to proceed with massive infrastructure projects as longer-term uplifting measures, and could continue to operate on a deficit budget in the current economic recession.

In sum, Hong Kong has indeed been well blessed by the China factor, the indirect fallout bonus from rising cross-strait tension, the fortunate timing of the crises, and the abundant financial resources that the SAR government still commands. Thus, even though these crises had shattered the confidence of many Hong Kong residents, key actors in the SAR are not entirely powerless in coping with these crises. The next section examines the profound transformations that the HKSAR has been undergoing as the actors and objective forces have interacted to make strategic decisions both to confront the challenges and to utilize the new opportunities for being a part of the PRC.

The Transformations

Democratic Compromise and a Weakened Democratic Party

A full-blown democracy crisis was soon averted after July 1, 1997, by the democratic compromise between Beijing and the Democratic Party. Ming Chan's chapter points out how DP leadership subtly modified its previous hostile stance toward the PRC leadership from harshly critical and condemning (following the June 4 Tiananmen Incident) to a more moderate critical tone (see chapter 3). The DP staged only a peaceful protest during the July 1, 1997, transition. It was also eager to participate in the 1998 elections, even though the Beijing-appointed Provisional Legislative Council (PLC) had so drastically changed the electoral rules that the democratic camp would have little chance to gain a majority in the post-1997 legislature. The DP diluted its anti-Beijing platform by emphasizing that it has always been "patriotic," as it has supported the PRC's resumption of sovereignty and has worked for Hong Kong's stability and prosperity.

In fact, Beijing has gradually yielded some limited political space for the Hong Kong democrats in the post-1997 era. The democrats were allowed to compete in the SAR elections, and local political protests were tolerated.

Beijing took no direct action even when local protesters shouted pro-democracy and pro–human rights slogans at Chinese communist leaders on their Hong Kong visit. Perhaps Beijing was confident that, once the DP was forced to operate under the regressive new electoral rules, it could not pose too much of a threat to the SAR regime as the Basic Law already entailed a restrictive framework to limit the power of the democratic forces. In the SAR's first legislative elections in 1998, only twenty seats were directly elected in the geographical constituencies, with the rest of the forty seats indirectly elected through functional constituencies (thirty seats) and through the small Election Committee (ten seats). In fact, the DP and its allies, because of their boycott of the PLC, failed to exert any influence on the design of new electoral rules that aimed to marginalize the democratic forces in the legislature.

First, the single-seat, first-past-the-post system in the 1995 geographical constituency elections was abandoned. Instead, the PLC adopted a proportional representation system for future SAR Legco direct elections. For the twenty directly elected seats in 1998, for example, Hong Kong was divided into five geographical constituencies, each returning three to five legislators. Candidates from either a party or a coalition would contest in each constituency. The number of seats allocated would depend on the percentage of votes they secured. This proportional representation system for the geographical seats aimed at intensifying the competition among the pro-democracy forces themselves. As Chan's chapter explains, under the proportional representation system, a political party participating in the direct election is required to put up a candidate list, and if there is more than one candidate, then the party candidates must be listed in ranking order for the geographical constituency. Candidates ranked at the top of the party list naturally stand a much better chance of getting elected than those with lower ranking. The need to work out an official party list of ranked candidates to contest the direct elections brought into the open the factional discords, personality clashes, and policy disagreements within the party ranks, as it was the case of the DP in 1998 and 2000.

Second, the PLC imposed a new parliamentary rule: Legco members cannot introduce bills that are related to public expenditure, political structure, or the operation of the government. As Benny Tai's chapter elucidates, for bills that are not related to these items, members still have to get the written consent of the chief executive if government policies are involved (see chapter 7). In other words, there is nothing of real significance that Legco members can introduce. This new rule is intended to marginalize the influence of democratic camp members in the Legco, as private member bills were important means for them to challenge the government on controversial issues and crucial decisions.

Third, the PLC also adopted a different procedure for the passage of private members bills and amendments. Tai explains that the passage of motions, bills, or amendments, introduced by Legco members to government legislation, would require a simple majority vote of each of the two groups of members present. The first group includes members returned by functional constituencies and the second group includes those returned by geographical constituencies through direct elections and by the Election Committee. In practice, it will be very difficult for the SAR Legco to pass any bill that is against the interests of the business class and the pro-Beijing bloc, whose combined strength has dominated the Legco since the 1998 elections.

Ming Chan shows that some DP "Young Turks," after feeling politically disempowered or even legislatively crippled by the above arrangements to roll back democracy, proposed a long-term walkout from both the Legco and the District Councils so as to take their fight against the SAR government directly into the street with public protests and demonstrations (see chapter 3). Although party senior leaders turned down their radical proposal, it created a deep internal division with the DP. The DP was deeply wounded by internal strife, unsure of its own class identity or socioeconomic constituencies, and unable to provide an effective platform on rice-bowl issues. These factors, along with the fading away of the negative fear-of-China factor and hence the direct relevance of its previous anti-Chinese communism stance, have led to the decline of the DP in electoral politics, as evidenced in the September 2000 Legco contests.

Shiu-hing Lo, Wing-yat Yu, and Kwok-fai Wan report that in the 1999 District Council elections, the democratic forces had lost their dominance in the electoral arena. The democratic forces received only about the same vote as the pro-Beijing camp, because the "patriotic forces" had much better coordination, organization, and mobilization than the democratic camp. Later, in the 2000 Legco elections, the DP saw its share of popular votes further decline to only 35 percent from 43 percent in 1998. Thus the once mythlike overwhelming electoral success record of the DP was finally broken.

Ngok Ma's chapter further delineates the new situation: Due to the change of the electoral system, a more pluralized cleavage structure in Hong Kong polity emerged after 1997 (see chapter 4). The change in cleavage patterns would pose a major challenge to the democrats in Hong Kong. Facing multiple new fault lines and the new proportional representation system, the democrats would find it extremely difficult to adopt a new ideological position or issue package to capture a wide range of supporters across multiple-issue fault lines, as they were able to do before 1997. The new pluralized cleavages would lead to the fragmentation of the democracy movement in Hong Kong, thus facilitating stronger executive control by the SAR regime.

Defending the Rule of Law Through Constitutional Compromise

How did the SAR government and the Court of Final Appeal (CFA) deal with the constitutional crisis? Benny Tai's chapter documents their constitutional repositioning in response to the constitutional challenge waged informally from the four mainland legal experts (see chapter 7). Instead of waiting for Beijing to formally invalidate the CFA's ruling as wrong, or declaring that the CFA had exceeded its authority in making such a decision (which then would have spelled the end of the CFA's authority), the SAR regime resorted to the measures described below, to preserve the rule of law in Hong Kong while trying to escape from the social and economic consequences of a massive influx of "legal" children immigrants from the mainland.

First, the secretary for justice representing the HKSAR government made an application to the CFA requesting a clarification of the constitutional jurisdiction of the HKSAR courts. The CFA accepted the application and exercised what it considered to be the inherent jurisdiction of the court to make a clarification. In its clarification, the CFA stated that the SAR courts have no power to question the authority of the NPC and its SCNPC to undertake any action, which is in accordance with the Basic Law and the procedure therein. Beijing seemed to be satisfied with this clarification, and the first wave of challenge against the CFA was settled after this act of the HKSAR judiciary's rearticulation of self-restraint.

Second, after a motion was approved in the HKSAR Legco, Chief Executive Tung Chee-hwa requested the central government's assistance to seek the SCNPC's reinterpretation of Basic Law Article 24(2)(3). As a result, the SCNPC did reinterpret the two provisions, which in effect overturned the CFA's original decisions. On the basis of the SCNPC's interpretation, the CFA was forced to make a constitution compromise; it reversed its previous ruling, and decided against those who applied for the right of abode in Hong Kong for their mainland children

As Tai explains, the CFA did not have many choices. The SCNPC had already issued an interpretation overruling the CFA's verdict. The CFA could not play with words to avoid direct conflict with the central government without changing its own stance. On the other hand, if the CFA refused to accept the authority of the SCNPC to issue such an interpretation, this would be a direct challenge to the supreme authority of the central government, and this might invite Beijing to interfere further with the affairs of the HKSAR. In sum, the CFA has decided that the constitution is far more important as the guardian of the rule of law than as the guardian of Hong Kong's high degree of autonomy and human rights, with the hope of avoiding open conflict with the central government so as to prevent any further direct interference from Beijing.

Governability Crisis and Executive Accountability

Anthony Cheung's chapter contends that facing the looming governability crisis, the new SAR government quietly toned down the highly unpopular civil service reform in order not to agitate civil servants further (see chapter 6). In February 2000 Lam Woon-kwong, who spearheaded the civil service reform, was replaced by Joseph Wong as the secretary for the civil service. The SAR government has given up the previous proposal to eventually turn all basic ranks (representing two-thirds of the civil service) into contract posts. It also conceded that a full-fledged performance-related pay system is difficult to develop.

In addition, Cheung reports that Chief Executive Tung Chee-hwa became interested in "executive accountability" when considering the question of governance. Tung noted that the Legco and the community have expressed the view that as principal officials (the chief secretary of administration, the financial secretary, the secretary of justice, and other secretaries) are involved in policy making and in playing leading roles in public affairs, they should be held accountable for the outcome of their policies.

But how to make principal officials accountable? Cheung outlines the several proposals. First, Tung's sympathizers and the pro-Beijing bloc have criticized the top civil servants under the leadership of Chief Secretary for Administration Anson Chan for not offering Tung sufficient support and full loyalty. Tung's supporters place the blame for the looming governability crisis on the lack of cooperation by the senior civil servants and their sheer incompetence. Subsequently, Tung's supporters used this opportunity to propose a more "presidential" style of executive government, with more loyal and politically reliable "outsiders" recruited from the private sector into the SAR government as principal officials. Tung could then pick his own team with top officials from the private sector rather than drawing them entirely from the existing pool of senior career civil servants inherited from the British colonial administration.

Second, senior officials nevertheless favor a civil service–dominated system. The regular civil service continues to be the main supply source for politically appointed policy bureau secretaries. What the senior officials prefer is the introduction of a new "political contract" for the secretaries who form a clear "political" layer, with existing senior civil servants invited to leave their civil service terms to accept appointment on new "ministerial" terms, that is, working in full tandem with the chief executive on both political and policy agenda, and being prepared to step down to take political responsibility for policy blunders or in case of policy disagreement.

Third, another proposal was offered by the Business and Professionals Federation, which envisaged that future Exco members will become "policy councilors," with clear policy responsibility, and will work closely with principal officials who have to relinquish their positions as career civil servants and be offered contract terms as appointed executive councilors themselves. These "policy councilors" will be appointed, will work full time, will be remunerated adequately, and will be expected to become spokespersons for their policy area, so as to explain and defend policies before the legislature. In practical terms, they will become full-time "ministers," overseeing senior officials who still head the various bureaus and departments, while the Exco will in effect become the real cabinet of the chief executive. The October 2001 policy speech tentatively suggested a combination of key elements from these three lines of thought on the new "political appointees" system that should become operational starting with the SAR chief executive's second term in July 2002.

Developmental State and Global High-Tech City

Berry Hsu's chapter discusses how the new SAR government responded to the challenge of the Asian financial crisis (see chapter 8). In August 1998, the global effects of the Asian financial crisis led to a major speculative attack on the Hong Kong dollar. In order to defend the local dollar's peg to the U.S. dollar and the local financial markets, the HKSAR government finally responded with a full-scale counterattack on August 15, 1998. Taking no decisive direct action would risk a 50 percent surge in interest rates and the substantial drop in the Hang Seng Index of the local stock market. This would further depress property prices, and would impose enormous pressure on the banking system that held the mortgages.

Hsu points out that in order to restore investor confidence in the financial markets, the SAR government decided to deploy its sizable Exchange Fund to purchase shares in selected "blue-chip" companies. As a result of the SAR regime's two-week direct intervention in the financial markets, all external speculative attacks faded. The total cost of the share acquisition by the SAR government amounted to US$15.2 billion. A consequence of such a colossal injection of funds was that it turned the SAR government into the single largest shareholder in the Hong Kong and Shanghai Banking Corporation (HSBC) and other locally listed business concerns. Subsequently, the regime did make profits on the initial investment in these acquired shares, but the public who later purchased units of a fund based on these shares have sustained losses due to the declining stock market since early 2001.

In addition, Hsu outlines the seven measures adopted by the SAR government to strengthen the currency board arrangements, and its thirty proposed measures to strengthen the order and transparency of the securities and futures market. Belatedly, the government tightened the rules on short selling and settlement; it also streamlined the autonomic trading systems that in the past had enabled speculators to take advantage of a delay in the settlement process.

The significance of the August 1998 official direct intervention is not only that it worked to defend the HK currency and strengthened its U.S. dollar–linked exchange rate, but also that it marked the advent of a developmental state in Hong Kong. The action of buying US$15.2 billion worth of stocks has gone far beyond the confines of the previously enshrined but hollow policy of "positive nonintervention," not to mention the once-celebrated colonial hallmark of a laissez-faire state. Since then, the SAR government has presented a new plan of transforming Hong Kong into a global high-tech city. The aim was to promote the development of a new technology-based and high-value-added sector in order to strengthen the long-term competitiveness of Hong Kong's increasingly knowledge-based economy.

The SAR government set up a high-powered Commission on Innovation and Technology (CIT), chaired by Professor Tien Chang-Lin of Berkeley, to guide Hong Kong's transformation into a high-tech center. In its first report, the CIT stated that Hong Kong will be an innovation-led, technology-intensive economy in the twenty-first century. In this vision, Hong Kong will be a leading city in the world for information technology (IT), a world hub for health food and pharmaceuticals based on Chinese medicine, a leading supplier in the world of high value-added components and products, a regional center for multimedia-based information and entertainment services, and a marketplace for technology transfer between mainland China and the rest of the world. In March 1999, the HKSAR government announced plans to build Cyberport, a US$1.7 billion technology park in Pokfulam aimed to create a strategic cluster of leading IT and service companies in Hong Kong in the shortest possible time. The project is expected to generate more than twelve thousand jobs in Hong Kong, while approximately four thousand jobs will be created in the construction industry to build Cyberport. Upon completion in 2002, Cyberport will generate demands for support services such as accounting, legal, and other back office functions. Such a full hand of government intervention in economic development seems to reflect Tung's paternalistic vision of his SAR regime's interactions with society. Lawrence Lai's chapter gives substance to this kind of interventionist approach to development planning and resource allocation (see chapter 10). However, the optimism of the Tung regime in such a "high-tech" grand vision for Hong Kong's rosy future developmental course has been reigned in by the dark realities of continuing recession that was recently further deepened by the second external blow assaulting the HKSAR in its first four years, the September 11, 2001, events' global effects.

Legitimacy Crisis and Soft Authoritarianism

How did the SAR government deal with the legitimacy crisis? Agnes Ku's chapter points out that the SAR government has appropriated the discourse of democracy and then incorporated it into the hegemonic discourse of governing success (see chapter 14). For instance, after repeated setbacks and glaring failures resulting in serious state-society disconnect, the HKSAR officialdom begins to actively mobilize its political machinery and communicative resources to maintain power by increasing publicity as well as strengthening its public relations skills. Senior officials work hard to develop better media publicity as a redress against a deficiency in their public communication skills. Their aim is to displace the democracy discourse through a modified paternalistic-administrative discourse that includes the practice of media publicity in its expectation for a more favorable public relations outcome.

Aside from improving its public relations skills, the SAR government is moving toward a practice which can be called "soft authoritarianism."[1] Tuen-yu Lau and Yiu-ming To's chapter argues that, since its establishment, the SAR government has entered a new age with obsolete laws (see chapter 13). It imposes restrictions on freedom of assembly and association, allegedly infringing human rights, by reviving discarded repressive provisions of the Public Order Ordinance and the Societies Ordinance that had been repealed by the colonial regime before 1997. These laws laid the foundation for the "soft authoritarianism" of the SAR government as they stipulate that demonstration with more than thirty participants should seek prior police approval, disguised in the form of a "no-objection" notice by the police. Association should first register with government approval before it becomes a legal organization. The concept of "national security" is also introduced as a criterion for the police to decide whether or not a demonstration or an association should be approved. Accordingly, the police will ban activities it regards as advocating the independence of Hong Kong, Taiwan, or Tibet. These repressive measures not only could undermine civil liberties but also curb the scope of freedom of speech and of the press.

Suzanne Pepper's chapter also points out that the Basic Law actually has provided the ground for authoritarianism because its Article 23 mandated special local legislation to prohibit subversion against the PRC Central Government, the theft of state secrets, and political activities by foreign organizations, as well as ties between them and counterparts in the SAR (see chapter 2). If Basic Law Article 23 were fully implemented, vigorously enforced as stated, and rigidly interpreted according to non–common law legal concepts as done elsewhere in the PRC, the implications would be grave indeed for Hong Kong's political life. The result would be prison terms, an underground existence, or at least drastically curtailed freedoms of speech and association for Hong Kong's most popular political leaders.

Nevertheless, the SAR government has been exercising obvious self-constraint in avoiding to invoke these repressive laws to deal with the legitimacy crisis. Except in a couple of cases where student protesters outside SAR government offices were arrested and prosecuted, the SAR administration has generally tolerated antiregime protests without making any arrest even though the protest movements leaders had declared in public that they would seek no prior approval from the police. Still, the SAR government has resorted to various means to intimidate these protesters, such as deploying a disproportionately very large police force supposedly to keep order and social peace (as sometimes there were many more policemen than protesters!), videotaping the demonstrations, and making public threats that the SAR government has reserved the right to prosecute even the nonarrested protesters later on (the police's preemptive seizure of a peaceful protesters' vehicle and arrest of its passengers some distance from the protest target site of a *Fortune* magazine global forum were ruled illegal by a local court in October 2001, perhaps a reflection of the HKSAR regime's obsession with internal security and overdeployment of suppressive capacity).

The Beijing authorities, too, have been using a strategy of "soft authoritarianism" to deal with the civil society in Hong Kong. Lau and To report that in March 2000 the Wharf Cable Television news channel interview of Anne Lu Hsiu-lien, then the Taipei regime's vice president–elect, provoked strong criticism by Wang Fengchao (deputy director of the PRC Central Government Liaison Office in Hong Kong). Wang charged that Hong Kong's mass media should fulfill its duty and responsibility to safeguard Chinese national unity and territorial integrity by refraining from reporting the views of "Taiwan independence" advocates. In October 2000, the criticisms of Hong Kong's mass media by PRC President Jiang Zemin, who labeled Hong Kong's journalists as "too simple and naive," sent shock waves to Hong Kong.

Like the SAR government, the PRC government so far has generally exercised considerable "self-constraint" and takes no further direct action to follow upon their criticisms of the Hong Kong media. Still, as Lau and To remark, repeated messages by Beijing officials served to forewarn or discipline Hong Kong's media, with the aim of establishing clear norms of political

correctness without resorting to enacting repressive press laws. Beijing officials are always ready to set guidelines for media practice, as well as issuing
warnings on unacceptable performance by individual journalists whom they
regard as having overstepped the proper bound of press freedom.

Future Trajectories

The above discussions on transformations illuminate how Hong Kong is
heading toward a pattern of "soft authoritarian developmentalism." The SAR
government is developmental in the sense that it is much more active in
guiding and promoting the economy with a very visible hand than the pre-
1997 colonial regime. Not only did it intervene in the stock market in 1998,
but it has also formulated a plan to propel the HKSAR into a global high-
tech city as well as launching numerous far-reaching reforms in civil service, housing, education, medical, and welfare, to increase Hong Kong's
quality of life and its economic competitiveness in the global arena. Perhaps to
some extent an active interventionist state is now needed to solve the developmental crisis, while strong economic performance will also do much in helping to solve the HKSAR regime's own lingering legitimacy crisis as well.

While an executive-led government facilitated the state's capacity to embark onto a developmental track, it also laid the foundation for "soft
authoritarianism." The weakening of the democratic camp and the constitutional compromise through which the CFA sets its own limits have
emboldened and empowered the SAR regime to impose its decision over the
civil society. The proposal for "executive accountability," if properly carried
out, would directly strengthen the loyalty of senior officials to the chief executive, as they not only will be appointed by and solely accountable to, but
serve only at the pleasure of and be easily dismissed by the chief executive.
Yet, this system will only strengthen the chief executive's direct control of
the SAR regime's decision process and buttress his personal command over
the entire state machinery, but not adding to the regime's accountability to
the Legco or to the public at large.

Since the Public Order Ordinance and the Society Ordinance, together
with Article 23 of the Basic Law, have already laid the legal groundwork for
authoritarianism in Hong Kong, it is due only to the self-constraint of both
the SAR government and the Beijing authorities that, until now, such
authoritarianism has been taking a relatively more subtle "soft" form of in-
timidation and surveillance, rather than being manifested through a "hard"
form of outright suppression, arrests, and imprisonment. In order to make
such soft authoritarianism work, the civil society also must play the soft
game. Thus, the DP has become only moderately critical of Beijing, the mass

media owners exercise self-censorship in reporting, protestors stage mostly peaceful demonstrations, and gradually more Hong Kong SAR residents are openly displaying stronger patriotic sentiments for Chinese national interests, such as the July 9, 2001, spontaneous popular celebrations with genuine enthusiasm on the streets of Hong Kong for Bejing's successful bid to host the 2008 Olympic Games.

However, since soft authoritarian developmentalism depends very much on the key actors' mutual self-constraint (rather than on repressive institutions and coercive procedures in public life) in order to function well, this is only a rather fragile and tacit pact among the actors. The trajectory of the HKSAR's development, therefore, is still very fluid and its future course is filled with great uncertainties. Using soft authoritarian development as the baseline, there seem to be three alternative paths of development.

First, the HKSAR could be transformed to an "authoritarian developmental regime" like that in mainland China today. If the democratic forces fail to exercise adequate self-constraint, if the protests in the civil society become too massive and violent, or if the HKSAR activists overtly support either the democratic activists on the mainland or the advocates for "Taiwan independence," this could provoke the SAR government to invoke Basic Law Article 23 (which has yet to be codified and enacted into local law) or the Societies Ordinance provisions. Hard-core authoritarianism then could be rationalized as a necessary evil in order to maintain SAR local order or Chinese national security and to promote rapid economic development for the cherished "stability and prosperity" of Hong Kong.

Second, the HKSAR could be transformed into a case of "democratic developmentalism" like that in South Korea. If the democratic forces were united, and if they received strong support from the aroused civil society for winning elections and dominating the legislature, they could eventually trim down the repressive laws, open the entire Legco for direct elections, and speed up the democratic process to elect the chief executive on a one-person–one-vote, universal franchise. Full-fledged liberal democracy then could be justified as a necessary and desirable step if Hong Kong wants to join the front rank of global financial hubs and high-tech centers, which are all located in advanced industrial democracies.

Finally, the HKSAR could be transformed into a caring and enlightened "populist welfare state" like that in the Scandinavian countries. The democratic forces become so strong, their popular impulses are so overwhelming, and the defeat of the pro-business conservative interests in elections is of such wide margins that the democrats could ultimately impose their own populist, proenvironment, and extensive entitlement welfare agenda on Hong Kong's development. The HKSAR government then would become a redistributive state, promoting equality, social justice, and grassroots democracy, perhaps at the expense of unchecked marketization and the pursuit of blind "GNPism."

At present, the HKSAR under Tung Chee-hwa's leadership seems to be embarking on the path of soft authoritarian developmentalism. With Beijing's blessing and the tycoons' endorsement, but despite the reservations of many in the middle class and the grassroots (including those in the patriotic bloc), it is clear that the present HKSAR regime is tilted more toward authoritarian developmentalism than toward democratic developmentalism, let alone populist welfarism. The second-term reelection of Tung Chee-hwa as SAR chief executive will only continue this major trend into the late 2000s, perhaps with an even stronger determination and a more effective hand, now that he has been baptized by the hard lessons of his disappointing first five-year tenure.

As mainland China has evolved very extensively through the last two decades of marketization, privatization, and international economic opening, the possibility that the PRC party-state will eventually adopt selected aspects of European-style social democratic ideologies and pluralistic political practices to further reform itself amid the strong globalization trends should not be entirely ruled out in the long run. The PRC's rising international prestige as an upcoming world power, which was clearly reflected in the October 2001 Asia-Pacific Economic Cooperation (APEC) summit in Shanghai, could be a sign for the future. The PRC's formal entry into the World Trade Organization (WTO) in late 2001 and Beijing's hosting of the 2008 Summer Olympic games, along with the mainland's exceptionally strong and uninterrupted economic growth all bode well for positive further reshaping of the Chinese state and society in the early decades of the new millennium. By then, the developmental paths of the Chinese mainland and the HKSAR might share many more common patterns and overlapping features, which would immeasurably enhance the full reintegration of these two parts of the modern Chinese nation.

Note

We want to thank Xueliang Ding for his comments on an earlier version of this chapter.

1. The concept of "soft authoritarianism" has been further developed in Alvin Y. So, "Social Protests, Legitimacy Crises, and the Impetus Toward Soft Authoritarianism in the Hong Kong SAR." In *The Tung Group: The First Five Year of the Hong Kong Special Administrative Region*, Siu-kai Lau, ed. (Hong Kong: Chinese University Press, forthcoming).

The Editors
and Contributors

The Editors

Ming K. Chan is a research fellow and executive coordinator of the Hong Kong Documentary Archives, Hoover Institution, Stanford University. He was a member of the history department, University of Hong Kong, from 1980 to 1997. He is general editor of the *Hong Kong Becoming China* series published by M.E. Sharpe, with an Asian paperback version by Hong Kong University Press. His edited volumes in this series include *The Hong Kong Basic Law: Blueprint for "Stability and Prosperity" Under Chinese Sovereignty?* (1991) and *Precarious Balance: Hong Kong Between China and Britain, 1842–1992* (1994). Ming Chan's most recent and forthcoming books are: *The Hong Kong Reader: Passage to Chinese Sovereignty* (M.E. Sharpe, 1996, coedited with G. Postiglione), *The Challenge of Hong Kong's Reintegration with China* (1997), *The China Factor and Hong Kong External Links, 1842–1997*, and *Historical Dictionary of the Hong Kong SAR and the Macau SAR* (with S.H. Lo).

Alvin Y. So is a professor in the Division of Social Science at the Hong Kong University of Science and Technology. His research interests are social class and development in Hong Kong, China, and East Asia. His recent publications include *Hong Kong's Embattled Democracy* (Johns Hopkins University Press, 1999), *Asia's Environment Movements: Comparative Perspective* (coedited, M.E. Sharpe, 1999), *Survey Research in Chinese Societies* (coeditor, 2001), *The Chinese Triangle of Mainland China-Taiwan-Hong Kong* (coeditor, 2001).

The Contributors

Anthony B. L. Cheung is a professor in the Department of Public and Social Administration at the City University of Hong Kong. With a main research focus on comparative public management reform in Asia, he has published extensively on privatization, civil service, and public-sector reforms.

He also writes about government and politics in Hong Kong and China. His articles have appeared in major international journals such as *International Review of Administrative Sciences, International Journal of Public Administration, Journal of Contemporary China, Asian Survey, Asian Journal of Public Administration,* and *Asian Journal of Political Science.* His recent books on Hong Kong are *The Civil Service in Hong Kong: Continuity and Change* (coauthor, 1998) and *Public Sector Reform in Hong Kong: Into the 21st Century* (coeditor, 2001).

Berry Fong-Chung Hsu, is an associate professor in law in the Department of Real Estate and Construction and a professorial fellow of the Asian Institute of International Financial Law at the University of Hong Kong. Dr. Hsu, a chartered engineer of the British Engineering Council, is also a barrister and solicitor of the Supreme Court of Victoria and the High Court of New Zealand. He is the author of numerous academic papers and monographs, including *Laws of Banking and Finance in the Hong Kong SAR* and *Laws of Taxation in the Hong Kong SAR.*

Agnes S. Ku is an assistant professor of sociology at the Division of Social Science, Hong Kong University of Science and Technology. She is the author of *Narratives, Politics, and the Public Sphere—Struggles over Political Reform in the Final Transitional Years in Hong Kong* (1999). Her recent publications include several articles on civil society, public sphere, identity politics, and democratic struggle in *Theory, Culture and Society, Sociological Theory* and *International Journal of Cultural Studies.*

Lawrence Wai-chung Lai worked as an executive officer, town planner, and environmental protection officer with the British Hong Kong government and is now associate professor in the Department of Real Estate and Construction, University of Hong Kong. He is a Registered Professional Planner in Hong Kong and has corporate memberships at the Royal Australian Planning Institute, the Hong Kong Institute of Planners, and the Chartered Institute of Transport. His current research focus is on the property rights aspects of urban planning and sustainable development.

Tuen-yu Lau is the director of the newly launched masters of communication program in digital media in the School of Communications at the University of Washington–Seattle. He has been a management executive for media companies in Hong Kong and Southeast Asia. He was a working journalist and news documentary producer for the leading TV network in Hong Kong in the early 1980s. He taught at Purdue University and was visiting professor at the University of California–Los Angeles (UCLA) and the University of Hong Kong, and a visiting scholar at the Hoover Institution, Stanford University. He is an editorial consultant for the Asia Pacific Media Network at UCLA.

Shiu-hing Lo teaches Hong Kong politics at the University of Hong Kong. His most recent work is *Governing Hong Kong: Legitimacy, Communication and Political Decay* (2002). He has also co-authored a number of articles and book chapters on Hong Kong politics with Wing-yat Yu and Kwok-fai Wan. He is working on several book projects on greater China subjects, including *Historical Dictionary of the Hong Kong SAR and Macau SAR* (with Ming K. Chan).

Francis T. Lui is a professor in the Department of Economics and the director of the Center for Economic Development at the Hong Kong University of Science and Technology. His research interests include endogenous growth models, social security systems, population economics, corruption, currency attacks, and the economies of Hong Kong and China. He has published six books and numerous articles in leading journals such as the *Journal of Political Economy*, the *Journal of Public Economics*, and the *Journal of Economic Dynamics and Control*. He is also a writer for the popular press and a well-known commentator on current economic affairs in Hong Kong.

Ngok Ma is an assistant professor in the Division of Social Science, Hong Kong University of Science and Technology. As a political scientist he specializes in the elections and party politics of Hong Kong on which he has published various book chapters and articles. His other research interests include political economy in Hong Kong, East European transition, and social movements in Hong Kong.

Suzanne Pepper is a Hong Kong–based American writer. She is the author, among other titles, of *Civil War in China: The Political Struggle, 1945–1949* (1978, 1980; 2d ed., 1999)

Gerard A. Postiglione is an associate professor and the director of the Center for Research on Education in China at the University of Hong Kong. His work on higher education focuses on how globalization is affecting the academy, especially in Hong Kong and mainland China. In recent years, he has edited a volume entitled *Asian Higher Education* (1997) and published a number of articles on higher education for the Organization for Economic Cooperation and Development (OECD), the American Council on Education, the Carnegie Foundation for the Advancement of Teaching, Comparative Education Review, Education and Society, and the Chronicle of Higher Education. He continues to be a general editor of the *Hong Kong Becoming*

China series by M.E. Sharpe, and of the *Hong Kong Culture and Society* series by Hong Kong University Press.

Chao Fen Sun is currently an associate professor and the chair of the Department of Asian Languages at Stanford University. His main research interests are the history of Chinese, Chinese syntax, and the sociocultural aspects of the Chinese languages. His major publications include *Studies on the History of Chinese Syntax* (editor); a 1997 *Journal of Chinese Linguistics* monograph, *Word-Order Change and Grammaticalization in the History of Chinese* (1996); and a number of articles on various topics in Chinese linguistics published in the *Journal of Chinese Linguistics, Language,* and other academic journals.

Benny Y. Tai is an assistant professor in Law at the University of Hong Kong, where he specializes in Hong Kong constitutional law. His research interests include human rights, legal education, administrative law, and comparative constitutional law. His recent publications include "Why Second-Generation Mainland Children Have No Right of Abode in Hong Kong" in the *Hong Kong Law Journal* (1999); "The Development of Constitutionalism in Hong Kong" in R. Wacks, ed., *The New Legal Order in Hong Kong* (1999); and "Constitutional Law" in A. Chen et al., eds., *General Principles of Hong Kong Law* (1999).

Yiu-ming To was a journalist before he joined the Hong Kong Baptist University, where he is now assistant professor in journalism. He is interested in studying political communication and press ethics, and is also an active freelance writer on public affairs. He is a three-time winner of the Human Rights Press Award for commentary (1999–2001).

Kwok-fai Wan is a political commentator on Hong Kong affairs. His University of Hong Kong masters thesis in philosophy focuses on China's policy toward Hong Kong. He coedited (with S.H. Lo) a special issue of *Chinese Law and Government* on Hong Kong's 2000 legislative elections. His commentaries on Hong Kong affairs focus on China's relations with Hong Kong, political and constitutional reforms, and public administration.

Wing-yat Yu teaches politics at the Hong Kong University of Science and Technology and at the University of Macau. His University of Hong Kong doctoral dissertation in progress focuses on party development and democratization in Hong Kong and Taiwan. He has published a number of articles and book chapters on Hong Kong's elections, grassroots politics, and political parties. He is also a political commentator on Hong Kong affairs.

Index